Lecture Notes in Computer Science 8640

Commenced Publication in 1973
Founding and Former Series Editors:
Gerhard Goos, Juris Hartmanis, and Jan van Leeuwen

T0213889

Irfan Awan   Muhammad Younas
Xavier Franch   Carme Quer (Eds.)

Mobile Web Information Systems

11th International Conference, MobiWIS 2014
Barcelona, Spain, August 27-29, 2014
Proceedings

 Springer

Volume Editors

Irfan Awan
University of Bradford
Department of Computing, Bradford BD7 1DP, UK
E-mail: i.u.awan@bradford.ac.uk

Muhammad Younas
Oxford Brookes University
Department of Computing and Communication Technologies
Oxford OX33 1HX, UK
E-mail: m.younas@brookes.ac.uk

Xavier Franch
Universitat Politècnica de Catalunya
Department of Sercice and Information System Engineering
08034 Barcelona, Spain
E-mail: franch@essi.upc.edu

Carme Quer
Universitat Politècnica de Catalunya
Department of Service and Information System Engineering
08034 Barcelona, Spain
E-mail: cquer@essi.upc.edu

ISSN 0302-9743   e-ISSN 1611-3349
ISBN 978-3-319-10358-7   e-ISBN 978-3-319-10359-4
DOI 10.1007/978-3-319-10359-4
Springer Cham Heidelberg New York Dordrecht London

Library of Congress Control Number: 2014945971

LNCS Sublibrary: SL 3 – Information Systems and Application,
incl. Internet/Web and HCI

Typesetting: Camera-ready by author, data conversion by Scientific Publishing Services, Chennai, India

Printed on acid-free paper

Springer is part of Springer Science+Business Media (www.springer.com)

Preface

This volume includes a collection of research articles presented at the 11th International Conference on Mobile Web Information Systems (MobiWis 2014), held in Barcelona, Spain, during August 27–29, 2014. The area of mobile web and information systems is growing at a rapid pace given the ubiquity of mobile devices and the advances in web technologies, network communication, and software systems. The number of mobile web users has been increasing in recent years both in the developed as well as the developing countries across the globe. According to mobiThinking (http://mobithinking.com/) China has more mobile web/Internet users than any other country. Similarly, other developing countries such as Egypt, India, and South Africa, etc., have been following significant growth in the use of mobile web over the last few years. Similarly, the United Nations specialized agency for Information and Communication Technologies, the ITU (International Telecommunication Union)[1] estimates that there are 2.3 billion mobile broadband subscriptions in the world; out of which 55% are in developing countries.

The International Conference on Mobile Web Information Systems (MobiWis) aims to advance research on and practical applications of mobile web and information systems. It provides a forum for researchers, developers, and practitioners from academia and industry in order to share research ideas, knowledge, and experiences in the areas of mobile web and information systems. MobiWis 2014 comprised a set of tracks which included (emerging) areas such as: mobile software systems, middleware/SOA for mobile systems, context- and location-aware services, data management in the mobile web, mobile cloud services, mobile web of things, mobile web security, trust and privacy, mobile networks, protocols and applications, mobile commerce and business services, HCI in mobile applications, social media, and adaptive approaches for mobile computing.

MobiWis 2014 attracted 75 submissions from various countries across the world. All the papers were peer-reviewed by the members of Program Committee. Based on the reviews 24 papers were accepted for the conference. The acceptance rate was 32%. The accepted papers covered a range of topics related to the theme of the conference. In addition to the research articles, MobiWis 2014 featured the following four invited talks:

- CLOUDs: A Large Virtualization of Small Things
  Prof. Keith Jeffery, Independent Consultant, Ex-Director IT at STFC Rutherford Appleton Laboratory, United Kingdom
- Internet of Things, People, and Processes
  Prof. Schahram Dustdar, Vienna University of Technology, Austria

---

[1] ITU: http://www.itu.int/en/ITU-D/Statistics/Pages/facts/default.aspx

- Cognitive Cars and Smart Roads - Applications, Challenges, and Solutions
  Prof. Azzedine Boukerche, University of Ottawa, Canada
- Mobile Cloud
  Prof. Fun Hu, University of Bradford, United Kingdom

These talks were delivered in conjunction with the co-located conference of the 2nd International Conference on Future Internet of Things and Cloud (Fi-Cloud 2014).

We would like to thank the invited speakers, Prof. Keith Jeffery, Prof. Schahram Dustdar, Prof. Azzedine Boukerche, and Prof. Fun Hu for delivering very interesting and visionary talks. We would also like to thank all authors for submitting their work to MobiWIS 2014 and for contributing to this volume and for presenting and discussing their papers during the conference. We highly appreciate their contributions to the MobiWis.

We also thank all the Program Committee members who provided valuable and constructive feedback to the authors and to the program chairs. We would like to thank the conference general chair, Schahram Dustdar and members of the Organizing Committee for their help and support in the organization of the conference. Special thanks also to Joyce El Haddad (Publicity Chair), Samia Loucif (Workshop Chair), Farookh Hussain (Journal Special Issue Coordinator), Hatem Musbah Ibrahim (Website Administrator) and the track chairs: Georgia M. Kapitsaki, Sven Casteleyn, Sergio Ilarri, Alberto Sillitti, Beniamino Di Martino, George Ghinea, Azizah Abd Manaf, Lisandro Zambenedetti Granville, Rainer Unland, Carlos Duarte, Hend S. Al-Khalifa, Bernady O. Apduhan, Tor-Morten Gronli, and Vincenzo De Florio.

We would like to thank the local organizing team of the Universitat Politècnica de Catalunya (Spain) for their great help and support. Our sincere thanks also go to the Springer LNCS team, Alfred Hofmann, Anna Kramer and Christine Reiss, for their valuable support in the approval and production of the conference proceedings.

We wish the conference participants a fruitful and enjoyable time at the conference and in Barcelona.

August 2014   Irfan Awan
                                                            Muhammad Younas
                                                               Xavier Franch
                                                                 Carme Quer

MobiWIS 2014 Organizing Committee

General Chair

Schahram Dustdar   Vienna University of Technology, Austria

General Vice-Chair

Xavier Franch   Universitat Politècnica de Catalunya, Spain

Program Co-chairs

Irfan Awan   University of Bradford, UK
Muhammad Younas   Oxford Brookes University, UK

Local Organizing Chair

Carme Quer   Universitat Politècnica de Catalunya, Spain

Track Chairs

Track 1: Mobile Software Systems
Chair

Georgia M. Kapitsaki   University of Cyprus, Cyprus

Track 2: Middleware/SOA for Mobile Systems
Chair

Sven Casteleyn   Universitat Jaume I, Castellón, Spain

Track 3: Context- and Location-aware Services
Chair

Sergio Ilarri   University of Zaragoza, Spain

Track 4: Data Management in the Mobile Web
Chair

Alberto Sillitti   Free University of Bolzano, Italy

Track 5: Mobile Cloud Services
Chair

Beniamino Di Martino   University of Naples, Italy

Track 6: Mobile Web of Things
Chair

George Ghinea   Brunel University, UK

Track 7: Mobile Web Security, Trust, and Privacy
Chair

Azizah Abd Manaf   Universiti Teknologi Malaysia, Malaysia

Track 8: Mobile Networks, Protocols, and Applications
Chair

Lisandro Zambenedetti
    Granville   Federal University of Rio Grande do Sul, Brazil

Track 9: Mobile Commerce and Business Services
Chair

Rainer Unland   Universität Duisburg-Essen, Germany

Track 10: HCI in Mobile Applications
Chair

Carlos Duarte   University of Lisbon, Portugal

Track 11: Social Media
Chair

Hend S. Al-Khalifa   King Saud University, Saudi Arabia

Track 12: General - Mobile Web and Information Systems
Chair

Bernady O. Apduhan   Kyushu Sangyo University, Japan

Track 13: Industry and Demo Track
Chair

Tor-Morten Gronli   Norwegian School of IT, Norway

Track 14: Adaptive Approaches for Mobile Computing
Chair

Vincenzo De Florio   University of Antwerp and iMinds Research
                               Institute, Belgium

Workshop Coordinator

Samia Loucif   ALHOSN University, UAE

Publicity Chair

Joyce El Haddad   University of Paris Dauphine, France

Journal Special Issue Coordinator

Farookh Hussain   University of Technology Sydney, Australia

Website Administrator

Hatem Musbah Ibrahim   University of Bradford, UK

Program Committee

Track 1: Mobile Software Systems

Achilleas Achilleos   University of Cyprus, Cyprus
Luca Berardinelli   Vienna University of Technology, Austria
Tommi Mikkonen   Tampereen teknillisen yliopiston, Finland
Nearchos Paspallis   UCLan Cyprus, Cyprus
Raquel Trillo   University of Zaragoza, Spain

Hong-Linh Truong   Vienna University of Technology, Austria
Nikolaos Tselikas   University of Peloponnese, Greece
Petri Vuorimaa   Aalto University, Finland
Michael Wagner   Schloss Dagstuhl - Leibniz Center for
                            Informatics, Germany
Marco Winckler   University Paul Sabatier Toulouse 3, France
Bin Xu   Tsinghua University, China

Track 2: Middleware/SOA for Mobile Systems

Schahram Dustdar   Technical University of Vienna, Austria
Florian Daniel   University of Trento, Italy
William Van Woensel   Dalhousie University, Canada
Salima Benbernou   Universite Paris Descartes, France
Peep Kungas   University of Tartu, Estonia
Abdelkarim Erradi   Qatar University, Qatar
Brahim Medjahed   University of Michigan at Dearborn, USA
Zaki Malik   Wayne State University, USA
Carlos Granell   European Commission, Joint Research Centre,
                            Italy
Xumin Liu   Rochester Institute of Technology, USA
Peter Dolog   Aalborg University, Denmark
Cesare Pautasso   University of Lugano, Switzerland

Track 3: Context- and Location-aware Services

Apostolos Papadopoulos   Aristotle University of Thessaloniki, Greece
Carlos Calafate   Technical University of Valencia, Spain
Christoph Quix   Fraunhofer FIT, Germany
Cristian Borcea   University Heights at Newark, USA
Cyril Ray   Naval Academy Research Institute (IRENav),
                            France
Diego Lopez-de-Ipina   Deusto Institute of Technology, Spain
Dragan Stojanovic   University of Nis, Serbia
Florence Sedes   University Paul Sabatier, France
Maria Luisa Damiani   Università degli Studi di Milano, Italy
Ouri Wolfson   University of Illinois at Chicago, USA
Philippe Pucheral   University of Versailles Saint-Quentin en
                            Yvelines, France
Raquel Trillo   University of Zaragoza, Spain
Riccardo Martoglia   University of Modena and Reggio Emilia, Italy
Thierry Delot   University of Valenciennes and Inria Lille,
                            France
Antonio Corral   University of Almeria, Spain

Track 4: Data Management in the Mobile Web

Ruth Breu	University of Innsbruck, Austria
Andrea Capiluppi	Brunel University, UK
Luis Corral	University of Bolzano, Italy
Francesco Di Cerbo	SAP, France
Grace Lewis	Canegie Mellon University, USA
Tommi Mikkonen	Tampere University of Technology, Finland
Davide Taibi	University of Kaiserslautern, Germany
Mikko Terho	Huawei, Finland
Aaron Visaggio	University of Sannio, Italy
Tony Wasserman	Canegie Mellon University, USA

Track 5: Mobile Cloud Services

Xavier Aubry	Appear Networks, Sweden
Rocco Aversa	Second University of Naples, Italy
Giuseppina Cretella	Second University of Naples, Italy
Vincent Dollet	Appear Networks, Sweden
Antonio Esposito	Second University of Naples, Italy
Silvia Fernandez Postigo	Telefonica, Spain
Massimo Ficco	Second University of Naples, Italy
Florin Fortis	Western University of Timisoara, Romania
Yannis Markoulidakis	Vodafone, Greece
Christine Morin	Inria, France
Francesco Moscato	Second University of Naples, Italy
Dana Petcu	Western University of Timisoara, Romania
Gregor Pipan	XLAB, Slovenia
Carles Sierra	CSIC, Spain
Vlado Stankowski	University of Lubljiania, Slovenia
Luca Tasquier	Second University of Naples, Italy
Salvatore Venticinque	Second University of Naples, Italy
Daniel Vladusic	XLAB, Slovenia
Theodora Varvarigou	National Technical University of Athens, Greece

Track 6: Mobile Web of Things

Johnson P. Thomas	Oklahoma State University, USA
Gabriel Miro-Muntean	Dublin City University, Ireland
Jarle Hansen	Evry, Norway
David Bell	Brunel University, UK
George Roussos	Birkbeck University, UK
Rajkumar Kannan	Bishop Heber College, India

Daniel Rodriguez Garcia	University of Alcala, Spain
Ramona Trestian	Middlesex University, UK
Dejene Ejigu	Addis Ababa University, Ethiopia
Tacha Serif	Yeditepe University, Turkey
Tor-Morten Gronli	Norwegian School of IT, Norway
Andre Hinkenjahn	Bonn Rhein Sieg University, Germany
Wu-Yuin Hwang	National Central University, Taiwan

Track 7: Mobile Web Security, Trust, and Privacy

Mazdak Zamani	Universiti Teknologi Malaysia, Malaysia
Mohd Shahidan Abdullah	Universiti Teknologi Malaysia, Malaysia
Liza Abdul Latiff	Universiti Teknologi Malaysia, Malaysia
Noor Azurati Salleh	Universiti Teknologi Malaysia, Malaysia
Aboul Ella Hassanien	Cairo University, Egypt
Nurul Huda Firdaus	Universiti Teknologi Malaysia, Malaysia
Tarek M. Gaber	Suez Canal University, Egypt
Mohd Nazri Mahrin	Universiti Teknologi Malaysia, Malaysia
Yoshiro Imai	Kagawa University, Japan
Suhaimi Ibrahim	Universiti Teknologi Malaysia, Malaysia

Track 8: Mobile Networks, Protocols, and Applications

Carlos A. Iglesias	Universidad Politecnica de Madrid, Spain
Paolo Nesi	University of Florence, Italy
Ignacio Soto	Universidad Carlos III, Spain
Francisco Cano	Satimo, France
Zhefu Shi	Microsoft, USA
Marco Manso	Rinicom, Portugal

Track 9: Mobile Commerce and Business Services

Andrzej Romanowski	Lodz University of Technology, Poland
Axel Hessler	DAI-Labor TU Berlin, Germany
Azzelarare Taleb-Bendiab	Edith Cowan University, Australia
David Taniar	Monash University, Australia
Dumitru Roman	University of Oslo, Norway
Ejub Kajan	State University of Novi Pazar, Serbia
Farookh Hussain	University of Technology, Australia
Frank-Dieter Dorloff	University of Duisburg-Essen, Germany
Guadalupe Ortiz Bellot	University of Cadiz, Spain
Hanno Hildmann	NEC Europe, Germany
Kalle Lyytinen	Case Western Reserve University, USA
Tarek Gaber	Suez Canal University, Egypt
Wenny Rahayu	La Trobe University, Australia
Wojciech Mazurczyk	Warsaw University of Technology, Poland
Wolfgang Deiters	Fraunhofer-Institute for Software and System Technology, Germany

Track 10: HCI in Mobile Applications

Borja Gamecho	University of the Basque Country, Spain
Fabio Paterno	National Research Council (CNR), Italy
Joanna Lumsden	Aston University, UK
Jose Coelho	University of Lisbon, Portugal
Luis Carrico	University of Lisbon, Portugal
Marco de Sa	Twitter, USA
Nadir Weibel	University of California at San Diego, USA
Roxanne Leitao	Sheffield Hallam University, UK
Sebastian Osswald	Technische Universitat Munchen, Germany
Shahriyar Amini	Carnegie Mellon University, USA
Teresa Romao	Universidade Nova de Lisboa, Portugal
Tiago Guerreiro	University of Lisbon, Portugal

Track 11: Social Media

Akiyo Nadamoto	Konan University, Japan
Jason J. Jung	Yeungnam University, Korea
Muna Al-Razgan	King Saud Univeristy, Saudi Arabia
Nesrine Zemirli	King Saud Univeristy, Saudi Arabia
Marika Luders	SINTEF ICT, Norway
Ashraf Khalil	Abu Dhabi University, UAE
Dade Nurjanah	Faculty of Technics - Telkom University, Indonesia
Hasan Tinmaz	Middle East Turkey University, Turkey
Shadi Aljawarneh	Isra University, Jordan
Salam Abdallah	Abu Dhabi University, UAE
Nabeel Al-Qirim	United Arab Emirates University, UAE
Chris Phethea	University of Southampton, UK

Track 12: General - Mobile Web and Information Systems

Agustinus Borgy Waluyo	Monash University, Australia
Fenghui Yao	Tennessee State University, USA
Xueyan Tang	Nanyang Technological University, Singapore
Haifeng (Kevin) Zhao	University of California at Davis, USA
Rafael Santos	Brazilian National Institute for Space Research, Brazil
Andre Gregio	Renato Archer IT Center (CTI), Brazil
Quang Nguyen	International University-VNU, Vietnam
Geerish Suddul	University of Technology, Mauritius

Track 13: Industry and Demo Track

Jarle Hansen	Systek AS, Norway
Florin Pop	Politehnica University of Bucharest, Romania

Table of Contents

Industrial and Practical Applications

Mobile Web Interfaces and Applications

Mobile Apps and Smart Phones

Mobile Commerce and Social Media

Online Change Detection for Energy-Efficient Mobile Crowdsensing

Viet-Duc Le, Hans Scholten, and P.J.M Havinga

Pervasive Systems, University of Twente
7522 NB Enschede, The Netherlands
{v.d.le,hans.scholten,p.j.m.havinga}@utwente.nl

Abstract. Mobile crowdsensing is power hungry since it requires continuously and simultaneously sensing, processing and uploading fused data from various sensor types including motion sensors and environment sensors. Realizing that being able to pinpoint change points of contexts enables energy-efficient mobile crowdsensing, we modify histogram-based techniques to efficiently detect changes, which has less computational complexity and performs better than the conventional techniques. To evaluate our proposed technique, we conducted experiments on real audio databases comprising 200 sound tracks. We also compare our change detection with multivariate normal distribution and one-class support vector machine. The results show that our proposed technique is more practical for mobile crowdsensing. For example, we show that it is possible to save 80% resource compared to standard continuous sensing while remaining detection sensitivity above 95%. This work enables energy-efficient mobile crowdsensing applications by adapting to contexts.

Keywords: Mobile Crowdsensing, Change Detection, Energy Efficiency, Resource Constraints, Computational Complexity, Adaptive Sensing.

1 Introduction

Recently mobile devices have a great improvement in both technology and popularity. For examples, Samsung Galaxy S5 is equipped with Quad-core 2.5 GHz Krait 400 and various sensors (e.g., accelerometer, gyro, proximity, compass, barometer, temperature, humidity, gesture and heart rate). That sensors are everywhere and are being designed into mobile devices offers researchers a rich and powerful computing platform to develop applications that leverage the sensing capability of these mobile devices. These applications are generally categorized into individual sensing and community sensing. Individual sensing pertains to the context of a particular device user, such as, running, walking, sleeping and health conditions. Community sensing attaches to environmental context which can be enhanced by combining sensory data gathered from individual devices. These contexts include air pollution, crowd density, road condition, and social events. In this word, we consider change detection for community sensing.

Community sensing has been known as mobile crowdsending [7], which is composed of participatory sensing and opportunistic sensing. Participatory sensing

I. Awan et al. (Eds.): MobiWis 2014, LNCS 8640, pp. 1–16, 2014.

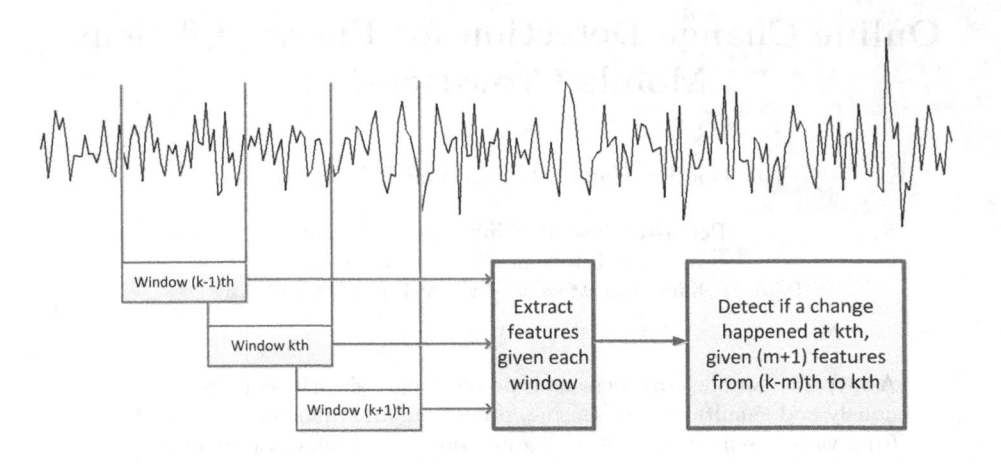

Fig. 1. Online change detection framework

requires the contribution of device users to sense contexts (e.g. report a road bump, taking a picture of fire). Conversely, opportunistic sensing autonomously senses contexts with minimum user involvement (e.g. continuously monitoring ambient temperature, device's locations). Technically, participatory sensing consumes less battery since it does not require continuously sensing like opportunistic sensing does. However, it is difficult to persuade numerous users to participate in sensing even with some incentives. In addition, participatory sensing may lead to biased results because the participants may provide incorrect information. Therefore, we focus on opportunistic sensing, which is more feasible to be deployed in large-scale networks.

Crowdsensing applications have exploited the microphone, GPS, accelerometer, gyroscope and pressure sensors. With the significantly developing of mobile devices, it is likely that more sophisticated and power-hungry sensors will be integrated in mobile devices in the future, such as, dust particle and gas sensors. Moreover, continuously uploading data to cloud servers is energy and bandwidth consumption. It also causes a considerable delay for real-time applications. Meanwhile, the capacity of battery and bandwidth are extremely limited. To avoid constantly invoking sensing, processing and uploading sensory data, the applications should be able to detect whether a context has changed. The power-hungry sensing, data processing and uploading just need to be executed around change points. Since contexts do not change very often throughout the day, change detection is a fundamental technique in energy-efficient mobile crowdsensing.

In this work, given sensory data, we introduce a new online change detection technique, called Frequency Likelihood Estimation (FLE). FLE provides low false positive while maintaining high true positive compared to current techniques. In other words, FLE enables researcher to develop energy-efficient applications in mobile crowdsensing including data sampling, data processing and data gathering with minimum resource consumption: computation, storage and battery. Figure 1 illustrates an overview of our scheme. In a nut shell, sensory data are split into predefined overlapping time windows. Data features are extracted from the measurements within a window. FLE estimates the change probability by modifying histogram-based outlier detection. Unlike the conventional techniques that build the histogram based on only historical features, FLE includes the current test feature. This solves the bin width problem, which the conventional techniques cannot. That conventional techniques use the KL divergence to detect changes also faces unstable determination of the threshold. FLE overcomes this issue by simply taking the absolute value of the samples. This method makes it easy to find a robust threshold to detect changes based on the frequency of the most left bin or the most right bin. The threshold can be defined by tuning the F-score.

To investigate the proposed technique, we first extracted data features given recorded audio data with various sounds, such as, footsteps, gun shots, sirens, etc. Then, we compare performance of our proposed technique FLE with one-class support vector machine and multivariate normal distribution, which are well-known in anomaly detection. The results show that the detecting change points using FLE is the most appropriate technique for online mobile crowdsensing applications in terms of energy efficiency.

The paper is organized as follows. Section 2 summarizes related work and discusses in more detail the novelty of this paper. Section 3 introduces the proposed detection through four subsections: descriptions, mathematical formulation, frequency likelihood estimation, complexity and evaluation metrics. Section 4 presents experiment setup and results. Finally, we conclude this work with Section 5.

2   Related Work

Online change detection has been known for various applications in sensing applications, such as, environment monitoring, remote sensing, intruder detection, fault detection, medical diagnostics, etc. It also has been used to automatically segment signals for postprocessing in data mining. However, to the best of our knowledge, change detection has not been widely used to save resource in mobile crowdsensing applications [2,14,15], especially to sampling adaptively, processing and uploading sensory data. Only several very recent work tackle the energy-efficiency problem by predicting the error based on data distribution. However, they focus on sampling framework rather then change detection techniques. For example, EmotionSense [14] and the Jigsaw [10] take a considerable delay from several seconds up to minutes because they require ruling feature extractions and classifiers to detect changes. Another example, EEMSS [16] recognizes user states as well as detects state transitions using hierarchial sensor management strategy. Since the sampling schedule is fixed after training phase, EEMSS is only work well with routine contexts that were trained. Moreover, none of the previous work clearly define the change detection concept and its roles in mobile crowdsensing.

In this paper, we formally introduce the benefit of using change detection techniques in resource-constrained mobile crowdsensing. To save the resources, devices should switch on power-hungry sensor, sensory data processing and uploading if and only if a change is detected. Since the main aim is to save resources, we propose a lightweight and efficient change detection technique, a variant of histogram-based anomaly detection using nonparametric statistical method to construct a profile of historical samples.

Histogram has been used in various applications [5, 6, 8]. In general, the techniques comprise two steps. The first step builds a profile given normal data. The second step checks whether the test sample is anomalous by measuring the frequency of the bin in which it falls. A key challenge for the conventional techniques is to determine an optimal size of the bins, which can be very dynamic under mobile crowdsensing circumstance. The test sample usually falls out of the learning profile even it is normal. Even if the anomalous sample falls into the constructed histogram, the frequency of the bin in which it falls might be as high as other bins.

There are also numerous algorithms for change detection, which are well reported in two surveys of Chandola et al. [3, 4]. However, classification-based techniques are most suitable for online change detection in dynamic contexts because of the lack of normal samples. As the page limit, only one-class support vector machine (OC-SVM) for outlier detection using Hamming distances [11] and multivariate gaussian distribution (MVN) in the Machine Learning course [12] are discussed in this work. OC-SVM is well known for its sensitivity and MVN is well known for its computational complexity. In particular, OC-SVM can deal with a small number of samples but requires high computation. Conversely, MVN is less effective but lightweight. In general, detecting change points from an online streaming data given short historical samples (say from 10 to 50 samples) is still an intricate research topic for mobile sensing platforms.

3   Change Detection in Opportunistic Sensing

In this section, we describe the concept and problem of change detection in the opportunistic sensing context. Given the problem definitions, we present FLE approach and evaluation metrics, based on which we study our approach in Section 4.

3.1   Description

As changes might be misclassified with conventional anomalies or outliers in data, again, we emphasize that their definitions are different in the context of mobile crowdsensing. An anomaly in data is defined as an unexpected pattern in a dataset, which typically indicates some kind of problem, such as, a road bump, a gun shoot or a defect of an engine. Changes not only include such anomalies but also are referred to as transitions of contexts, such as the sequential sounds in Figure 2. Since data next to transitions like in Figure 2 do not have significant

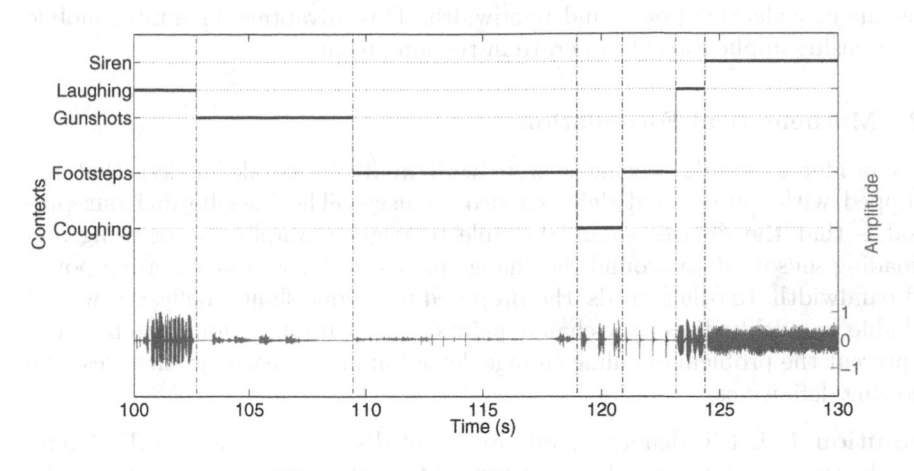

Fig. 2. A random sequence of sounds

dissimilarity in pattern with previous ones, a good anomaly detection technique might be ineffective under such circumstance. Assume that such changes can be detected and do not happen very often throughout the day, we describe how they would be used to reduce energy and bandwidth consumption in mobile crowdsensing through sensing, processing and uploading sensory data.

Most mobile crowdsensing applications require continuous sensing, which is the burden of battery. One of the solutions is that these applications just activate a minimum set of sensors to monitor the contexts. The rest can be idle to save the resource. A detected change can be used to invoke idle sensors to enhance information of collected data for better context inference. For examples, sound sensors can be use to detect if there is a sounds. If so, a camera is turned on to record the scene. By doing this, most power-hungry sensors stay in the sleep mode most of the time to prolong battery life.

Current approaches mine sensory data at individual devices to trigger other sensors in sensing or to avoid the overhead of uploading data to cloud servers. However, constantly processing data and data mining is also power hungry for mobile devices. The solution is detecting changes by some lightweight technique such as FLE in this paper. The reason is that change detection in our approach does not aim know what the context is by using data mining like in other approaches. Indeed, knowing that the current context has changed is fairly enough to trigger other sensors, data mining and data uploading processes.

Change detection also plays a key role in raw data gathering among mobile devices for high level context awareness. Most applications just need to know the transitions of contexts. For instance, knowing when a user changes from walking to running and then to sitting is barely enough to calculate how many calories have been burned. Therefore, storing, carrying and forwarding only sensory data sampled around change points significantly save bandwidth of networks.

In resume, change detection can be used to avoid constantly waking up sensors, data mining blocks and communication modules in mobile devices, which consume considerable power and bandwidth. This advantage facilitates mobile crowdsensing applications to operate in the long term.

3.2   Mathematical Formulation

We consider a mobile sensing system with multiple mobile devices that are equipped with sensors and daily carried by users. The idea beyond our proposal is that the devices should be able to trigger sampling, processing and uploading sensory data around the change points in order to save sensing power and bandwidth. In other words, the proposed technique should be featherweight and able to quickly detect the change points on-fly with minimum false positive. To present the problem of online change detection more clearly, we first describe following definitions.

Definition 1. Let $\mathbb{T}$ denote an infinite set of discrete instants $t \in \mathbb{T}$. Therefore, the timestamp value, which is assigned to each consecutive sample, can be regarded as natural numbers from $\mathbb{N}$. We define time intervals $(t_1, t_2] = \{t \in \mathbb{T}, t_1 < t \leq t_2\}$, $[t_1, t_2) = \{t \in \mathbb{T}, t_1 \leq t < t_2\}$ and $[t_1, t_2] = \{t \in \mathbb{T}, t_1 \leq t \leq t_2\}$.

Definition 2. At an arbitrary t, a data stream X is considered as an ordered sequence of the sample x_t, obtained with timestamp t. Without loss of generality, we define window W_t is a set of temporal samples spanning ω units backwards from time t, $W_t = \{x_i, i \in (t - \omega, t]\}$, where ω is called as the window size.

Definition 3. To control the transition of successive windows W, we define sliding step of ϑ time units. Upon sliding, window W_t^k at sliding step k^{th} subject to $t = k\vartheta + \omega$, $W_t^k = \{x_i, i \in (k\vartheta, k\vartheta + \omega]\}$ includes not only fresh ϑ samples but also a $\omega - \vartheta$ of samples from the previous window. For notational simplicity, we let $W^k = W_t^k$ be the window at sliding step k^{th}.

Definition 4. For better representing information of data, we define data features or window features are features extracted by mechanism $\mathcal{H}(\cdot)$. At any sliding step k^{th}, a feature is computed by $F^k = \mathcal{H}(W^k)$ or $F^k = \mathcal{H}(x_i)$, $i \in (k\vartheta, k\vartheta + \omega]$. Note that F^k is a feature vector with p numerical attributes that represent data W^k. Therefore, the feature F^k can be also expressed as a row vector of p elements, $F^k = (a_1^k, a_2^k, \ldots, a_p^k)$.

Definition 5. Since the accumulative number of features F in feature domain $\mathbb{R}^p$ can be very large and we only need to temporally keep a finite number of historical features, we define the historical data at sliding step k^{th} is a set of temporal features spanning m units before the current k^{th}, $\Gamma^k = \{F^i, i \in [k - m, k)\}$, where m is called as the history length. For better visualizing, we express Γ_k as a $m \times p$ matrix

$$\Gamma^k = \begin{bmatrix} a_1^{k-m} & a_2^{k-m} & \ldots & a_p^{k-m} \\ a_1^{k+1-m} & a_2^{k+1-m} & \ldots & a_p^{k+1-m} \\ \ldots & \ldots & \ldots & \ldots \\ a_1^{k-1} & a_2^{k-1} & \ldots & a_p^{k-1} \end{bmatrix}. \tag{1}$$

From above definitions, we have the mathematical formulation of change detection. Given $\Gamma^k = \{F^i,\ i \in [k-m, k)$ is the training set and F^k is the test sample, where $m \in \mathbb{N}$ is considered as the number of observations. By assuming that observed features belong to a single class, change detection detects if the current feature value F^k belongs to another class. Mathematically, the problem is to find the statistical model probability $p(F)$. Then if

$$
\begin{cases}
p(F^k) \geq \epsilon, & \text{context is remained} \\
p(F^k) < \epsilon, & \text{context has changed}
\end{cases}
\tag{2}
$$

where ϵ is a threshold, which can be chosen in advance or tuned by maximizing the F-measure in statistics.

In other words, given a streaming data X sampled from consecutive contexts that composes n change points and have the length $\mathcal{T}$ time units, window size ω, sliding step ϑ and current timestamp value t_c, the change detection needs to be able to:

- have lightweight computation.
- detect as many as real change points,
- detect changes quickly within a certain delay,
- keep false detection as less as possible.

3.3   Frequency Likelihood Estimation

Our hypothesis is that most change detections are whether too sensitive to outliers or too robust with statistical dispersion (underlying of statistical samples). This characteristic makes these change detections suitable in detecting outliers that are significantly different from the dispersion like normal distribution, but not suitable to detecting changes that cannot be seen clearly. To detect the changes among sounds efficiently, we propose the lightweight Frequency Likelihood Estimator FLE, a nonparametric-based technique preliminarily described in [9]. The technique is termed "frequency likelihood" since we modify the conventional frequency histogram of consecutive samples. We reemphasize that using histogram to detect anomalies has been used in previous work. However, histogram-based techniques have to endure the issues caused by the highly dynamic contexts. In particular, a small amount of samples measured in a dynamic environment typically is not normal distributed, even left-skewed or right-skewed. Determining a fixed threshold also struggled with the dynamic. Furthermore, the conventional histogram based change detection HBOS [8] constructs the bin width solely based on historical samples. However, the number of historical samples are quite short for online detection. Therefore, HBOS has poor performance since the test samples usually fall out of the predefined histogram. Indeed, our new method is able to deal with such issues.

Given temporary dataset $m + 1$ samples including training set Γ^k and test sample F^k, which is expressed as a $(m + 1) \times p$ matrix

$$
\mathcal{D} = \begin{bmatrix}
a_1^{k-m} & a_2^{k-m} & \cdots & a_p^{k-m} \\
a_1^{k+1-m} & a_2^{k+1-m} & \cdots & a_p^{k+1-m} \\
\cdots & \cdots & \cdots & \cdots \\
a_1^k & a_2^k & \cdots & a_p^k
\end{bmatrix}, \tag{3}
$$

for each attribute column of $\mathcal{D}$, FLE first counts the amount of elements that fall into each disjoint category, also called bin. Let b denote the total number of bins, FLE for each attribute i, $i = 1, \ldots, p$, is a function $p_{i,j}$ that must satisfy:

$$
m + 1 = \sum_{j=1}^{b} p_{i,j}. \tag{4}
$$

In general, b is set to $b < (m+1)$ to make use of the histogram. Unlike HBOS using only m samples, FLE includes the test sample F^k in constructing the histogram. This solve the case test sample falling out of histogram. It also turns out that the frequency $p_{i,j}$ at bin j will have the highest value for attribute i if there exists a change. That the highest values of frequencies in the modified histogram are almost similar makes it feasible to chose a constant threshold.

Another issue is that the position of the maximum frequency is highly dynamic and depends on which bin most samples fall into. Consequently, repeatedly finding the location of the means consumes more mobile platform's resources. FLE can overcome this issue by taking the absolute values of given data as the data set $\mathcal{D}$. As a result, this technique always pushes the mean and outliers to the most left bin (called least significant bin LSB) and the most right bin (called most significant bin MSB). Therefore, we only need to simply count the frequencies of LSB and MSB. The change probability of test data $|F_i^k|$ of the ith attribute, denoted by $\widetilde{p}(|F_i^k|)$, can be estimated by:

$$
\widetilde{p}(|F_i^k|) = p_{i,1} + p_{i,b}, \tag{5}
$$

where $p_{i,1}$ and $p_{i,b}$ are the frequencies of LSB and MSB regarding to the ith attribute, respectively. Note that HBOS has to count frequencies of all bins, which requires more computation.

As our goal is to detect anomalies, we aggregate such individual change probability for all attributes of a feature by finding the maximum value. We remark that using join probability will results in limiting the possibility to detect outlier since $\widetilde{p}(|F_i^k|)$ may have very small values. For instance, a buzzer emits considerable amplitude in high frequency but not in low frequency. Choosing the max probability is a suitable solution to increase possibility of detecting the buzzer sound. Hence, the estimate change probability given current feature observation F^k is

$$
\widetilde{p}(|F^k|) = max\{\widetilde{p}(|F_i^k|)\}, \; i = 1, \ldots, p. \tag{6}
$$

To match (6) with the problem definition (2), we take the complement of the change probability as the imaginary density probability:

$$p(|F^k|) \leftarrow 1 - \widetilde{p}(|F^k|). \tag{7}$$

Using above (7), we can detect changes using the condition described by (2).

3.4   Complexity

Given a temporary dataset $\mathcal{D}$ including training set Γ^k and test sample F^k. The total number of entities in $\mathcal{D}$ is $p \times (m + 1)$. For each attribute of feature F_i, FLE uses $m+1$ elements. Therefore, it requires $m+1$ operations to find the min and max values. It also needs another $m + 1$ operations to count the frequency density of LSB and MSB. Therefore, the complexity, or big-O of FLE is:

$$O(2(m + 1)p) \simeq O(mp), \tag{8}$$

where m is the history length and p is the dimension of the data feature. We remark that the conventional histogram HBOS requires b, the number of bins, iterations to compute frequency density for each element. Therefore, the complexity of FLE is b times less than that of HBOS, which is $O(mbp)$. Moreover, the complexity of FLE is much less than that of OC-SVM $O(m^3p^3)$ and even the well-known lightweight MVN $O(m^2p^2 + p^3)$.

Regarding to the framework in Figure 1, the total computational complexity, denoted by C, computed by summing feature extraction and detection technique costs. For example, the computational cost of FLE with the MedianX feature extraction is

$$C = O(q(mp + \omega)), \tag{9}$$

where q is the total quantity of sliding steps.

3.5   Evaluation Metrics

Since detecting changes from streaming data always has a delay, we leverage true positive (TP) and false negative (FP) [13] by adding latency parameter ζ in milliseconds. For better understanding, we interpret these definitions in context change detections. Assume that we expect there is no change of context, null hypothesis (H_0). Let H_a denote the alternative hypothesis, there is a change happened within previous ζ ms. The error types then can be redefined:

- TP_ζ is the total number of sliding steps when real changes are detected within the acceptable latency ζ. The number of correctly detecting a change when H_a is true.
- FP is the total number of sliding steps when the technique wrongly alarms that there is a change. The number of falsely detecting a change when H_0 is true.

Table 1. Features used in the experiments

Feature spaces	Notations	Description	p	Complexity
spectral	PSDP	Power spectral density peak	1	$O(\omega \log_2 \omega)$
	SBC	Spectral subband centroids	4	$O(\omega \log_2 \omega)$
	SBCR	Spectral subband centroid ratio	4	$O(\omega \log_2 \omega)$
cepstral	MFCC	Mel-frequency cepstral coefficients	20	$O(2\omega \log_2 \omega + \omega)$
principal	PCA	Principal component analysis	20	$O(\omega \log_2 \omega + \frac{\omega^2}{4})$
temporal-spectral	DWT	Discrete wavelet transform	4	$O(\omega \log_2 \omega)$
temporal	ZCR	Zero-corssing rate	1	$O(\omega)$
	MinX	Minimum amplitude	1	$O(\omega)$
	MaxX	Maximum amplitude	1	$O(\omega)$
	IqrX	Interquartile range	1	$O(\omega)$
	MedianX	Median amplitude	1	$O(\omega)$
	MeanX	Mean amplitude	1	$O(\omega)$
	StdX	Standard variance amplitude	1	$O(\omega)$

The value of ζ is set based on application requirements. However, it should not be less than the period of the shortest context. For example, we set ζ to 1000 ms in our experiment. Base on these errors, we define following metrics to evaluate the performance of change detection: Sensitivity S and Efficiency E.

$$S = 100\frac{TP_\zeta}{n} \tag{10}$$

and

$$E = 100(1 - \frac{FP}{q}). \tag{11}$$

We remark that sensitivity does not count the changes detected later than 1 s. To evaluate how fast changes can be detected, we investigate the required latency L_S to obtain the expected sensitivity S. Together with the aforementioned computational complexity C, these three metrics perfectly represent the change detection problem defined in Section 3.2. High sensitivity S means high detected change points. High efficiency E means less false detection. Remark that execution time of algorithms does not really represent their computational costs since it heavily depends on the implementation optimization. Therefore, we prefer the computational complexity over the execution time.

4   Experiments

In this section, we first describe the experiment setup and then analyze the results. The following experiments are aimed to evaluate (i) FLE together with several change detection techniques, that are OC-SVM and MVN and (ii) thirteen types of feature extractions shown in Table 1. In particular, we focus on the performances of such techniques when combined with different feature types, especially light computational features.

4.1   Experiment Setup

Without loss of generality, we generated a database by randomly mixing 200 sound tracks of 10 common sounds (20 tracks per sound), which we may encounter in daily life: babies crying, bells ringing, cars horning, humans coughing, dogs barking, footsteps, glass breaking, gun shoots, human laughing and siren. Sound tracks are downloaded from the free database [1], and have various lengths from 1 second to 10 seconds. Through our experiment on Nexus 7, we experienced realtime processing takes considerable and unpredictable extra delay for each window, up to 500 ms. The major cause comes from microphone hardware, thread interrupts and sound echoes. Therefore, we process offline the database as an online stream of audio with 20 ms windows and 10 ms sliding steps. We extract thirteen different features described in Table 1, which cover most common feature spaces. Remark that the Blackman - Harris window is used to reduce leakage within a Fourier Transform analysis.

We compared the change detection using FLE against OC-SVM and MVN. OC-SVM is one of the best anomaly detection technique in term of sensitivity and MVN is one of the best in term of computational complexity, which are used most for anomaly detection. We set the bin length b to 10 ($b \leq m$) for FLE, the radius of radial basis function kernel γ to $1/p$ for OC-SVM and the significant level of t-distribution α to 0.05 for MVN as common setting values used in other work. The metrics described in Section 3.5 are used to evaluate performance in terms of sensitivity, latency and efficiency. The detection algorithms were repeatedly run with different length of historical sliding steps, from 10 to 50 steps, or 100 ms to 500 ms. More than 500 ms is not practical since the time between two consecutive change points can be 1 s.

4.2   Experiment Results

Since the length of a sound track in our database can be 1 s, we only count detected changes with the delay less than 1 s. In addition, the sensitivity S is very critical in most applications. Therefore, the runs having sensitivity below 95% will be ignored in our analysis.

Although we conducted the experiment with various features, we only show results of the features best presenting for each feature space. They are MedianX, SCR, PSDP, MFCC, PCA, and DWT. Figure 3 shows the performance of change detection algorithms with the MedianX feature, the numerical value separating the higher half of window W_t from the lower half. By looking at both Figure 3(a) and (b), we observe that FLE scores best in term of efficiency as shown in Figure 3(b), while being able to detect real changes at high rate as shown in Figure 3(a) as we expected. Conversely, MVN fails to detect change points when the history length is over 200 ms as shown in Figure 3(a). Therefore, the high efficiency of MVN as shown in Figure 3(b) is meaningless. In fact, MVN is not be able to detect changes when the history length is above 200 ms. OC-SVM performance is more suitable when latency is important.

Since the ZCR feature has been used heavily in sound analysis, we consider ZCR in our study too besides the MeanX, even both of them are in

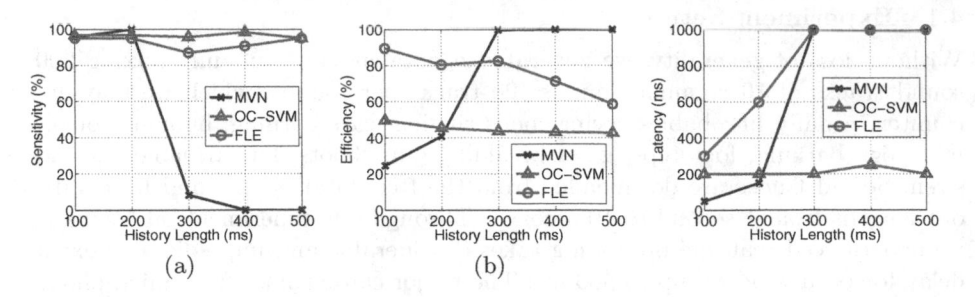

Fig. 3. Change detection performance with the MedianX feature (a) Sensitivity, (b) Efficiency and (c) Latency

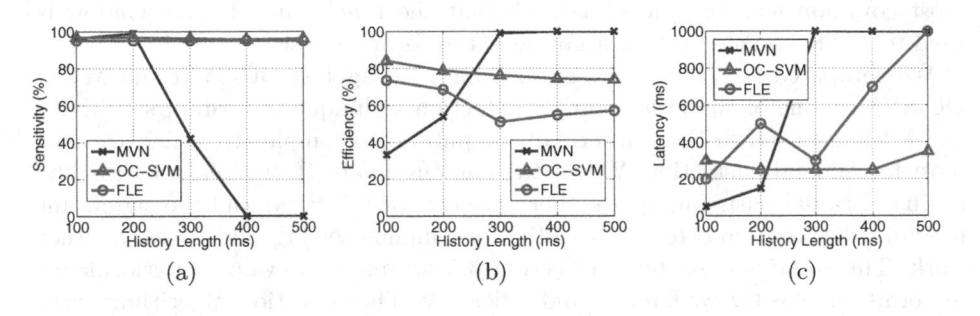

Fig. 4. Change detection performance with the ZCR feature (a) Sensitivity, (b) Efficiency and (c) Latency

temporal space. The results are shown in Figure 4. Efficiency of FLE is around 60%, a bit below our expectation. However, the efficiency is still good enough for most sensing applications. OC-SVM scores best when using the ZCR feature: high sensitivity, high efficiency and short latency. This is due to that OC-SVM is originally designed for classification and ZCR is more informative than MeanX, especially when applying on sounds. Contrary to FLE and OC-SVM, MVN with the ZCR feature performs as poor as with the MeanX feature.

Figure 5 shows the performance metrics of change detection with the PSDP feature when varying the history length parameter. Both FLE and OC-SVM yield good results: high sensitivity ratios, high efficiency ratios and acceptable latency. FLE is better in term of the efficiency and OC-SVM is better in term of the latency. Since the sensitivity ratios of MVN are very poor when the history length is greater than 20 steps, its efficiency and latency results in Figure 5(b) and Figure 5(c) are meaningless.

By looking at performance results with MFCC shown in Figure 6, we draw the same conclusions as with PSDP. The similarity is due to that both PSDP and MFCC represent the frequency aspect.

Figure 7 shows the results when apply changes detection using the PCA feature. And again, both FLE and OC-SVM perform well in terms of sensitivity,

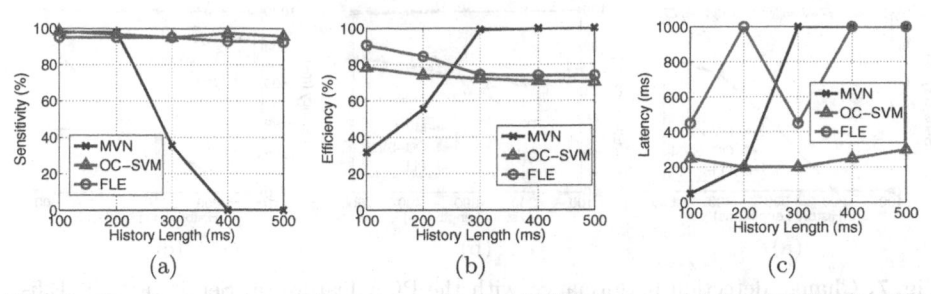

Fig. 5. Change detection performance with the PSDP feature (a) Sensitivity, (b) Efficiency and (c) Latency

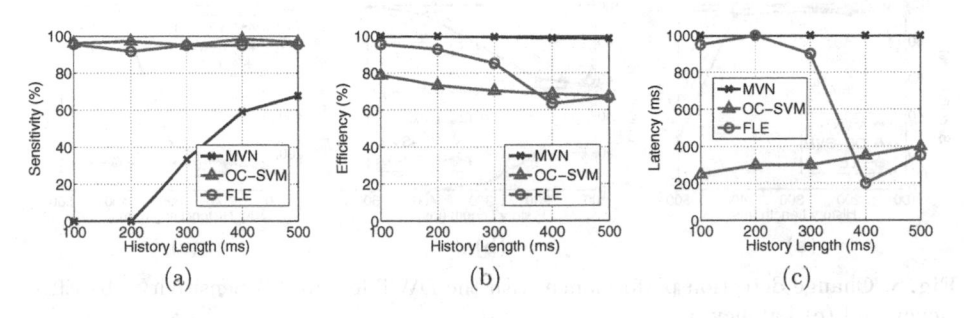

Fig. 6. Change detection performance with the MFCC feature (a) Sensitivity, (b) Efficiency and (c) Latency

efficiency and latency. Contrary to FLE and OC-SVM, MVN is not able to detect more than 95% of real changes. In addition, we observe that there using PCA gives shorter latency than using MFCC. However, using PCA gives low efficiency, which means more falsely detections.

We have investigated change detection methods with features extracted in time and frequency domains. We going on with a feature in time-frequency domain, the DWT feature. The experimental results are shown in Figure 8. Surprisingly, FLE has very low efficiency. In other words, FLE is not suitable for energy-efficiency sensing with DWT. This is not what we expected. The fact is that DWT provides higher time resolution of high frequencies and lower time resolutions of lower frequencies. A small change in sensory data will results in a significant change in the historical pattern. This leads to very high sensitivity and short latency, but low efficiency. Due to the high resolution, MVN is able to detect well real changes with acceptable efficiency.

Above conclusive results can be summarized as in Table 2 by averaging performance values of history lengths. In the table, the hyphen "-" indicates the value is meaningless. MVN is unsuitable to change detection in our assumption because it is not sensitive to context changes. Overall, OC-SVM performs

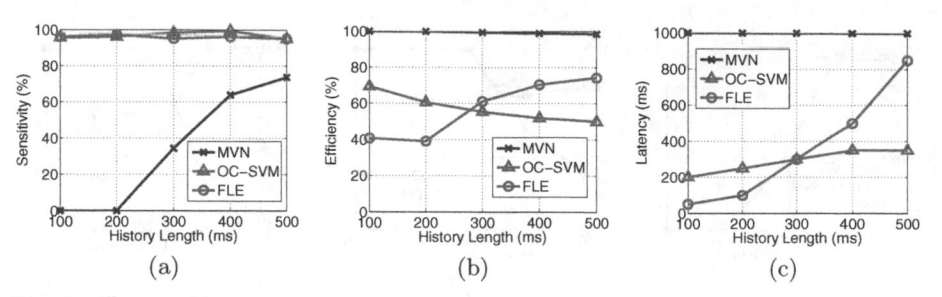

Fig. 7. Change detection performance with the PCA feature (a) Sensitivity, (b) Efficiency and (c) Latency

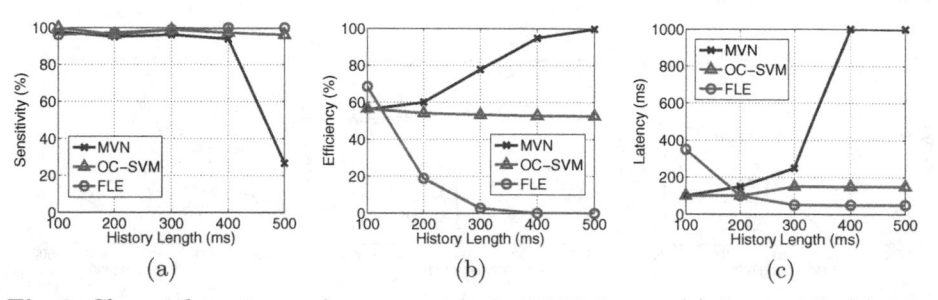

Fig. 8. Change detection performance with the DWT feature (a) Sensitivity, (b) Efficiency and (c) Latency

best in terms of sensitivity and latency. OC-SVM is able to detect more than 97% changes points within approximate 300 ms. We also observed that FLE is more efficiency than others, especially with the featherweight feature MedianX. In addition, the computational cost of the combination of FLE and MedianX is the least, see the numerical example calculated by (9) in Table 3. Since the objective of our problem is lightweight computing and high detection efficiency, FLE with MedianX is a suitable solution for the energy-efficient problem. Moreover, FLE also performs well when using more complex features such as PSDP and MFCC. This is more than what we expected. In addition, the results clearly lead to the conclusion that OC-SVM is suitable for applications of which high sensitivity and fast respond are more important than resource saving.

Table 2. Average performance values of history lengths

Performance	MedianX			ZCR			PSDP			MFCC			PDA			DWT		
	S	E	L_S	S	E	L_S	S	E	L_S	S	E	L_S	S	E	L_S	S	E	L_S
MVN	41	-	-	47	-	-	46	-	-	32	-	-	34	-	-	82	-	-
OC-SVM	97	45	210	96	78	280	97	73	240	97	72	320	97	57	290	98	54	130
FLE	93	76	780	95	61	540	94	80	780	95	81	680	96	57	360	98	18	120

Table 3. Numeric computation complexity of change detections with historical length is 200 ms, given the experimental dataset comprised of 81105 sliding windows (160 samples per window)

Big O	MedianX	ZCR	PSDP	MFCC	PDA	DWT
MVN	4.55E+07	4.55E+07	1.28E+08	1.38E+10	1.42E+10	6.19E+08
OC-SVM	6.62E+08	6.62E+08	7.44E+08	5.19E+12	5.19E+12	4.16E+10
FLE	*1.46E+07*	**1.46E+07**	**9.66E+07**	**2.35E+08**	**6.47E+08**	**1.02E+08**
HBOS	2.92E+07	2.92E+07	111E+08	5.27E+08	9.39E+08	1.60E+08

5 Conclusion

In this paper, we propose the nonparametric-based change detection FLE to detect change points of contexts. The technique is featherweight, sensitive and efficient compared to existing ones such as MVN and OC-SVM. Particularly, FLE estimates the density probability of a test sample using the frequency sum of the least and the most significant bins of the modified histogram. The complexity of FLE is only $O(mp)$, which is much lighter than the complexity of MVN, OC-SVM and even HBOS. Although the proposed method can be applied on various sensory data types, we conducted the experiment on sound data since audio signal is more complex then others in terms of the environmental noises, the tempos and the dynamics. The experimental results are consistent with our analysis. The results show that FLE can detect more than 95% change points in limited time while saving 80% resource compared with standard continuous sensing. This work makes continuous sensing applicable for mobile crowdsensing applications. A testbed including sound recognition has been planned.

Acknowledgements. This work is supported by the SenSafety project in the Dutch Commit program, www.sensafety.nl.

References

1. Findsounds, http://www.findsounds.com
2. Beach, A., Gartrell, M., Akkala, S., Elston, J., Kelley, J., Nishimoto, K., Ray, B., Razgulin, S., Sundaresan, K., Surendar, B., Terada, M., Han, R.: Whozthat? evolving an ecosystem for context-aware mobile social networks. Netwrk. Mag. of Global Internetwkg 22(4), 50–55 (2008)
3. Chandola, V., Banerjee, A., Kumar, V.: Anomaly detection for discrete sequences: A survey. IEEE Transactions on Knowledge and Data Engineering 24(5), 823–839 (2012)
4. Chandola, V., Banerjee, A., Kumar, V.: Anomaly detection: A survey. ACM Comput. Surv. 41(3), 15:1–15:58 (2009)
5. Eskin, E.: Modeling system calls for intrusion detection with dynamic window sizes. In: Proc. DISCEX (2001)
6. Fawcett, T., Provost, F.: Activity monitoring: Noticing interesting changes in behavior. In: Proc. SIGKDD, pp. 53–62 (1999)

7. Ganti, R., Ye, F., Lei, H.: Mobile crowdsensing: current state and future challenges. IEEE Communications Magazine 49(11), 32–39 (2011)
8. Goldstein, M., Dengel, A.: Histogram-based outlier score (hbos): A fast unsupervised anomaly detection algorithm. In: Stefan Advances in Konwledge Discovery and Data Mining. LNCS, pp. 577–593. Springer (206)
9. Le, V.D., Scholten, H., Havinga, P.: Flead: Online frequency likelihood estimation anomaly detection for mobile sensing. In: Proceedings of the 2013 ACM Conference on Pervasive and Ubiquitous Computing Adjunct Publication, UbiComp 2013 Adjunct, pp. 1159–1166. ACM, New York (2013)
10. Lu, H., Yang, J., Liu, Z., Lane, N.D., Choudhury, T., Campbell, A.T.: The jigsaw continuous sensing engine for mobile phone applications. In: Proceedings of the 8th ACM Conference on Embedded Networked Sensor Systems, SenSys 2010, pp. 71–84. ACM, New York (2010)
11. Manevitz, L.M., Yousef, M.: One-class svms for document classification. J. Mach. Learn. Res. 2, 139–154 (2002)
12. Ng, A.: Machine learning, https://class.coursera.org/ml/lecture/97
13. Olson, D.L., Delen, D.: Advanced DataMining Techniques. Springer (2008)
14. Rachuri, K.K., Musolesi, M., Mascolo, C., Rentfrow, P.J., Longworth, C., Aucinas, A.: Emotionsense: A mobile phones based adaptive platform for experimental social psychology research. In: Proceedings of the 12th ACM International Conference on Ubiquitous Computing, Ubicomp 2010, pp. 281–290. ACM, New York (2010)
15. Sherchan, W., Jayaraman, P.P., Krishnaswamy, S., Zaslavsky, A., Loke, S., Sinha, A.: Using on-the-move mining for mobile crowdsensing. In: Proceedings of the 2012 IEEE 13th International Conference on Mobile Data Management (Mdm 2012), MDM 2012, pp. 115–124. IEEE Computer Society, Washington, DC (2012)
16. Wang, Y., Lin, J., Annavaram, M., Jacobson, Q.A., Hong, J., Krishnamachari, B., Sadeh, N.: A framework of energy efficient mobile sensing for automatic user state recognition. In: Proceedings of the 7th International Conference on Mobile Systems, Applications, and Services, MobiSys 2009, pp. 179–192. ACM, New York (2009)

A Hybrid Approach to Web Service Composition Problem in the PlanICS Framework*

Artur Niewiadomski[1], Wojciech Penczek[1,2], and Jaroslaw Skaruz[1]

[1] ICS, Siedlce University, 3-Maja 54, 08-110 Siedlce, Poland
{artur.niewiadomski,jaroslaw.skaruz}@uph.edu.pl
[2] ICS, Polish Academy of Sciences, Jana Kazimierza 5, 01-248 Warsaw, Poland
penczek@ipipan.waw.pl

Abstract. The paper deals with the concrete planning problem – a stage of the Web Service Composition in the PlanICS framework. A novel (hybrid) planning technique based on a combination of a Genetic Algorithm and a Satisfiability Modulo Theories Solver is introduced. The experimental results of the hybrid algorithm are compared with these obtained using "pure" planning methods.

1 Introduction

Service-Oriented Architecture (SOA) [2] exploits the idea of composing simple functionalities, accessible via well-defined interfaces, in order to satisfy more sophisticated objectives. The problem of finding such a composition is hard and known as the Web Service Composition (WSC) problem [1,2,9].

The system PlanICS [4] is a framework aimed at WSC, which allows for adapting existing real-world services. The main assumption in PlanICS is that all the web services in the domain of interest as well as the objects that are processed by the services, can be strictly classified in a hierarchy of *classes*, organised in an *ontology*. Another key idea is to divide the planning into several stages. The first phase deals with *classes of services*, where each class represents a set of real-world services, while the other phases work in the space of *concrete services*. The first stage produces an *abstract plan* composed of service classes [5]. Next, the offers are retrieved by the offer collector (OC) (a module of PlanICS) and used in the concrete planning (CP). As a result of CP a *concrete plan* is obtained, which is a sequence of offers satisfying predefined optimization criteria. Such an approach enables to reduce dramatically the number of web services to be considered, and inquired for offers.

This paper deals with the concrete planning problem, shown to be NP-hard [7]. Our previous papers employ several techniques to solve it: a genetic algorithm (GA) [10], numeric optimization methods [8], and Satisfiability Modulo Theories (SMT) Solvers[7]. The results of our extensive experiments show that the proposed methods are complementary, but every single one suffers from

---

* This work has been supported by the National Science Centre under the grant No. 2011/01/B/ST6/01477.

I. Awan et al. (Eds.): MobiWis 2014, LNCS 8640, pp. 17–28, 2014.

some disadvantages. This observation is the motivation to *combining the power of SMT with the potential of GA*, which is the main contribution of this paper.

The principal disadvantage of an SMT-based solution is often a long computation time, which is not acceptable in the case of a real-world interactive planning tool. On the other hand, a GA-based approach is relatively fast, but it yields solutions, which are far from optimum and of low probability. Thus, our aim is to exploit the advantages of both methods by combining them into one hybrid algorithm. In the paper we present two new hybrid algorithms and compare their efficiency with the pure SMT- and GA-based planner on several benchmarks.

The rest of the paper is structured as follows. In Section 2 the PlanICS framework is introduced and the Concrete Planning Problem (CPP) is defined. Section 3 presents the main ideas of our hybrid approach as well as some technical solutions. Next, the preliminary experimental results are presented and discussed, followed by conclusions.

2   Concrete Planning Problem

This section introduces the main ideas of the PlanICS framework and gives all the necessary definitions for defining the concrete planning problem.

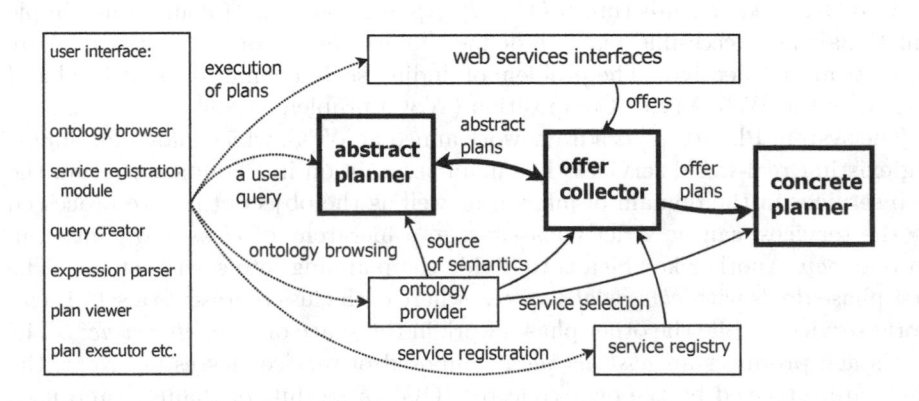

Fig. 1. A diagram of the PlanICS system architecture. The bold arrows correspond to computation of a plan, the thin arrows model the planner infrastructure, while the dotted arrows represent the user interactions.

An ontology contains a system of *classes* describing the types of the services as well as the types of the objects they process [6]. A class consists of a unique name and a set of the attributes. By an *object* we mean an instance of a class. By a *state* of an object we mean a valuation of its attributes. A set of objects in a certain state is called a *world*. A key notion of PlanICS is that of a *service*. We assume that each service processes a set of objects, possibly changing values of their attributes, and produces a set of new (additional) objects. We say that a service *transforms* a world. The types of the services available for planning are defined as elements of the branch of classes rooted at the *Service* concept. Each service type stands for a description of a set of real-world services of similar features.

The main goal of the system is to find a composition of services that satisfies a user query. The query interpretation results in two sets of worlds: the initial and the expected ones. Moreover, the query may include additional constraints, especially *quality constraints*, the sum of which is used to choose the best from all the potential solutions. Thus, the task of the system is to find such a set of services, which transform some initial world into a world matching some expected one in such a way that the value of the quality function is maximized. Fig.1 shows the general Planics architecture.

In the first stage of the composition an *abstract planner* matches services at the level of input/output types and the abstract values[1] [5]. The result of this stage is a *Context Abstract Plan* (CAP), consisting of a multiset of service types (defined by a representative sequence), contexts (mappings between services and the objects being processed), and a set of final worlds[2] containing objects that fulfil the user query.

In the second planning stage CAP is used by the *offer collector* (OC), i.e., a tool which in cooperation with the service registry queries real-world services. The service registry keeps an evidence of real-world web services, registered accordingly to the service type system. During the registration the service provider defines a mapping between the input/output data of the real-world service and the object attributes processed by the declared service type. OC communicates with the real-world services of types present in a CAP, sending the constraints on the data, which can potentially be sent to the service in an inquiry, and on the data expected to be received in an offer in order to keep on building a potential plan. Usually, each service type represents a set of real-world services. Moreover, querying a single service can result in a number of offers. Thus, we define offer sets as the main result of the second planning stage.

Definition 1 (Offer, Offer set). *Assume that the n-th instance of a service type from a CAP processes some number of objects having in total m attributes. A single offer collected by OC is a vector $P = [v_1, v_2, \ldots, v_m]$, where, for $1 \le j \le m$, v_j is a value of a single object attribute processed by the n-th service of the CAP. An offer set O^n is a $k \times m$ matrix, where each row corresponds to a single offer and k is the number of offers in the set. Thus, the element $o^n_{i,j}$ from O^n is the j-th value of the i-th offer collected from the n-th service type instance from the CAP.*

The responsibility of OC is to collect a number of offers, where every offer represents one possible execution of a single service. However, other important tasks

---

[1] At this planning stage it is enough to know if an attribute does have a value, or it does not, so we abstract from the concrete values of the object attributes.

[2] The user query q defines a set of initial and expected worlds. A CAP for q transforms some initial world into a set of final worlds, where at least one of them has to match one of the expected worlds. See [5] for details.

of OC are as follows: (1) building a set of constraints resulting from the user query and from semantic descriptions of service types, and (2) a conversion of the quality constraints expressed using objects from the user query to an *objective function* built over variables from offer sets. Thus, we can formulate CPP as a constrained optimization problem.

Definition 2 (CPP). *Let n be the length of CAP and let $\mathbb{O} = (O^1, \ldots, O^n)$ be the vector of offer sets collected by OC such that for every $i = 1, \ldots, n$*

$$O^i = \begin{bmatrix} o^i_{1,1} & \cdots & o^i_{1,m_i} \\ \vdots & \ddots & \vdots \\ o^i_{k_i,1} & \cdots & o^i_{k_i,m_i} \end{bmatrix}, \text{ and the } j\text{-th row of } O^i \text{ is denoted by } P^i_j. \text{ Let } \mathbb{P} \text{ denote}$$

the set of all possible sequences $(P^1_{j_1}, \ldots, P^n_{j_n})$, such that $j_i \in \{1, \ldots, k_i\}$ and $i \in \{1, \ldots, n\}$. The Concrete Planning Problem is defined as:

$$max\{Q(S) \mid S \in \mathbb{P}\} \text{ subject to } \mathbb{C}(S), \tag{1}$$

where $Q : \mathbb{P} \mapsto \mathbb{R}$ is an objective function defined as the sum of all quality constraints and $\mathbb{C}(S) = \{C_j(S) \mid j = 1, \ldots, c \text{ for } c \in \mathbb{N}\}$, where $S \in \mathbb{P}$, is a set of constraints to be satisfied.

Finding a solution of CPP consists in selecting one offer from each offer set such that all constraints are satisfied and the value of the objective function is maximized. This is the goal of the third planning stage and the task of a *concrete planner*.

3   Hybrid Solution

The analysis of several CPP instances, which are hard to solve by "pure" SMT- and GA-based planners, is our main motivation for combining both the methods. The main disadvantage of the SMT-based solution is often a long computation time which is not acceptable in the case of a real-world interactive planning tool. On the other hand, the GA-based approach is relatively fast, but it yields solutions, which are far from optimum and of low probability. Thus, our aim is to exploit the advantages of both the methods by combining them into one hybrid algorithm.

3.1   Overview

The main idea is as follows. The base of our hybrid approach is the standard GA aimed at solving CPP. GA is a non deterministic algorithm maintaining a population of potential solutions during an evolutionary process. A potential solution is encoded in a form of an individual, which, in case of CPP, is a sequence of natural values. In each iteration of GA a set of individuals is selected in order to apply genetic operations such as the standard one-point crossover and mutation. This leads to obtaining a new population passed to the next iteration of GA. The selection of an individual and thus the promotion of its offspring to the next generation depends on the value of the *fitness function*. The fitness value of an individual is the sum of the optimization objective and the ratio of the number of the satisfied constraints to the number of all the constraints (see Def. 2), multiplied by some constant β:

$$fitness(I) = q(S_I) + \beta \cdot \frac{|sat(\mathbb{C}(S_I))|}{c}, \qquad (2)$$

where I stands for an individual, S_I is a sequence of the offer values correspond-ing to I, $sat(\mathbb{C}(S_I))$ is a set of the constraints satisfied by a candidate solution represented by I, and c is the number of all the constraints. The parameter β is to reduce both the components of the sum to the same order of magnitude and to control the impact of the components on the final result[3].

The main idea of our new hybrid approach consists in the modification of the standard GA. After every couple of iterations of GA, several top-ranked individuals are processed by the SMT-based algorithm. Given an individual I, the procedure searches for a similar, but improved individual I', which represents a solution satisfying all the constraints and having a greater value of the objective function at the same time. The similarity between I and I' consists in sharing a number of genes. We refer to the problem of finding such an individual as to the *Search for an Improved Individual (SFII)*.

3.2 Encoding

The SMT-based procedure combined with GA is based on the encoding exploited in our "pure" SMT-based concrete planner [7]. The idea is to encode *SFII* as an SMT formula which is satisfiable if such an individual exists. First, we initialize an SMT-solver allocating the set $\mathcal{V}$ of all necessary variables:

- **oid**^{i}, for $i = 1\ldots n$, where n is the length of the abstract plan. These vari-ables are used for storing the identifiers of the offers constituting a solution. A single **oid**^{i} variable takes a value from 1 to k_i.
- **o**^i_j, for $i = 1\ldots n$, $j = 1\ldots m_i$, where m_i is the number of the offer values in the i-th offer set. They are used for encoding the values of S, i.e., the values from the offers chosen as a solution. From each offer set O^i we extract the subset R^i of offer values, which are present in the constraint set and in the quality function, and we allocate only the variables relevant for the plan.

Next, using the variables from $\mathcal{V}$, we encode the offer values, the objective function, and the constraints, as the formulas shared by all calls of our SMT-procedure. The offer values from the offer sets $\mathbb{O} = (O^1, \ldots, O^n)$ are encoded as the following formula:

$$ofr(\mathbb{O}, \mathcal{V}) = \bigwedge_{i=1}^{n} \bigvee_{d=1}^{k_i} \left(\mathbf{oid}^i = d \wedge \bigwedge_{o^i_{d,j} \in R^i} \mathbf{o}^i_j = o^i_{d,j} \right). \qquad (3)$$

---

[3] The value of β depends on the estimation of the minimal and the maximal quality function value.

The formulae $ctr\big(\mathbb{C}(S), \mathcal{V}\big)$ and $qual\big(Q(S), \mathcal{V}\big)$, denoted as **ctr** and **q** for short, encode the constraints and the objective function, respectively. Due to the space limit the details are omitted here.

Let $I = (g_1, \ldots, g_n)$ be an individual, $M = \{i_1, \ldots, i_k\}$ be the set of indices of the genes allowed to be changed, and $q(S_I)$ be the value of the objective function, where $n, k \in \mathbb{N}$. Hence, the *SFII* problem is reduced to the satisfiability problem of the following formula:

$$\bigwedge_{i \in \{1, \ldots, n\} \setminus M} (\mathbf{oid}^i = g_i) \wedge ofr(\mathbb{O}, \mathcal{V}) \wedge \mathbf{ctr} \wedge (\mathbf{q} > q(S_I)) \tag{4}$$

That is, the formula (4) is satisfiable only if there exists an individual $I' = (g'_1, \ldots, g'_n)$ satisfying all the constraints, where $\forall_{i \notin M} \, g_i = g'_i$ and $q(S_{I'}) > q(S_I)$, i.e., sharing with I all genes of the indices outside M and having a higher value of the objective function than I. If the formula is satisfiable, then the values of the genes changed are decoded from the model returned by the SMT-solver, and the improved individual I' replaces I in the current population.

3.3 Hybrid Variants

Although, we have presented the general idea of a hybrid algorithm, there are still a number of problems that need to be solved in order to combine GA and SMT. Moreover, they can be solved in many different ways. The crucial questions that need to be answered are as follows. When to start the *SFII* procedure for the first time? How many times and how often *SFII* should be run? How many genes should remain fixed? How to choose genes to be changed? Since there are many possibilities to deal with the above problems, we started from the simplest solution which randomly selects genes to be changed. The solutions to the remaining questions we treat as parameters in order to develop the first version of our hybrid solution, called Random Hybrid (RH). Its pseudo-code is presented in Algorithm 1.

After analyzing the experimental results (see Section 4) we found that the results are slightly better than those obtained using GA and SMT separately, however they could still be improved, especially in terms of a higher probability and a lower computation time. Thus, we introduced several improvements in the RH algorithm and we implemented the Semi-Random Hybrid (SRH) algorithm. The most important improvements introduced in SRH are as follows.

The *selectGenes* procedure (see line 11 of Algorithm 1) is not completely random any more. In the first place the genes violating some constraints are chosen to be changed. Then, additional gene indices are selected randomly until we get a set of size gn. This change allows to increase the probability of finding a solution.

The next improvement aims at reducing the computation time. It consists in running the *SFII* procedure only if an individual violates some constraints. Thus, in case of SRH the lines from 11 to 15 in Algorithm 1 are executed conditionally, only if the individual I violates some constraints. In the next section we compare both the approaches and discuss the results obtained.

1 **Procedure RandomHybrid(*st*, *ind*, *int*, *gn*, *N*)**
    Input: *st*: when to start *SFII* for the first time, *ind*: the number of individuals
        to pass to *SFII* during a single GA iteration, *int*: how often run *SFII*,
        gn: the number of genes to change by *SFII*, *N*: the number of GA
        iterations
    Result: an individual representing the best concrete plan found, or *null*

```
 2  begin
 3  │   initialize(); // generate initial population, initialize SMT solver
 4  │   evaluate(); // compute fitness function for all individuals
 5  │   for (i ← 1; i ≤ N; i ← i + 1) do
 6  │   │   selection(); crossover(); mutation(); // ordinary GA routines
 7  │   │   evaluate();
 8  │   │   if (i ≥ st) ∧ (i mod int = 0) then
 9  │   │   │   BI ← findBestInd(ind); // a set of ind top individuals
10  │   │   │   foreach I ∈ BI do
11  │   │   │   │   M ← selectGenes(I, gn); // a set of gene indices to be
    │   │   │   │       changed
12  │   │   │   │   I' ← runSFII(M);
13  │   │   │   │   if I' ≠ null then
14  │   │   │   │   │   I ← I'; // replace I by I' in the current population
15  │   │   │   │   end
16  │   │   │   end
17  │   │   end
18  │   end
19  │   {best} ← findBestInd(1);
20  │   if constraintsSatisfied(best) then
21  │   │   return best; // if a valid solution has been found
22  │   else
23  │   │   return null
24  │   end
25  end
```

Algorithm 1. Pseudocode of the RandomHybrid algorithm

4 Experimental Results

In order to evaluate the efficiency of our hybrid algorithms on 'difficult' bench-marks, we have used for the experiments six instances of CPP that have been hardly solved with our "pure" SMT- and GA-based planner [7]. All the instances represent plans of length 15. Each offer set of Instance I, III, and V contains 256 offers, which makes the number of the potential solutions equal to $256^{15} = 2^{120}$. In the case of Instance II, IV, and VI, each offer set consists of 512 offers, which results in the search space size as large as $512^{15} = 2^{135}$. The objective functions used are as follows:

$$Q_{1,2} = \sum_{i=1}^{n} o_{j_i,1}^{i}, \qquad Q_{3,4} = \sum_{i=1}^{n} (o_{j_i,1}^{i} + o_{j_i,2}^{i}), \qquad Q_{5,6} = \sum_{i=1}^{n} o_{j_i,3}^{i}. \qquad (5)$$

The set of the constraints of Instances from I to IV is defined as follows:

$$\mathbb{C}_{1,2,3,4} = \{(o^i_{j_i,2} < o^{i+1}_{j_{i+1},2}) \mid i = 1, \ldots, n-1\}. \tag{6}$$

In the case of Instance V and VI, which are based on an example from [7], the constraints are the following:

$$\mathbb{C}_{5,6} = \{(o^1_{j_1,1} \leq 100), (o^1_{j_1,2} + o^2_{j_1,2} > 50), (o^i_{j_i,5} = o^{i+1}_{j_{i+1},1}) \mid i = 1, \ldots, n-1\}. \tag{7}$$

Besides the parameters introduced already in Section 3.3, the standard parameters of GA, used in the hybrid algorithms, have been set to the same values as in the pure GA, that is, the population size - 1000, the number of iterations - $N = 100$, the crossover probability - 95%, and the mutation probability - 0.5%. Moreover, all the experiments with the hybrid algorithms have been performed using $st = 20$, that is, the first *SFII* procedure starts with the 20th iteration. Every instance has been tested 12 times, using a different combination of the remaining parameter values (see Tables from 1 to 3), and every experiment has been repeated 30 times on a standard PC with 2.8GHz CPU and Z3 [3] version 4.3 as SMT-solving engine.

The preliminary results of applying our hybrid algorithms to Instances I - VI are presented in Tables 1, 2, and 3, where the columns from left to right display the experiment label, the parameter values, and for each Instance and each hybrid variant the total runtime of the algorithm (**t[s]**), the average quality of the solutions found (**Q**), and the probability of finding a solution (**P**). For reference, we report in the two bottom rows (marked with SMT and GA, respectively) the results of the pure SMT- and GA-based planner[4]. One can easily see that the quality values obtained in almost every experiment are higher than these returned by GA. However, in several cases either the runtime or the probability is hardly acceptable. On the other hand, for many parameter combinations we obtain significantly better results in terms of the runtime (comparing to the pure SMT) or the probability (in comparison with the pure GA). We marked in bold the results that we find the best for a given instance and a hybrid variant.

Although the results are very promising and encouraging, as one could expect, the hybrid solutions are clearly a trade-off between the three measures: the quality, the probability, and the computation time of the pure algorithms. It is easy to observe that for many parameter valuations the hybrid solutions outperform each pure planning method provided one or two measures are taken into account only. Moreover, the Semi-Random Hybrid algorithm outranks in almost all cases the Random Hybrid one in terms of the computation time and the probability of finding a solution. On the other hand, since RH runs SMT-solver much more often than SRH, it also finds solutions of better quality than SRH, but at the price of a much longer computation time.

---

[4] The pure GA-based planner has used the same parameters values as the hybrid ones. The test has been performed on the same machine.

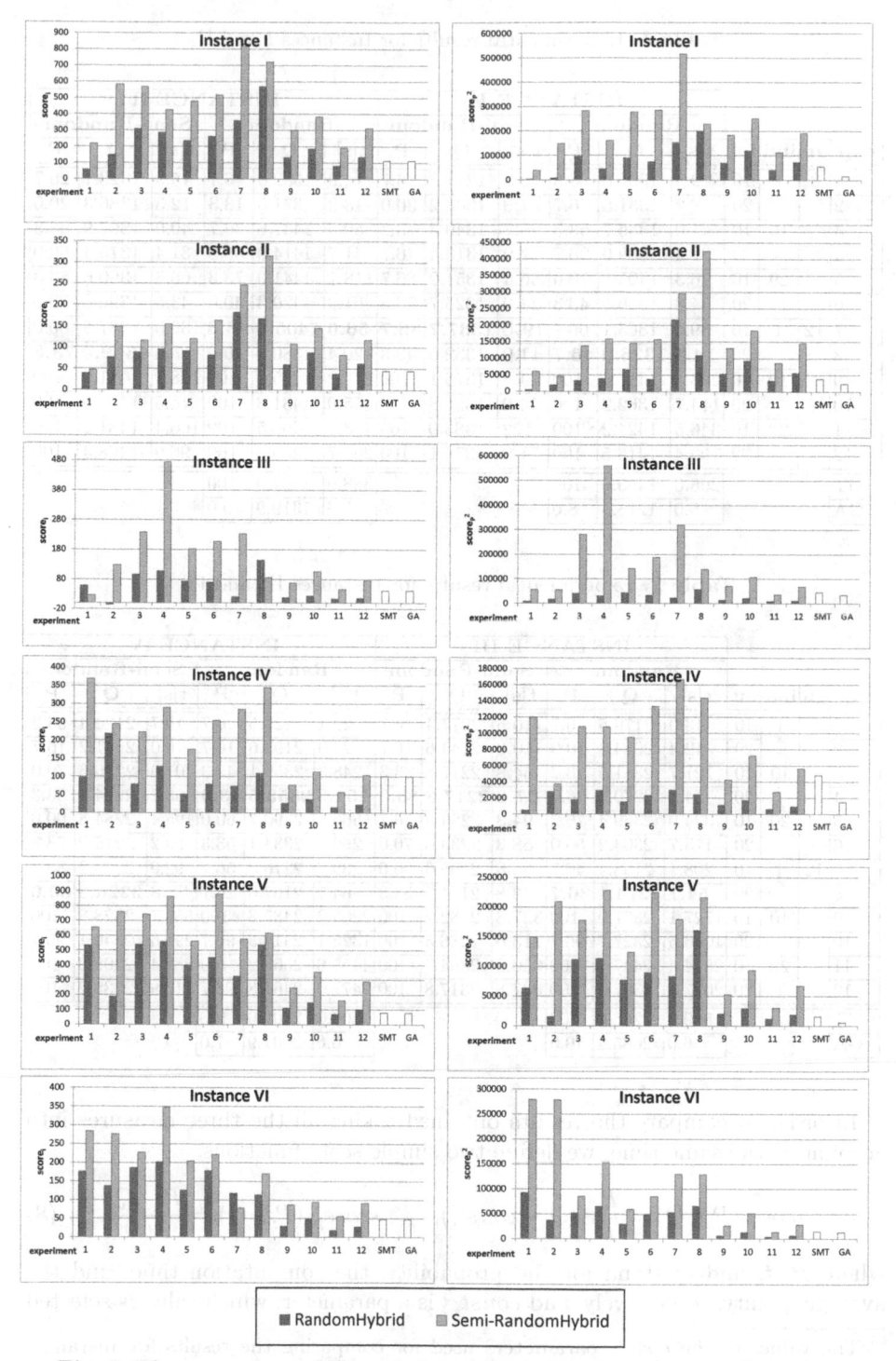

Fig. 2. The comparison of the experimental results using two score functions

Table 1. Experimental results for Instances I and II

| | | | | INSTANCE I | | | | | | INSTANCE II | | | | | |
| | | | | Random | | | Semi-Random | | | Random | | | Semi-Random | | |
exp	gn	ind	int	t[s]	Q	P	t[s]	Q	P	t[s]	Q	P	t[s]	Q	P
1	8	1	10	9.3	1305.0	3.3	9.3	1271.2	16.7	14.9	1382.0	6.7	15.9	1323.1	26.7
2			20	8.2	1331.5	6.7	7.9	1303.2	30.0	13.2	1371.5	13.3	12.3	1386.3	20.0
3		10	10	41.0	1386.7	53.3	25.7	1349.3	73.3	59.5	1437.6	36.7	40.0	1367.9	63.3
4			20	22.4	1389.0	26.7	17.9	1313.4	46.7	41.7	1414.0	33.3	31.4	1375.4	60.0
5		20	10	76.3	1405.8	70.0	36.4	1351.2	86.7	118.1	1441.0	73.3	66.3	1390.6	83.3
6			20	34.3	1356.5	43.3	24.9	1325.7	73.3	61.9	1420.3	40.0	43.5	1396.3	70.0
7	12	1	10	39.6	1363.1	66.7	**19.5**	**1337.7**	**86.7**	**56.6**	**1405.3**	**93.3**	30.0	1387.5	80.0
8			20	**14.5**	**1326.9**	**46.7**	11.0	1332.5	43.3	20.4	1380.0	40.0	**17.4**	**1369.9**	**73.3**
9		10	10	203.6	1417.6	100	74.8	1373.1	100	273.2	1455.8	100	108.1	1411.3	100
10			20	114.7	1362.2	100	54.0	1356.8	100	155.9	1431.3	100	76.5	1405.9	100
11		20	10	346.5	1424.2	100	122	1383.9	100	443.1	1460.5	100	166.4	1431.2	100
12			20	196.4	1416.5	100	71.9	1374.1	100	261.7	1455.3	100	96.9	1408.4	100
SMT				266.0	1443.0	100				388.0	1467.0	100			
GA				5.0	1218.5	8.0				5.6	1319.9	10.0			

Table 2. Experimental results for Instances III and IV

| | | | | INSTANCE III | | | | | | INSTANCE IV | | | | | |
| | | | | Random | | | Semi-Random | | | Random | | | Semi-Random | | |
exp	gn	ind	int	t[s]	Q	P	t[s]	Q	P	t[s]	Q	P	t[s]	Q	P
1	8	1	10	13.0	2176.5	6.7	10.5	2077.4	16.7	22.1	2229.5	6.7	19.7	2124.4	33.3
2			20	12.4	2054.3	10.0	10.9	2144.6	16.7	22.0	2193.6	16.7	16.0	2141.2	16.7
3		10	10	121.7	2311.5	46.7	54.8	2217.8	83.3	248.3	2359.1	43.3	101.0	2226.6	70.0
4			20	54.2	2279.4	26.7	**27.6**	**2217.8**	**83.3**	151.9	2353.5	43.3	58.7	2224.4	53.3
5		20	10	324.9	2369.4	76.7	94.3	2284.3	76.7	566.8	2390.7	60.0	195.4	2284.8	90.0
6			20	175.7	2304.2	50.0	58.3	2233.0	70.0	290.8	2334.1	53.3	89.2	2215.2	73.3
7	12	1	10	208.1	2153.4	46.7	55.8	2205.6	90.0	239.7	2216.3	56.7	92.9	2223.2	83.3
8			20	**54.1**	**2274.1**	**36.7**	43.8	2131.7	53.3	64.1	2167.0	26.7	**55.8**	**2226.3**	**60.0**
9		10	10	1727.1	2377.9	100	327.3	2282.2	100	2205.2	2485.3	100	553.7	2328.8	100
10			20	1066.5	2327.7	96.7	213.0	2286.5	100	1325.1	2414.3	96.7	291.6	2246.1	96.7
11		20	10	2814.4	2447.1	100	650.8	2364.7	100	4455.6	2568.2	100	882.4	2408.3	100
12			20	2027.1	2387.3	100	337.8	2317.8	100	2477.0	2469.8	96.7	416.9	2338.2	100
SMT				500.0	2266.0	100				500.0	2409.0	100			
GA				6.0	2085.4	10.0				6.6	2001.9	7.0			

In order to compare the results obtained taking all the three measures into account at the same time, we define two simple score functions:

$$score_i(P, t, Q) = \frac{P}{t} \cdot (Q - const_i), \qquad score_{p^2}(P, t, Q) = \frac{P^2 \cdot Q}{t}, \qquad (8)$$

where P, t, and Q stand for the probability, the computation time, and the average quality, respectively, and $const_i$[5] is a parameter, which value is selected

---

[5] The values of the $const_i$ parameters used for comparing the results for Instances I-VI are as follows: 1150, 1295, 2061, 1906, 386, 514, respectively.

Table 3. Experimental results for Instances V and VI

exp	gn	ind	int	INSTANCE V						INSTANCE VI					
				Random			Semi-Random			Random			Semi-Random		
				t[s]	Q	P	t[s]	Q	P	t[s]	Q	P	t[s]	Q	P
1	8	1	10	12.0	560.0	36.7	16.3	546.1	66.7	25.4	584.1	63.3	20.5	572.1	100
2			20	8.8	486.0	16.7	10.8	509.5	66.7	17.4	585.3	33.3	16.4	564.3	90.0
3		10	10	55.0	704.1	93.3	34.1	648.0	96.7	156.1	804.8	100	81.9	699.9	100
4			20	**36.2**	**638.2**	**80.0**	22.7	596.1	93.3	**96.8**	**722.8**	**93.3**	**40.6**	**660.1**	**96.7**
5		20	10	94.9	777.9	96.7	51.8	687.1	96.7	298.7	888.1	100	131.8	783.0	100
6			20	52.0	667.3	83.3	**28.2**	**634.1**	**100**	165.9	808.9	100	81.5	694.4	100
7	12	1	10	69.8	620.2	96.7	31.8	569.6	100	124.4	660.3	100	42.2	546.8	100
8			20	30.4	561.1	93.3	23.0	532.6	96.7	75.1	608.8	90.0	42.5	588.6	96.7
9		10	10	420.0	852.8	100	139.9	731.4	100	1385.4	928.5	100	294.7	769.0	100
10			20	264.1	774.5	100	66.5	620.8	100	619.6	814.4	100	122.3	628.9	100
11		20	10	807.4	935.5	100	275.7	832.7	100	2614.5	993.3	100	643.2	874.4	100
12			20	461.9	852.6	100	100.7	675.7	100	1464.6	927.3	100	260.1	750.9	100
SMT				500.0	781.0	100				500.0	755.0	100			
GA				5.1	436.0	8.0				5.9	537.8	12.0			

for each Instance i from I to VI, to make the scores of the pure GA- and SMT-based algorithm equal. These scores are then selected as the benchmarks for the comparison given in Fig. 2. The dark- and light-grey bars correspond to the results obtained with the RH and SRH algorithm, respectively.

The $score_i$ function aims at comparing the results under the assumption that both the pure planning methods are equally effective as far as the three measures are concerned. On the other hand, the $score_{p^2}$ function gives priority to the solutions having a high probability. Obviously, this way, one can define a number of other score functions in order to compare the results according to a personal preference. Notice that another interesting remark can be made about the hybrid parameter values. Namely, the bold values in Tables 1, 2, and 3, as well as the highest chart bars in Figure 2 most often correspond to parameter combinations of the experiment 4, 7, and 8. However, the study of only six instances does not allow us to draw any broad conclusions. Therefore, in our future work we are going to investigate whether these parameter values guarantee to obtain good results in general.

5   Conclusions and Future Work

In this paper two prototypes of the hybrid concrete planner have been implemented and several experiments have been performed. The experimental results show that even when using a straightforward strategy of combining the SMT- and GA-based approach, one can obtain surprisingly good results. We believe that the method proposed is of a high potential. Our plan is to further improve the efficiency of our hybrid approach in terms of: a better quality of solutions, lower computation times, as well as higher probabilities of finding solutions. Moreover, using the experience gained from the concrete planning, we intend to develop also a hybrid solution for the abstract planning stage.

References

1. Ambroszkiewicz, S.: Entish: A language for describing data processing in open distributed systems. Fundam. Inform. 60(1-4), 41–66 (2004)
2. Bell, M.: Introduction to Service-Oriented Modeling. John Wiley & Sons (2008)
3. de Moura, L.M., Bjørner, N.: Z3: An efficient SMT solver. In: Ramakrishnan, C.R., Rehof, J. (eds.) TACAS 2008. LNCS, vol. 4963, pp. 337–340. Springer, Heidelberg (2008)
4. Doliwa, D., Horzelski, W., Jarocki, M., Niewiadomski, A., Penczek, W., Półrola, A., Szreter, M., Zbrzezny, A.: PlanICS - a web service compositon toolset. Fundam. Inform. 112(1), 47–71 (2011)
5. Niewiadomski, A., Penczek, W.: Towards SMT-based Abstract Planning in Plan-ICS Ontology. In: Proc. of KEOD 2013 International Conference on Knowledge Engineering and Ontology Development, pp. 123–131 (September 2013)
6. Niewiadomski, A., Penczek, W., Półrola, A.: Abstract Planning in PlanICS Ontology. An SMT-based Approach. Technical Report 1027, ICS PAS (2012)
7. Niewiadomski, A., Penczek, W., Skaruz, J.: SMT vs Genetic Algorithms: Concrete Planning in PlanICS Framework. In: CS&P, pp. 309–321 (2013)
8. Niewiadomski, A., Penczek, W., Skaruz, J., Szreter, M., Jarocki, M.: SMT versus Genetic and OpenOpt Algorithms: Concrete Planning in the PlanICS Framework (accepted to Fundam. Inform.) (2014)
9. Rao, J., Su, X.: A survey of automated web service composition methods. In: Cardoso, J., Sheth, A.P. (eds.) SWSWPC 2004. LNCS, vol. 3387, pp. 43–54. Springer, Heidelberg (2005)
10. Skaruz, J., Niewiadomski, A., Penczek, W.: Automated abstract planning with use of genetic algorithms. In: GECCO (Companion), pp. 129–130 (2013)

Analysis of Offloading as an Approach for Energy-Aware Applications on Android OS:
A Case Study on Image Processing

Luis Corral, Anton B. Georgiev, Alberto Sillitti, Giancarlo Succi,
and Tihomir Vachkov

Free University of Bozen-Bolzano
Piazza Domenicani 3, 39100 Bolzano-Bozen, Italy
{luis.corral,anton.georgiev,asillitti,gsucci,
tihomir.vachkov}@unibz.it

Abstract. Energy consumption on mobile devices has been studied with the objective of finding ways to extend the device's autonomy, responding to a clear requirement from the end user. Computation offloading is an energy aware design technique that moves the execution of software routines outside the mobile device. In this paper, we illustrate a case study of an energy aware image processing application for Android mobile systems, which exercises process offloading to describe a quantitative outline of its actual contribution to save energy in a mobile device. We compared the battery consumption of local and remote executions of selected benchmarks, finding that even though in some cases it is actually more economical to offload the process, the expenses of overhead and network usage have a high impact on the energy required by the application.

Keywords: Android, Consumption, Design, Energy, Green, Mobile, Offloading.

1   Introduction

The evolution of mobile devices as personal portable computers has triggered the need of more energy, to keep up with the requirements of more powerful hardware and software features. Currently, with an average usage, smartphones can hardly resist 24 hours without exhausting the energy supplies. From the user point of view, the capability of the device's battery is a key quality when choosing a new smartphone. Since the device's autonomy is a strong requirement in mobile devices, energy-aware mobile design has been the focus of numerous research works, both from hardware and software perspective.

From hardware point of view, manufacturers explore new technologies that aim to create better batteries, or that pursue the reduction of the energy required by the electronic components of mobile devices. Nevertheless, it has not been possible to keep the hardware evolution along with the fast pace of the mobile software development, which constantly increases the demand of power resources. From the software point of view, different techniques have been studied: economic system profiling, to select the

I. Awan et al. (Eds.): MobiWis 2014, LNCS 8640, pp. 29–40, 2014.

settings, that reduce the energy consumed [1]; code optimization which aims to restructure the code for energy awareness [2]; method reallocation [3] and process offloading [4], which focus on moving the heaviest computations to the places where the energy required to execute them is minimum.

In this work, we deepen the discussion on one of the software-oriented approaches by proposing a case study of computation offloading, implemented in an Android OS application. We study the ways to implement computation offloading, and we analyze its benefits and tradeoffs on a mobile software system. As a case study, we created a mobile software application that executes software benchmarks, including the option of offloading computational job into a remote environment. We measured the energy consumed by the application when executing locally the complete set of functionality, and when part of the job was offloaded, with the goal of describing a quantitative outline of the actual contribution of the offloading technique to save energy in a mobile device. We found that even though in some cases it is actually more economic to offload the process, the expenses of overhead and network usage have also a high impact on the energy consumption of the offloaded application.

The rest of the paper is structured as follows: Section 2 presents the problem statement; Section 3 introduces our approach in the form of an offloading-enabled Android OS application; Section 4 shows our experimental setup and data collection plan; Section 5 discusses the obtained results; Section 6 presents the related work and Section 7 summarizes this work and draws conclusions.

2   Reducing Energy Consumption on Mobile Devices

A critical principle of mobile devices is their ability to excel away from a continuous energy supply. However, the performance and high usage of hardware components demanded by modern mobile applications causes that the battery constantly exhausts its reserves. One of the software-based approaches to tackle this problem is energy-aware application design, which contributes to economize battery resources throughout different practices of architecting, design and software implementation. In this way, an energy-aware application specifically focuses on demanding a smaller amount of power while offering the required features with an acceptable level of performance.

One of the most recent approaches for energy-aware software design in the mobile context is process offloading. Process offloading is a technique in which heavy computation jobs are sent to remote computers with the purpose of saving energy on the local machine, to the expenses of response overhead while the application is waiting. At the end of the remote execution, the result is sent back to the local machine.

Several research works [1, 4] have discussed different techniques to implement process offloading, claiming that it leads to considerable energy savings. In principle, it may be evident that process offloading should free the mobile's processing resources required to complete a given task; nevertheless, one should bear in mind that the phone should spend a relative amount of energy to establish a connection with the remote infrastructure, send the request and the associated information, wait until the task is completed, receive the result and close the connection. If this investment of energy is less than the one that the phone has to spend on executing the operation using its own processing resources, offloading can be considered beneficial.

A sustained answer to this issue involves the comparison of the investment associated to executing the same task in two contexts: locally and offloaded. In this fashion, one may compare the overall amount of energy spent by an application of comparable computational job executed locally or offloaded in a remote server. To accomplish a fair comparison, such server should be able to execute the required job in an equivalent implementation to the one in the phone.

In this work we investigate the possible energy savings achieved through process offloading of a heavy computational tasks such as matrix multiplication and image processing. Hence, we established the following work hypothesis:

H1. Image processing application's energy efficiency can be improved by offloading its heavy computational tasks to external infrastructure

From our hypothesis, we defined a research question:

RQ1. How much more energy efficient is a matrix multiplication or image processing job executed outside of the client device?

To answer this question in a quantitative way, it is necessary to build an experimental setup with an Android application and a server counterpart, which enables us to collect data about the energy spent by several processing tasks executed in the cellphone and in the external infrastructure. This experiment will help in identifying the scenarios where offloading a computational job to external infrastructure will be an energy efficient solution. Finally, the computational task to exercise the methods should be prepared in the context of image processing mobile applications.

3   Our Approach: An Offloading-Enabled Image Processing Android Application

Our proposal is to analyze the energy consumption optimization of an image processing applications through offloading the heavy computations to a remote environment. After designing and executing the experiment we will have a set of energy measurements of various load levels. The data collected should be sufficiently expressive to compare the two types of execution.

3.1   Benchmarks

For our experiment we selected two benchmarks with various workloads in order to analyze the benefits of process offloading.

•   *Matrix multiplication* - the input is a text file with two matrices. A separate Java program was developed to generate such file with random values of the elements of the matrices (allows the adjustment of the dimension of both arrays). The actual input is a string indicating the full path to the file, but if offloading comes into act, all the bytes of the file are sent over the Internet. The system must read the input file from the phone storage, convert the matrices from text format into numerical two-dimensional arrays and apply the "dot product" multiplication. The output of the operation is two-dimensional array of integers written to another text file and stored in the phone with different name.

- *Image filter* - the input is an image file of the most used formats (i.e. PNG, BMP, JPG, JPEG, GIFF). In this case the actual input parameter of the system's functions is a string indicating the full path to the file, but when the execution is offloaded to the remote server, all the bytes of the file are sent over the Internet. The server method reads the input file and applies the same algorithm with the same settings for filtering. In both cases the resulting image file is stored on the phone.

The benchmarks were selected in a way to enable us to analyze the impact of offloading on the image processing routines. We included the matrix multiplication scenario, because of the fact that many image filters methods contain this routine as part of their algorithm.

Additionally, the implementations of the image filter and the matrix multiplication in combination with the different loads aim to not only collect data for the energy spent by a heavy computational job, but also simulates various real-world image processing applications' behavior.

3.2   Our System's Architecture

The aim of our system is to run the benchmarks we selected with different loads in two different execution environments while tracking the amount of energy the specific application consumed. To achieve that we used an open-source measurement application – PowerTutor [5], which measures the energy every apps consumed. To avoid imprecisions, a given experiment is run 100 times automatically with the same input parameter values and in the same execution environment. Thus, the difference in battery utilization is more obvious.

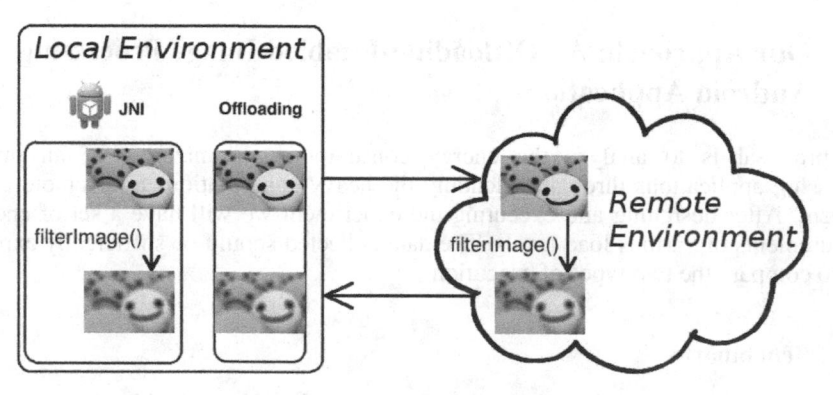

Fig. 1. Architecture of the execution environments

On figure 1 is depicted the execution flow in our two cases, when we execute the computation locally or in a remote environment.

Local Environment - Android Application

The starting point of the execution flow in the client Android mobile application is the main activity. In order to take advantage from the JNI, the shared libraries with the C++ code are loaded in that specific class. When the benchmark is selected, an internal auxiliary method is invoked, in which a very simple *if* statement simulates a decision for offloading. The experiment presented in this paper would behave equally with a complex and precise decision-making and the measurements would not be altered. Moreover, in this method can be specified different input values of the computational loads in order to measure the performance in vast situations. If the execution flow is switched to local processing, the respective native method is called. Otherwise the offloading process starts in a new thread.

The first step in the multiplication of the matrices job is for the method to take a string indicating the path to the file to be processed. With purpose of the experiment, different files can be specified to measure behavior of various matrices size. Once the plain text file with the matrices is open, its content is saved into a string. According to the syntax structuring the information about the matrices, this string is split first around the "~" symbol to obtain the matrices, then around the ";" symbol to retrieve the rows of each matrix. At this point a program can execute an algorithm for the actual multiplication. The product is parsed into a string, which is written in a .txt file and stored in the internal permanent phone memory. To finalize the method the path to the outcome is returned to the Android application.

In the case of the image processing benchmark the flow is analogical. The difference is that the STL does not dispose methods, which can be used for the purpose of the image filter, so the external OpenCV libraries were included. The source image is loaded into an object and a kernel is initialized. The size of the kernel must be the same in the two implementations in order to have the same level of blur on the image. Invoking the filter2D method with arguments source image object, destination image object, additional coefficient for depth, the kernel, delta encoding and border option, the picture is modified and written in the destination object. A little formatting of the path to specify where the graphics file will be written and afterwards the outcome is stored. The function returns the path to the resulting file to the Android application, which later shows it on the GUI.

Remote Environment - Server-Side Application

The role of the remote environment in our experiment is to receive a computational task alongside with the load, execute it using identical algorithm with the one in the client mobile application, and return the result of the execution back to the client. To implement it we used only Java programming language. As mentioned before, the benchmarks to be executed on the phone and on the cloud are the same but implemented in different language. Nevertheless, the all algorithms are equivalent and produce the same result.

4   Experimental Setup

To achieve the comparison we implemented an Android app with offloading capabilities to stress the two execution environments' processes. With the goal of simulating real world scenario, those tasks should provide the possibility to adjust the computational load and to adjust the amount of data being exchanged between the local and the remote environment over the Internet.

Our experiment consists of running the Android application that we developed and measure how much energy it needs to perform a given task. To do so we used

PowerTutor, which is an open-source application that records the power consumption at application level. It can report the amount of power, measured in Joule, which a given application employs. To increase precision of the obtained readings, the application quits after the last execution statement to avoid consuming energy while staying idle.

The experiment was performed using three different test beds – LG Nexus 4, Galaxy Samsung Galaxy Nexus and Thl 220W. Their specification is shown in the Table1.

Table 1. Specification of our mobile test beds

LG Nexus 4 specification
CPU - Dual 1.4 GHz, ARM cortex A9 architecture
RAM - 1 GB
Display - 5.29" WXGA HD sAMOLED, screen resolution: 800x1280, 16 million Internal Color Depth
Connectivity - Wi-Fi a/g/b/n, 2.4 GHz / 5 GHz, 3G
Samsung Galaxy Nexus specification
CPU – 1.2 GHz Dual-core, OMAP, TI
RAM – 1 GB
Display – 4.65", 720x1280
Connectivity – Wi-Fi 802.11 a/b/g/n, 3G
THL W220S specification
CPU – MTK MT6592, 8x 1.7 GHz, Octacore, A7
RAM – 1 GB
Display – 5. 0" OGS, 720x1280, HD
Connectivity – Wi-Fi 802.11 a/b/g/n, 3G

To establish the connection with the external infrastructure and to send and receive the needed information, we used the Wi-Fi capabilities of the mobile devices.

The display is one of the most energy hungry components. It is playing a key role since it consumes a lot of power when switched on. In real world scenarios, while a job is running, the user has to wait for the outcome, usually the person is doing something else or at least the display is on. The experiment is valid and correct regardless to the above statement, since this condition is equal to all the tasks. PowerTutor provides functionality, which shows the percentage of the total energy spent for the exercise each device consumed. When tasks are executed remotely, the display consumes most of the power, even when big files have to be sent and received. This is due to the fact that the actual work is done in the remote environment and the only energy spent by the local device is the one of transferring and waiting for the files needed for the job.

5   Collected Data Interpretation

After executing the selected benchmarks with all the different workloads we collected more than 900 readings. Due to the space limitations we will show a summary of the collected energy samples in Table 2.

Table 2. Summary of the collected energy samples

Benchmark	File size	Load	Local	Remote
Samsung Galaxy Nexus				
Matrix	96 Bytes	[2x3] * [3x4]	4.24 J	9.40 J
Matrix	8 KB	[20x30] * [30x40]	4.96 J	9.48 J
Matrix	524 KB	[200x300] * [300x400]	36.14 J	15.82 J
Matrix	1.5 MB	[350x700] * [700x400]	170.21 J	26.94 J
Matrix	2.9 MB	[500x1000] * [1000x500]	411.15 J	48.20 J
Image	8 KB	52x39	6.52 J	9.52 J
Image	123 KB	209x241	9.50 J	11.50 J
Image	512 KB	477x356	14.42 J	17.16 J
Image	340 KB	1024x683	32.76 J	27.56 J
Image	532 KB	1920x1200	97.52 J	65.40 J
LG Nexus 4				
Matrix	96 Bytes	[2x3] * [3x4]	6.24 J	9.80 J
Matrix	8 KB	[20x30] * [30x40]	6.76 J	10.56 J
Matrix	524 KB	[200x300] * [300x400]	47.84 J	22.82 J
Matrix	1.5 MB	[350x700] * [700x400]	209.42 J	37.72 J
Matrix	2.9 MB	[500x1000] * [1000x500]	522.24 J	63.72 J
Image	8 KB	52x39	6.52 J	10.40 J
Image	123 KB	209x241	9.50 J	13.82 J
Image	512 KB	477x356	14.42 J	20.16 J
Image	340 KB	1024x683	32.76 J	37.74 J
Image	532 KB	1920x1200	97.52 J	67.00 J
THL W220S				
Matrix	96 Bytes	[2x3] * [3x4]	7.24 J	11.2 J
Matrix	8 KB	[20x30] * [30x40]	8.08 J	12.2 J
Matrix	524 KB	[200x300] * [300x400]	45.92 J	25.8 J
Matrix	1.5 MB	[350x700] * [700x400]	159.12 J	27.06 J
Matrix	2.9 MB	[500x1000] * [1000x500]	400.96 J	49.06 J
Image	8 KB	52x39	7.50 J	11.02 J
Image	123 KB	209x241	10.52 J	14.44 J
Image	512 KB	477x356	14.84 J	17.60 J
Image	340 KB	1024x683	32.76 J	31.02 J
Image	532 KB	1920x1200	95.7 J	74.92 J

As stated in our research question the comparison between the two execution environments is one of the goals of this work. To communicate better the results that we obtained and summarized we created separate plot for each test bed and benchmarks depicted on Figure 2.

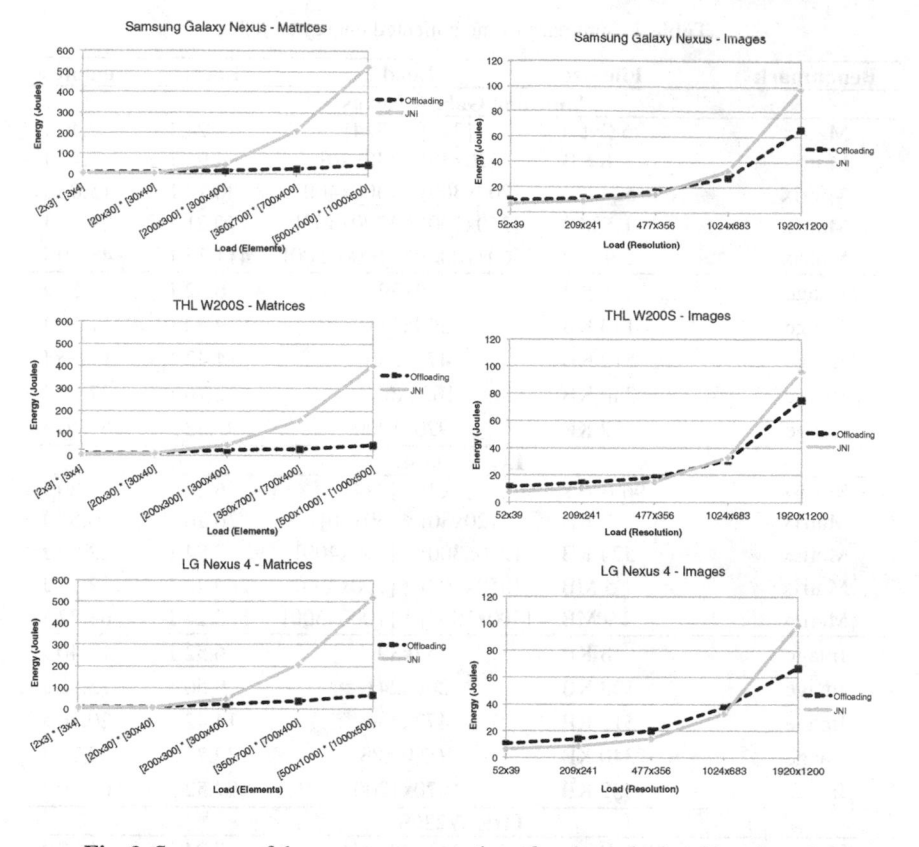

Fig. 2. Summary of the energy consumption of each test bed and benchmark

5.1   Data Analysis

From the data collected with PowerTutor, we can make conclusions about the outcome of the experiment. In the scenarios described in this paper, it is not always the case that offloading is beneficial. An example of such case is when little load is given to one of the selected benchmarks. It is evident from the results that in these situations it is pointless to transmit data over the Wi-Fi adapter, keep the connection alive while waiting for a result and finally receive the actual result rather than just call local functions which will make the processor to spend less energy. However for the cases of heavy computations, we can conclude that offloading is advantageous. When big load is given to the app, the processor is free of all those instructions involved in computing the result. Therefore, in this case the amount of battery drained is lower.

It can be noticed from the results in the Table 2 that the volume of energy that is drained from the battery is not constant even with identical conditions of the tests execution. One of the reasons for that is the invocation of JNI functions while which other processes running on the phone may require some CPU usage at the time the benchmark is executing. Low-level kernel processes have precedence over application processes. Similar discussion can be developed for the memory available for execution. The above statements are valid also for the offloading flow of execution, but in the server environment. In addition, other external factors may reflect the overall performance of the remote execution process. For example, the exchange rate between the two parts is unsteady due to the nature of the wireless connections. Often there is the so-called "*noise*" along the track and radio waves of other hardware may interfere with the Wi-Fi or 3G connection. Therefore, the values regarding the offloading are more variable.

5.2   Research Questions Revisited

The values obtained as result of our experimentation in the different test beds lead to the partial confirmation of our work hypothesis that aimed to find a connection between the placement of the executed method and the amount of energy invested by the cellphone to complete it.

H1. Image processing application's energy efficiency can be improved by offloading its heavy computational tasks to external infrastructure

The data provided by our experiments do not allow us to confirm this work hypothesis categorically. A combination of factors that include the computational complexity, of the method, the data load and the network usage are of paramount importance to determine if the offloaded execution of the image processing method will really lead to energy savings. We were able to identify cases in which the local execution proved to be more economic than the remote one, due to the fact that the network usage was intense, and the use of network interfaces in a cellular phone require a significant investment of energy.

We detailed as well answer to our research question:

RQ1. How much more energy efficient is a matrix multiplication or image processing job executed outside of the client device?

From Table 2 we can see that in the best case, one can save up to 800% of the energy consumption when offloading a matrix multiplication method to an external infrastructure. For image processing task we reached maximum gain of 30%. However, as already discussed, it is important to consider the cases and conditions when the computational job is offloaded, as we could as well identified cases where the local execution performed better.

6   Related Work

From the software point of view, different approaches have been studied. For instance, provided that the overall energy consumption of a software piece may be related to its performance [6], existing techniques of code optimization (refactoring and restructuring) have been explored to reduce energy consumption [2]. In the same track, reverse engineering has been considered, although its application is more complex and not every developer is able to conduct it properly. Another way for saving energy is through method reallocation [3]. Reallocation is a technique which, taking advantage of the organization of the operative stack within the mobile device, locates the execution of heavy tasks in the level where they consume less energy [7, 8]. For example, it is well known that C or C++ perform faster than Java in certain conditions, which may imply the consumption of less energy. Then, if the software architecture allows it, one can use the Java support of native interface with C/C++ language and reallocate computationally heavy methods to C or C++ implementations. For example, this support is possible on Android OS [9], and in this way, hybrid applications can be attractive for developers as they can benefit from the advantages of both languages, including power economization and increasing the overall quality of their products [10, 11, 12, 13].

In a different track, other research efforts concentrate on moving the heaviest computations out of the device via Internet to a remote infrastructure. This technique is also called offloading, cyber foraging or remote execution. There are several ways to implement offloading: the simplest one is to send some parameters to the server, specifying what operation is going to be performed and other parameters for the calculation, and the result is then returned back to the phone. With this technique, the energy resources required to execute the computation are surrogated to an external infrastructure, to the expenses of the overhead of sending and receiving the information. This can imply, however, that the mobile device invests energy for the Wi-Fi or 3G modules to set up and maintain the connection, and to receive the results processed by the cloud infrastructure.

In the design phase of our experiment we were searching for a heavy computational job to be implemented, in order to find out if and in which cases offloading is more energy efficient compared to the local execution. Image processing is an example of such complex task that has high demand of hardware resource of its execution environment, which leads to vast energy consumption. To cope with this problem, several research works try to offload the computation of such elaboration outside the mobile device. Chun et al. [14] designed a system, which migrates a thread to its clone on a remote cloud infrastructure. In the final phase, the thread is accommodated back in the mobile client. In their work the authors [15] present an approach, where the smartphone requests web services on service providers' servers. Their design brings several advantages, for instance excellent encapsulation, loose coupling, standard protocols and integration capabilities. The paper of Tae-Hyun Kim [16] is concentrated on backlight power reduction using efficient image compensation. They identified the problem of spending a lot of energy when an image is shown to the user in daylight. In such situation the display brightness is on maximum, since the human eye perceives the image dark. Their light algorithm for image compensation performs in the so-called Discrete Cosine Transform domain, which re-calculates the pixels in a way that it is easy to avoid to rise up the display brightness when viewing and image. In a different track several architectures [17, 18, 19, 20] include the widely used OpenCV library, which we used in our experiment, for efficient image processing and object recognition.

7   Conclusions

In this paper, we discussed the importance of energy aware design to achieve more efficient mobile apps in the context of the Android Operating Systems. We implemented the code offloading technique to the built a mobile application that is able to execute the same image processing method both locally and remotely; and we calculated the energy consumed by the application when it selects to execute the code in the cellular phone or in an external infrastructure.

To determine what approach is more convenient from the energy awareness point of view, we conducted a survey executing systematically the local and remote image processing and matric multiplication methods and calculating the energy consumed by both implementations. We investigated the cases in which local execution was more efficient than remote execution, and the cases where offloading the code resulted in a more economic implementation. The computational complexity, data load and potential network usage stand out as the most important factors to consider when deciding whether to execute locally or offload a particular method.

Mobile devices are currently the most important platform for the introduction and utilization of software products and services. The trends show a consistent growth in computing capabilities, number of users and distributed products, configuring a rich field of research of extraordinary potential and impact. Currently, it is necessary to count on the methods to assure the efficient execution of mobile apps in a way that the battery life meets and exceeds the requirements and expectations of the end user. To do it, energy awareness techniques grow as an instrumental design tool for software engineers to increase their knowledge of the way that the devices use their resources towards overcoming the energy challenges, satisfying the needs of the end user, and helping developers in creating better mobile solutions.

References

1. Chen, H., Luo, B., Shi, W.: Anole: a case for energy-aware mobile application design. In: 2012 41st International Conference on Parallel Processing Workshops (ICPPW), pp. 232–238. IEEE (2012)
2. Gottschalk, M., Jelschen, J., Winter, A.: Energy-client Code by Refactoring. Carl von Ossietzky Universität, Oldenburg, Germany
3. Corral, L., Georgiev, A.B., Sillitti, A., Succi, G.: Method Reallocation to Reduce Energy Consumption: An Implementation in Android OS. In: Proceedings of the 29th Symposium on Applied Computing. ACM (2014)
4. Shivarudrappa, D., Chen, M., Bharadwaj, S.: COFA: Automatic and Dynamic Code Offload for Android. University of Colorado, Boulde
5. Zhang, L., Tiwana, B., Qian, Z., Wang, Z., Dick, R.P., Mao, Z.M., Yang, L.: Accurate on-line power estimation and automatic battery behavior based power model generation for smartphones. In: Proceedings of the Eighth IEEE/ACM/IFIP International Conference on Hardware/Software Codesign and System Synthesis, pp. 105–114. ACM
6. Corral, L., Sillitti, A., Succi, G.: Mobile multiplatform development: An experiment for performance analysis. In: 9th International Conference on Mobile Web Information Systems (MobiWIS 2012). Procedia Computer Science, vol. 10, pp. 736–743. Elsevier (2012)
7. Corral, L., Georgiev, A.B., Sillitti, A., Succi, G.: A Method for Characterizing Energy Consumption in Android Smartphones. In: Proceedings of the 2nd International Workshop on Green and Sustainable Software (GREENS 2013), in connection with ICSE 2013, pp. 38–45. ACM (2013)

8. Corral, L., Georgiev, A.B., Sillitti, A., Succi, G.: Can Execution Time Describe Accurately the Energy Consumption of Mobile Apps? An Experiment in Android. In: Proceedings of the 2nd International Workshop on Green and Sustainable Software (GREENS 2014), in connection with ICSE 2014. ACM (2014)
9. Georgiev, A.B., Sillitti, A., Succi, G.: Open Source Mobile Virtual Machines: An Energy Assessment of Dalvik vs. ART. In: Corral, L., Sillitti, A., Succi, G., Vlasenko, J., Wasserman, A.I. (eds.) OSS 2014. IFIP AICT, vol. 427, pp. 93–102. Springer, Heidelberg (2014)
10. Corral, L., Sillitti, A., Succi, G.: Software Assurance Practices for Mobile Applications. A Survey of the State of the Art. Computing. In: Special Issue on Mobile Web and Information Systems. Springer (2014)
11. Corral, L., Sillitti, A., Succi, G.: Agile software development processes for mobile systems: Accomplishment, evidence and evolution. In: Daniel, F., Papadopoulos, G.A., Thiran, P. (eds.) MobiWIS 2013. LNCS, vol. 8093, pp. 90–106. Springer, Heidelberg (2013)
12. Corral, L., Sillitti, A., Succi, G., Garibbo, A., Ramella, P.: Evolution of mobile software development from platform-specific to web-based multiplatform paradigm. In: Proceedings of the 10th SIGPLAN Symposium on New Ideas, New Paradigms, and Reflections on Programming and Software (ONWARD 2011), pp. 181–183. ACM (2011)
13. Corral, L., Janes, A., Remencius, T.: Potential advantages and disadvantages of multiplatform development frameworks – A vision on mobile environments. Procedia Computer Science 10, 1202–1207
14. Chun, B.G., Ihm, S., Maniatis, P., Naik, M., Patti, A.: Clonecloud: elastic execution between mobile device and cloud. In: Proceedings of the Sixth Conference on Computer Systems, pp. 301–314. ACM
15. Liang, Y., Xiao, Y., Huang, J.: An Efficient Image Processing Method Based on Web Services for Mobile Devices. In: 2nd International Congress on Image and Signal Processing, CISP 2009, pp. 1–5. IEEE (2009)
16. Kim, T.H., Choi, K.S., Ko, S.J.: Backlight power reduction using efficient image compensation for mobile devices. IEEE Transactions on Consumer Electronics 56(3), 1972–1978 (2010)
17. Deepthi, R.S., Sankaraiah, S.: Implementation of mobile platform using Qt and OpenCV for image processing applications. In: 2011 IEEE Conference on Open Systems (ICOS), pp. 284–289. IEEE (September 2011)
18. Willow Garage, Inc., Willow garage (August 2009), http://www.willowgarage.com/
19. Farrugia, J.P., Horain, P., Guehenneux, E., Alusse, Y.: GPUCV: A framework for image processing acceleration with graphics processors. In: 2006 IEEE International Conference on Multimedia and Expo, pp. 585–588. IEEE (2006)
20. Hiromoto, M., Nakahara, K., Sugano, H., Nakamura, Y., Miyamoto, R.: A specialized processor suitable for AdaBoost-based detection with Haar-like features. In: IEEE Conference on Computer Vision and Pattern Recognition, CVPR 2007, pp. 1–8. IEEE (2007)

Optimizing QoS-Based Web Services Composition by Using Quantum Inspired Cuckoo Search Algorithm

Serial Rayene Boussalia and Allaoua Chaoui

MISC Laboratory, Constantine 2 University, 25000 Constantine, Algeria
seriel.rayene@gmail.com, a_chaoui2001@yahoo.com

Abstract. Optimization of web services composition is one of the most interesting challenges at present, since the composition of web services become a promising technology in a variety of areas. In fact, on the internet many services provide the same functionality. So, for one user request a set of compositions is proposed. In order to have the best one, we propose in this paper an approach based on the use of the Quantum Inspired Cuckoo Search Algorithm with the QoS as optimization criteria, to satisfy the user's queries. More precisely, we propose two contributions: In the first one, we define an appropriate quantum representation for solutions. While in the second one, we propose a new randomized heuristic generating solutions starting from the user's request. And globally, with our approach we will optimize the QoS-based web services composition in order to satisfy the user query by capturing his constraints. To illustrate our approach, we have implemented it as a prototype of a system and applied it on a text translation case study. The results obtained from this illustration are encouraging and express the feasibility and effectiveness of our approach.

Keywords: Web services composition, Web service, Quality of service (QoS), Optimization methods, Combinatorial optimization, Cuckoo Search Algorithm, Quantum Computing.

1 Introduction

Web services are software components with atomic features on the internet that provide a new way to develop applications that meet its needs in order to make the web more dynamic. Web services seem to be the most suitable solution for interoperability, which is used to transmit data between different applications of an organization [1].

Web services offer a new interesting concept which consists of creating a new complex web service by composing existing ones; this concept is the process of the web services composition [2]. Indeed, the aim of the web services composition is to determine a suitable combination of web services, according to user's request that could not be satisfied by a single web service [3]. However, the large number of web services available on the internet with different implementations offering

I. Awan et al. (Eds.): MobiWis 2014, LNCS 8640, pp. 41–55, 2014.
© Springer International Publishing Switzerland 2014

the same functionality [4], led to many solutions of web services composition for one user's request. So, we need a web services composition optimization, to get the best one. In this context, The quality of service (QoS) attributes are the non-functional properties of web services which emerge as the key differential factors for selecting and composing web services [5]. Moreover, the choice of the best web services composition becomes an NP-Hard optimization problem [6] that can be modelled as a problem of multidimensional knapsack [7]. The optimization of the web services composition consists to find the best combination of web services for giving the best web services composition using optimization methods to optimize predefined QoS parameters [6]. In order to deal with this hard optimization problem, different optimization methods have been proposed.

The present study is designed to investigate the use of a Quantum Inspired Cuckoo Search Algorithm [8] to deal with the web services composition problem. The remainder of the paper is organized as follows:Section 1 is an introduction, section 2 recalls the related work; section 3 is reserved for the background, section 4 introduces the proposed approach, section 5 presents a case of study and discusses the experiments. Finally, section 6 gives some conclusions of our work and the directions for future work.

2   Related Work

In the literature, the problem of optimizing web services composition with the QoS as optimization criteria has been intensively studied and different approaches have been proposed in the past few years. Researchers in this area have focused on different sub-topics and proposed their own assertions and results.

J. Wang And Y. Hou [9] used a genetic algorithm to find an optimal web services composition. Their method is based on an abstract workflow where each abstract task is associated to a set of concrete web services with different values of quality of service(QoS). In this approach the genetic algorithm is used to make a correspondence between concrete and abstract web services in order to determine the workflow of the optimal web services composition. The solution of the composition is coded as a binary string where each position corresponds to an abstract task and indicates the selected concrete service to perform.

J. Xu and S. Reiff-Marganiec [10] proposed an algorithm of selection based on the immune system in the context of the web services composition. This approach has as input a workflow that corresponds to a composition of abstract web services, a set of web services with their specific matrix of quality of service(QoS), and the parameters for the algorithm. And as a result, it provides as output an instance of the workflow with concrete web services coded in a binary system.

Zhang et al [11] used Ant Colony Optimization for the QoS-based web services composition. With this approach, web services composition can be stated as the problem of finding a concrete web service for each abstract candidate web service extracted from a static web service composition graph. The aim is to find the near-optimal web services composition from a candidate web services composition graph.

Maolin Tang et al[12] proposed the use of A Hybrid Genetic Algorithm for the Optimal Web Services Selection Problem in Web Services Composition. In this approach, a genetic individual is mapped on a composition solution encoded using discrete representations (e.g. integer, binary). This genetic-based technique is based on a static workflow and starts from an initial population that is randomly generated and it uses a local optimizer to improve the individuals in the population and utilizes a knowledge based crossover operator.

Jianjun Li et al [13] developed an intelligent optimization algorithm for Web services composition, by combining frog leaping algorithm with the accuracy of the particle swarm optimization algorithm. Each frog (particle) represents a solution of the problem which is a web services composition. Starting with a randomly generated population, this algorithm can find the best one from a lot of web services composition schemes by optimizing an aggregated QoS function.

All those proposed approaches are statics, they are based on the use of static workflows to realize the web services compositions. But, in this paper we propose a dynamic approach, in which we investigate the use of a Quantum Inspired Cuckoo Search Algorithm [8] to deal with the web services composition problem. This efficient approach performs a global optimization in the search space by optimizing an aggregated QoS function and capturing the user's QoS constraints. Our approach starts from an initial population generated according to the user's request with a new randomized heuristic that we proposed, and uses a qubit representation for the search space and a set of quantum operators that operate on it. Our choice is motivated by the ability of this new algorithm to handle large space of potential solutions[8].

3   Background

This section recalls the theoretical background required for developing our proposed approach of using the Quantum Inspired Cuckoo Search Algorithm to optimize the QoS-based web services composition.

3.1   The Web Services Composition

The web services composition refers to the process of combining the functionality of multiple web services within the same business process, in order to meet a complex request that one web service can not satisfy alone [14]. Further, the web services composition includes several activities that correspond to the different phases of its life cycle [15], from the description to the implementation. In general, the life cycle of the web services composition consists of publishing, discovering, and executing the composition. However, for a single user request, several potential compositions can be proposed because many web services can have the same functionality [4]. So that, another activity is added in the life cycle of the web services composition which is the selection of the best web services composition that satisfies the user's constraints.

3.2   QoS-Optimization of Web Services Composition

The QoS-optimization of the web services composition consists of selecting and interconnecting the appropriate web services provided by different web services providers, with the aim of optimizing a set of predefined parameters to guaranty the overall quality of this composition [16]. The quality of services parameters (QoS)are the non-functional descriptions of web services [7], that correspond to the modalities for achieving its functions, and generally their values are provided by the Service Provider while publishing the web service [17]. These non-functional parameters characterize each web service and determine the candidate ones for each task of a complex user's request. The computation of the overall QoS depends on the web services composition, this composition is evaluated by computing the aggregated QoS function based on the values of its QoS parameters. Then, when the aggregated QoS functions of all possible web services combinations are calculated, the best combination of web services that does not violate the QoS constraints set by the user is selected [18].

3.3   Quantum Inspired Cuckoo Search Algorithm

The Quantum Inspired Cuckoo Search Algorithm (QICSA) integers the principles of quantum computing in the core of the cuckoo search algorithm, trying to increase the optimization capacities of the cuckoo search algorithm[8]. The particularity of the quantum inspired cuckoo search algorithm is the quantum representation it adopts which allows representing the superposition of all potential solutions for a given problem[19].

Cuckoo Search Algorithm. Cuckoo search algorithm is a recent bioinspired algorithm [20], it is based on the style life of Cuckoo birds. In fact, Cuckoos have an aggressive strategy of reproduction,their female hack nests of other birds to lay their eggs fertilized. Sometimes, the egg of cuckoo in the nest is discovered and the hacked birds discard or abandon the nest and start their own brood elsewhere[19]. For more details, the cuckoo search algorithm proposed by Yang and Deb [20] is describe in Algorithm 1.

The cuckoo search algorithm is characterised by its simplicity. In fact, it has few parameters to set comparing with other population metaheuristic algorithms, such as particle swarm optimization and ant colony optimisation algorithm[19].

Overview of Quantum Computing. Quantum computing has attracted prevalent interest and has induced intensive investigations and researches since it appears more powerful than its classical counterpart. Indeed, the parallelism that the quantum computing provides reduces clearly the algorithmic complexity. Such an ability of parallel processing can be used to solve combinatorial optimization problems which require the exploration of large solutions spaces [21]. For more details, the reader is refereed to [8].

In the following, we recalls the basic ideas of our proposed approach.

Algorithm 1. Cuckoo search algorithm [20]
1: **Input :**   Problem data
2: **Output :**   Problem solution
3: **begin**
4: Initial Initial a population of n host nests xi;
5: **while** t < MaxGeneration **do**
6:     Get a cuckoo (say i) randomly by Lévy flights;
7:     Evaluate its quality/fitness Fi;
8:     Choose a nest among n (say j) randomly;
9:     **if** Fi > Fj **then**
10:       Replace j by the new solution;
11:     **end if**
12:     Abandon a fraction (pa) of worse nests;
13:     Build new ones at new locations via Lévy flights;
14:     Keep the best solutions;
15:     Rank the solutions and find the current best;
16: **end while**
17: **end**

4   Proposed Approach

The development of our proposed approach QICSA-WSC (the use of Quantum Inspired Cuckoo Search Algorithm to find the best Web Services Composition) is based mainly on a quantum representation of the search space associated with the formulated problem and a QICSA dynamic is used to explore this space using quantum operations.

The schema of our proposed approach is presented in Figure 1, where the user is supposed to enter his request(input, output) and his QoS constraints thought the interaction module, and the role of our approach is to return the best web services composition using the composition and optimization module.

The most essential module in the schema (Figure 1)is the composition and optimization module, it represents globally our approach. This module accomplishes its role by three essential actions: The first one is the generation of the initial population (a set of compositions), the second one is the evaluation of the solutions(compositions)with the objective function and the selection of the best solution with the selection operator which is similar to the elitism strategy used in genetic algorithms[19]. Finally, the third action and the most important one, is applying the main quantum cuckoo dynamics. This action is done by four operations inspired from quantum computing and cuckoo search algorithm: Quantum Measurement, Quantum Mutation, Quantum Interference and Levy flights operations.

4.1   Problem Definition and Formulation

The problem of finding the best web services composition without enumerating all possible combinations is considered as an optimization problem. That problem is

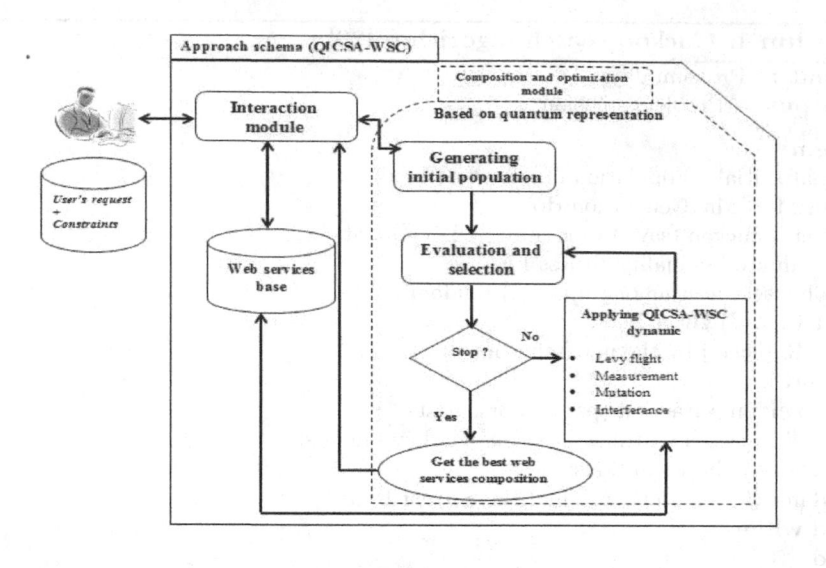

Fig. 1. QICSA-WSC schema

modelled as a problem of multidimensional knapsack which is known as NP-Hard optimization problem [6]. This model is due to three factors that determine the complexity of this problem which are [7] : The number of tasks to be performed, the number of candidate web services for each task and the number of parameters of quality of services to optimize.

To evaluate the multi-dimensional quality of a given web services composition (WSC), an objective function (fitness)is used. This fitness is an aggregated function (QoS) that maps the attributes of the QoS (time, cost, availability, reputation) into a single real value, in order to sort and rank candidate web services. Formally, we model the optimization problem we are addressing as follows:

$$Min\,QoS(WSC) \;=\; \Sigma_{i=1}^{n}\,qos(S_i) \tag{1}$$

Subject to constraints:

$$\Sigma_{i=1}^{n}\,q_1 * S_i \;\leq\; Tmax \tag{2}$$

$$\Sigma_{i=1}^{n}\,q_2 * S_i \;\leq\; Cmax \tag{3}$$

$$\prod_{i=1}^{n}\,q_3 * S_i \;\geq\; Amin \tag{4}$$

$$\frac{1}{n} * \Sigma_{i=1}^{n}\,q_4 * S_i \;\geq\; Rmin \tag{5}$$

With:

$S_i = 1$ if the service i is candidates in the current WSC; else 0.

n: Number of available web services.

And:

$$qos(S) = \Sigma_{i=1}^{4} w * q_i \qquad (6)$$

Where:

q_i : Parameter of QoS of the web service S,

$\quad q_i \in \{Time, Cost, Availability, Reputation\}$

w: The weight attributed to each QoS q_i.

In the above model the objective function (Equation(1)) minimizes the aggregated QoS function of potential web services compositions that correspond to a user request, satisfying all global constraints expressed in Equation (2), Equation (3), Equation (4)and Equation(5). Equation (6) calculates the aggregated function of QoS for each web service; this function allows merging the attributes of QoS in one real value, by assigning the same weight $w = 0.25$ to each one.

4.2   Quantum Representation of Web Services Composition

In order to easily apply quantum principles on the web services composition optimization problem, we need to map potential solutions (compositions) into a quantum representation that could be easily manipulated by quantum operators. The solution of the problem which is a web services composition is represented as binary vector (Figure 2) satisfying the following criteria:

- For n web services, the size of the binary vector that represents a composition is n, each element of the vector is a web service.
- The presence of 1 in the position (i) of the solution's vector indicates that the web service i is a candidate web service in the current composition's solution.

The following example shows a binary solution for a web service composition instance of 10 web services. According to the example the services 1, 3, 6, 7 are candidates in the proposed solution, and the others are not.

$$[1 \quad 0 \quad 1 \quad 0 \quad 0 \quad 1 \quad 1 \quad 0 \quad 0 \quad 0]$$

Fig. 2. Binary representation of web service composition solution

In terms of quantum computing, each variable emplacement is represented as a quantum register. One quantum register contains a superposition of all possible variable positions. Each column $\binom{\alpha_i}{\beta_i}$ represents a single qubit and corresponds to the binary digit 1 or 0. The probability amplitudes α_i and β_i are real values satisfying $|\alpha|^2 + |\beta|^2 = 1$. For each qubit, a binary value is computed according to its probabilities $|\alpha|^2$, $|\beta|^2$ and can be interpreted as the probabilities to have respectively 0 or 1 [8].

4.3   The Construction Phase: The Proposed Stochastic Heuristic

The construction of the initial population is a crucial phase in our approach; it consists to build gradually feasible initial solutions. Within the aim of reducing the runtime complexity, we have proposed a new efficient and scalable stochastic heuristic to generate this initial population of the web services composition optimization problem. This new proposed heuristic has the aim to generate randomly a number of individuals in the initial population giving feasible solutions starting from the user's request. Each solution must fulfil the user's end-to-end QoS requirements and ensure its preferences. The construction of a solution starts from finding a web service that corresponds to the request's input and finishes by finding the one that meets the expected request's output. So, a solution is a successive collection of candidate web services combined together to satisfy the user's request. For more details, the proposed random heuristic is described in Algorithm 2.

Algorithm 2. Heuristic for generating initial solution

1: **Input :**   Existing web services, $request_{input}$, $request_{output}$
2: **Output :**   The best web services composition solution;

3: **begin**
4: Initiate web services composition solution to zero;
5: Find randomly service S_i such as $request_{input} = Si_{input}$;
6: $S_{candidate} = S_i$;
7: Put the value 1 in the position i of the vector's solution;
8: **while** $request_{output}$ not found **do**
9:    Find randomly service S_i such as $Si_{input} = Scandidate_{output}$;
10:    $S_{candidate} = S_i$;
11:    Put the value 1 in the position i of the vector's solution;
12: **end while**
13: **end**

4.4   Quantum Inspired Cuckoo Search Algorithm Operators

The main four operators used by the quantum inspired cuckoo search are: Quantum Measurement, Quantum Mutation, Quantum Interference and Levy flights operations. The algorithm uses these operators to evolve the entire swarm (population) through generations.

Quantum Measurement Operator. This operation transforms by projection the quantum vector into a binary vector [8]. With this operator, we can get infeasible solutions. To improve this kind of solutions which didn't correspond to the user's request, we have proposed a new improvement heuristic. For the web services composition optimization problem, this operation is accomplished as follows (Algorithm 3).

Algorithm 3. Measurement operator

1: **Input** :   Quantum solution S_q;
2: **Output** :   Binary solution S_b;

3: **begin**
4: Generate a random value $Pr \in [0, 1]$;
5: **while** $i < n$ **do**
6:    **if** $Pr < S_q[i]$ **then**
7:        $S_b[i] = 1$;
8:    **else**
9:        $S_b[i] = 0$;
10:   **end if**
11: **end while**
12: **if** S_b not feasible **then**
13:    Apply Improvement Heuristic;
14: **end if**
15: **end**

Quantum Interference Operator. This operation increases the amplitude that corresponds to the best composition (solution) and decreases the amplitudes of the bad ones. The quantum interference has the aim of moving the state of each qubit in the direction of the best solution in progress. To be accomplished, this operation uses a unit transformation which achieves a rotation whose angle is a function of the amplitudes α_i, β_i. The rotation angle's value $\delta\theta$ should be well set in order to avoid premature convergence. In our algorithm, the rotation angle has the value $\delta\theta = $ pi/20 [8].

Quantum Mutation Operator. This operator is inspired from the evolutionary mutation. It consists of moving from the current solution to one of its neighbours. This operator allows exploring new solutions and thus enhances the diversification capabilities of the algorithm. In each generation, this quantum mutation is applied with a probability, for what it is recommended to use a small values in order to keep a good performance of the quantum inspired cuckoo search [8].

Levy Flights Operator. This operator is used to generate new solutions x^{t+1}, by providing a random walk (Equation(7)). In fact, a random walk is formed essentially by a consecutive random steps of a cuckoo. Those random steps are drawn from a Levy distribution for large steps which has an infinite variance with an infinite mean (Equation (8))[20].

$$x_i^{t+1} = \alpha \oplus Levy(\lambda) \tag{7}$$

$$Levy \sim \mu = t^{-\lambda} \tag{8}$$

where $\alpha > 0$ is the step size, it depends on the scales of the problem of interest. In general, we set $\alpha = O(1)$. The product $\oplus$ means entry-wise multiplications[20]. This product (entry-wise) is similar to the used multiplication in PSO, but here the random walk via Levy flight is more efficient in exploring the search space as its step length is much longer in the long run [19].

4.5   Outlines of the Proposed Algorithm

Here, we describe how the representation scheme including quantum representation and quantum operators has been embedded within a cuckoo search algorithm and resulted in a hybrid stochastic algorithm used to solve the web services composition problem. Firstly, a swarm of p host nests (solutions) is created at random positions to represent all possible solutions and n-p host nests is generated with the proposed greedy heuristic of population construction. The developed algorithm called QICSA-WSC progresses through a number of generations according to the QICSA dynamics.

During each iteration, the best solution is found and the global one is then updated if a better one is found and the whole process is repeated until reaching a stopping criterion. For more details, the proposed QICSA can be described in Algorithm 4.

5   Prototype and Experimentation

In order to evaluate and validate our approach, we implemented a Java-based prototype under Windows 7 Operating System and the environment Net-Beans IDE 7.3. Then, to demonstrate its efficiency we tested it on a text translation case study. To analyse the performances of our approach and evaluate its optimality rates on this case study we have conducted an experiment study that shows its feasibility and effectiveness.

5.1   Case Study

Although it exist different use cases for the web services composition, we have chosen a prototype example of a text translation use case system, for the reason that it concretes clearly the process of the web services composition. More precisely, when we can't translate directly a text from a language to another, the solution is the use of a multiple web services combination to realize this complex translation. Although, with our use case system, the user enters a text in an

---

Algorithm 4. QICSA algorithm for WSC

1: **Input :** Problem data
2: **Output :** Problem solution

3: **begin**
4: Construct an initial population of n host nests;
5: **while** not stop criterion **do**
6:    Apply Lévy flights operator to get cuckoo randomly;
7:    Apply randomly a quantum mutation ;
8:    Apply measurement operator;
9:    Apply improvement heuristic;
10:   Evaluate the quality/fitness of this cuckoo;
11:   Apply Interference operator;
12:   Replace some nests among n randomly by the new solution according to its fitness;
13:   A fraction $(pa)$of the worse nests are abandoned and new ones are built via Lévy flights;
14:   Keep the best solutions (or nests with quality solutions);
15:   Rank the solutions and find the current best;
16: **end while**
17: **end**

---

input language and asked to translate it in an output language. So, the user is supposed to enter his request (the input language, and the output language)and his QoS constraints. And the role of our optimization approach is to meet his queries with the best web services composition. Our optimization approach is realized by combining (composing) the most appropriate web services (these services are defined by their inputs languages, outputs languages and their QoS values).

Example. To evaluate our approach, we suppose the following user's request:

The user enters his input language: $Request_{input}=$ German, and his output language which is: $Request_{output}=$ Spanish.

Then his QoS constraints, and they are:
$Tmax = 400sec$
$Cmax = 80Dollar$
$Amin = 0, 5$
$Rmin = 1$

To satisfy this request, our approach is proceeded as follow:

During the first phase, the system will respond to the user query by applying the randomized heuristic to generate the 10 nests (solutions) of the population, and return the best initial web services composition.

Once the best initial solution is defined, the system executes the optimization phase a number of iterations (450 iterations for this example) and returns the final best web services composition.

The obtained results are summarized in Table 1.

Table 1. Request's results

	The solution	QoS Value
Best initial solution	german arabic 2, arabic turkish 7 , turkish arabic, arabic french 4, french english 4, english italian 5, italian spanish	469.9125
Optimal solution	german turkish, turkish italian, italian spanish	44.767498

Figure 3 shows the evolution of the QoS function during the optimization phase (for the example's request). The quick convergence to the optimal solution illustrates the applicability and efficiency of the proposed QICSA-WSC.

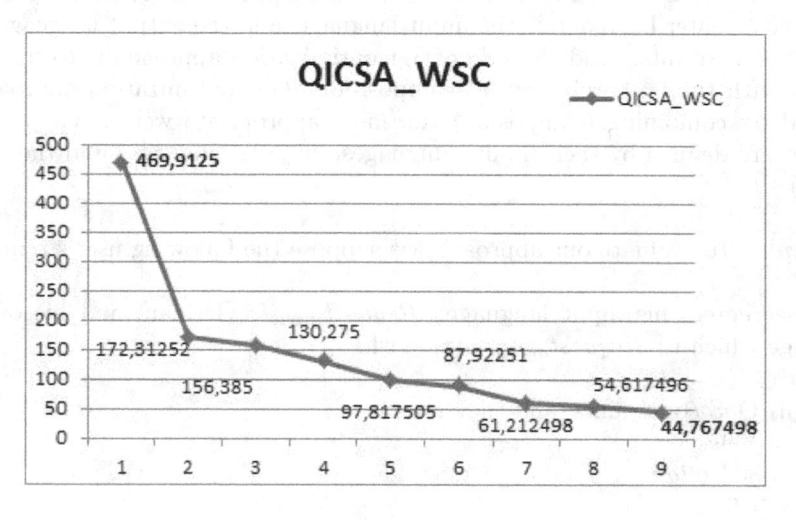

Fig. 3. The optimization evolution

5.2   Experimentation

Our initial intention was to test our approach on a great corpus of real services and compare it with other proposed approaches. However, a lack of availability of the appropriate services appeared, so for the need of the application, we have developed (extended) a data set inspired from [22], where we have different classes of services. Each class contains instances of services having the same functionality, and we assume that the total number of candidate services= 100.

This used data is a set of translator's web services; each web service is defined by its input, output and QoS (time, cost, availability and reputation) parameters. The value of each QoS attribute is generated by a uniform random process which respects the bounds specified in Table 2.

Table 2. The QoS bounds

QoS criterion	Bounds values
Time	[0 , 300] (sec)
Cost	[0 , 30](Dollar)
Availability	[0.7 , 1.0]
Reputation	]0 ,5]

In our experiment, the adopted quantum inspired cuckoo search algorithm uses the following attributes(they are chosen empirically):

Population size=10 nests.
Number of iterations $\in [50, 1000]$.
The weights of the QoS parameters: $w = 0.25$.

While in our approach we are minimizing the QoS aggregated function, the optimality rate is defined as follows (Equation (9)):

$$Optimality_{rate} = 1 - \left(\frac{QoS_{optimal_s olution}}{QoS_{initial_s olution}}\right) \tag{9}$$

Figure 4 below indicates the optimality rate according to the iteration number, for the same example.

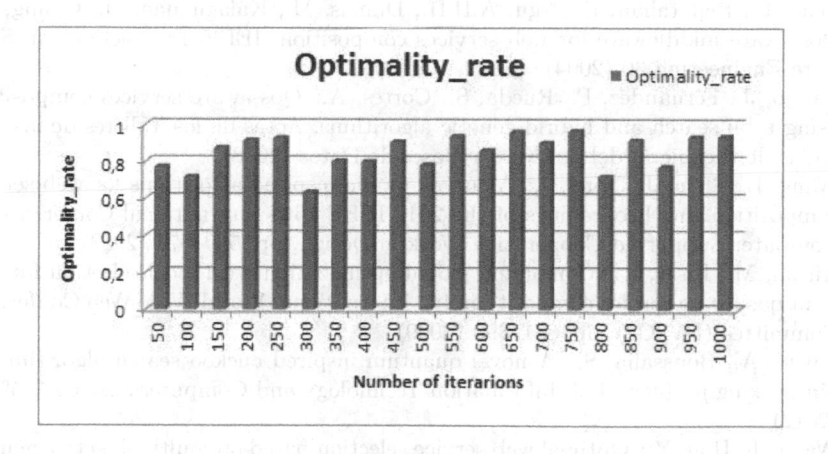

Fig. 4. The optimality rate

We contrast that with our proposed approach QICSA-WSC we can reach an optimality rate between 0.7 and 0.96 regardless of the number of iterations, but we notice that with a high number of iterations it gives better results. This observation confirms the effectiveness of our approach and it feasibility.

But, we note that the response time is not reasonable, if we exceed 1000 iterations.

6   Conclusion and Perspectives

This paper dealt with the optimization of the web services composition problem. Our objective was optimizing the web services composition using QoS as an optimization criteria. So, we have proposed a new approach based on the use of the quantum inspired cuckoo search algorithm. The approach is realized with two contributions: The definition of an appropriate quantum representation for solutions, and the proposition of a new randomized heuristic to evaluate our approach, we have realized a prototype of our system and applied it on a text translation case study. The obtained results are very encouraging and express the feasibility and effectiveness of our approach.

In a future work, we plan to treat the problem of the optimization of semantic web service composition. To use another meta-heuristic for the optimization and to compare the obtained results.

References

1. Kreger, H.: Web service conceptual architecture. IBM Software Group (2001)
2. Kellert, P., Toumani, F.: Les web services sémantiques. revue I3, hors-série Web sémantique (2004)
3. Talantikite, H., Aissani, D., Boudjlida, N.: Les web services complexes: Découverte, composition sélection, et orchestration (2011)
4. Zeng, L., Benatallah, B., Ngu, A.H.H., Dumas, M., Kalagnanam, J., Chang, H.: Qos-aware middleware for web services composition. IEEE Transactions on Software Engineering 30 (2004)
5. Parejo, J., Fernandez, P., Rueda, S., Cortes, A.: Qos-aware services composition using tabu search and hybrid genetic algorithms. Actas de los Talleres de las Jornadas de Ingeniería del Software y Bases de Datos (2008)
6. Wang, L., Shen, J., Yong, J.: A survey on bio-inspired algorithms for web service composition. In: Proceedings of the 2012 IEEE 16th International Conference on Computer Supported Cooperative Work in Design, pp. 569–574 (2012)
7. Alrifai, M., Risse, T.: Combining global optimization with local selection for efficient qos-aware service composition. In: International World Wide Web Conference Committee (IW3C2), pp. 881–890 (2009)
8. Layeb, A., Boussalia, S.: A novel quantum inspired cuckoo search algorithm for bin packing problem. I. J. Information Technology and Computer Science 5, 58–67 (2012)
9. Wang, J., Hou, Y.: Optimal web service selection based on multi- objective genetic algorithm. In: Proc. of the International Symposium on Computational Intelligence and Design, vol. 1, pp. 553–556 (2008)

10. Xu, J., Reiff-Marganiec, S.: Towards heuristic web services composition using immune algorithm. In: Proc. of the International Conference on Web Services, pp. 238–245 (2008)
11. Zhang, W., Chang, C., Feng, T., Jiang, H.: Qos-based dynamic web service composition with ant colony optimization. In: Proceedings of the 34th Annual Computer Software and Applications Conference, vol. 1, pp. 493–502 (2010)
12. Tang, M., Ai, L.: A hybrid genetic algorithm for the optimal constrained web service selection. In: IEEE Congress on: Evolutionary Computation, pp. 1–8 (2010)
13. Li, J., Yu, B., Chen, W.: Research on intelligence optimization of web service composition for qos. In: Liu, C., Wang, L., Yang, A. (eds.) ICICA 2012, Part II. CCIS, vol. 308, pp. 227–235. Springer, Heidelberg (2012)
14. Gustavo, A., Casati, F., Kuno, H., Machiraju, V.: Web services: Concepts, architecture and applications. Springer (2004)
15. Yang, J., Papazoglou, M.P.: Service components for managing the life-cycle of service compositions. In: The 14th International Conference on Advanced Information Systems Engineering, vol. 29, pp. 97–125 (2004)
16. Lécué, F., Mehandjiev, N.: Seeking quality of web service composition in a semantic dimension. Journal of Latex Class Files 6(1) (2007)
17. Bhuvaneswari, A., Karpagam, G.: Qos considerations for a semantic web service composition. European Journal of Scientific Research 65(3), 403–415 (2011)
18. Barreiro Claro, D., Albers, P., Hao, J.: Selecting web services for optimal composition. In: Proceedings of the 2nd International Workshop on Semantic and Dynamic Web Processes, pp. 32–45 (2005)
19. Layeb, A.: A novel quantum inspired cuckoo search for knapsack problems. The International Journal of Bio-Inspired Computation 3(5), 297–305 (2011)
20. Yang, X.S., Deb, S.: Engineering optimisation by cuckoo search. Int. J. Mathematical Modelling and Numerical Optimisation 1(4), 330–343 (2010)
21. Tein, L.H., Ramli, R.: Recent advancements of nurse scheduling models and a potential path. In: Proc. 6th IMT-GT Conference on Mathematics, Statistics and its Applications, pp. 395–409 (2010)
22. Yu, Q., Bouguettaya, A.: Foundations for efficient web service selection. Springer Science Business Media (2010)

Towards a Context-Aware Mobile Recommendation Architecture

María del Carmen Rodríguez-Hernández and Sergio Ilarri

Department of Computer Science and Systems Engineering
University of Zaragoza, Zaragoza, Spain
{692383,silarri}@unizar.es

Abstract. Nowadays, the huge amount of information available may easily overwhelm users when they need to take a decision that involves choosing among several options. On the one hand, it is necessary to identify which items are relevant for the user at a particular moment and place. On the other hand, some mechanism would be needed to rank the different alternatives. Recommendation systems, that offer relevant items to the users, have been proposed as a solution to these problems. However, they usually target very specific use cases (e.g., books, movies, music, etc.) and are not designed with mobile users in mind, where the context and the movements of the users may be important factors to consider when deciding which items should be recommended.

In this paper, we present a context-aware mobile recommendation architecture specifically designed to be used in mobile computing environments. The interest of context-aware recommendation systems has been already shown for certain application domains, indicating that they lead to a performance improvement over traditional recommenders. However, only very few studies have provided insights towards the development of a generic architecture that is able to exploit static and dynamic context information in mobile environments. We attempt to make a step in that direction and encourage further research in this area.

Keywords: context-awareness, recommendation systems, mobile computing.

1 Introduction

Since the emergence of *Recommendation Systems* (*RS*) in the last decade of the 20th century, their use has increased in different application scenarios. For example, they have been proposed for the recommendation of books, music, movies, news, and even friends in social networks. They are particularly popular in e-commerce, as providing relevant recommendations to customers can help to improve their satisfaction and increase product sales. However, these recommendation systems are far from perfect, and sometimes the user is overwhelmed with irrelevant information, leading to his/her frustration and potential desensitization: the user feels disturbed and unhappy with the recommendations provided

I. Awan et al. (Eds.): MobiWis 2014, LNCS 8640, pp. 56–70, 2014.

and will tend to ignore them in the future even if some of them happen to be relevant.

Most RS operate in a *two-dimensional* (2D) *User × Item* space. However, considering only information about the users and items is not enough in applications such as the recommendation of vacation packages. In this case it is important not only to determine which items should be recommended, but also when these recommendations should be provided and how to combine them in a ranked list. Moreover, traditional collaborative filtering techniques generally take into account all the collected ratings of the items to generate the recommendation models; these techniques assume that the context is homogeneous, but actually a user can assign different ratings to the same item in diverse contexts, as the relevance and interest of a specific item for a user may depend on his/her current context. Therefore, additional contextual information should be considered in the recommendation process. Examples of contextual information are the location, the time, the weather (e.g., the current temperature), the user's mood, the user's current activity, the user's current goals, the presence of other people accompanying the user, and the network/communication capabilities.

With advances in the fields of ubiquitous and mobile computing, the lack of analysis of contextual information in recommendation systems has been strongly criticized. So, researches and developers have mainly focused on solving classic problems of recommendation systems, such as the *cold start* problem, *spam vulnerability*, *high dimensionality*, and many others. Recently, researchers working on recommendation systems have recognized the need to investigate them in domains where the context information is relevant. A pioneer proposal in the field of context-aware recommendation systems is [1]. In order to improve the recommendations based on contextual information, the authors extend the classical 2D paradigm to a *multidimensional recommendation model* (*MD model*) that provide recommendations based on multiple dimensions: *User × Item × Context*. RS that incorporate context information in the recommendation process were denominated *Context-Aware Recommender Systems* (*CARS*).

However, CARS is still an emerging field. Indeed, Adomavicius and Jannach claimed recently that there is still much research needed in the field of CARS [2]. Most researchers so far have worked on research issues related to the problem of understanding and representing the context. So, they basically have tried to determine how the context could be modeled in recommendation systems. Other researchers have proposed different recommendation algorithms which include contextual information in the recommendation system. In [3], existing techniques for building context-aware recommendations are evaluated and compared.

Despite these efforts, the design of flexible and generic architectures and frameworks to support an easy development of CARS has been relatively unexplored. Recently, in [4] a software framework to build complex context-aware applications was introduced, but there is still significant work that needs to be done in this area.

In this paper, we introduce a context-aware mobile recommendation architecture which facilitates the use of context-aware recommendation capabilities in mobile computing environments. The rest of the paper is organized as follows. In Section 2 we review the related work. Section 3 presents a motivating scenario where a context-aware architecture like the one proposed in this paper would be useful. In Section 4 we describe the design of our proposed context-aware mobile recommendation architecture. Finally, Section 5 presents our conclusions and points out some directions for future work.

2   Related Work

A *Recommendation System* (*RS*) is an application which suggests (relevant) items to users. It tries to adapt its proposals to each user individually, based on his/her preferences. These recommendations can be seen as an advice about relevant items that are considered of interest for a particular user. For example, in a scenario of books the recommendations should be books that are expected to be relevant for the user (and so they should be read before others), in a scenario of travel destinations the recommendations would be places that according to the user preferences will be more attractive for the user, in the context of a digital newspaper the recommendations would be the news that the user could find interesting, in the context of movies the recommendations would be movies that the user would probably like, etc. Depending on how the recommendations are obtained, a recommendation system can be classified in one of three categories [5]:

- *content-based* recommenders: the user is recommended items similar to the ones the user preferred in the past.
- *collaborative filtering* recommenders: the user is recommended items that people with similar tastes and preferences liked in the past.
- *hybrid* recommenders: they combine collaborative filtering and content-based methods.

Generally, the user preferences towards the potentially relevant items are conditioned by his/her context. However, one of the fundamental problems that traditional 2D recommendation models exhibit is that the contextual information (e.g., the time, with whom the user is with, the weather conditions, what the user is doing, etc.) is excluded from consideration. To avoid this problem, in [1] the authors proposed that the recommendation procedure should incorporate contextual information. For this purpose, various recommendation paradigms have been categorized according to three different types of methods [6, 7] :

- *pre-filtering*, where the contextual information is used to filter the data set before applying traditional recommendation algorithms.
- *post-filtering*, where the contextual information is considered only in the final step of the process. So, contextual information is initially ignored and the ratings are predicted using any conventional 2D recommendation system taking all the input data available (potential items to recommend) into account. Then, the resulting set of recommendations is adjusted (contextualized) for each user by using contextual information.

– *contextual modeling*, where the context information is used directly in the modeling technique.

So, pre-filtering and post-filtering methods consider the context as an additional filtering step that can be applied to any traditional recommendation algorithm, either to restrict its input (pre-filtering) or its output (post-filtering). On the other hand, contextual modeling recommendation systems imply a radically different approach, as the context information directly affects the generation of the recommendation models.

A critical issue for the contextual modeling paradigm is obviously the development of context models, such as those proposed in [8–10]. The problem with these proposals is that they model information for a very specific application domain, and so their domain-specific models cannot be easily reused in other recommendation scenarios. For this reason, within the research community there is a need to solve this problem by defining a generic, abstract, contextual framework for modeling *Context-Aware Recommender Systems* (*CARS*). There are also some proposals that try to exploit available contextual information and be more generic, but they have some limitations. Thus, in [11] the authors emphasize that those approaches usually represent information that either concerns particular application domains (e.g., tourism, movies, etc.) or more abstract domains (e.g., products, web services, e-learning, etc.), but that a truly generic contextual model for CARS was missing, which motivated their work. As an example, [12] presents a generic model using an ontology, which can be used in different types of recommender systems and models data, context, and the recommendation process itself. Recently, [11] carried out a study to try to determine whether a more generic modeling approach could be applied for CARS. As a result of the study, the authors proposed a novel generic contextual modeling framework for CARS, which was theoretically evaluated with positive results.

In recommendation systems, it is important to balance the potential trade-off between not offering some relevant items in the recommendations and providing some irrelevant items. In the first situation, we would miss the opportunity to suggest the user items that he/she may found very interesting. In the second, we could end up overloading the user with irrelevant information, which in turn could lead to an eventual user's desensitization and distrust in the system. Particularly in mobile environments, where the user is moving and the context is highly dynamic, it is important to provide precise recommendations and avoid overloading the user with the suggestion of many items. Generally, mobile devices such as smartphones have important limitations in comparison to traditional mobile or desktop computers; for example, they usually provide restricted input facilities (e.g., lack of a comfortable keyboard). Therefore, a recommendation system should try to relieve the user from having to type or introduce significant information as an input, favoring implicit recommendations (based on the context and user preferences) over explicit (query-based or user-initiated) recommendations. Along these lines, [13] proposes a proactive recommender system that pushes recommendations to the user when the current situation (i.e., the context) is considered appropriate, without explicit user requests.

Recently, a new class of ubiquitous context-aware recommendation systems, called *UbiCARS*, has been proposed in [14]. The idea is to combine characteristics of both ubiquitous systems and CARS. Systems in this category are ubiquitous in the sense that they capture information from the environment and react on it. At the same time, they are context-aware because they consider the context in the recommendation process by using multidimensional contextual datasets. As an example, we could consider the case of recommending nearby items to a user while he/she is shopping. This kind of system could be based on the use of NFC (Near Field Communication) or other similar technologies to read RFID (Radio Frequency IDentification) tags and identify products in the vicinity of the user, as well as product information that can be useful in that context. These kinds of systems, as well as others in very different scenarios, could be developed based on the architecture that we propose in this paper.

A software framework named *Hybreed* [4], for building complex context-aware applications, has also been proposed. The framework is based on a notion of context quite generic. An interesting feature is that the user of the framework (a developer of recommendation systems or a researcher working in this field) can use different recommendation algorithms (e.g., item/user-based collaborative filtering, item-average recommender, random recommender, slope-one, content-based algorithms, rule-based recommenders, as well as combinations of them). Besides, it provides recommendations for both individual users and groups of users. It also includes methods to generate context-aware recommendations. Finally, it incorporates data from external data sources (e.g., user's profile information, semantic networks, etc.) and is able to store and manage the information in databases (e.g., MySQL or HSQL). However, there are still elements pending for future work, as identified by the authors, such as developing and providing advanced learning algorithms as part of the framework or the development of a processing engine that supports distributed and asynchronous workflows. Moreover, privacy issues were not addressed.

Some of the open research problems identified in [15] have been addressed to a certain extent in recent studies. For example, in [3] the authors performed an evaluation and comparison of the effectiveness (accuracy vs. diversity) of the existing paradigms, in order to identify strengths and weaknesses of each paradigm and to determine which one is better in different circumstances (a qualitative comparison among the paradigms had been presented before in [16]). Moreover, the inclusion of *diversity* as an important element in context-aware recommendation systems was considered for the first time in [17]: the idea is that the users should be provided with recommendations that are diverse enough rather than very similar to each other, which is an idea that had been exploited before in Information Retrieval (IR) contexts [18].

As shown in this section, the field of context-aware recommendation systems has started to emerge quite recently. However, aspects related to mobile users and mobile computing are usually ignored in this field. The aim of our architecture is to combine ideas of the existing research, as well as to incorporate other relevant elements for context-aware mobile recommendations. Our goal is to contribute to bridge the gap not only between recommendation systems [19] and context-aware computing [20, 21], but also between context-aware recommendation systems [15] and mobile computing [22, 23].

3 Motivating Scenario

This section describes a sample scenario to illustrate the interest of a context-aware mobile recommendation architecture. The scenario shows some of the main benefits provided by the architecture that we propose in this paper, as well as the interest of having a flexible and global CARS framework for mobile users.

Alice gets up on a rainy Saturday at 7:30 am. She needs to buy some food for the week, but she does not know exactly what she should buy and where she should go. Fortunately, she has installed on her mobile device (a mid-range smartphone) the application *MOcCARSin* (*MObile Context-Aware Recommendation System*), which recommends (proactively or through explicit queries) products of interest, considering Alice's enriched profile from opinions issued in the past about products in different contexts as well as additional contextual information obtained from the environment (e.g., via sensors).

So, Alice decides to use the application in order to receive recommendations of supermarkets where she can go, given her current circumstances. First, she introduces in the system the *keyword* "food" as the query. Automatically, the system enriches this input with additional context information that is relevant in her context, such as the *hour* and *day of the week*, the *weather conditions*, her *current location*, and even information about the persons that are with Alice at the moment. The system identifies that Alice is probably interested in buying food, as the likelihood that she would like to have lunch or dinner at that time of the day is unlikely; breakfast does not seem a plausible option either because Alice's coffee machine broadcasted a "coffee ready" message a few minutes ago (by using *M2M*, or *Machine to Machine*, communications). So, the system asks Alice "Do you need to buy food?" and she confirms.

Then, the system considers the different context parameters and Alice's preferences to suggest her a place where she can buy food. It knows that Alice prefers medium-price supermarkets rather than more expensive high-quality ones or small shops specialized in specific types of products. However, in this case the closest supermarket is quite far, it is raining, Alice does not have a car, the public transportation system is not working yet at this time, and Alice's brother (who could drive her to the supermarket) is not with her at the moment. So, the system considers interesting to include in the list of suggestions a small food store located a few blocks from her home. Alice finally selects a supermarket, and so the system suggests her to take a taxi or wait until 9:00 when the bus service starts. Alice decides to take a taxi, and so the system recommends her several taxi companies (ranked based on ratings from other users), continuously showing on a map the up-to-date locations of taxis nearby along with contact information of the taxi companies.

Once in the supermarket, the system automatically suggests products that she usually buys, products whose stock in her fridge is decreasing (this information was provided by her fridge before leaving home), as well as other products that she has never purchased but she might like. For each product suggested, the system provides optional information such as its name, price, and appropriate routes to reach the supermarket's section where the product is located. If Alice selects a set of products at the same time, then the system is able to suggest Alice a route that optimizes the retrieval of all those products. As the supermarket may include several floors, the system exploits a hierarchical indoor map to obtain the appropriate walking directions, including (if necessary) taking stairs or an elevator. Information about products is obtained from a web service provided by the supermarket, as well as from other customers that may disseminate and share dynamically (through a mobile peer-to-peer network) information about specific offers that they have seen. Moreover, Alice has accepted to share information about her current shopping cart with the supermarket, which the marketing department exploits to offer her customized offers and related products (e.g., since Alice has bought strawberries the system offers her whipped cream at a special price).

By using NFC, the system is able to provide Alice with information about products that she is currently observing, as the supermarket has deployed an appropriate mechanism to query this information (such as RFID tags). For example, the system can identify product features such as its ingredients or caloric content, its price, and its expiry date. Alice is in a gluten-free diet, and so the system warns her if she tries to pick up products that contain gluten. It also prevents Alice from choosing specific products whose expiry date is too close in time, taking into account her consumer habits (she is used to leave products in the fridge for a long time).

When Alice considers that the shopping is finished, the system alerts Alice that she is just 3 euros below the threshold that would entitle her to a free delivery at home. As she does not have a car, she decides to buy a couple of chewing gum packets and ask for home delivery during the afternoon.

After getting out of the supermarket, the weather has improved considerably. Alice starts walking home and she receives a recommendation to have lunch in a restaurant located nearby. It is a good time to eat and she is hungry. Besides, the restaurant offers Chinese food, which is Alice's preferred meal. So, she decides to accept the recommendation. The system suggests Alice to ask Bob, Alice's best friend, to join her, as he also loves Chinese food. Alice contacts Bob and he accepts, but he is not nearby, so he takes his own car to go there. As Bob also enjoys the benefits of MOcCARSin, he types "parking car" and introduces the address of the restaurant in his application to try to find available parking spaces near the restaurant. The system collects and offers him information about available parking spaces (obtained from repositories with information about parking lots and garages, data collected from parking sensors, etc.) that may be relevant, and some parking spots support even booking them in advance subject to payment.

In the meanwhile, Alice decides to buy a present for Bob. He loves books, so she asks for appropriate book recommendations. As Bob is sharing with

Alice information about his preferences and the books that he has already read, MOcCARSin has no problem in suggesting Alice an appropriate book for Bob.

While Bob and Alice enjoy lunch in the restaurant. Bob invites Alice to go to the cinema to watch a movie afterwards. Alice accepts, but she has to choose and she has no idea. Again, MOcCARSin comes to the rescue. By simply introducing the keyword "cinema movies" the system is able to provide recommendations about interesting movies being shown in cinemas in the vicinity. User preferences related to the price, type of cinema (preferred size, audio and video capabilities offered, comfort and additional services, etc.), and thematics of the movies, are analyzed automatically during the recommendation process. Moreover, as Alice shares many interests with her friends, she trusts particularly recommendations from people in her close social network.

The above example illustrates the benefits of a mobile context-aware architecture to provide useful recommendations in a variety of scenarios. In the rest of this paper, we describe an architecture that would accommodate several components needed to make this a reality.

4   Context-Aware Mobile Recommendation Architecture

Figure 1 shows a high-level view of the architecture designed to facilitate the creation of CARS for mobile computing environments. It provides several traditional recommendation algorithms, such as *collaborative filtering based on users/items, slope-one,* and *Singular Value Decomposition (SVD). Knowledge-based recommendation* [24] algorithms also fit in the proposed architecture; they could be used to recommend items affected only by the user's needs and preferences but not by ratings (e.g., in a scenario where parking spaces are recommended to a driver the suitable recommendations are usually based on objective criteria rather than ratings). On the other hand, content-based recommendation models can be exploited by applying Artificial Intelligence techniques. Besides, it is possible to combine several recommendation algorithms in order to improve the accuracy of the recommendations; for hybridization of recommenders several strategies can be applied [24], such as *weighting* (applying several algorithms at the same time and weigh their scores to obtain an overall score) and *switching* (choosing the recommendation model more appropriate based on the available information). In addition, the architecture accommodates different context-aware recommendation paradigms (*pre-filtering, post-filtering,* and *contextual modeling*) in a privacy-preserving way.

The architecture is suitable for both *indoor* and *outdoor* scenarios, as the specifics of each environment would be exploited internally by the system (e.g., by considering appropriate positioning technologies to obtain the location of the user in that environment, to determine if the mobility of the user is completely free or constrained to specific path networks such as roads or a building layout, etc.). Besides, no assumption is made regarding the availability of complete information in the local knowledge base of the user device, the communication technology used (WiFi, 3G, etc.), or the possibility to query central servers

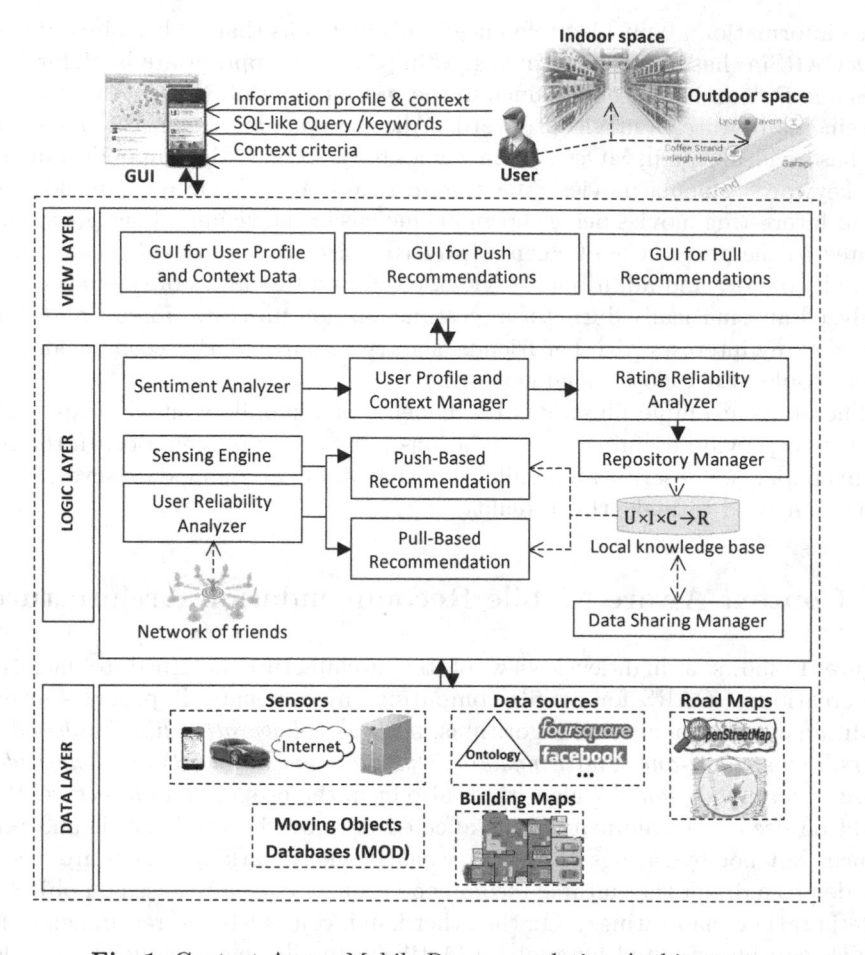

Fig. 1. Context-Aware Mobile Recommendation Architecture

and/or opportunistically query other mobile devices through a mobile peer-to-peer architecture [23]. The architecture should adapt to the available options. Whatever the scenario, the user should receive appropriate recommendations for his/her current context in real-time, by following a best-effort approach.

Static context information obtained from the user's profile as well as dynamic context data obtained from the environment are considered in the recommendation process. A *sensing engine* exploits information from sensors and other available data sources (e.g., geospatial information services, social networks, web services, etc.) to obtain relevant context information. The architecture is very generic in terms of contextual modeling, as we consider the generic modeling approach proposed in [11], which can be adjusted to any domain.

Both *push-based recommendations* (proactive recommendations, received without explicit requests from the user) and *pull-based recommendations* (reactive recommendations, obtained as an answer to a query submitted by the user and evaluated by the system as a continuous query) are supported. In both cases, the system could simply query data available on the local knowledge base (data pushed from other mobile peers, introduced by the user, or obtained from other services and cached locally) and/or access other data repositories, as required.

The proposed architecture includes strategies to deal with well-known problems in recommendations systems, such as: the problem of *cold start* and *sparse data*, by supporting hybrid recommendations models (e.g., content-based and collaborative filtering) and the possibility to exploit data available outside the local knowledge base (queried through a mobile peer-to-peer architecture and/or by directly contacting central servers or repositories) in order to obtain missing useful information (e.g., when the recommendation system needs information about other users with a similar profile); the problem of *high dimensionality*, by employing the SVD model; the problem of *vulnerability spam*, by allowing the use of techniques to identify false information injection attacks as well as to discard information judged as unreliable through a *reliability analysis* (e.g., collaborative filtering can be constrained to consider only, or assign more confidence to, information provided by friends [25]); and the problem of *too similar or redundant recommendations*, by ensuring diversity through the use of similarity measures and clustering techniques. Moreover, it considers the possibility to obtain numerical ratings for items from opinions expressed in natural language, by exploiting supervised learning methods for *sentiment analysis* [26].

So, in this architecture we tried to include the main elements that can be interesting for context-aware recommendations in a variety of mobile computing scenarios. By combining and adapting/extending the architecture components, it is possible to fine-tune and adapt the architecture to specific needs. In the rest of this section, we describe each of the architecture levels in more detail.

4.1   View Layer

This layer reflects the main components of the Graphical User Interface (GUI). Through the GUI, the user can perform the following main actions: define and manage information to include in his/her profile (e.g., his/her name, birth date, age, sex, occupation, home city, friends, etc.), indicate his/her preferences about items (votes), submit queries, and receive recommendations.

The user's preferences may be reflected in the system through explicit or implicit ratings. *Explicit ratings* can be expressed numerically (e.g., values in the range 1-5, 0-10, etc.) or by using literal expressions (e.g., "good", "poor", etc.). Numeric ratings may be quite subjective (they depend heavily on the user's tendency to assign higher or lower scores), but on the other hand literal expressions need to be translated to numeric values for the recommendation process. *Implicit ratings* are obtained through analysis of the user's behavior (e.g., purchases of specific products, visits to certain places, etc.). It is important to emphasize that the ratings assigned by the users may depend on the existing context when the rating was made. So, this contextual information is stored along with the ratings.

Moreover, the user can receive push-based recommendations and pull-based recommendations. Push-based recommendations are provided to the user based only on the user's profile and the current context, without a previous request by the user. On the other hand, pull-based recommendations are provided as an answer to a *query* explicitly submitted by the user (by using keywords related to the type of item required, by filling application forms and templates, by selecting among predefined queries, or by directly expressing advanced SQL-like queries). The user can enter, along with the query, *soft and hard constraints* for the items as well as hints regarding the *context criteria* that should be considered for that type of item during the recommendation process.

4.2   Logic Layer

This layer contains the main modules of the system. The module *User Profile and Context Manager* is responsible for managing (inserting, modifying, and removing) information of the user profile and context. The information can be stored in a local knowledge base through the module *Repository Manager*, which allows the access to the local knowledge base. Access to external knowledge bases is also possible thanks to the *Data Sharing Manager*.

A module called *Sentiment Analyzer* is able to interpret an opinion in natural language (e.g., an opinion expressed in free text) and to determine if the opinion is positive, negative, o neutral, to assign it a rating automatically. It applies techniques for *sentiment classification* [26]. Methods of supervised learning, Naïve Bayes [27], Support Vector Machines (SVMs) [28], and regression methods [29], can be used.

A module *Rating Reliability Analyzer* protects against profile injection attacks (attacks that try to artificially increase or decrease the relevance of some items by injecting fake ratings). This module applies different attack detection methods [30] and its filtered output is used to update the corresponding local knowledge base by using the module *Repository Manager*.

The *Push-Based Recommendation* module is based on the pre-filtering paradigm, adapted for mobile environments by including a continuous reevaluation of constraints and context update (see Figure 2). Firstly, a *Context analysis* is performed in order to detect when the system should provide a recommendation to the user. For this analysis, the system uses the local knowledge base, which contains information about the user profile and the context. The context information exploited can be *static* (derived from the user profile) or *dynamic* (e.g., physical and social context information, detected by sensors, geospatial information services, social networks, web services, semantic networks, etc.). If a recommendation should be pushed to the user, then an *Obtaining contextualized data* task is performed, which filters the appropriate data for the current context. Then, a *creating/updating 2D recommender* task takes place. Finally, the resulting list of items can be provided.

Figure 3 illustrates the main steps of the *Pull-Based Recommendation* module. First, the user introduces a query in the GUI (*STEP 0: Query*). In this step, the query introduced by the user is transformed by the system into an

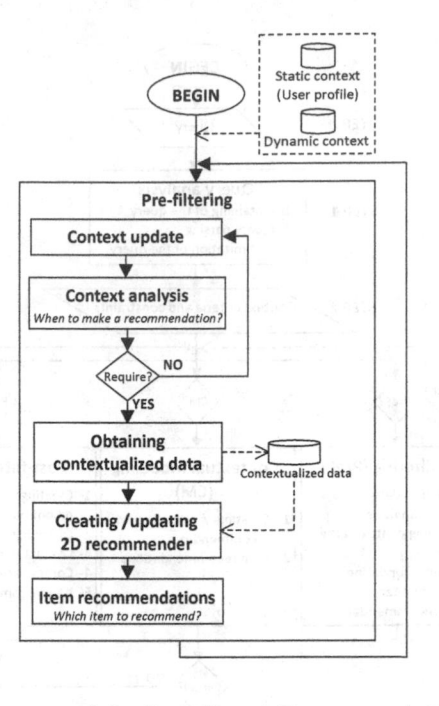

Fig. 2. Main steps of the Push-Based Recommendation module

SQL-like query (unless the user already introduced an advanced query in this format), and identifies its key parts, to facilitate its internal processing (*STEP 1: Query analysis*); the query parsing includes a lexical, syntactic, and semantic analysis. Then, the query can be optimized by applying diverse transformations to the query (e.g., the simplification of complex expressions and the elimination of redundant predicates). Afterwards, the user can specify (optionally) hints regarding *context criteria* that should be taken into account during the recommendation process, as well as soft and hard constraints (*STEP 2: Context criteria and constraints*). Finally, a certain paradigm is considered to obtain the recommendation (*STEP 3*). The type of paradigm executed depends either on the final implementation of the architecture (provided by the system developer) and/or the type of items to recommend. The study performed in [3] provides a comparison of paradigms for context-aware recommendation in terms of the accuracy and diversity of the recommendations they provide, which is useful to determine which methods are more appropriate under certain circumstances.

With the *pre-filtering* paradigm, first a *context update* is performed. Then, a *context analysis* takes place to provide *contextualized data*. The contextualized data allows *creating/updating a 2D recommender*. Finally, the *item recommendations* are provided to the user. The *post-filtering* paradigm is similar to the pre-filtering but inverting the order of steps; as an example of post-filtering step, filtering the candidate items according to specific location-dependent constraints [31] could be considered (e.g., filtering the items based on their distance

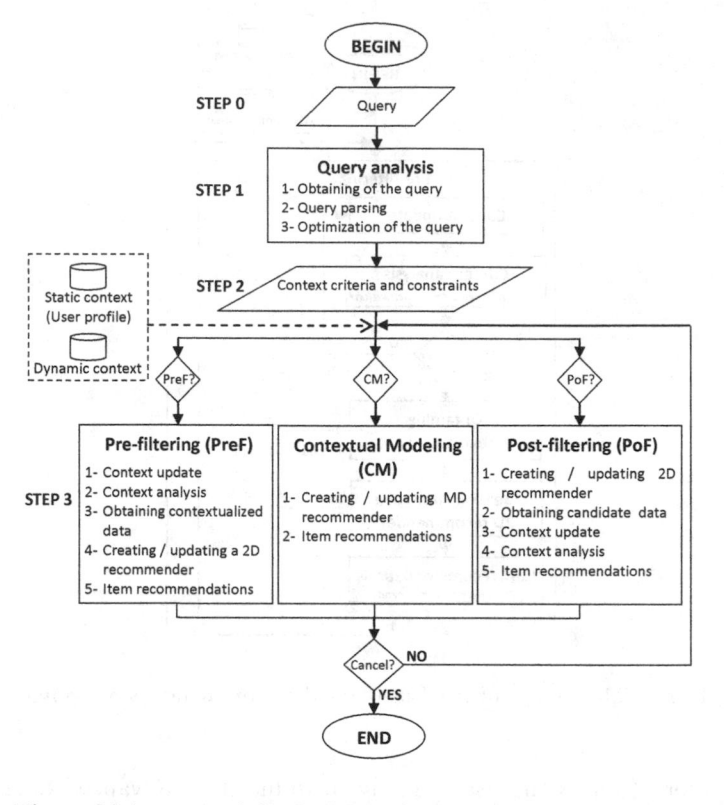

Fig. 3. Main steps of the Pull-Based Recommendation module

from the user). Finally, in the *contextual modeling* paradigm the context information is used directly in the recommendation model.

It should be noted that in a mobile environment, where the context is constantly changing, the recommendations should be kept up-to-date over time. For that purpose, the recommendation modules include a loop. For example, both the *Context Analysis* and *Context Update* tasks must be executed periodically, with a certain frequency.

4.3 Data Layer

This layer provides access to data relevant for the recommendation process, such as maps of the environment or external data sources. Besides, the mobile device of the user can exchange data with others in a peer-to-peer way.

5 Conclusions and Future Work

In this paper, we have introduced an architecture for context-aware recommendations in mobile environments. The architecture is generic, extensible, and can be adapted to the requirements of specific types of recommendations. We have shown its interest and justified its design. This is a first step to contribute to bridging the gap between recommender systems and mobile computing. We are currently implementing a framework based on this architecture, based on Apache Mahout, and we plan to evaluate it in different scenarios.

Acknowledgments. This work has been supported by the CICYT project TIN2010-21387-C02-02, DGA-FSE, and a Banco Santander scholarship held by the first author.

References

1. Adomavicius, G., Sankaranarayanan, R., Sen, S., Tuzhilin, A.: Incorporating contextual information in recommender systems using a multidimensional approach. ACM Transactions on Information Systems 23(1), 103–145 (2005)
2. Adomavicius, G., Jannach, D.: Preface to the special issue on context-aware recommender systems. User Modeling and User-Adapted Interaction 24(1-2), 1–5 (2014)
3. Panniello, U., Tuzhilin, A., Gorgoglione, M.: Comparing context-aware recommender systems in terms of accuracy and diversity: Which contextual modeling, pre-filtering and post-filtering methods perform the best. User Modeling and User-Adapted Interaction 24(1-2), 35–65 (2014)
4. Hussein, T., Linder, T., Gaulke, W., Ziegler, J.: Hybreed: A software framework for developing context-aware hybrid recommender systems. User Modeling and User-Adapted Interaction 24(1-2), 121–174 (2014)
5. Adomavicius, G., Tuzhilin, A.: Toward the next generation of recommender systems: A survey of the state-of-the-art and possible extensions. IEEE Transactions on Knowledge and Data Engineering 17(6), 734–749 (2005)
6. Adomavicius, G., Tuzhilin, A.: Context-aware recommender systems. In: ACM Conference on Recommender Systems (RecSys 2008), pp. 335–336. ACM (2008)
7. Adomavicius, G., Tuzhilin, A.: Context-Aware Recommender Systems. In: Recommender Systems Handbook, pp. 217–253. Springer (2011)
8. Yu, Z., Zhou, X., Zhang, D., Chin, C.Y., Wang, X., Men, J.: Supporting context-aware media recommendations for smart phones. IEEE Pervasive Computing 5(3), 68–75 (2006)
9. Santos, O., Boticario, J.: Modeling recommendations for the educational domain. Procedia Computer Science 1(2), 2793–2800 (2010)
10. Sielis, G., Mettouris, C., Papadopoulos, G., Tzanavari, A., Dols, R., Siebers, Q.: A context aware recommender system for creativity support tools. Journal of Universal Computer Science 17(12), 1743–1763 (2011)
11. Mettouris, C., Papadopoulos, G.: Contextual modelling in context-aware recommender systems: A generic approach. In: Haller, A., Huang, G., Huang, Z., Paik, H.-y., Sheng, Q.Z. (eds.) WISE 2011 and 2012. LNCS, vol. 7652, pp. 41–52. Springer, Heidelberg (2013)
12. Loizou, A., Dasmahapatra, S.: Recommender systems for the Semantic Web. In: ECAI 2006 Recommender Systems Workshop (2006)
13. Woerndl, W., Huebner, J., Bader, R., Gallego-Vico, D.: A model for proactivity in mobile, context-aware recommender systems. In: Fifth ACM Conference on Recommender Systems (RecSys 2011), pp. 273–276. ACM (2011)

14. Mettouris, C., Papadopoulos, G.: Ubiquitous recommender systems. Computing 96(3), 223–257 (2014)
15. Adomavicius, G., Mobasher, B., Ricci, F., Tuzhilin, A.: Context-aware recommender systems. AI Magazine 32(3), 67–80 (2011)
16. Panniello, U., Tuzhilin, A., Gorgoglione, M., Palmisano, C., Pedone, A.: Experimental comparison of pre- versus post-filtering approaches in context-aware recommender systems. In: Third ACM Conference on Recommender Systems (RecSys 2009), pp. 265–268. ACM (2009)
17. Gorgoglione, M., Panniello, U., Tuzhilin, A.: The effect of context-aware recommendations on customer purchasing behavior and trust. In: Fifth ACM Conference on Recommender Systems (RecSys 2011), pp. 85–92. ACM (2011)
18. Agrawal, R., Gollapudi, S., Halverson, A., Ieong, S.: Diversifying search results. In: Second ACM International Conference on Web Search and Data Mining (WSDM 2009), pp. 5–14. ACM (2009)
19. Bobadilla, J., Ortega, F., Hernando, A., Gutiérrez, A.: Recommender systems survey. Knowledge-Based Systems 46, 109–132 (2013)
20. Chen, G., Kotz, D.: A survey of context-aware mobile computing research. Technical Report TR2000-381, Dartmouth College, Computer Science, Hanover, NH, USA (2000)
21. Baldauf, M., Dustdar, S., Rosenberg, F.: A survey on context-aware systems. International Journal of Ad Hoc and Ubiquitous Computing 2(4), 263–277 (2007)
22. Mascolo, C., Capra, L., Emmerich, W.: Mobile computing middleware. In: Gregori, E., Anastasi, G., Basagni, S. (eds.) NETWORKING 2002. LNCS, vol. 2497, pp. 20–58. Springer, Heidelberg (2002)
23. Luo, Y., Wolfson, O.: Mobile P2P databases. In: Encyclopedia of GIS, pp. 671–677. Springer (2008)
24. Burke, R.: Hybrid web recommender systems. In: Brusilovsky, P., Kobsa, A., Nejdl, W. (eds.) Adaptive Web 2007. LNCS, vol. 4321, pp. 377–408. Springer, Heidelberg (2007)
25. Avesani, P., Massa, P., Tiella, R.: A trust-enhanced recommender system application: Moleskiing. In: ACM Symposium on Applied Computing (SAC 2005), pp. 1589–1593. ACM (2005)
26. Liu, B.: Sentiment analysis and subjectivity. CRC Press, Taylor and Francis Group, Boca Raton, FL (2010)
27. Duda, R., Hart, P., Stork, D.: Pattern Classification, 2nd edn. Wiley-Interscience (2000)
28. Vapnik, V., Cortes, C.: Support-vector networks. Machine Learning 20(3), 273–297 (1995)
29. Kramer, S., Widmer, G., Pfahringer, B., Groeve, M.D.: Prediction of ordinal classes using regression trees. Foundations of Intelligent Systems 47(1-2), 1–13 (2001)
30. Mobasher, B., Burke, R., Bhaumik, R., Williams, C.: Toward trustworthy recommender systems: An analysis of attack models and algorithm robustness. ACM Transactions on Internet Technology 7(4), 23:1–23:41 (2007)
31. Ilarri, S., Mena, E., Illarramendi, A.: Location-dependent query processing: Where we are and where we are heading. ACM Computing Surveys 42(3), 12:1–12:73 (2010)

Beyond Responsive Design: Context-Dependent Multimodal Augmentation of Web Applications

Giuseppe Ghiani, Marco Manca, Fabio Paternò, and Claudio Porta

CNR-ISTI, HIIS Laboratory, Via G. Moruzzi 1,
56124 Pisa, Italy
{giuseppe.ghiani,marco.manca,fabio.paterno,
claudio.porta}isti.cnr.it

Abstract. Context-dependent adaptation is becoming a continuous necessity since we access our applications in more and more variegated contexts. Multimodality can be a significant support in such changing settings. We present a solution for obtaining automatic augmentation of Web applications in such a way as to enable them to exploit various combinations of graphical and vocal modalities. We report on the software architecture supporting such augmentations and its underlying context manager, as well as some example applications and first user tests.

Keywords: Adaptation, Context-Awareness, Multimodal Interfaces, Vocal Interaction, Web applications.

1   Introduction

One consequence of the explosion of mobile technology has been that we use our applications more and more in dynamic contexts of use. Such contexts can vary in aspects related to the users (their preferences, abilities, physical and emotional state, etc.), the technology (devices, connectivity, interaction modalities, etc.), environment (noise, light, etc.), and social aspects (privacy, trust, etc.).

Responsive design [14] has recently been widely adopted by many Web developers and designers since it provides support for adapting to various device features through fluid layout and stylesheets. It moreover provides the possibility of associating various visual attributes with groups of devices identified by some features detected through media queries.

However, in many cases responsive design is not enough for various reasons:

- The contextual changes that this approach is able to detect are limited to device and window resolution, and orientation, while many other aspects may vary in the context of use that can have an impact on the user experience;
- The changes that it is possible to specify are limited to hiding/showing some elements and changing the graphical attributes; no support for multimodality is provided.

The idea behind model-based approaches [3] is to have declarative descriptions that can be used to provide implementation-independent descriptions in which the

I. Awan et al. (Eds.): MobiWis 2014, LNCS 8640, pp. 71–85, 2014.
© Springer International Publishing Switzerland 2014

purpose of each interface element is described. This approach is meaningful as is demonstrated by the fact that HTML5 has adopted it by providing more semantic tags, even if it is limited to only graphical user interfaces. Model-based approaches involve the effort of using an additional description level. This is justified by its potential support for adaptation, which is particularly effective when it involves the use of different modalities.

In this paper, we present a novel solution that addresses the limitations of responsive design. Instead of media queries we use a context manager, a software infrastructure able to detect any type of contextual change in terms of technology, users, and environments. Then, in order to better support the user, a server is able to provide for various adaptations, including augmenting the accessed Web pages in such a way as to exploit multimodality, in particular various combinations of graphical and vocal modalities. The adaptations to perform are expressed through adaptation rules in the format event/condition/actions in which the triggering events are detected by the context manager, and the action part indicates the adaptation effects that can even exploit the vocal modality still using standard HTML, CSS, and JavaScript. We have focused on the vocal modality, in various combinations with the graphical one, since it is spreading quickly thanks to rapid improvements in TTS/ASR technology (e.g., Google speech) and can support various types of input and output, including non-speech sounds. Our environment also supports vibro-tactile feedback.

In the paper, after discussion of related work, we introduce a modality-based classification of the possible adaptations that can be supported by our solution, and describe its software architecture. We provide a description of the context manager supporting it, and report on two user tests. Lastly, we draw some conclusions and provide indications for future work.

2   Related Work

One type of approach to obtaining context-dependent applications is represented by the Context Toolkit [19], which provides explicit mechanisms to handle context-dependent events. While such toolkits allow creating context-dependent applications, we provide a solution that makes any Web application context-dependent by merely requiring designers and developers (who could be different from those who created the original application) to provide only the desired adaptation rules to the adaptation engine. Thus, we focus on adaptations of Web applications, an area that has been addressed by previous work, e.g. [12] proposed a solution for automatically retargeting Web sites through the use of machine learning techniques applied to existing designs. Our support provides broader dynamic adaptation based on context dependent adaptation rules, interpreted by our adaptation server. It is worth noting that our approach does not require rewriting or manually modifying the existing applications. We instead propose a middleware that is targeted to support developers/designers who want to augment their applications with limited effort and/or to third parties needing to augment the capabilities of Web-based applications (e.g., municipalities that aim to improve Web accessibility within the smart city).

Although adaptation of Web mobile applications has been investigated, there are still many issues to solve in this area. Researchers have tried to automate the adaptation of Web pages for touch devices. W3Touch [15] is an example tool for supporting Web pages adaptation according to user interaction by using missed links and frequent zooming as indicators of layout issues, but the adaptation rules supported do not consider the use of multimodality. We aim to an architecture able to take as input existing (Web) applications and dynamically generate multimodal versions according to the context of use.

FAME [7] provides a framework to guide the development of adaptive multimodal applications. A conceptual basis for adaptive multimodal systems and a set of guidelines for driving the development process is furnished, but no support for automatic application development is given. A survey [10] about trends in context of use exploitation in mobile HCI has provided a classification of context aspects. According to the study, the most exploited aspects are related to user social dimensions and physical environments. A more recent study about mobile multimodality has led to some further guidelines for developers of context-aware adaptive multimodal mobile applications [8]. As in our vision, context-awareness is a medium for providing the combination of interaction modalities that best suit the current situation. The flexibility of our approach, as described in the following sections, lies in the extensible adaptation rules that: (1) can take into account the context of use; (2) allow adding and tuning the level of multimodality to better suit users in each run-time context. This is a type of Web augmentation, where the rendering of an existing application is augmented to improve user experience [6], different e.g. from mashup techniques, aiming to build new applications out of existing Web resources.

We enable the combination of vocal and graphical modalities both in input and output in various ways, similar to those indicated by the CARE (Complementarity, Assignment, Redundancy, and Equivalence) properties [5].

Multimodal augmentation can even support people with permanent or transient disabilities that may have problems in accessing the original Web applications, thus being a possible solution for personalised dynamic accessibility [9].

An approach to generating accessible user interfaces from multimodal design patterns is presented in [18], which requires the use of a statecharts-based notation in the authoring of the adaptive applications. Another framework for developing adaptive multimodal interfaces was introduced in [1], while our approach can be applied to any existing Web interactive application independently of how they were developed. We propose to express adaptation through rules structured in the event/condition/actions format. The event is something happening at a given time, the condition (optional) is a constraint to be satisfied, and the action describes how the application should change in order to perform the requested adaptation. A similar language for adaptation rules was used in [16] in an approach that supported adaptation as well, but without considering multimodality. Multimodal adaptation was tackled by the GUIDE project as well [4]. In that case, the authors mainly focused on adaptation for elderly people based on user capabilities models while in this work we aim to address a wider set of contextual aspects.

3   Adaptation Classification According to Modalities Use

In this section we introduce a classification of four adaptation types that illustrate the space of possible adaptations that our environment can support. In the rest of the paper we focus on the types that involve multimodality, since context-dependent multimodal augmentation is the main contribution of this work. Here we also mention graphical-to-graphical adaptation scenarios just to indicate that we are able to address them, but we do not go in depth on this part since in this paper our focus is on multimodal support.

Graphical-to-graphical adaptation. In some cases there is a need to change the user interface within the same modality. One example can be a person walking in a noisy environment. This context implies that the user is not able to pay much attention through the visual channel since s/he is walking but cannot use the vocal modality because of the noise. In this context a useful adaptation [11] can be increasing the size of the graphical elements (fonts, buttons, etc.) in order to make them more easily perceivable and selectable.

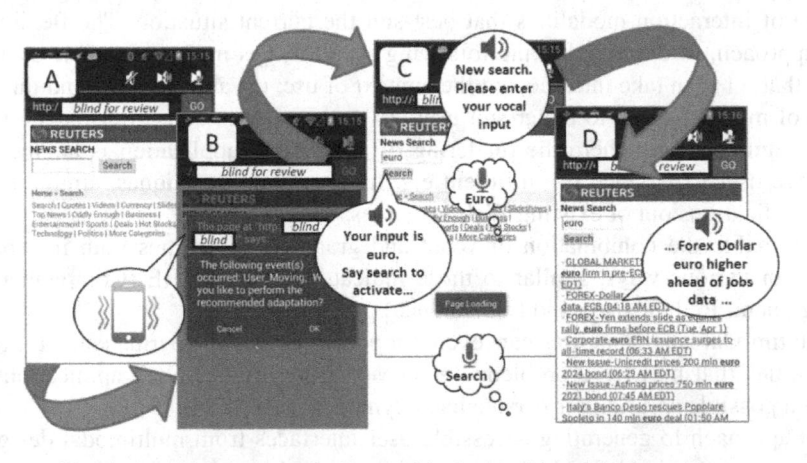

Fig. 1. An example scenario for graphical-to-multimodal adaptation

Graphical-to-multimodal adaptation. There are cases in which exploiting other modalities can allow users to overcome limitations inherent in the graphical one. For example, when the context of use limits the degree of attention to the visual modality, e.g. walking on a crowded street or while driving, such limitation can be counterbalanced by exploiting the vocal modality for supporting information rendering and interaction. Thus, some information can be rendered in a redundant way in order to ensure that it is perceived by the user, while the input can be entered either through one modality or another. This is the type of scenario that has received limited support so far, and the main contribution of this work is to provide a solution that works even for existing Web applications and not only for those developed with specific authoring tools. An example is shown in Figure 1. A graphical Web application is accessed (A) when the user is sitting. When the user starts an activity that makes full graphical interaction difficult (e.g., walking), the Platform detects the context change, triggers a vibrating alert, and asks for confirmation to perform the adaptation (B) before providing the appropriate multimodal version (C). The graphical page is thus augmented with vocal input and output. At the beginning a vocal prompt is provided ("New search. Please enter your vocal input"). The user enters "euro" vocally and confirms. Then, the multimodal version of the search results (D) is rendered. When the user skips the search form through the next command, the text content of the page is rendered vocally.

Multimodal-to-graphical adaptation. If for some reason multiple modalities can no longer be exploited at the same time, then it can be useful to change the user interface in such a way as to exploit only the graphical modality. This type of adaptation is not particularly complex since it is mainly based on disabling one modality and forcing all information rendering and interaction to be performed graphically. Thus, when dealing with a multimodal user interface that was originally graphical, the multimodal-to-graphical adaptation actually consists on restoring the original interface version.

Multimodal-to-multimodal adaptation. It may happen that once the original graphical application has been augmented in terms of multimodality due to some contextual change, at some point a new contextual change may require different multimodal support. Indeed, even within multimodal support there can be various possibilities depending on how the modalities involved are exploited. For example, in the case of low multimodality for interactive elements, the input can be entered either vocally or graphically, while prompts and feedback are rendered only graphically. On the other hand, in the case of high multimodality all interactions are rendered through both modalities. Likewise, output textual elements can be rendered vocally in different ways: totally or partially or only on request depending on the parameters specified in the adaptation rules.

4   Software Architecture of the Adaptation Platform

Our platform for multimodal augmentation is server-based. It includes a proxy and an adaptation server composed of a number of modules, which also use model-based languages for supporting adaptation. In such languages it is possible to have descriptions at various abstraction levels. We have considered the use of abstract and concrete descriptions. In the former the specification is independent of the actual interaction modalities used, while in the latter the description depends on such interaction modalities but it is still independent of the implementation languages used. We have adopted the MARIA language [17] since it provides both an abstract language and concrete refinements of such language for various platforms (graphical, vocal, multimodal, etc.) and it is publicly available along with an authoring environment. In the following we first introduce the various modules (graphically represented in Figure 2) and then describe how they communicate with each other.

Orchestrator. It is mainly the interface between the adaptation server and the external world. It coordinates the access to and interactions among the various modules of the adaptation server.

Navigation Proxy. In addition to the usual proxy functionalities the proxy that we have implemented inserts some scripts in the navigated pages in order to allow communication between such pages and the orchestrator module. These scripts are used to trigger and perform the forwarding of the DOM of the currently accessed page to the server, and to dynamically load the adapted page.

Reverser. This tool is able to create the MARIA graphical concrete description of any existing Web page. For this purpose, it parses the page DOM, saves the content of the script nodes in a separate file, adds the information related to CSSs to a cache memory, including information related to elements created dynamically through JavaScript. Then, it starts a depth-first analysis of the DOM tree nodes (except when there are elements that can be associated with labels; in this case the labels are searched through a breadth-first analysis). For each node the reverse engineering tool identifies the type, the relevant CSSs and events. The analysis considers CSSs that can be external to the Web page, internal to the page with the STYLE element, and in any HTML element with the *style* attribute, including the case of nested CSSs. Then, it creates the corresponding elements, with the associated attributes and events, in the logical concrete descriptions. In contrast to previous reverse engineering tools [2], this module is also able to handle recently introduced HTML 5 and CSS 3 elements.

Adaptation Engine. The purpose of this module is to decide what adaptation should take place. For this purpose it uses adaptation rules written in an XML-based format according to the event/condition/action template. When new rules are added the adaptation engine subscribes to be notified of their events by the context manager. In this way when the relevant events occur the associated actions are triggered. Such actions can vary from small changes (e.g. change of font size) to the change of the platform used for rendering the user interface (as in the case of graphical-to-multimodal adaptation).

Multimodal Adapter. The multimodal adapter performs the transformation from the graphical concrete description to the multimodal one. Since both are XML-based descriptions it has been implemented as an XSLT transformation. The action part of the adaptation rules can specify the parameters for this transformation. For instance, it is possible to indicate if the images must be vocally annotated (i.e. by synthesizing the "alt" attribute), if users have to confirm the entered vocal input, if the multimodal support has to list all the choice elements in case of a single choice interactor. The classification of the interactive elements provided by the MARIA language together with the CARE properties provide a powerful way to customise the multimodality level. Since the user interface specification has a hierarchical structure, it is possible, through the CARE properties, to associate the type of desired multimodality at different granularity levels. It is also possible to associate a multimodality property to all the elements that share a certain semantics (e.g. single selection object, text edit, function activation) according to the classification of the abstract MARIA language. In the MARIA multimodal Concrete User Interface (CUI), the interaction elements can be decomposed into three different parts: input, prompt and feedback. In the adaptations rules it is possible to indicate the CARE value for each part, thus specifying how users can interact with interaction elements with a very fine level of granularity. Usually the Multimodal Adapter extracts vocal information from the graphical page, for instance the vocal prompt value is derived from the label text of the interactor element. If the element has no label then the multimodal adapter adds a default vocal prompt. Regarding text content, the way to vocally render it can be specified as well (e.g., synthesize the whole text or only the heading part, synthesize it automatically or when selecting it, etc.).

Context Manager. It supports the possibility of detecting any change in the context of use. It has a client/server architecture in which the clients are context delegates whose task is to detect various types of contextual events and inform the server, which will then communicate them to the adaptation server, if it had subscribed for their notification. A more detailed description of this important component follows in the next section.

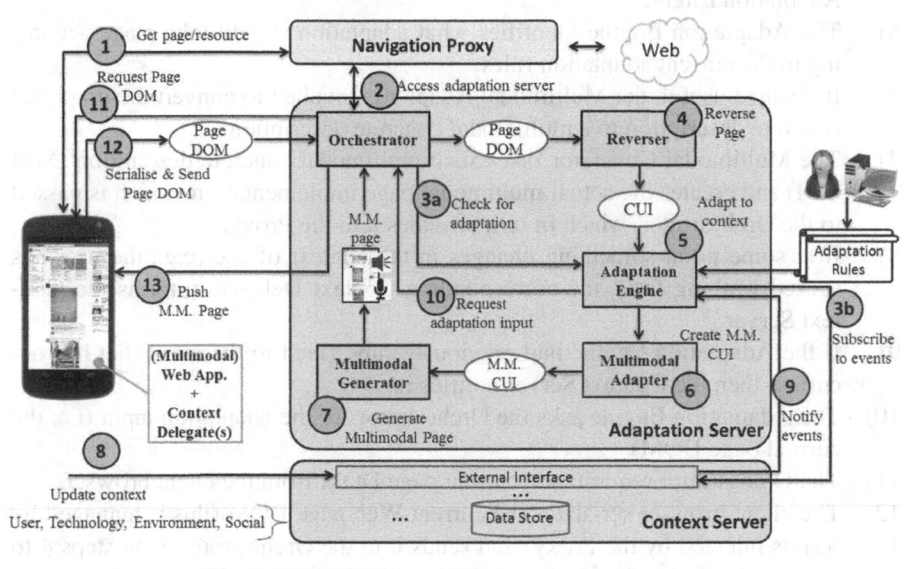

Fig. 2. The architecture of the proposed environment

Multimodal Generator. The adaptation server also exploits a generator of multimodal interfaces from model-based descriptions, which was introduced in [13]. That work, however, relied on existing multimodal model-based descriptions of the interactive Web application, and was not able to support adaptation of existing Web applications, as presented in this paper.

Communication among components. Figure 2 shows the steps through which the multimodal augmentation takes place (the numbers in Figure 2 provide an indication of the corresponding step):

1) The Web application is accessed through the Proxy, which enhances it (e.g. by modifying links/references, injecting additional scripts). The user interacts with the modified Web application in the same way as without any proxy.

2) The Proxy passes the annotated page DOM to the Orchestrator module of the Adaptation Server.

3) a) The Orchestrator queries the Adaptation Engine to check whether an adaptation is needed for the current page (i.e. whether, according to the adaptation rules, the page should be adapted to the current context). If adaptation is needed, then the Orchestrator sends the page DOM to the Reverser; otherwise, the Proxy receives back the current page and provides it to the client browser without any change.

   b) At the first user access the Adaptation Engine subscribes to the relevant context events according to the available adaptation rules associated with the current user and application.

4) The Reverser creates the concrete description (CUI) and provides it to the Adaptation Engine.

5) The Adaptation Engine identifies what adaptation should take place according to the current adaptation rules.

6) If deemed useful, the Multimodal Adapter is invoked to convert the graphical concrete description to a multimodal concrete description.

7) The Multimodal Generator takes such multimodal concrete description (MM CUI) and creates the actual multimodal page implementation, which is passed to the Orchestrator, which in turn provides it to the Proxy.

8) If at some point something changes in the context of use (e.g., the user has started walking fast), the corresponding Context Delegate informs the Context Server.

9) If the Adaptation Engine had previously subscribed to the event that has occurred, then the Context Server notifies it.

10) The Adaptation Engine asks the Orchestrator for the adaptation input (i.e. the current page DOM).

11) The Orchestrator requests the current page DOM from the client browser.

12) The client browser serializes the current Web page DOM (this is managed by scripts injected by the Proxy) and sends it to the Orchestrator, then steps 4 to 7 are performed again.

13) The Orchestrator pushes the current multimodal page to the client browser.

5   Context Information Management

The context manager is composed of a context server and a number of context delegates and it has the aim of detecting, communicating, and manipulating context information. In particular, the context delegates are modules devoted to detecting contextual information. A context delegate, upon sensing several context parameters, updates the corresponding attributes in the context server. Context delegates can be deployed in the user device or in the environment.

The context manager supports contextual information manipulation at various abstraction levels. Delegates and server exploit a REST interface, which allows delegates to update various entities in the server even without knowing their structures exactly. Some of the RESTful services defined so far are: UserEnvironment, which includes attributes such as noise/light/temperature; UserLocationBluetoothBeacon, for the state (e.g. signal strength) of a Bluetooth beacon detected by the device; UserPhysiologicalActivity, for user respiration and heart rate.

In order to automatically update the previously mentioned resources, we have implemented a number of context delegates for Android devices. One example senses Bluetooth beacons (e.g. Bluetooth embedded devices, dongles, etc.) available in the environment and provides the context server with their identifier (name, MAC address) and Received Signal Strength Indicator (RSSI). Two other different delegates are devoted to updating the user environment: one for the light and one for the noise level. The former parameter is provided by the device light sensor; the latter is obtained by analysing the audio input amplitude provided by the embedded microphone. A context delegate has also been developed for interfacing with physiological monitoring hardware with Bluetooth interface. The physiological monitor is a belt that can be comfortably worn and senses several parameters (e.g. heart rate, ECG-variability, respiration rate, user movements). The above cited context delegates and related data are exploited at run time depending on the adaptation rules.

Besides the basic operations for creating, updating and removing information, the Context Manager also hosts mechanisms for subscribing to information changes. Subscription is a way for an external module to be asynchronously notified when something changes in the context, and thus it is fundamental for the multimodal context-aware adaptation platform. We use an Event subscription mechanism, i.e. a mechanism for a subscriber to be notified only when one or more conditions are met. Conditions can refer to one or more attributes. The attributes are identified through a path in their hierarchical structure that represents the context model (e.g., the noise level attribute is defined as an environment sub-entity). Notifications are sent via HTTP POST. Subscriptions are carried out at run-time according to pre-defined adaptation rules structured as event-conditions-actions, as previously discussed.

We designed the context manager to be able to detect any relevant contextual information: in the server a lower layer stores and manages information as a set of structured entities, while the external interface allows access to such information at different abstraction levels. The benefit of the low level way of storing information is flexibility. Low level entities are basic data containers, able to store an arbitrary number of attributes and/or reference to other entities (e.g. user, device, etc.). Overall, the context manager architecture is extensible, since it is easy to add new delegates for detecting further contextual events without having to change the implementation of the other modules.

6   User Tests

We have carried out two user tests in order to assess some aspects characterizing context-based multimodal augmentation and to what extent they are considered useful and usable with respect to the standard way to access Web applications.

A first user test involved ten users (6 male, 4 female) between 21 and 45 y.o. (mean 30.4), who were requested to interact with the English mobile Wikipedia home page (http://en.m.wikipedia.org) in order to find information about cities and countries. Only four users had previous experience in the use of UIs combining graphical and vocal modalities. None of them was involved in the project. Interaction occurred through an Android smartphone equipped with support for multimodal Web user interface execution obtained through an instance of a WebView component and libraries accessing the Google Text-To-Speech and Augmented Speech Recognition. The calls to the functionalities of such libraries are created by the generator for MARIA multimodal concrete descriptions.

In the test, the users first had to search for a city, and find out its population, and then to search for a country and find its surface area. The city and country names were the same for all users, in order to maintain homogeneity in task complexity.

Users had to complete the tasks through a multimodal augmented version of Wikipedia automatically obtained through our adaptation environment according to the context of use. When a contextual change triggers an adaptation various events happen on the device during this adaptation transition: a pop-up announces the contextual change and the possibility of triggering multimodal adaptation; if accepted, there is vibrotactile feedback and a pop-up informing the user of the progression of the adaptation transition in percentage. The contextual factor for triggering the adaptation was the environment noise, detected by a context delegate running in background on the smartphone.

In order to evaluate our platform, we defined a list of relevant aspects related to usability and usefulness. Such aspects, listed in the following, were rated with a value on a 1-5 scale, with 5 as the most positive score (min and max value are expressed into square brackets):

a) Awareness of context-dependent interface adaptation [3,5]; mean: 4.1; std.: 0.88;
b) Adaptation appropriateness [1,4]; mean: 3.4; std.: 0.97;
c) Adaptation continuity [1,5]; mean: 3.2; std.: 1.03;
d) Rendering of adaptation transition [1,5]; mean: 2.4; std.: 1.35;
e) Impact of the adaptation in decreasing interaction complexity [1,5]; mean: 3.2; std.: 1.03;
f) Impact of adaptation in improving user experience [1,5]; mean: 3.2; std.: 1.03;
g) Utility of multimodal augmentation for improving Web applications usability [2,5]; mean: 3.7; std.: 0.82.

In order to help users in subjectively rating the system, each possible score in the questionnaire was associated to a short textual description. For instance, in the first question, 1/2/3/4/5 values on the Scale were described as *"My awareness was very low/low/borderline/high/very high"*, respectively.

Overall, we can argue that users were quite aware of the context-dependent inter-face adaptation being performed, in particular thanks to the vibrotactile notification following the contextual change. Other issues emerged on adaptation appropriateness, which received lower ratings. This may be due to minor inconsistencies the users found in the adapted page (e.g. links not immediately visible because of their altered layout).

The way adaptation transition was rendered received the lowest mean score. A possible explanation for this is the server-side delay, i.e. page adaptation taking much longer than simple loading.

Among the positive informal considerations, participants highlighted the benefits that the multimodality can provide in various situations, such as when hands free interaction is needed, and/or when it is not possible/safe to look at the screen. One participant also mentioned possible benefits in the social aspects of interaction that can arise from such multimodal adaptations (e.g., accessibility for the visually im-paired). We also got some positive observations on the potential of multimodal adap-tation, for which our platform was considered to be a good starting point.

In general, the main technical issue with the multimodal augmented version seemed to be the latency of the adaptation process. The preliminary results collected and the issues pointed out by the participants helped us to create an improved version of the platform. In particular, the adaptation process latency, which was considered a serious lack, was reduced by reducing the computation complexity (especially for the Reverser module) and by installing all the modules in a single server, which led to minimal network communications.

In December 2013 we performed a second user test taking into account the indica-tions and issues pointed out by the users during the first test. We decided to assess the same aspects as in the previous test, thus the assessment questionnaire was similar, though we added one more question about the adaptation responsiveness.

Twelve users participated in the second user test (8 male, 4 female), with ages ranging between 21 and 36 (mean 30). Users were recruited from within the personnel of our organization was among those who were not involved in the project. They par-ticipated voluntarily   and had to perform three tasks for different applications.

Walking with noise scenario: the users had to walk in a noisy scenario and interact with the original (i.e. not adapted) Web site at http://m.foxbusiness.com. After enter-ing a search into the form and pressing the submit button, the context changed (the noise level decreased) and the adaptation process started. Users then had to insert a different text input and listen to the voice synthesis of the search results. In the result-ing multimodal version we had: redundant (vocal and graphical) text output, and only graphical input/prompt/feedback of interaction elements.

Fitness scenario: the user was doing gymnastics. Initially s/he accessed the original Web site at http://us.mobile.reuters.com/search and performed a search through the non-adapted page. During an exercise s/he had to change position from standing to lying down and had to continue the interaction with the opened page. When the user was laying down, the physiological delegate running on the device was able to interpret this change and trigger the page adaptation. The user could then insert the input vocally and listen to the voice synthesis of the search results. In the resulting multimodal version we had: redundant (vocal and graphical) text output, while in the interaction elements the input was equivalent, prompt and feedback were redundant, and the ask for confirmation parameter was false. Because the user was able to see the entered vocal input graphically, we decided not to ask for vocal confirmation of the input.

User driving scenario: we simulated a car through a large screen showing a street view video and users had a steering wheel. The user started this scenario outside the room (outside the car) and performed a search in the original Web site at http://eurometeo.mobi.en. When the user entered the room and sat at the desk with the large screen and wheel, the adaptation took place. The context manager detected when the user was inside the car thanks to a context delegate for Bluetooth beacons. When the Bluetooth beacon with the strongest signal was the car's, then the adaptation was triggered. In this scenario users could insert the input only vocally (the input field was not visible) and the output was redundant (graphical and vocal). In this way, users could interact with the interface while driving without taking their hands off the wheel. In the resulting multimodal version we had: redundant (vocal and graphical) text output, input/prompt/feedback of interaction elements only vocal, ask for confirmation true. In this scenario the input prompt and feedback part of the interaction elements (text edit and submit button) were only vocal. This means that they were not visible but it was possible to interact with them vocally; for this reason and in order not to distract the user while driving we decided to ask the user to confirm the entered input.

Therefore, for each task, users interacted with the original, non-adapted Web site through the graphical modality to perform a search and to read the results. After that, the context changed and the adapted page was loaded, and users had to perform the same task, with different search input and different result output, through the adapted page.

The following aspects were rated (Scale and values as for the previous test):

a) Awareness of context-dependent interface adaptation [4,5]; mean: 4.3; std.: 0.49;
b) Adaptation appropriateness [3,5]; mean: 4.08; std.: 0.52;
c) Adaptation continuity [3,5]; mean: 4.17; std.: 0.58;
d) Rendering of adaptation transition [3,5]; mean: 4.0; std.: 0.74;
e) Impact of the adaptation in decreasing interaction complexity [1,5]; mean: 3.58; std.: 1.16;
f) Impact of adaptation in improving user experience [3,5]; mean: 4,17; std.: 0.58;
g) Utility of multimodal augmentation for improving Web applications usability [3,5]; mean: 4.0; std.: 0.74;
h) Adaptation responsiveness [3,5]; mean: 3.92; std.: 0.67.

All aspects received greater ratings than in the previous test (excluding h, absent in the first test).

The rating on Awareness of the Adaptation process is slightly higher than in the first test. This is presumably because with respect to the previous version of the system, the vibrotactile notification has been combined with a pop-up also including information about the event that triggered the adaptation.

The Adaptation Appropriateness received good ratings, higher than the first user test. We believe this improvement is due to the new version of the multimodal generator, which has been updated in order to solve minor layout issues mentioned by the users of the first test.

The Adaptation Continuity and the Rendering of Adaptation transition received significantly higher ratings than previously (especially the latter). This is likely due to the improvements to the system that reduced the adaptation process latency. This is confirmed also by the good ratings of the adaptation responsiveness.

The Impact of the adaptation in decreasing interaction complexity received borderline ratings (nearly the same rating as the first test). This seems to be due to the accented English pronunciation of the participants. The problem of erroneous vocal input recognition is not due to the multimodal adaptation system, but is influenced by the distance from the microphone, the loudness of the voice and user pronunciation.

Two users did not like the need to press OK to confirm the adaptation when the pop-up appears because it forced them to manually interact with the interface even though the system adapted the page to interact vocally.

We have logged the interaction times for each scenario performed by each user. Scenario A (walking with noise) took between 97 and 490 seconds (mean 245, std. 132). For scenario B (fitness), interaction times were between 110 and 410 seconds (mean 198, std. 96). Completion times for scenario C (driving) was between 120 and 308 (mean 185, std. 52). Although a proper time comparison across modalities would have implied to perform the same task in the same settings, it is interesting to observe that scenario A, which took longer on average, relied on only-graphical input. Scenarios B and C (with multimodal and only-vocal input, respectively) took less time. Since the scenarios order was shuffled for the various users, we would exclude that this is due to a learning effect. In particular, scenario C, where vocal interaction was dominant, was the one whose tasks were performed most quickly. It is also worth highlighting that the standard deviation for interaction times was lower for scenario C than for B. In addition, scenario B had, in turn, a lower standard deviation than A (the one without vocal input). This may indicate that vocal interaction, which already brings undeniable benefits (e.g. accessibility) does not negatively affect task completion time.

The other statistical tests we have performed, e.g. considering ratings on system responsiveness and on perceived improvement in user experience, did not highlight any significant correlation between task completion time and subjective ratings.

We plan to perform a more extensive user study in the future by involving a larger set of users in order to get more statistically significant information.

7   Possible Platform Deployment

In order to highlight the benefits of the proposed approach for augmenting Web applications, in this section we explain how our platform can be deployed and exploited. To this end, there are two main modes depending on the organizations involved.

In within-organization deployment the adaptation platform can be deployed in and managed by the same organization that hosts the Web application(s) to be augmented. In this case, those responsible for configuring the platform are internal to the organization, e.g., the developers/designers responsible for managing the Web applications. It is worth noting that the existing Web applications do not need manual modifications or upgrades to be integrated with the adaptation platform.

In cross-organization deployment the organization hosting and managing the adaptation platform can be different from the one providing the original Web applications. An example use case is represented by a company or institution needing to provide (a subset of) users with augmented versions of existing Web interfaces with minimal effort. Examples might be a municipality wishing to furnish multimodal access to tourist information; a transportation company needing to provide its drivers with accessible versions of a pre-existing application for logistics, etc.

It should be noted that, in both deployments, end users access the Web applications through the (proxy of the) Augmentation Platform.

The formal issues arising from this kind of deployment, such as the need for agreements between the two organizations involved to comply with local/international rules, are beyond the scope of this paper.

8   Conclusions

We have presented a novel solution for multimodal augmentation of Web applications in mobile scenarios. It exploits an adaptation server receiving events from a distributed context manager and able to trigger adaptations according to externally specified rules. The server also exploits a model-based description language to perform the transformation from a graphical to a multimodal concrete description.

A video showing example applications of our platform for multimodal augmentation is available at: http://youtu.be/7Y670aWNUDM .

We have reported on user tests, which gave positive feedback and indications for further refinements. The proposed approach provides more flexible and general support than that currently provided in responsive design, which is not able to address many types of contextual events or provide dynamic and customizable multimodality.

Future work will be dedicated to making the adaptation server publicly available for external use, improve its performance, and move some of its functionality to cloud support. Since creating/editing adaptation rules still require some basic technological knowledge, we also aim to provide end users with intuitive interfaces for the customization of such rules. This would allow them to directly modify the context-dependent behaviour of their Web applications also in terms of multimodality.

References

1. Avouac, P.-A., Lalanda, P., Nigay, L.: Autonomic management of multimodal interaction: DynaMo in action. In: Proc. EICS 2012, pp. 35–44. ACM (2012)

2. Bellucci, F., Ghiani, G., Paternò, F., Porta, C.: Automatic Reverse Engineering of Interactive Dynamic Web Applications to Support Adaptation across Platforms. In: Proc. IUI 2012, pp. 217–226. ACM (2012)
3. Cantera, J.M., González, J., Meixner, G., Paternò, F., Pullmann, J., Raggett, D., Schwabe, D., Vanderdonckt, J.: Model-Based UI XG Final Report,
   http://www.w3.org/2005/Incubator/model-based-ui/XGR-mbui-20100504/
4. Coelho, J., Duarte, C.: The Contribution of Multimodal Adaptation Techniques to the GUIDE Interface. In: Stephanidis, C. (ed.) Universal Access in HCI, Part I, HCII 2011. LNCS, vol. 6765, pp. 337–346. Springer, Heidelberg (2011)
5. Coutaz, J., Nigay, L., Salber, D., Blandford, A., May, J., Young, R.: Four Easy Pieces for Assessing the Usability of Multimodal Interaction: the CARE Properties. In: Proc. INTERACT 1995, pp. 115–120. Chapman and Hall (1995)
6. Díaz, O., Arellano, C., Azanza, M.: A language for end-user web augmentation: Caring for producers and consumers alike. ACM Transactions on Web (2), 9 (2013)
7. Duarte, C., Carriço, L.: A conceptual framework for developing adaptive multimodal applications. In: Proc. IUI 2006, pp. 132–139. ACM (2006)
8. Dumas, B., Solórzano, M., Signer, B.: Design Guidelines for Adaptive Multimodal Mobile Input Solutions. In: Proc. MobileHCI 2013, pp. 285–294. ACM (2013)
9. Gajos, K.Z., Hurst, A., Findlater, L.: Personalized dynamic accessibility. Interactions 19(2), 69–73 (2012)
10. Jumisko-Pyykkö, S., Vainio, T.: Framing the Context of Use for Mobile HCI. International Journal of Mobile-Human-Computer-Interaction (IJMHCI) 3(4), 1–28 (2010)
11. Kane, S.K., Wobbrock, J.O., Smith, I.E.: Getting off the treadmill: Evaluating walking user interfaces for mobile devices in public spaces. In: Proc. MobileHCI 2008, pp. 109–118. ACM Press (2008)
12. Kumar, R., Talton, J.O., Ahmad, S., Klemmer, S.R.: Bricolage: Example-Based Retargeting for Web Design. In: Proc. CHI 2011, pp. 2197–2206. ACM (2011)
13. Manca, M., Paternò, F., Santoro, C., Spano, L.D.: Generation of Multi-Device Adaptive MultiModal Web Applications. In: Daniel, F., Papadopoulos, G.A., Thiran, P. (eds.) MobiWIS 2013. LNCS, vol. 8093, pp. 218–232. Springer, Heidelberg (2013)
14. Marcotte, E.: Responsive Web Design, A Book Apart (2011),
   http://www.abookapart.com/products/responsive-web-design
15. Nebeling, M., Speicher, M., Norrie, M.C.: W3Touch: Metrics-based Web Page Adaptation for Touch. In: Proc. CHI 2013, pp. 2311–2320. ACM (2013)
16. Octavia, J.R., Vanacken, L., Raymaekers, C., Coninx, K., Flerackers, E.: Facilitating Adaptation in Virtual Environments Using a Context-Aware Model-Based Design Process. In: England, D., Palanque, P., Vanderdonckt, J., Wild, P.J. (eds.) TAMODIA 2009. LNCS, vol. 5963, pp. 58–71. Springer, Heidelberg (2010)
17. Paternò, F., Santoro, C., Spano, L.D.: MARIA: A Universal Language for Service-Oriented Applications in Ubiquitous Environment. ACM Transactions on Computer-Human Interaction 16(4), 19:1–19:30 (2009)
18. Peissner, M., Häbe, D., Janssen, D., Sellner, T.: MyUI: generating accessible user interfaces from multimodal design patterns. In: Proc. EICS 2012, pp. 81–90. ACM Press (2012)
19. Salber, D., Anind, D., Abowd, G.: The context toolkit: Aiding the development of context-enabled applications. In: Proc. CHI 1999 Conference, pp. 434–441. ACM (1999)

Wherever You Go – Triggers of Location Disclosure for Check-in Services

Stephanie Ryschka and Markus Bick

ESCP Europe Business School, Berlin, Germany
{sryschka,mbick}@escpeurope.eu

Abstract. Privacy concerns have been identified as a major barrier to location-based services (LBS) usage. As opposed to previous studies treating location data as a universal term, this work aims at opening the black box of location data by showing the impact of the different characteristics of a user's location. Due to the exploratory nature, qualitative interviews and a focus group are applied. By investigating voluntary and proactive location disclosure for check-in services, this study reveals two major location characteristics triggering the associated disclosure intention: hedonism and perceived uniqueness. Finally, the practical and theoretical contribution of this study consists of an enriched understanding of location data in the context of LBS usage.

Keywords: Location-Based Services, Check-In Services, Information Disclosure, Qualitative Research.

1 Introduction

Mobile apps and devices rank among the top ten strategic technology trends for 2013 [1]. What especially distinguishes mobile from desktop applications is their new value propositions which are derived from context-awareness. Location represents the key enabler for several context-aware services (such as way- or friendfinding, location-aware shopping, or information services) [2]. Besides conventional voice services, these mobile, value-added services have naturally become a new opportunity for providers to create revenue [3]. However, from a user perspective, these location-based services (LBS) represent a double-edged sword, leading to the gratification of needs by these services on the one hand and the disclosure of personal location, and hence privacy concerns, on the other hand [4].

A vast stream of literature concentrates on the impact of privacy concerns on IS usage (see e.g. [5] for an overview of online concerns) which also includes LBS privacy concerns in particular [6],[7]. For LBS, privacy concerns form a special focus of attention since data collection is expanded to a variety of elements such as time, identity, entities and for these special services in combination with location [8]. This comprehensive form of data collection is thus the basis of prevalent privacy concerns.

Research focuses mainly on the factors balancing users' perception of LBS, such as perceived benefits on the one hand and privacy concerns on the other hand [7].

I. Awan et al. (Eds.): MobiWis 2014, LNCS 8640, pp. 86–99, 2014.

Traditional models such as UTAUT are adapted to LBS by integrating perceived risk and privacy concerns [9]. Heng et al., 2012 expanded this body of research by examining the impact of perceived personal control and its antecedents on context-specific concerns for LBS [10].

However, to this point, the notion of privacy concerns is treated in a general manner when it comes to the context and the type of location data people a willing to keep private [11]. Users might perceive some information as worth protecting while regarding some information as less privacy sensitive. As privacy concerns create a major barrier to LBS usage [12];[6], exploring what characteristics of location data determine what exactly users are or are not willing to provide will create a starting point to act on these triggers for other occasions where people refrain from sharing so far.

The present paper will focus on this obstructive side of LBS usage, namely concerns regarding location disclosure. In contrast to previous studies, which examined location data as a universal term, this work aims at opening the black box of location data by uncovering the impact of the different characteristics of a user's location. With a more nuanced consideration of location, this study aims to reveal different perceptions of location data and the associated disclosure intention. By investigating voluntary and proactive location disclosure (e.g., for check-in services), this study aims at answering the following research question: What triggers the decision of sharing vs. not sharing a location with respect to its characteristics?

2   Theoretical Background

The following section defines LBS and classifies check-in services within the category. Subsequently, the collection of location data from a user's perspective is presented.

2.1   Location-Based Services (LBS)

Location-based services are a subcategory of context-aware services. A context-aware service makes use of a context subsystem aiming at supporting users in performing tasks more efficiently and reaching their goals [2]. This context subsystem, in its narrow sense, is given by time, identity and location [8].

For LBS, the central pillar is represented by acquiring and utilizing information about the user's geographic context. For the scope of this paper, LBS are defined as any kind of network-based, mobile information services that account for and result from the positional information taken from a mobile device to provide value added services to the user, depending on their geographic context and individual preferences [13], [14], [15]. The major benefits of these services are provided by the integration of a time-dependent value, a position-dependent value – namely locatability – and by user-dependent values, namely personalization [16].

These services can be classified in either person-oriented LBS or device-oriented LBS [17]. Person-oriented LBS are primarily based on the integration of the user's geographic position into the service. Device-oriented LBS create value for the user by locating another device, which could be e.g. a free car for carsharing or a lost phone. Furthermore, these services can be distinguished from a user point of view by either actively requesting the service (pull) or automatically receiving the service (push) [14]. The several service categories range from navigation or directory services to location-based advertising [13].

Within these classifications, the intentions of the user and the recognition of those intentions by the service play a significant role. Bradley and Dunlop provide a set of possible cases of what user and service can know about the user's intentions [18]. The present study focuses on the explicit relationship between service and user, since this implies the user's awareness of revealing their location to the service. In contrast to e.g., mapping services where most users are not aware of sharing their location with the provider of the service, an explicit relationship assumes the user's awareness of sharing their geographical position. This is a pre-condition for successfully investigating users' perceptions of location disclosure.

Finally, the LBS concept consists of multiple layers. For this reason, the underlying research focuses on mobile services delivered via smartphones due to their high market penetration in contrast to tablets for example. Looking forward, smartphone application revenues are expected to remain at more than triple those of tablet application revenues up to 2015 [19]. Moreover, the focus is on location-based business-to-consumer (B2C) services, as this allows us to concentrate particularly on the influence of individual triggers of location disclosure. Location-based business-to-business (B2B) service adoption processes provoke additional potential organizational effects and non-voluntary usage which should be studied in a next step. This means in turn that our study will examine mobile services in the private (leisure) domain.

Table 1. Characteristics and resulting value propositions of LBS [20]

	Characteristic	Example
Value	Location + Time + Identity	Foursquare, Facebook Places, Google Latitude
	Location + Time	In-car navigation, Telstra Whereis, Mobile Google Maps
	Location	Paper maps, Desktop Google Maps

Furthermore, this work focuses on check-in services as a subcategory of LBS. These services allow users to share a location announcement within a more or less bounded system [11]. Check-in services are particularly suitable for this study, since they rely on voluntary and therefore conscious disclosure of location. Hence, an active cognitive engagement of this location disclosure is well suited to investigate the triggers for these decisions. Additionally, compared to other LBS, check-in services provide a high level of value for their users (see Table 1). By conflating the contextual elements of location, time and identity, check-in services constitute a sophisticated class of LBS which comprises all elements of interest for exploring the triggers of location disclosure.

2.2   Location Data

LBS users can be seen as technology users on the one hand, but also – in contrast to traditional IS users – as service consumers on the other hand [21],[22]. Traditional service consumption involves the exchange of goods or services in return for money or other goods and services. This is called first exchange. For mobile services and LBS, this relation is given by the exchange of the (personalized) service in return for the consumer's (location) data, called second exchange [23].From a user's point of view, providing their location is thus considered to be a sacrifice in the LBS usage context.

Research on data privacy is not new, but results of web privacy research cannot be directly applied to LBS privacy research [24]. Due to the ubiquitous nature of the service, the mobile device is constantly linked to the physical position of its user. As a consequence a greater amount and richer information about the user can be collected. Additionally, location data "cannot lie", which means that one can for example state that one is exercising every day in a web profile while location data reveals no gym attendance for weeks [16].

What does this location data add to traditional data collected from a user? First of all, location data provides mostly real-time information, which transforms privacy invasion into "a critical and acute concern" [6]. Additionally, this location-based information is not only perceived as geographical data given by latitude and longitude. From a philosophical point of view, for the user, location is equivalent to a place to which he attributes a certain meaning [16]. The location is linked to a locale which can be described by its shape and boundaries. This locale is given a sense by adding personal and emotional connections and hence rendering it as a place in the user's perceptive world (see Figure 1) [25].

This concept is comparable to pure data (location) which is put into context (locale) and by interpretation turned into knowledge [26]. As a consequence, one gains knowledge about the user by investigating their location data. This knowledge can be a powerful source for uncovering a vast amount about the users' beliefs, preferences and behavior [16].

Knowledge about the user's place is much more powerful compared to single identity and time data as it can be used in two ways. For push services, the service can directly influence the users' course of action (e.g. by directing them to the store on the left or right) [16] and for pull services, especially, check-in services as instances of service consumption are directly linked to the communication of that knowledge [27].

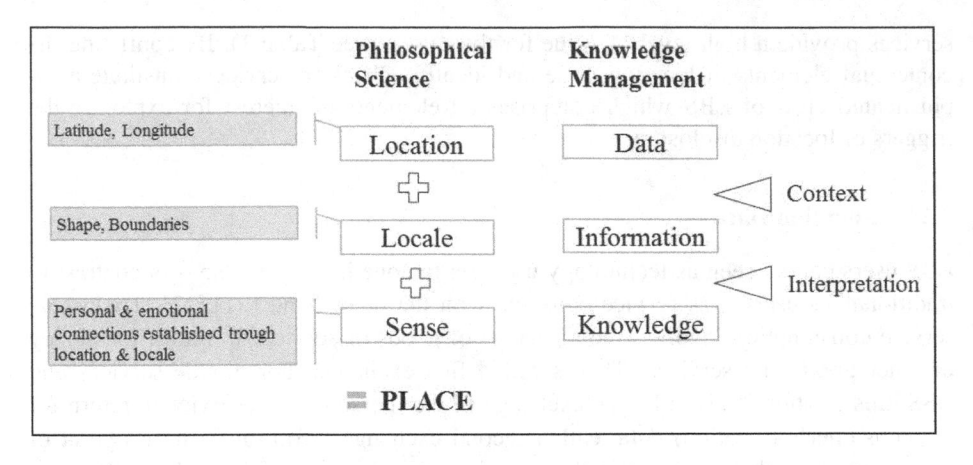

Fig. 1. The meaning of location data from a user's perspective based on [25],[26]

According to the concept of self-presentation and self-disclosure, people are willing to reveal information about themselves if this information is consistent with the way they would like to be seen by others [27]; [28]. In contrast to the established frame of sacrificing location privacy in return for service personalization or monetary compensation, location disclosure does not necessarily have to be valued negatively.

Thus, in some instances users might agree to share their place while in others they would heavily refuse. This study will focus on these services and locations as they can serve as the starting point for differentiating the perception of the value of a user's location. This study aims at opening the black box of location by investigating how to distinguish these locations by means of a qualitative study.

3   Methodology

The data collection was carried out by means of a focus group and qualitative interviews. Qualitative interviews were applied, as they are particularly appropriate for exploratory, theory building studies [29], [30] and for elaborating on complex issues with open-ended questions, which can be easily followed-up if necessary [31]. A focus group was chosen to complement the interviews with insights from collective interaction, which enables more spontaneous expressive and emotional statements than more cognitive individual interviews [32]. Additionally focus groups are particularly suitable for qualitative studies of motivational structures [33].

Since the pre-test revealed that users are not fully aware of the mechanism and functionalities of check-in services, the semi-structured interviews started with a 5min video introducing check-in services and their capabilities based on the case of foursquare. Subsequently, the definition of check-in services and prominent examples were presented to the participants before completing the questionnaire on demographics (gender, age) and usage frequency. The information on usage frequency built the starting point for the interviews. The focus group followed the same procedure, apart from setting the focus on discussion among the participants instead of discussion between the interviewer and the participants [33].

Due to the exploratory nature of the study, purposeful sampling was applied to achieve conceptual representativeness [34]. Maximum variation sampling was chosen to ensure relevant cases with maximum heterogeneity related to gender and usage intensity [35], [36]. The focus group was composed of light and non-users of check-in services as the interviews revealed that their cognitive and emotional processes are difficult to capture in a one-to-one setting (see Table 2). 5 participants are considered as an optimal size for this kind of inquiry [33]. Theoretical saturation was attained after the focus group with 5 participants and 5 single interviews, one additional interview was pursued to control for theoretical saturation (see Figure 2).

Table 2. Sample characteristics

	Inter-viewee	Age	Gender	Usage LBS	Usage Frequency LBS	Usage Check-In	Usage Frequency Check-In
Semi-struc-tured inter-views	A	27	M	yes	daily	yes	several times a week
	B	26	W	yes	several times a month	yes	once a month or less
	C	33	M	yes	daily	yes	several times a week
	D	26	W	yes	daily	no	
	E	27	W	yes	daily	yes	several times a week
	F	30	W	yes	daily	yes	once a month or less
Focus group	1	26	M	yes	several times a month	yes	once a month or less
	2	25	M	yes	several times a month	yes	once a month or less
	3	25	M	yes	several times a month	no	
	4	26	M	yes	several times a month	no	
	5	25	M	yes	several timesa month	yes	once a month or less

The sample consists of graduate and PhD students since they belong to the group of heavy smartphone users and have shown to be appropriate for LBS research [24], [21], [4]. The average interview lasted 21 minutes, while the interview length varied between 16 and 33 minutes (excluding the time of the video, the check-in service definition and the completion of the demographics questionnaire). With the prior consent of the participants, the interviews were recorded and subsequently transcribed according to Kuckartz, 2007 [37]. In total, 65 pages of transcribed material were analyzed. For the analysis, open coding following Grounded Theory was applied [38]. This analytical process allowed the identification of potential concepts and their dimensions. Whenever possible, invivo codes were applied to ensure the highest measure of validity of the results [39]. By subsequently applying first selective and then using axial coding, the codes were reduced and put back together by linking them to each other, to their contexts, their causes and interactions.

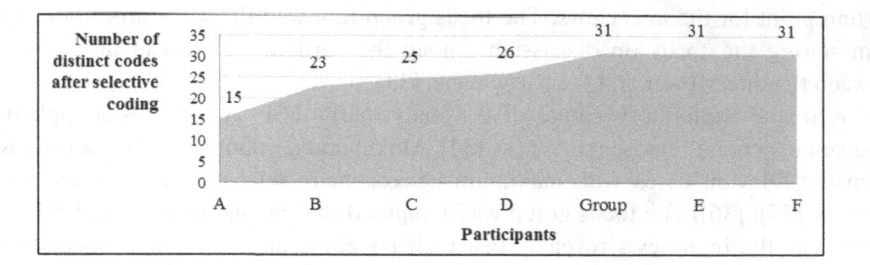

Fig. 2. Theoretical saturation of selective codes

4   Results

Based on the analysis of the interviews and the focus group, two prominent characteristics determining voluntary location disclosure were revealed. Hedonic characteristics and perceived uniqueness predominantly trigger the disclosure intention of location for check-in services. As proposed in section 2.2, the projection of the users' thoughts to the potential receiver and their perception of the location information was found to be a key element.

4.1   Hedonism

Predominantly, the disclosure of the users' location is seen as the transmission of a certain message linked to the characteristics of this location. Most of the participants revealed that they first think of the receiver of this kind of message before checking into a location. Location disclosure tends to act primarily as a way of sending a positive message in the sense of pleasure, as emphasized for example by Interviewee 3:

"For me, sharing location acts as sending a nice message. That's also how I perceive it from my friends. When I see one of my friends checking into a nice location I think: What a pleasure for him or her to be there!" (Interview 3)

If the user is at a location which evokes positive emotions, he or she intends to transmit these emotions to the receivers of their location data. For a particular instance, this is described by Interviewee 1:

"For instance in case of the location of my graduation ceremony, I simply wanted others to witness this occasion and to feel happy for me." (Interview 1)

In general, fun and enjoyment frequently constitute the decision criteria for location disclosure, as for instance shown by interviewee 4:

"Well, if I enjoy a special situation and I am having fun at a location, then I'm willing to publish this." (Interview 4)

Furthermore, linked to these characteristics, event locations tend to be prominent locations whose sharing is considered worth trading against privacy concerns. Even for users most hesitant to share their location data, an event creates such strong emotions that it can trigger a location check-in as made clear by focus group participant 1:

"I think it has to be a certain kind of event character. So, when I experience some-thing really really cool, then I really want to share it with others. E.g. being at Wemb-ley stadium for the Champions League final was simply great!" (Focus group P1)

Even users who are currently refraining from using check-in services, these kinds of characteristics and elements would constitute a potential trigger for sharing their location. However, they reported that if they experienced something that they consi-dered overwhelmingly fun then it would be worth sharing, such as bungee-jumping for focus group participant 3:

"It has to have a funny side or something cool or crazy, such as bungee-jumping. If I were to do such a thing, I would definitely be willingly to reveal the bridge from which I jump for this special occasion." (Focus group P3)

However, the qualitative interviews also revealed that there seems to be a certain maximum threshold for the transmission of locations with the above presented charac-teristics. As addressed in section 2.2, the users pay attention to their self-presentation by means of location disclosure. Thus, most of them stressed that they keep an eye on their sharing frequency, as highlighted by interviewee 5:

"But sometimes, I stop sharing it. You don't want to be associated only with having fun all day long." (Interview 5)

In summary, all the characteristics presented above can be captured in the hedonic nature of a location. Predominantly applied for consumer research to product catego-ries or brands, hedonic attitudes result "from sensations derived from the experience of using products" [40]. Items for measuring hedonism include for instance being perceived as pleasant, nice, agreeable and happy [41]. Referring to the statements presented above, the hedonic attributes tend not only to be applicable and relevant for product consumption but can also be expanded to characterizing the perception of locations. As presented in Table 1, in this case, the value proposition of the LBS of location+time+identity is released due to the hedonic nature of the location. This re-sults contrast previous findings [42], which revealed that participants willingness to disclose their location was highest when being depressed.

4.2   Uniqueness

Apart from the hedonic nature, a second prominent characteristic triggering location disclosure was identified. A location is predominantly considered noteworthy when being disclosed. Noteworthiness for a location can be further elaborated by the fol-lowing interview statements:

"I only check-in at highlights... because I only check-in at places that are special in a certain way." (Interview 5)

"Well, the main decision focus is: is this somehow something special, some place that is out of the norm?" (Interview 2)

Thus, a location which is perceived as special is more likely to be revealed. The term "highlight", emphasizes the notion of limited frequency which means in turn that the location has to be perceived as somehow special. The term "special" was elabo-rated upon and made concrete during the interviews in the following way:

"It's something that's highly ranked, meaning that it's a really really good restaurant with a famous name, a famous brand and the food is really extraordinary. And it has to be somehow exclusive in some way. That's how I would define a special place." (Interview 2)

"There are two criteria. First, it has to be a place where I am not staying all the time. Secondly, it also has to be a particular place not only for me but also in the sense that other people perceive it as a particular place." (Interview 3)

"I wouldn't check-in at the Starbucks around the corner, but there is e.g. a coffee shop in London with a unique high-tech machine that has already been discussed in several magazines. There I would definitely check-in." (Interview 2)

The specialness of a place is thus derived from its perceived exclusivity and the way in which it is perceived by others. This can be further underlined or triggered by having been selected as a unique place by previous visitors or different types of media.

Again, the shaping of one's identity has been stressed as an important factor. Communicating a visit to unique places fulfills the aim of representing a person that does not belong to the mainstream, as highlighted by focus group participant 4:

"If you set yourself apart from the masses, because you experience something unique, that would be something to reveal. In contrast to a simple Mallorca holiday which nearly everyone is doing – that's not showing the ideal picture of yourself." (Focus group P4)

Condensing all of the above, a central element which triggers location disclosure can be determined as the perceived uniqueness of the location. For product categories, perceived uniqueness is the extent to which the customer regards the product as different from other products in the same category [43]. This perceived uniqueness can be linked to desirability of objects and generates value for the consumer in terms serving the meta-preference of defining themselves as distinct from others [44]. Items for measuring perceived uniqueness are given by the terms "highly unique, being one of a kind, and really special" [44] which is highly consistent with the interview statements. The location transmits knowledge about the user (see Fig.1) and helps in shaping their self-presentation (see section 2.2). In the present study, perceived uniqueness has consequently been shown to also be a valid trigger in the case of location disclosure.

Linked to the user's perception of uniqueness of a place is also the notion of frequency. Commonly, a place perceived as exclusive and special is not visited on a daily basis. Thus, users might be more willingly to reveal a visit since their privacy is not that strongly threatened – usage patterns and routines cannot that easily be derived from these check-ins. This is congruent with the suggestion of improving location privacy by reducing the length of location traces [16].

4.3   Context

In addition to the identification of the two major triggers of voluntary location disclosure, several contextual elements have also been explored (see figure 3).

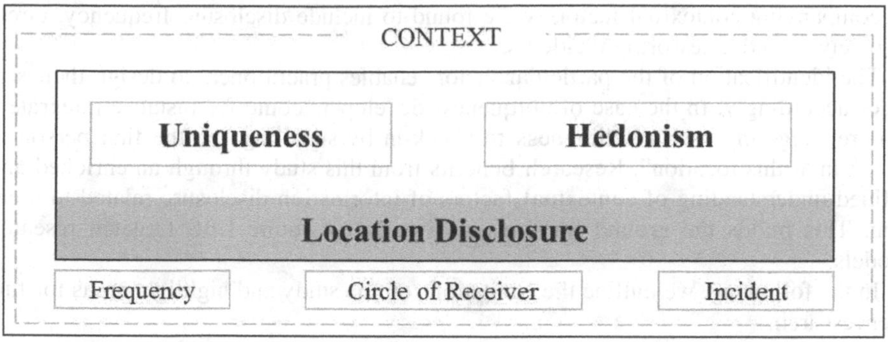

Fig. 3. Triggers of location disclosure for check-in services

In contrast to previous studies, such as [6], none of the participants mentioned compensation or gamification as triggers of location disclosure. On the one hand, this could be due to a limited number of compensation offers for check-ins. On the other hand, users indicated several times the importance of the communication aspect. This in turn is linked to their strong preference for sharing their location by means of face-book places rather than foursquare as users indicated they wanted to share with their friends. Thus, the circle of receivers represents an important contextual factor. This was emphasized by referring to the publishing of different locations according to whether receivers were close friends, simply facebook friends or the public.

Additionally, the possibility of having a different level of precision for location da-ta was not relevant for the disclosure decision. Differing levels of accuracy (e.g. sub-urb, pinpoint at the street address level, or manual location entry) were proposed to impact privacy concerns [45] but interviewees indicated that they perceive check-ins without exact coordinates as not being meaningful. This was seen as an either or decision: they either provided the exact location or no location at all. Thus, the proposition of maintaining "a coarse level of granularity for any location estimate" [16] for reducing location privacy concerns might not represent a uniformly applica-ble solution.

Furthermore, a noteworthy incident accompanying presence at a certain location can represent an additional trigger for location disclosure. Given a non-hedonic place such as a fast food restaurant, can become worth mentioning if the user is experienc-ing something that renders him pleased or happy such as finding a 100 euro note at this location (an example mentioned during one of the interviews). This is also valid for less unique places such as train stations, if the departure from that train station represents the beginning of a unique journey which, when shared together with the location information, becomes a place worth disclosing.

5   Discussion

By means of a qualitative study, several triggers for voluntary location sharing have been revealed. Two prominent characteristics of a location – hedonism and unique-ness– were found to differentiate between location disclosure and non-disclosure.

Accompanying contextual factors were found to include disclosure frequency, circle of receivers and noteworthy incidents.

The identification of the particular factors enables practitioners to design their services accordingly. In the case of uniqueness developers could for instance integrate a feature triggering user's willingness to check-in by signaling "be the first person to check-in at this location". Research benefits from this study through an enriched and refined understanding of contextual factors of information disclosure related to location. This builds the ground for the development of future LBS targeted research models.

In the following, we outline the limitations of this study and highlight areas for further research.

5.1   Limitations

The results of this study should be considered within the framework of some limitations.

First of all, the generalizability of results is limited, due to the exploratory and hence qualitative nature of the study. Linked to this, the results might be limited by cultural specificities, as the interviews took place with German participants. In countries where Foursquare has been far more successful, such as the United States, results might differ.

Secondly, the results might involve a social desirability bias [46]. Participants indicated that they wanted to share fun and unique locations with their friends to involve them in a positive experience. However, the location disclosure could also be a tool for making friends feeling jealous about a current location.

Thirdly, the results rely on voluntary and hence controlled location disclosure. They can thus only establish a starting point for services involving passive location disclosure.

5.2   Further Research

Based on the limitations of the study, there are various areas for further research.

Firstly, further studies should expand the data collection to different cultures. This could shed light on how cultural variables influence contextual factors and triggers of location disclosure in different countries.

Secondly, research should build on current findings and examine the impact of the revealed location triggers. A quantitative scenario-based experiment could show how hedonism, uniqueness and their interaction have an impact on the perceived value or sacrifice of location disclosure. Further contextual variables, such as the circle of receivers or frequency could be integrated into the experiment to examine their interaction with the two main triggers of location disclosure.

Thirdly, further research should expand this body of knowledge by studying passive location disclosure. As this mostly involves no cognitive engagement, a field study tracking user behaviour in cases when location disclosure is enabled and not enabled location disclosure might be beneficial. A starting point could also be given by analysing applications for which users have constantly enabled location tracking versus applications where this is not the case.

References

1. Gartner: Gartner Identifies the Top 10 Strategic Technology Trends for (2013), http://www.gartner.com/it/page.jsp?id=2209615
2. Aaltonen, A., Huuskonen, P., Lehikoinen, J.: Context awareness perspectives for mobile personal media. Information Systems Management 22, 43–55 (2005)
3. Kuo, Y.-F., Yen, S.-N.: Towards an understanding of the behavioral intention to use 3G mobile value-added services. Computers in Human Behavior 25, 103–110 (2009)
4. Xu, H., Luo, X., Carroll, J.M., Rosson, M.B.: The personalization privacy paradox: An exploratory study of decision making process for location-aware marketing. Decision Support Systems 51, 42–52 (2011)
5. Awad, N.F., Krishnan, M.S.: The personalization privacy paradox: an empirical evaluation of information transparency and the willingness to be profiled online fpr personalization. MIS Quarterly 30, 13–28 (2006)
6. Xu, H., Teo, H.-H., Tan, B.C.Y., Agarwal, R.: The Role of Push–Pull Technology in Privacy Calculus: The Case of Location-Based Services. Journal of Management Information Systems 26, 135–173 (2009)
7. Gupta, S., Xu, H., Zhang, X.: Balancing privacy concerns in the adoption of Location-Based Services: an empirical analysis. International Journal of Electronic Business 9, 118–137 (2011)
8. Kwon, O., Choi, K., Kim, M.: User acceptance of context-aware services: selfefficacy, user innovativeness and perceived sensitivity on contextual pressure. Behaviour & Information Technology 26, 483–498 (2007)
9. Zhou, T.: Examining Location-Based Services Usage From The Perspectives of Unified Theory of Acceptance And Use of Technology And Privacy Risk. Journal of Electronic Commerce Research 13, 135–144 (2012)
10. Xu, H., Teo, H.-H., Tan, B.C.Y., Agarwal, R.: Effects of Individual Self-Protection, Industry Self-Regulation, and Government Regulation on Privacy Concerns: A Study of Location-Based Services. Information Systems Research 23, 1342–1363 (2012)
11. Zhao, L., Lu, Y., Gupta, S.: Disclosure Intention of Location-Related Information in Location-Based Social Network Services. International Journal of Electronic Commerce 16, 53–90 (2012)
12. Junglas, I.A., Johnson, N.A., Spitzmüller, C.: Personality traits and concern for privacy: an empirical study in the context of location-based services. European Journal of Information Systems 17, 387–402 (2008)
13. Dhar, S., Varshney, U.: Challenges and business models for mobile location-based services and advertising. Commun. ACM 54, 121–128 (2011)
14. Gerpott, T.J., Berg, S.: Determinanten der Nutzungsbereitschaft von standortbezogenen Mobilfunkdiensten. Wirtschaftsinf 53, 267–276 (2011)
15. Yun, H., Han, D., Lee, C.C.: Extending UTAUT to Predict the Use of Location-Based Services. In: Galletta, D.F., Liang, T.-P. (eds.) Association for Information Systems (2011)
16. Wicker, S.B.: The Loss of Location Privacy in the Cellular Age. Communications of the ACM 55, 60–68 (2012)
17. Spiekermann, S.: General Aspects of Location Based Services. In: Schiller, J.H., Voisard, A. (eds.) Location-Based Services, pp. 5–25. Morgan Kaufmann Publishers, San Francisco (2004)
18. Bradley, N.A., Dunlop, M.D.: Toward a Multidisciplinary Model of Context to Support Context-Aware Computing. Human-Computer Interaction 20, 403–446 (2005)

19. McCarthy, J.: Mobile app internet recasts the software and services landscape. Forrester ABT Future Report (2011)
20. Finn, M.: I am here now: determining value in location based services. Telecommunications Journal of Australia 61, 1–10 (2011)
21. Kim, B., Han, I.: The role of utilitarian and hedonic values and their antecedents in a mobile data service environment. Expert Systems with Applications 38, 2311–2318 (2011)
22. Bick, M., Bruns, K., Sievert, J., Jacob, F.: Value-in-Use of Mobile Technologies. In: Back, A., Bick, M., Breunig, M., Pousttchi, K., Thiesse, F. (eds.) MMS 2012: Mobile und Ubiquitäre Informationssysteme. Proceedings zur 7. Konferenz Mobile und Ubiquitäre Informationssysteme, Braunschweig, pp. 56–67. Köllen Druck+Verlag GmbH, Bonn (2012)
23. Culnan, M.J., Bies, R.J.: Consumer Privacy: Balancing Economic and Justice Considerations. J. Social Issues 59, 323–342 (2003)
24. Ho, S.Y.: The effects of location personalization on individuals' intention to use mobile services. Decision Support Systems 53, 802–812 (2012)
25. Agnew, J.A.: Place and politics. The geographical mediation of state and society Allen & Unwin, Boston (1987)
26. Lehner, F.: Wissensmanagement. Grundlagen, Methoden und technische Unterstützung Hanser, München (2012)
27. Kaplan, A.M.: If you love something, let it go mobile: Mobile marketing and mobile social media 4x4. Business Horizons 55, 129–139 (2012)
28. Gilly, M., Schau, H.: We Are What We Post? Self-Presentation in Personal Web Space. The Journal of Consumer Research 30, 385–404 (2003)
29. Daniels, J.D., Cannice, M.V.: Interview Studies in International Business Research. In: Marschan-Piekkari, R., Welch, C. (eds.) Handbook of Qualitative Research Methods for International Business, pp. 185–206. Edward Elgar, Cheltenham (2005)
30. Flick, U.: An Introduction to Qualitative Research. SAGE Publications Ltd. (2009)
31. Ghauri, P.N., Grønhaug, K.: Research Methods In Business Studies: A Practical Guide. Pearson Education (2005)
32. Kvale, S.: Doing Interviews. Sage Publications, London (2007)
33. Lamnek, S.: Qualitative Sozialforschung. Band 2 Methoden und Techniken. Psychologie-Verl.-Union, München [u.a.] (1995)
34. Glaser, B.G., Strauss, A.L.: The discovery of grounded theory. Strategies for qualitative research Aldine Transaction, New Brunswick, N.J (1999)
35. Ritchie, J., Lewis, J., Elam, G.: Designing and Selecting Samples. In: Ritchie, J., Lewis, J. (eds.) Qualitative Research Practice. A Guide for Social Science Students and Researchers, pp. 77–108. Sage Publications, London (2003)
36. Patton, M.Q.: Qualitative research and evaluation methods. Sage Publications, Thousand Oaks (2002)
37. Kuckartz, U.: Qualitative Evaluation. Der Einstieg in die Praxis VS. Verl. für Sozialwiss, Wiesbaden (2007)
38. Strauss, A., Corbin, J.M.: Basics of Qualitative Research – Techniques and Procedures for Developing Grounded Theory. Sage Publications, Thousand Oaks (1990)
39. Wrona, T.: Fortschritts- und Gütekriterien im Rahmen qualitativer Sozialforschung. In: Zelewski, S. (ed.) Fortschritt in den Wirtschaftswissenschaften, pp. 189–216. Springer Fachmedien, Wiesbaden (2007)
40. Voss, K.E., Spangenberg, E.R., Grohmann, B.: Measuring the Hedonic and Utili-tarian Dimensions of Consumer Attitude. Journal of Marketing Research 40, 310–320 (2003)
41. Batra, R., Ahtola, O.: Measuring the hedonic and utilitarian sources of consumer attitudes. Marketing Letters 2, 159–170 (1991)

42. Consolvo, S., Smith, I.E., Matthews, T., LaMarca, A., Tabert, J., Powledge, P.: Location disclosure to social relations: why, when, & what people want to share. In: Proceedings of the SIGCHI Conference on Human Factors in Computing Systems, pp. 81–90. ACM, Portland (2005)
43. Tian, K., Bearden, W., Hunter, G.L.: Consumers' Need for Uniqueness: Scale Development and Validation. Journal of Consumer Research 28, 50–66 (2001)
44. Franke, N., Schreier, M.: Product uniqueness as a driver of customer utility in mass customization. Marketing Letters 19, 93–107 (2008)
45. Fusco, S.J., Michael, K., Michael, M.G.: Using a social informatics framework to study the effects of location-based social networking on relationships between people: A review of literature. In: 2010 IEEE International Symposium on Technology and Society (ISTAS), pp. 157–171 (2010)
46. Fisher, R.J.: Social Desirability Bias and the Validity of Indirect Questioning. Journal of Consumer Research 20, 303–315 (1993)

Stochastic Resource Allocation for Uplink Wireless Multi-cell OFDMA Networks

Pablo Adasme[1], Abdel Lisser[2], and Chen Wang[2]

[1] Departamento de Ingeniería Eléctrica,
Universidad de Santiago de Chile, Avenida Ecuador 3519, Santiago, Chile
pablo.adasme@usach.cl
[2] Laboratoire de Recherche en Informatique,
Université Paris-Sud XI, Bâtiment 650, 91190, Orsay Cedex, France
{abdel.lisser,chen.wang}@lri.fr

Abstract. In this paper, we propose a (0-1) stochastic resource allocation model for uplink wireless multi-cell OFDMA Networks. The model
maximizes the total signal to interference noise ratio produced in a multi-
cell OFDMA network subject to user power and subcarrier assignment
constraints. We transform the proposed stochastic model into a deterministic equivalent binary nonlinear optimization problem having quadratic
terms and second order conic constraints. Subsequently, we use the deterministic model to derive an equivalent mixed integer linear programming
formulation. Since the problem is NP-Hard, we propose a simple reduced
variable neighborhood search (VNS for short) metaheuristic procedure
[6,7]. Our preliminary numerical results indicate that VNS provides near
optimal solutions for small and medium size instances when compared to
the optimal solution of the problem. Moreover, it provides better feasible
solutions than CPLEX when the instances dimensions increase. Finally,
these results are obtained at a significantly less computational cost.

Keywords: Wireless multi-cell OFDMA networks, resource allocation,
mixed integer linear programming, variable neighborhood search.

1 Introduction

Orthogonal frequency division multiple access (OFDMA) is a wireless multi-
carrier transmission scheme currently embedded into modern technologies such
as IEEE 802.11a/g WLAN and IEEE 802.16a. It has also been implemented in
mobile WiMax deployments ensuring high quality of service (QoS) [10,14]. In a
wireless OFDMA network, multiple access is achieved by assigning different sub-
sets of subcarriers (subchannels) to different users using orthogonal frequencies.
In theory, this means that interference is completely minimized between subcarriers which allows simultaneous data rate transmissions from/to several users
to/from the base station (BS). We can have an OFDMA system consisting of one
or more BSs surrounded by several mobile users within a given radial transmission area. The former is known as a single-cell OFDMA network while the latter

I. Awan et al. (Eds.): MobiWis 2014, LNCS 8640, pp. 100–113, 2014.
© Springer International Publishing Switzerland 2014

forms a multi-cell OFDMA network. The last one is by far the highest complex scenario since it involves the interference generated among different users [1]. Interference between the BSs is also possible as long as their radial transmissions overlap each other. The interference phenomenon is mainly caused by the fact that different users and BSs use the same frequency bands either for uplink and/or downlink transmissions. In the uplink case, the transmission of signals is performed from the users to the BS whereas in the downlink case, this is done in the opposite direction. In this paper, we propose a (0-1) stochastic resource allocation model for wireless uplink multi-cell OFDMA networks. The proposed model maximizes the total signal to interference noise ratio (SINR) produced in a multi-cell OFDMA network subject to user power and subcarrier assignment constraints. The SINR is defined as the ratio between the power of a signal over the sum of different powers caused by other interfering signals plus the absolute value of the Additive White Gaussian Noise (AWGN). Maximizing SINR is relevant in a multi-cell OFDMA network as it allows selecting the best subcarriers for the different users while simultaneously exploiting multi-user diversity. The multi-user diversity phenomena occurs since subcarriers perceive large variations in channel gains which are different for each user and then each subcarrier can vary its own transmission rate depending on the quality of the channel. The better the quality of the channel, the higher the number of bits that can be transmitted. On the other hand, the interfering signals in a particular subcarrier can be efficiently detected using any multi-user detection scheme [12]. We transform the proposed stochastic model into a deterministic equivalent binary nonlinear optimization problem having quadratic terms and second order conic constraints. Finally, we use the deterministic model to derive an equivalent mixed integer linear programming formulation. This allows computing optimal solutions and upper bounds directly using its linear programming (LP) relaxation. Since the problem is NP-Hard, we propose a simple reduced variable neighborhood search (VNS) metaheuristic procedure to come up with tight near optimal solutions [6,7]. We choose VNS mainly due to its simplicity and low memory requirements [7]. Our numerical results indicate that VNS provides near optimal solutions for most of the instances when compared to the optimal solution of the problem. Moreover, it provides better feasible solutions than CPLEX when the instances dimensions increase. Finally, these solutions are obtained at a significantly less computational cost.

Several mathematical programming formulations for resource allocation in OFDMA networks have been proposed in the literature so far. In [1], the authors present a table with 19 papers published until 2007 where only two of them deal with multi-cell OFDMA networks either for uplink and downlink transmissions. More recent works can be found in [8,11,15]. In [8], the authors address the problem of inter-cell interference (ICI) management in the context of single frequency broadband OFDMA based networks. Whereas in [15], the problem of resource allocation in multi-cell OFDMA networks under the cognitive radio network (CRN) paradigm is considered. Finally, in [11] the problem of energy efficient communication in the downlink of a multi-cell OFDMA network is considered where user scheduling and power allocation are jointly optimized. As far as we know, stochastic programming or VNS algorithmic procedures have not been investigated so far for resource allocation in multi-cell OFDMA networks. In this paper, we adopt a simple scenario based approach to handle the expectation in the objective function of our stochastic formulation [5]. This is a valid assumption in stochastic programming framework as one may use historical data for instance [3,5]. On the other hand, we use a second order conic programming (SOCP) approach to deal with the probabilistic user power constraints [9]. For this purpose, we assume that the entries in the input power matrices are independent multivariate random variables normally distributed with known means and covariance matrices. The normal distribution assumption is motivated by its several theoretical characteristics amongst them the central limit theorem.

The paper is organized as follows. Section 2 briefly introduces the system description and presents the stochastic multi-cell OFDMA model. In Section 3, we transform the stochastic model into a deterministic equivalent mixed integer linear programming problem. Subsequently, in Section 4 we present our VNS algorithmic procedure. In Section 5, we conduct numerical tests to compare the optimal solution of the problem with those obtained with the LP relaxation and with the VNS approach, respectively. Finally, in section 6 we give the main conclusions of the paper and provide some insights for future research.

2   System Description and Problem Formulation

In this section, we give a brief system description of an uplink wireless multi-cell OFDMA network and formulate a stochastic model for the problem.

2.1   System Description

A general system description of an uplink wireless multi-cell OFDMA network is shown in Figure 1. As it can be observed, within a given radial transmission area, the BSs and users simultaneously transmit their signals. This generates interference and degrades the quality of wireless channels. These type of networks may arise in many difficult situations where infrastructure less approaches are mandatorily required. Mobile ad hoc networks (MANETS) or mesh type networks are examples of them commonly used in emergency, war battlefield or natural disaster scenarios where no strict planning of the network is possible due to short time constraints. In a multi-cell OFDMA network, the interference phenomena is a major concern in order to efficiently assign subcarriers to users.

Each BS must perform the allocation process over time in order to exploit the so-called multi-user diversity and hence increasing the capacity of the system [2]. Different modulation types can be used in each subcarrier. The modulation types depend on the number of bits to be transmitted in each subcarrier. Commonly, M-PSK (M-Phase Shift Keying) or M-QAM (M-Quadrature Amplitude Modulation) modulations are used in OFDMA networks [13].

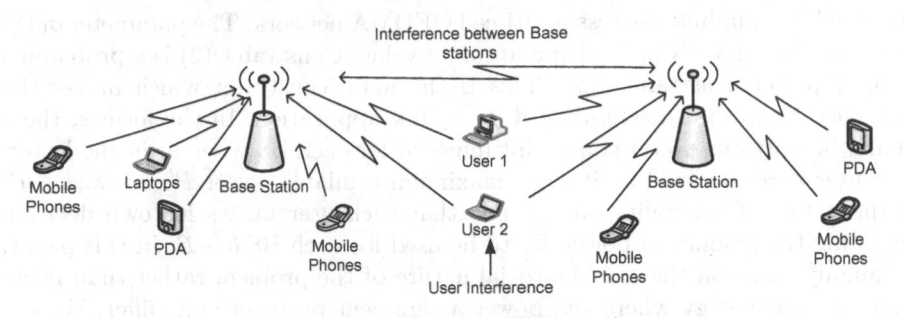

Fig. 1. System Description

In the next subsection, we propose a (0-1) stochastic resource allocation model to efficiently assign subcarriers to users in an uplink wireless multi-cell OFDMA network.

2.2 Stochastic Formulation

We consider an uplink wireless multi-cell OFDMA network composed by a set of $\mathcal{N} = \{1,..,N\}$ subcarriers in each BS, a set of $\mathcal{K} = \{1,..,K\}$ users and a set of $\mathcal{B} = \{1,..,B\}$ BSs. The BSs are surrounded by several mobile users within a given radial transmission range as depicted in Figure 1. Each BS has to assign a set of subcarriers to a set of users within a given frame[1]. The allocation process is performed by each BS dynamically in time depending on the quality of the channels in order to exploit multi-user diversity. The stochastic model we propose can be written as follows

P_0 :

$$\max_{x} \; \mathbb{E}_\xi \left\{ \sum_{b=1}^{B} \sum_{k=1}^{K} \sum_{n=1}^{N} \left(\frac{Q_{k,n}^b(\xi) x_{k,n}^b}{\sum_{\{w=1,w\neq b\}}^{B} \sum_{\{v=1,v\neq k\}}^{K} Q_{v,n}^w(\xi) x_{v,n}^w + |\sigma_0(\xi)|} \right) \right\} \quad (1)$$

$$\text{st: } \mathbb{P} \left\{ \sum_{n=1}^{N} p_{k,n}^b(\omega) x_{k,n}^b \leq P_k^b \right\} \geq (1-\alpha), \quad \forall k \in \mathcal{K}, b \in \mathcal{B} \quad (2)$$

$$\sum_{k=1}^{K} x_{k,n}^b \leq 1, \quad \forall n \in \mathcal{N}, b \in \mathcal{B} \quad (3)$$

$$x_{k,n}^b \in \{0,1\}, \quad \forall k, n, b \quad (4)$$

where $\mathbb{E}\{\cdot\}$ denotes mathematical expectation and $\mathbb{P}\{\cdot\}$ a probability measure. The decision variable $x_{k,n}^b = 1$ if user k is assigned subcarrier n in BS b, otherwise $x_{k,n}^b = 0$. The objective function (1) maximizes the total expected SINR

---

[1] A frame is a packet in which the data to be transmitted is placed. Each frame is composed by T time slots and N subcarriers.

produced in an uplink wireless multi-cell OFDMA network. The parameter $\sigma_0(\xi)$ represents the AWGN and $|\cdot|$ the absolute value. Constraint (2) is a probabilistic user power constraint [5,9]. This is the main constraint which makes the difference between a downlink and an uplink application. In the former, there should be only one power constraint imposed for each BS whereas in the latter, each user is constrained by its own maximum available power $P_k^b, k \in \mathcal{K}, b \in \mathcal{B}$. Without loss of generality, we assume that each user makes his own decision regarding the amount of power P_k^b to be used for each BS $b \in \mathcal{B}$. In this paper, we mainly focus on the combinatorial nature of the problem rather than using a specific technology where the power assignment protocol may differ. For example, both technologies WiMAX and long term evolution (LTE) use OFDMA, however both operate under different protocols. Therefore, in order to avoid specific technological aspects, in our numerical results presented in section 5, we generate these power values randomly. We further assume that the entries in each input matrix $(Q_{k,n}^b) = (Q_{k,n}^b(\xi))$ and input vector $(p_{k,n}^b) = (p_{k,n}^b(\omega))$ are random variables. In general, the entries in matrix $(Q_{k,n}^b(\xi))$ can be computed as $(Q_{k,n}^b(\xi)) = (p_{k,n}^b(\omega)H_{k,n}^b(\chi))$, where each entry in matrix $(H_{k,n}^b(\chi))$ represents the channel gain associated to the channel link of user k when using subcarrier n of $b \in \mathcal{B}$. The probabilistic constraint (2) imposes the condition that each power constraint must be satisfied at least for $(1 - \alpha)\%$ of the cases where $\alpha \in [0, 0.5)$ represents the risk of not satisfying some of these constraints. Constraint (3) indicates that each subcarrier in each BS should be assigned to at most one user. Finally, constraint (4) are domain constraints for the decision variables. In the next section, we present a simple equivalent deterministic formulation for P_0.

3   Deterministic Equivalent Formulation

In order to obtain a simple deterministic equivalent formulation for P_0, we assume that the input vectors $(p_{k,\bullet}^b(\omega))$ $\forall k, b$ are independent multivariate random variables normally distributed with known means $(\bar{p}_{k,\bullet}^b)$. Also, let $\Sigma^{kb} = (\Sigma_{ij}^{kb}), \forall i, j \in \mathcal{N}, k \in \mathcal{K}, b \in \mathcal{B}$ be the corresponding covariance matrices for each vector $(\bar{p}_{k,\bullet}^b)$. For sake of simplicity, we assume that the input matrices $(Q_{k,n}^b(\xi))$ and the input parameter $\sigma_0(\xi)$ are discretely distributed which might be the case when using sample data in order to approximate any unknown source of uncertainty [3,5]. This allows considering finite sets of scenarios such as $\left\{ (Q_{k,n}^{b,1}), (Q_{k,n}^{b,2}), ..., (Q_{k,n}^{b,S}) \right\}$ and $\{\sigma_0^1, \sigma_0^2, ..., \sigma_0^S)\}$ with probabilities $Pr(s) \geq 0, s \in \mathcal{S} = \{1, 2, ..., S\}$ such that $\sum_{s \in \mathcal{S}} Pr(s) = 1$. In particular, each $\sigma_0^s, s \in \mathcal{S}$ is generated according to a normal distribution with zero mean and standard deviation equal to one. Thus, an equivalent deterministic formulation for P_0 can be written as [9]

$$P_1: \quad \max_x \sum_{b=1}^{B} \sum_{k=1}^{K} \sum_{n=1}^{N} \sum_{s=1}^{S} \left(\frac{Pr(s)Q_{k,n}^{b,s}x_{k,n}^b}{\sum_{\{w=1, w \neq b\}}^{B} \sum_{\{v=1, v \neq k\}}^{K} Q_{v,n}^{w,s}x_{v,n}^w + |\sigma_0^s|} \right) \quad (5)$$

$$\text{st:} \quad \sum_{n=1}^{N} \bar{p}_{k,n}^{b} x_{k,n}^{b} + F^{-1}(1-\alpha) \sqrt{\sum_{i=1}^{N} \left(\sum_{j=1}^{N} \Sigma_{i,j}^{k,b} x_{k,j}^{b} \right)^2} \leq P_k^b,$$

$$\forall k \in \mathcal{K}, b \in \mathcal{B} \tag{6}$$

$$\sum_{k=1}^{K} x_{k,n}^{b} \leq 1, \quad \forall n \in \mathcal{N}, b \in \mathcal{B} \tag{7}$$

$$x_{k,n}^{b} \in \{0,1\}, \quad \forall k, n, b \tag{8}$$

where $F^{-1}(1-\alpha)$ denotes the inverse of $F(1-\alpha)$ which is the standard normal cumulative distribution function.

3.1 Mixed Integer Linear Programming Formulation

In order to obtain an equivalent mixed integer linear programming formulation for P_1, we introduce variables $t_{k,n}^{b,s}, \forall k, n, b, s$ in the objective function (5) and square both sides of constraint (6). This allows writing P_1 equivalently as

$$P_2: \quad \max_{x,t} \sum_{b=1}^{B} \sum_{k=1}^{K} \sum_{n=1}^{N} \sum_{s=1}^{S} Pr(s) t_{k,n}^{b,s} \tag{9}$$

$$\text{st:} \quad \sum_{\{w=1, w \neq b\}}^{B} \sum_{\{v=1, v \neq k\}}^{K} Q_{v,n}^{w,s} t_{k,n}^{b,s} x_{v,n}^{w} + t_{k,n}^{b,s} |\sigma_0^s| \leq$$

$$Q_{k,n}^{b,s} x_{k,n}^{b}, \forall k, n, b, s \tag{10}$$

$$\left(F^{-1}(1-\alpha) \right)^2 \sum_{i=1}^{N} \left(\sum_{j=1}^{N} \Sigma_{i,j}^{k,b} x_{k,j}^{b} \right)^2 \leq \left(P_k^b - \sum_{n=1}^{N} \bar{p}_{k,n}^{b} x_{k,n}^{b} \right)^2$$

$$\forall k \in \mathcal{K}, b \in \mathcal{B} \tag{11}$$

$$P_k^b \geq \sum_{n=1}^{N} \bar{p}_{k,n}^{b} x_{k,n}^{b}, \forall k \in \mathcal{K}, b \in \mathcal{B} \tag{12}$$

$$\sum_{k=1}^{K} x_{k,n}^{b} \leq 1, \forall n \in \mathcal{N}, b \in \mathcal{B} \tag{13}$$

$$x_{k,n}^{b} \in \{0,1\}, \forall k, n, b \tag{14}$$

Afterward, we consider separately each quadratic term in constraint (11) and introduce linearization variables $\varphi_{v,n,k}^{w,b,s} = t_{k,n}^{b,s} x_{v,n}^{w}$ with $(v \neq k, w \neq b)$ and $\theta_{k,j,l}^{b} = x_{k,j}^{b} x_{k,l}^{b}, \forall k \in \mathcal{K}, j, l \in \mathcal{N}$ with $(j \neq l)$ and $b \in \mathcal{B}$. This leads to write the following mixed integer linear program

$$P_{MIP}:$$

$$\max_{x,t,\varphi,\theta} \sum_{b=1}^{B} \sum_{k=1}^{K} \sum_{n=1}^{N} \sum_{s=1}^{S} Pr(s) t_{k,n}^{b,s} \tag{15}$$

$$\text{st:} \quad \sum_{\{w=1,w\neq b\}}^{B} \sum_{\{v=1,v\neq k\}}^{K} Q_{v,n}^{w,s}\varphi_{v,n,k}^{w,b,s} + t_{k,n}^{b,s}|\sigma_0^s| \leq Q_{k,n}^{b,s}x_{k,n}^b, \quad \forall k,n,b,s \quad (16)$$

$$\varphi_{v,n,k}^{w,b,s} \leq Mx_{v,n}^w, \quad \forall v,n,k,w,b,s,(v\neq k,b\neq w) \quad (17)$$

$$\varphi_{v,n,k}^{w,b,s} \leq t_{k,n}^{b,s}, \quad \forall v,n,k,w,b,s,(v\neq k,b\neq w) \quad (18)$$

$$\varphi_{v,n,k}^{w,b,s} \geq Mx_{v,n}^w + t_{k,n}^{b,s} - M, \quad \forall v,n,k,w,b,s,(v\neq k,b\neq w) \quad (19)$$

$$\varphi_{v,n,k}^{w,b,s} \geq 0, \quad \forall v,n,k,w,b,s, \quad (20)$$

$$\left(F^{-1}(1-\alpha)\right)^2 \sum_{i=1}^{N}\left[\sum_{j=1}^{N}(\Sigma_{ij}^{kb})^2 x_{k,j}^b + \sum_{j=1}^{N}\sum_{l=1,j\neq l}^{N}\Sigma_{ij}^{kb}\Sigma_{il}^{kb}\theta_{k,j,l}^b\right] \leq$$

$$\left((P_k^b)^2 - 2\sum_{n=1}^{N}\bar{p}_{k,n}^b P_k^b x_{k,n}^b + \sum_{n=1}^{N}(\bar{p}_{k,n}^b)^2 x_{k,n}^b + \sum_{j=1}^{N}\sum_{l=1,j\neq l}^{N}\bar{p}_{k,j}^b\bar{p}_{k,l}^b\theta_{k,j,l}^b\right)$$

$$\forall k \in \mathcal{K}, b \in \mathcal{B} \quad (21)$$

$$P_k^b \geq \sum_{n=1}^{N}\bar{p}_{k,n}^b x_{k,n}^b, \quad \forall k,b \quad (22)$$

$$\sum_{k=1}^{K} x_{k,n}^b \leq 1, \quad \forall n \in \mathcal{N}, b \in \mathcal{B} \quad (23)$$

$$\theta_{k,j,l}^b \leq x_{k,j}^b, \quad \forall k \in \mathcal{K}, j,l(j\neq l), b \in \mathcal{B} \quad (24)$$

$$\theta_{k,j,l}^b \leq x_{k,l}^b, \quad \forall k \in \mathcal{K}, j,l(j\neq l), b \in \mathcal{B} \quad (25)$$

$$\theta_{k,j,l}^b \geq x_{k,j}^b + x_{k,l}^b - 1, \quad \forall k \in \mathcal{K}, j,l(j\neq l), b \in \mathcal{B} \quad (26)$$

$$x_{k,n}^b \in \{0,1\}, \quad \forall k,n,b \quad (27)$$

$$\theta_{k,j,l}^b \in \{0,1\} \quad \forall k \in \mathcal{K}, j,l \in \mathcal{N}, b \in \mathcal{B} \quad (28)$$

where constraints (17)-(19) and (24)-(26) are standard linearization constraints [4] for constraints (10) and (11) in P_2, respectively. The parameter $\mathcal{M}$ is a bigM positive value. Model P_{MIP} allows obtaining optimal solutions and upper bounds for P_1. In the next section, we propose a VNS algorithmic procedure to compute feasible solutions for P_1 as well.

4   Variable Neighborhood Search Procedure

VNS is a recently proposed metaheuristic approach [6,7] that uses the idea of neighborhood change during the descent toward local optima and to avoid valleys that contain them. We define only one neighborhood structure as $Ngh(x)$ for P_1 as the set of neighbor solutions x' in P_1 at a distance "h" from x where the distance "h" corresponds to the number of 0-1 values which are different in x' and x, respectively. We propose a reduced variable neighborhood search procedure [6,7] in order to compute feasible solutions for P_1. The VNS approach mainly consists in solving the following equivalent problems

P_1^{VNS} :

$$\max_x \sum_{b=1}^{B}\sum_{k=1}^{K}\sum_{n=1}^{N}\sum_{s=1}^{S}\left(\frac{Pr(s)Q_{k,n}^{b,s}x_{k,n}^{b}}{\sum_{\{w=1,w\neq b\}}^{B}\sum_{\{v=1,v\neq k\}}^{K}Q_{v,n}^{w,s}x_{v,n}^{w}+|\sigma_0^s|}\right) +$$

$$\mathcal{M}\sum_{k=1}^{K}\sum_{b=1}^{B}\min\left\{P_k^b - \sum_{n=1}^{N}\bar{p}_{k,n}^b x_{k,n}^b - F^{-1}(1-\alpha)\sqrt{\sum_{i=1}^{N}\left(\sum_{j=1}^{N}\Sigma_{i,j}^{k,b}x_{k,j}^b\right)^2},0\right\}$$

st: $\sum_{k=1}^{K}x_{k,n}^b \leq 1, \quad \forall n \in \mathcal{N}, b \in \mathcal{B}$

$x_{k,n}^b \in \{0,1\}, \forall k,n,b$

Where $\mathcal{M}$ is a positive bigM value. The VNS procedure we propose is depicted in Algorithm 4.1. It receives an instance of problem P_1 and provides a feasible solution for it. We denote by $(\bar{x}, \bar{f})$ the final solution obtained with the algorithm

---

Algorithm 4.1. VNS approach

Data: A problem instance of P_1
Result: A feasible solution $(\bar{x}, \bar{f})$ for P_1
$Time \leftarrow 0$; $\mathcal{H} \leftarrow 1$; $count \leftarrow 0$; $x_{k,n}^b \leftarrow 0, \forall k,n,b$;
foreach $b \in \mathcal{B}, k \in \mathcal{K}$ and $n \in \mathcal{N}$ do
    Draw a random number r in the interval $(0,1)$;
    if $(r > 0.5)$ then
        $x_{k,n}^b \leftarrow 1$;

Let $(\bar{x}, \bar{f})$ be the an initial solution for P_1^{VNS} with objective function value $\bar{f}$;
while $(Time \leq maxTime)$ do
    for $i = 1$ to $\mathcal{H}$ do
        Choose randomly $k' \in \mathcal{K}, b' \in \mathcal{B}$ and $n' \in \mathcal{N}$;
        $x_{k,n'}^{b'} \leftarrow 0, \quad \forall k \in \mathcal{K}$;
        Draw a random number r in the interval $(0,1)$;
        if $(r > 0.5)$ then
            $x_{k',n'}^{b'} \leftarrow 1$;

    Let (x^*, g^*) be a new feasible solution found for P_1^{VNS} with objective function value g^*;
    if $(g^* > \bar{f})$ then
        $\mathcal{H} \leftarrow 1, (\bar{x}, \bar{f}) \leftarrow (x^*, g^*)$; $Time \leftarrow 0$; $count \leftarrow 0$;
    else
        Keep previous solution; $count \leftarrow count + 1$;
    if $(count > \eta)$ then
        $count \leftarrow 0$;
        if $(\mathcal{H} \leq K)$ then
            $\mathcal{H} \leftarrow \mathcal{H} + 1$;
        else
            $\mathcal{H} \leftarrow 1$;

$(\bar{x}, \bar{f}) \leftarrow (\bar{x}, \bar{f})$;

---

where $\bar{f}$ represents the objective function value and $\bar{x}$ the solution found. The algorithm is simple and works as follows. First, it computes randomly an initial feasible solution $(\tilde{x}, \tilde{f})$ for P_1^{VNS} that we keep. Next, the algorithm performs a variable neighborhood search process by randomly assigning to $\mathcal{H} \leq K$ users a different subcarrier and a different BS. Initially, $\mathcal{H} \leftarrow 1$ and it is increased in one unit when there is no improvement after new "η" solutions have been evaluated. On the other hand, if a new current solution is better than the best found so far, then $\mathcal{H} \leftarrow 1$, the new solution is recorded and the process goes on. Notice that the value of $\mathcal{H}$ is increased until $\mathcal{H} = K$, otherwise $\mathcal{H} \leftarrow 1$ again after new "η" solutions have been evaluated. This gives the possibility of exploring in a loop manner from local to wider zones of the feasible space. The whole process is repeated until the cpu time variable "$Time$" is less than or equal to the maximum available "$maxTime$". Note we reset "$Time = 0$" when a new better solution is found. This allows searching other "$maxTime$" units of time with the hope of finding better solutions.

5   Numerical Results

We present numerical results for P_1 using CPLEX 12 and the proposed VNS algorithm. We generate a set of 1000 samples of realistic power data using a wireless channel from [16] while the entries in matrices $(Q_{k,n}^{b,s})$ are computed as $(Q_{k,n}^{b,s}) = p_{k,n}^{b,s} H_{k,n}^{b,s}, \forall s \in \mathcal{S}$ where the values of $p_{k,n}^{b,s}$ are also generated using the wireless channel from [16]. Each maximum available power value $P_k^b, \forall k, b$ is set equal to $P_k^b = 0.4 * \sum_{n=1}^{N} \bar{p}_{k,n}^b$ where each $\bar{p}_{k,n}^b \ \forall k, n, b$ corresponds to the average over the set of 1000 samples. The channel values $H_{k,n}^{b,s}$ are generated according to a standard Rayleigh distribution function with parameter $\sigma = 1$.

The input parameter $\sigma_0^s, \forall s \in \mathcal{S}$ is normally distributed with zero mean and standard deviation equal to one. We calibrated the value of $\eta = 50$ in Algorithm 4.1. Finally, we set $\alpha = 0.1$ and the bigM value $\mathcal{M} = 10^{10}$. A Matlab program is implemented using CPLEX 12 to solve P_{MIP} and its linear programming relaxation LP_{MIP} and the proposed VNS Algorithm 4.1. The numerical experiments have been carried out on a AMD Athlon 64X2 Dual-Core 1.90 Ghz with 1.75 GoBytes of RAM under windows XP. In Table 1, column 1 gives the instance number and columns 2-4 give the instances dimensions. In columns 5, 7 and 6, 8, we provide the optimal solutions of P_{MIP}, LP_{MIP}, and the cpu time in seconds CPLEX needs to solve them. Similarly, in columns 9-10, we present the best solution found and the cpu time in seconds VNS Algorithm 4.1 requires to reach that solution. We arbitrarily set the maximum cpu time available for CPLEX to be at most 1 hour. While for the VNS algorithm, we set in all our tests the maximum available time to $maxTime = 100$ seconds. We also mention that whenever the variable $Time$ in Algorithm 4.1 reaches the 100 seconds, it means the algorithm did not find any better solution within this amount of time, therefore we subtract this amount to the complete registered time. The latter provides the exact cpu time VNS approach requires to obtain that solution. Finally, in columns 11 and 12, we provide gaps we compute as $\frac{LP_{MIP} - P_{MIP}}{P_{MIP}} * 100$ and $\frac{|VNS - P_{MIP}|}{P_{MIP}} * 100$ respectively. We also mention that the preliminary numerical results presented in Table 1 are obtained using only $S = 4$ scenarios in

Table 1. Feasible solutions obtained using CPLEX and VNS with S=4 scenarios

#	Instances Dimensions			Linear programs				VNS Approach		Gaps	
	K	N	B	P_{MIP}	$Time$	LP_{MIP}	$Time$	VNS	$Time$	$LP\%$	$VNS\%$
1	4	8	3	187.1625	6.88	237.5973	1.05	178.5370	21.53	26.9471	4.6085
2	8	8	3	384.3661	26.30	479.5605	3.14	384.3661	151.72	24.7666	0
3	12	8	3	293.9304	181.63	367.4731	7.77	293.9304	5.59	25.0205	0
4	14	8	3	1525.0840	145.00	1822.3541	16.50	1464.9243	32.45	19.4920	3.9447
5	4	8	5	604.5217	20.61	768.5897	2.97	575.5403	179.19	27.1402	4.7941
6	8	8	5	583.8594	409.56	735.0504	22.74	574.7517	86.28	25.8951	1.5599
7	12	8	5	305.6647	3600	406.9006	45.91	298.0767	86.19	33.1199	2.4824
8	14	8	5	46832.5618	3600	67656.9540	50.05	44682.1000	40.73	44.4656	4.5918
9	4	16	3	1403.5467	37.95	1707.7717	4.50	1395.5805	50.66	21.6754	0.5676
10	8	16	3	599.1510	133.49	730.1556	9.94	599.1510	11.47	21.8650	0
11	12	16	3	660.5156	1796.75	834.0475	30.44	660.5156	14.71	26.2722	0
12	14	16	3	1445.0892	3600	1741.4093	21.63	1515.0978	37.52	20.5053	4.8446
13	4	16	5	40616.6713	836.81	53810.3188	10.83	34136.6073	198.95	32.4833	15.9542
14	8	16	5	595.1008	3600	874.2042	27.31	543.9943	310.23	46.9002	8.5879
15	12	16	5	811.7762	3600	1331.2226	72.23	780.8005	50.12	63.9889	3.8158
16	14	16	5	*	*	1783.3788	66.98	1113.9113	131.86	*	*
17	4	32	3	767.3340	3600	1261.3962	24.55	841.8803	62.17	64.3869	9.7150
18	8	32	3	3686.4326	3600	5998.2713	103.74	3720.8249	92.26	62.7121	0.9329
19	12	32	3	993.0576	3600	1506.5105	55.55	995.9633	146.50	51.7042	0.2926
20	14	32	3	1454.5490	3600	2454.8796	115.69	1530.6112	160.04	68.7726	5.2293
21	4	32	5	240.6614	3600	4364.5604	147.28	2443.5389	128.41	1713.5687	915.3430
22	8	32	5	739.9245	3600	5062.2949	248.47	2567.0373	277.26	584.1637	246.9323
23	12	32	5	*	*	4818.1842	292.50	2736.2113	372.58	*	*
24	14	32	5	*	*	2831.4831	603.98	1586.3495	740.02	*	*

*: No solution found due to CPLEX shortage of memory.

P_{MIP}. From Table 1, we mainly observe that the gaps obtained with the VNS approach are lower than 5% for most of the instances. In particular, we obtain optimal solutions for instances 2-3 and 10-11, and best feasible solutions than CPLEX for the instances 17-24. Moreover, for the larger size instances 21-24, the differences between the solutions obtained with P_{MIP} and VNS are notably larger which confirms that the proposed VNS approach outperforms CPLEX significantly. Besides, these solutions are obtained at a considerably lower cpu time. This observation can also be verified by looking at the upper bounds of the optimal solutions obtained with LP_{MIP} which, by far, overpass the solutions obtained with P_{MIP}. This is not the case for the VNS approach. In summary, we see that the gaps are better when the number of users increase. This is an interesting observation as these type of networks are designed for multiple access purposes. Regarding the cpu times, we observe that VNS can find better feasible solutions at a significantly less computational cost than CPLEX. This is the case in about 83.3% of the instances. Particularly, for instances 7-8, 12, 14-16, and 17-24 where the cpu time required by CPLEX to get these solutions is at least one hour. On the other hand, the cpu time required by CPLEX to solve the LP relaxations grows considerably when the instances dimensions increase. Finally, we observe that the gaps obtained with the LP relaxation deteriorates rapidly when the instances dimensions increase. In order to give more insight regarding the number of scenarios considered in P_{MIP}, in Table 2 we present further numerical results using $S = 8$. The column information is exactly the same as in Table 1. From Table 2, we observe that the gaps obtained with VNS algorithm

Table 2. Feasible solutions obtained using CPLEX and VNS with S=8 scenarios

#	Instances Dimensions			Linear programs				VNS Approach		Gaps	
	K	N	B	P_{MIP}	$Time$	LP_{MIP}	$Time$	VNS	$Time$	$LP\%$	$VNS\%$
1	4	8	3	396.0058	17.80	494.4254	1.80	359.6266	23.17	24.8531	9.1865
2	8	8	3	294.5774	72.69	343.9400	7.33	294.5774	18.61	16.7571	0
3	12	8	3	378.1765	189.66	457.9363	38.55	363.0186	88.31	21.0906	4.0081
4	14	8	3	382.0399	304.97	446.0401	22.92	375.1456	99.72	16.7522	1.8046
5	4	8	5	1645.5083	63.64	1946.0497	7.02	1367.9773	216.03	18.2644	16.8660
6	8	8	5	988.6564	715.42	1224.7990	26.53	811.7008	31.23	23.8852	17.8986
7	12	8	5	2475.8996	3600	3438.1747	90.45	2258.9482	36.36	38.8657	8.7625
8	14	8	5	818.3844	3600	1088.7688	114.09	799.9939	65.89	33.0388	2.2472
9	4	16	3	680.5390	723.66	871.3750	10.94	671.8174	386.89	28.0419	1.2816
10	8	16	3	420.1876	268.45	509.4053	27.16	412.1617	167.61	21.2328	1.9101
11	12	16	3	965.5496	703.63	1163.4646	51.66	965.5496	186.19	20.4977	0
12	14	16	3	*	*	984.4130	81.28	732.6627	248.62	*	*
13	4	16	5	1357.7920	3600	1964.5528	22.81	1031.8239	21.08	44.6873	24.0072
14	8	16	5	980.9758	3600	1454.2974	79.11	929.1635	138.29	48.2501	5.2817
15	12	16	5	*	*	1583.5987	178.19	1036.2983	575.86	*	*
16	14	16	5	*	*	2363.6524	490.03	1606.6579	244.51	*	*
17	4	32	3	10481.2140	3600	13788.7161	51.72	9495.2439	344.46	31.5565	9.4070
18	8	32	3	786.9654	3600	1092.8612	143.33	754.8404	382.65	38.8703	4.0821
19	12	32	3	*	*	1585.6223	106.89	1081.1442	269.78	*	*
20	14	32	3	*	*	1420.6889	167.36	1087.8288	401.65	*	*
21	4	32	5	*	*	5959.0736	111.61	3372.2211	467.43	*	*
22	8	32	5	*	*	1447.7113	357.77	873.4855	466.66	*	*
23	12	32	5	*	*	*	*	2889.0945	583.05	*	*
24	14	32	5	*	*	*	*	6652.0679	893.88	*	*

*: No solution found due to CPLEX shortage of memory.

slightly deteriorates when compared to Table 1. In this case, they are in average lower than 7% approximately. In particular, we obtain near optimal solutions for instances 2-4, 8-11, and 18. We know that these solutions are near optimal since the solutions obtained with P_{MIP} are obtained in less than 1 hour of cpu time. Otherwise they should only be considered as best feasible solutions found with CPLEX. We also see that CPLEX can not solve large scale instances and that the gaps obtained with VNS get tighter when the number of users increase. Regarding the cpu times, we observe that VNS can find better feasible solutions at a significantly less computational cost than CPLEX. Finally, the cpu time required by CPLEX to solve the LP relaxations grows even faster than in Table 1 when the instances dimensions increase. Next, we further consider a more realistic demanding situation where the number of users is significantly larger. These numerical results are presented below in Tables 3 and 4, respectively. The column information in these tables is exactly the same as in the previous tables. In particular Table 3 presents numerical results using $S = 4$ whereas in Table 4 we use $S = 8$ scenarios. In these tables, we mainly observe that finding optimal solutions with CPLEX becomes rapidly prohibitive. In fact, we can only find feasible solutions for instances 1, 2 and 9 in Table 3 and for instance number 1 in Table 4 using the linear programs. On the opposite, using VNS approach still allows finding feasible solutions up to instances with $K = 100$ users. Although, the cpu times are considerably larger when compared to Tables 1 and 2, respectively. This confirms again that the proposed VNS approach is competitive.

Table 3. Feasible solutions obtained with CPLEX and VNS for larger number of users using S=4 scenarios

#	Instances Dimensions			Linear programs				VNS Approach		Gaps	
	K	N	B	P_{MIP}	Time	LP_{MIP}	Time	VNS	Time	LP%	VNS%
1	20	8	3	270.5294	951.79	338.7968	14.40	270.5294	57.42	25.2347	0
2	30	8	3	490.9271	3600	593.0366	44.20	495.8847	116.24	20.7993	1.0098
3	50	8	3	*	*	263.2351	539.21	126.3258	105.54	*	*
4	100	8	3	*	*	*	*	275.0429	134.03	*	*
5	20	8	5	*	*	773.6433	82.67	583.6842	507.71	*	*
6	30	8	5	*	*	671.2375	365.91	543.9147	755.11	*	*
7	50	8	5	*	*	*	*	446.9953	363.37	*	*
8	100	8	5	*	*	*	*	4138.8963	348.22	*	*
9	20	16	3	607.2990	3600	745.4151	59.20	662.6294	394.06	22.7427	9.1109
10	30	16	3	*	*	1587.8095	181.55	1424.2695	1597.67	*	*
11	50	16	3	*	*	*	*	5865.1871	1276.79	*	*
12	100	16	3	*	*	*	*	1272.3440	223.53	*	*
13	20	16	5	*	*	2783.0741	162.20	1299.5881	1234.41	*	*
14	30	16	5	*	*	*	*	8524.1006	652.28	*	*
15	50	16	5	*	*	*	*	1917.7369	212.81	*	*
16	100	16	5	*	*	*	*	2832.1584	886.86	*	*
17	20	32	3	*	*	3770.3202	230.89	2426.4821	2902.60	*	*
18	30	32	3	*	*	*	*	2428.6924	3853.00	*	*
19	50	32	3	*	*	*	*	675.1841	174.92	*	*
20	100	32	3	*	*	*	*	1677.3204	615.92	*	*
21	20	32	5	*	*	*	*	2507.8547	1422.99	*	*
22	30	32	5	*	*	*	*	880.2869	1555.05	*	*
23	50	32	5	*	*	*	*	724.5287	922.64	*	*
24	100	32	5	*	*	*	*	453.1134	4000.73	*	*

*: No solution found due to CPLEX shortage of memory.

Table 4. Feasible solutions obtained with CPLEX and VNS for larger number of users using S=8 scenarios

#	Instances Dimensions			Linear programs				VNS Approach		Gaps	
	K	N	B	P_{MIP}	Time	LP_{MIP}	Time	VNS	Time	LP%	VNS%
1	20	8	3	304.9070	926.97	363.6304	62.98	250.3734	226.53	19.2594	17.8853
2	30	8	3	*	*	346.1478	104.80	317.3865	155.50	*	*
3	50	8	3	*	*	*	*	192.7712	402.53	*	*
4	100	8	3	*	*	*	*	328.1000	60.58	*	*
5	20	8	5	*	*	1929.2130	284.56	1220.2991	1099.84	*	*
6	30	8	5	*	*	*	*	2063.0753	331.43	*	*
7	50	8	5	*	*	*	*	736.4978	185.36	*	*
8	100	8	5	*	*	*	*	140.0601	619.28	*	*
9	20	16	3	*	*	4902.3964	144.20	4290.7134	492.44	*	*
10	30	16	3	*	*	*	*	7289.1626	1133.05	*	*
11	50	16	3	*	*	*	*	532.0673	737.55	*	*
12	100	16	3	*	*	*	*	242.7288	478.31	*	*
13	20	16	5	*	*	*	*	1142.8744	1158.90	*	*
14	30	16	5	*	*	*	*	687.1994	1739.78	*	*
15	50	16	5	*	*	*	*	990.0482	403.17	*	*
16	100	16	5	*	*	*	*	615.1829	2235.63	*	*
17	20	32	3	*	*	3926.1787	327.11	2156.4379	1687.58	*	*
18	30	32	3	*	*	*	*	819.6241	585.23	*	*
19	50	32	3	*	*	*	*	14159.5528	427.56	*	*
20	100	32	3	*	*	*	*	2154.5143	1071.48	*	*
21	20	32	5	*	*	*	*	100865.1824	3447.88	*	*
22	30	32	5	*	*	*	*	2255.9878	1005.44	*	*
23	50	32	5	*	*	*	*	1787.8574	2139.78	*	*
24	100	32	5	*	*	*	*	828.8698	6320.64	*	*

*: No solution found due to CPLEX shortage of memory.

In general, when looking at the four tables presented, we observe that solving P_{MIP} and LP_{MIP} is considerably harder than solving the proposed VNS approach. However, the proposed linear programs still provide an alternative way to compute optimal solutions and upper bounds for the multi-cell OFDMA problem. Also, we observe that the VNS approach outperforms the solutions obtained with CPLEX in most of the cases, especially when the instances dimensions increase. Additionally, we observe that the number of scenarios $s \in S$ directly affects the performance of CPLEX when solving the linear programs. This can be explained by the fact that using more scenarios implies using more variables in the linear programs. This is not the case for the VNS approach where the number of variables in P_1^{VNS} does not depend on the number of scenarios. Finally, we observe that the linear programs can not be solved efficiently when considering a larger number of users in the system. Hence, the number of scenarios and the number of users can be considered as bottlenecks for the proposed linear programs. On the other hand, the performance of the VNS approach deteriorates when incrementing the number of users and the number of subcarriers either separately or simultaneously.

6   Conclusions

In this paper, we propose a (0-1) stochastic resource allocation model for uplink wireless multi-cell OFDMA Networks. The model maximizes the total signal to interference noise ratio produced in a multi-cell OFDMA network subject to user power and subcarrier assignment constraints. We transformed the stochastic model into a deterministic equivalent binary nonlinear optimization problem having quadratic terms and second order conic constraints. Subsequently, we use the deterministic model to derive an equivalent mixed integer linear programming formulation. Finally, we proposed a reduced variable neighborhood search metaheuristic procedure [6,7] to compute feasible solutions. Our preliminary numerical results provide near optimal solutions for most of the instances when compared to the optimal solution of the problem. Moreover, we find better feasible solutions than CPLEX when the instances dimensions increase. Finally, we obtain these feasible solutions at a significantly less computational cost.

As future research, we plan to study new stochastic and algorithmic approaches for the problem.

Acknowledgments. The author Pablo Adasme is grateful for the financial support given by Conicyt Chilean government through the Insertion project number: 79100020.

References

1. Amzallag, D., Armarnik, T., Livschitz, M., Raz, D.: Multi-Cell Slots Allocation in OFDMA Systems. In: 16th Mobile and Wireless Communications Summit (IST), pp. 1–5 (2007)

2. Cao, Z., Tureli, U., Liu, P.: Optimum subcarrier assignment for OFDMA uplink. In: IEEE International Conference on Communications, pp. 11–15 (2003)
3. Delage, E., Ye, Y.: Distributionally Robust Optimization under Moment Uncertainty with Application to Data-Driven Problems. Operations Research 58(3), 596–612 (2010)
4. Fortet, R.: Applications de lálgebre de boole en recherche operationelle. Revue Francaise de Recherche Operationelle 4, 17–26 (1960)
5. Gaivoronski, A., Lisser, A., Lopez, R., Hu, X.: Knapsack problem with probability constraints. Journal of Global Optimization 49, 397–413 (2011)
6. Hansen, P., Mladenovic, N., Perez Brito, D.: Variable Neighborhood Decomposition Search. Journal of Heuristics 7, 335–350 (2001)
7. Hansen, P., Mladenovic, N.: Variable neighborhood search: Principles and applications. European Journal of Operational Research 130, 449–467 (2001)
8. Hernández, A., Guio, I., Valdovinos, A.: Interference Management through Resource Allocation in Multi-Cell OFDMA Networks. In: IEEE 69th Vehicular Technology Conference VTC, pp. 1–5 (2009)
9. Lobo, M., Vandenberghe, L., Boyd, S., Lebret, H.: Applications of Second-Order Cone Programming. Linear Algebra and its Applications 284, 193–228 (1998)
10. Sternad, M., Svensson, T., Ottosson, T., Ahlen, A., Svensson, A., Brunstrom, A.: Towards Systems Beyond 3G Based on Adaptive OFDMA Transmission. In: Proceedings of the IEEE, vol. 95, pp. 2432–2455 (2007)
11. Venturino, L., Risi, C., Buzzi, S., Zappone, A.: Energy-efficient coordinated user scheduling and power control in downlink multi-cell OFDMA networks. In: IEEE 24th International Symposium on Personal Indoor and Mobile Radio Communications (PIMRC), pp. 1655–1659 (2013)
12. Verdu, S.: Multiuser Detection. University of Cambridge, Cambridge, United Kingdom (1998)
13. Wong, I.C., Zukang, S., Evans, B.L., Andrews, J.G.: A low complexity algorithm for proportional resource allocation in OFDMA systems. In: IEEE Workshop on Signal Processing Systems, pp. 1–6 (2004)
14. Yaghoobi, H.: Scalable OFDMA physical layer in IEEE 802.16 WirelessMAN. Intel Technology Journal 8, 201–212 (2004)
15. Zhaorong, Z., Jianyao, Z., Jingjing, L., Weijiang, L., Yunjie, R.: Resource Allocation Based on Immune Algorithm in Multi-Cell Cognitive Radio Networks with OFDMA. In: Fifth International Conference on Computational and Information Sciences (ICCIS), pp. 1644–1647 (2013)
16. Zukang, S., Jeffrey, G., Evans, B.: Short Range Wireless Channel Prediction Using Local Information, Signals, Systems and Computers. In: Conference Record of the Thirty-Seventh Asilomar Conference, vol. 1, pp. 1147–1151 (2003)

Improving the Performance and Reliability of Mobile Commerce in Developing Countries

Ibtehal Nafea[1] and Muhammad Younas[2]

[1] Computer Science College, Taibah University, Saudi Arabia
e.t.nafea@gmail.com
[2] Department of Computing and Communication Technologies,
Oxford Brookes University, Oxford, UK
m.younas@brookes.ac.uk

Abstract. Mobile commerce (m-commerce) is currently more widely adapted in developed countries than the developing countries. Developing countries lag behind due to inappropriate technological infrastructure for the provisioning of m-commerce services. Though there exist various obstacles of adapting m-commerce services in developing countries, this paper addresses the performance and reliability issues. In particular, it considers the limited bandwidth of wireless networks and the capacity of underlying web servers involved in processing m-commerce requests. If m-commerce requests are not processed efficiently then they are more likely to be dropped wherever the network connection can be intermittent as in developing countries. This paper proposes an approach which is based on the class-based priority scheme that distinguishes m-commerce requests from other requests. The idea is to give high priority to the requests coming from mobile devices (over wireless networks) as compared to requests coming from standard PC/laptops (over standard Internet (wired) connections) as the later can tolerate longer delay and are less susceptible to connection failures. The proposed approach is formally specified and is implemented as a prototype tool. Experimental results demonstrate that the proposed approach significantly improves the performance and reliability m-commerce requests.

Keywords: E-commerce services, Mobile commerce, Priority scheduling, Performance.

1 Introduction

Mobile Commerce (or m-commerce) is defined as buying and selling of goods and services over the Internet using mobile devices such as mobile phones [15]. Mobile phones have been used for a variety of purposes ranging from voice calls to text messages through to social networking and online shopping. Increasingly, customers research products online via computers and mobile devices prior to making any purchase decision. It is anticipated that mobile phones would replace our wallets and the payment cards, e.g., using NFC (Near Field Communications) technology in the

I. Awan et al. (Eds.): MobiWis 2014, LNCS 8640, pp. 114–125, 2014.
© Springer International Publishing Switzerland 2014

near future. Mobile service provisioning and consumption is more common in developed countries. For example, 34% of mobile phone users have made a purchase using their mobile phone compared to 19 percent in 2011 (Source: DC Financial Insights, 2012). In addition, according to recent US Holiday Shopping Survey, results show that 33% of US shoppers use their smartphones when comparing prices while in a store and 13% using their mobile phone to receive mobile text reminders of sales (http://www.accenture.com/us-en/Pages/insight-holiday-2013-shopping-trends.aspx).

However, developing countries still lack appropriate technological infrastructure for m-commerce services. The authors in [16] identify various factors that have negative impact on the adaption of m-commerce in developing countries. These include, network infrastructure, service cost, hardware and handsets costs, trust and security, cultural and user acceptance. In terms of network infrastructure, 2G networks are common in developing countries which are sufficient for simple SMS communication but not for m-commerce services such as online shopping or online payment. Most of the m-commerce services need 3G networks but this requires large investment by the mobile network operators. For instance, authors in [17, 18] identify internet broadband in Saudi Arabia is more expensive than developed countries. This research also identifies security, trust and privacy issues related to online shopping and that small business lack appropriate online payment mechanisms in Saudi Arabia.

For the successful provisioning of m-commerce services tackling all such issues are equally important. But this paper addresses the performance and reliability issues of m-commerce services. In particular, it takes into account the limited bandwidth of wireless networks and the capacity of underlying web servers involved in processing the m-commerce requests. If m-commerce requests are not processed efficiently then they are more likely to be dropped wherever the network connection can be intermittent as in developing countries.

This paper proposes an approach which is based on the class-based priority scheme that distinguishes m-commerce requests from other requests. The idea is to give high priority to the requests coming from mobile devices (over wireless networks) as compared to requests coming from standard PC/laptops (over standard Internet (wired) connections) as the later can tolerate delay and are less susceptible to failure. The proposed approach is formally specified and is implemented as a prototype tool. Experimental results demonstrate that the proposed approach significantly improves the performance and reliability m-commerce requests.

These m-commerce applications process large number of users' requests which incur excessive load on the underlying servers. Such excessive load generally results in performance degradation of the servers, i.e. response time of requests may increase or servers may drop requests. This paper focuses on the extremely important challenges to today's mobile and e-commerce applications and the development of class-based priority scheme which classifies requests into high and low priority requests. Requests by paying customers should be favoured over others (e.g. search or browse). By assigning class-based priorities at multiple service levels, E-commerce web servers can perform better and can improve the performance of high priority requests without causing adverse effects on low priority effects. In this paper the buy requests received from mobile devices should generally get higher priority as such requests are more likely to lose due to the lack of reliability that related to network connectivity's. Due to space limitations, only the buy requests are considered in this paper.

The remainder of the paper is structured as follows. Section 2 describes related works. Section 3 presents the generalized architecture of the proposed approach. Section 4 presents the implementation of the proposed approach. Section 5 describes the experimental results and their analysis. Section 6 concludes the paper.

2   Related Work

Various research studies have been conducted in order to investigate the issues that hinder the adoption of m-commerce in developing countries. For instance, research study conducted in [13] is related to Bangladesh which is a developing country but has a significance usage of mobile phones — estimated to be 65% (~98.5 million of population) by February 2013. This study identified the main barriers to m-commerce adoption in developing countries. The study involved fact finding methods such as interviewing people from different background including bankers, solution providers, telecoms, retailers and government officials. The paper found that the major barriers to the adoption of m-commerce in Bangladesh are lack of literacy, trust and conflict of interest between telecoms and banks.

There are many other barriers to m-commerce such as perceived risk, lack of knowledge, government regulation, poor accessibility, poor readability, less navigable page designs and cost. For example, Sambhanthan et al. [3] explore the accessibility issues in commercial websites in developing countries, through a study of Sri Lankan hotel websites. The issues identified in this study include poor accessibility for users with visual and mobility impairments, and lack of conformance to W3C accessibility principles. In addition, the availability of high speed networking in different regions of developing countries is also an issue. For instance, accessing the web contents from rural areas with poor network bandwidth is still a major challenge. This is due to the lack of resources in deploying appropriate network cables in rural areas. To alleviate such issues mobile devices and wireless networks can be used which do not require the deployment of network cables. According to Hyun et al [14] it is critical for hotels to utilize m-commerce in tourism promotion to survive in an era of increasing mobile adaptation. Though the deployment of wireless networks in rural areas is useful for standard voice calls or sending/receiving SMS messages they lack support for m-services.

The above studies provide useful insights into the issues faced by adopting m-commerce in developing countries. But they neither address the underlying technical issues nor propose any solutions to deal with the wireless networking or server side processing in m-commerce applications.

The work in [19] takes account of the underlying network capabilities in order to improve the performance of mobile transactions. It proposes a pre-emptive resume scheduling which gives higher priority to the control messages of transactions (e.g., transaction commit or abort) compared to the data processing operations of a transaction. However, this work addresses only transactional applications and their control messages and does not take into account the wireless connectivity or other operations (e.g., browse, buy) of m-commerce applications. The work in [20] concerns mobility management of roaming users in m-commerce applications. It analytically models scarce channels in wireless network cells in order to maximize channel utilization and to efficient handle roaming requests. However, this work does not consider the priority in terms of network connectivity nor it considers the underlying (web) server processing which is the focus of this work.

The (web) server's behaviour has a strong relation to successful completion of m-commerce (or e-commerce) requests. For example, if the server becomes overloaded the response time can grow to unacceptable levels that can lead to the user leaving the website. To maintain acceptable response time and minimise server overload, clusters of multiple web servers have been developed [2, 1]. Cache servers also help to improve the performance of web servers [4], by reducing the response time in real-world dynamic web applications.

Mechanisms to schedule requests have been proposed to improve the performance of web servers [5, 6, 7]. Request scheduling refers to the order in which concurrent requests should be served. This section describes the existing techniques that are relevant to scheduling techniques for web-based E-commerce services at a user level, such as modifying the inclusion of a scheduler process in a web server to decide the order in which the requests should be handled to improve the mean response time. Kernel level such as controlling the order in which socket buffers are contacted to the network, or both (user and kernel levels). These techniques adopted non-traditional request ordering policies, such as: shortest remaining processing time first (SRPT). The main idea underlying these techniques is to classify the requests and schedule them in a given order, as a result of providing different quality of service (QoS) levels to each group, by assigning different priorities to the different requests.

For example, to implement policies based on SRPT, firstly scheduling to prioritise the service of short static web content requests is needed in front of the long requests [11, 12]. These studies conclude that SRPT scheduling provides a better response time to short requests at relatively low costs to the long requests. However, Crovella et al. [11] indicate that the application level scheduling does not provide fine enough control over the order in which packets enter the network. The other problem is that in traditional UNIX network stack implementations, processing for all connections is handled in an aggregate manner. That is, outgoing packets are placed on the wire in response to the arrival of acknowledgements. This means that if many connections have data ready to send, and if the client and network are not the bottleneck, then data will be sent from the set of connections and acknowledgements will arrive, which is not under application control.

3   The Proposed Approach

The proposed approach extends our previous work [21] to improve the performance and reliability of m-commerce applications in developing countries. Generally, in the m-commerce (or e-commerce) setup, users interact with a number of (web) servers through a series of requests in order to acquire required information or make purchases. Example of such requests include: search for particular products, browse information about a specific item, browse/read product reviews, select items, add items to cart, and make payment. Figure 1 represents the proposed architecture of the m-commerce or e-commerce services. Our approach is to design and develop Priority Scheduling Mechanism (PSM) in order to enable request classification and to provision required level of performance and reliability to m-commerce applications. We therefore deploy a middleware component, named PSM, in the standard m-commerce or e-commerce web server architecture.

In it, the proposed PSM system receives requests from different clients either through PC or mobile devices. In the case of PC, requests are submitted to the PSM using standard Internet. In the case of mobile devices requests are submitted through the wireless networks in addition to the standard Internet. For instance, mobile devices can first send requests to the base stations which in turn send the requests using the standard (wired) networks. PSM classifies the requests and submit them to the (web) servers. Web server then passes the requests to the application server and then to the database server. Results of the requests are processed and sent back to the client devices (PC or mobile devices).

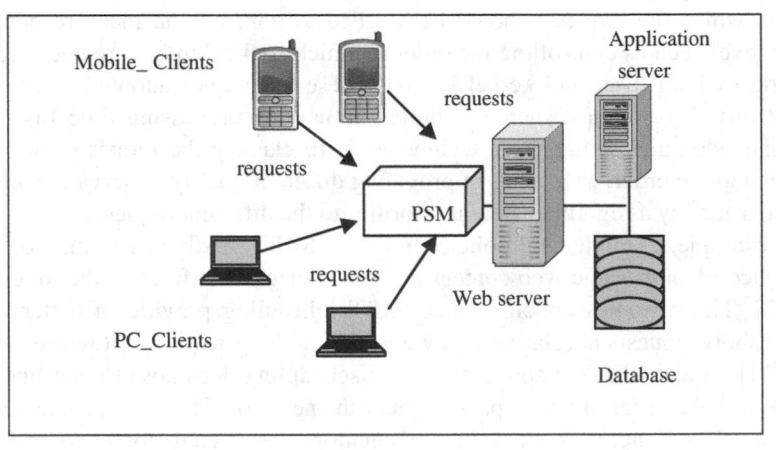

Fig. 1. Priority scheduling model architecture

The PSM is designed and developed using a combination of different techniques and models which are described as follow:

Session-Based Admission Control: Sessions are created for each client in the PSM system; this includes the different types of request, such as: browse and buy from PC or mobile client. Each client has a handler which can be a session-based control for client's session because the handler controls the session and met the query only if the system got a capacity to do it.

Service Differentiation: Different priorities are given to each class, service differentiation is implemented by means of scheduling; in other words, scheduling mechanisms need to not only classify requests, but also identify the difference between them. The proposed approach implements mechanisms in order to classify the client requests into different classes, in accordance with the type of request.

Service Degradation Technique: The acceptance probability of low priorities requests are adjusted in this proposed mechanism gives a small delay to processing these requests rather than rejecting them.

Request Scheduling: As previously mentioned, this work applies request scheduling in the form of the priority scheduling mechanism that distinguishes classes of requests and schedules these classes in a priority order. It prioritizes the service of Mobile buy requests over other requests (as detailed below).

The proposed approach employs priority scheduling queuing model in order to classify requests into different classes. In it, four different types of requests are classified, including: 'Mobile_browse', 'Mobile_ buy', 'PC_browse',' and 'PC_buy'. 'Mobile_buy' requests are given high priority compared to other requests. The rationale is that these requests should be processed efficiently in order to avoid disconnection that may occur due to poor wireless network connectivity. Compared to Mobile_browse requests Mobile_buy requests should also be prioritised as the latter are more likely to be converted to purchasing orders which will generate money for the service provider. A second priority is given to 'PC_buy' and a third priority is given to 'Mobile_browse'. A lowest priority is given to 'PC_browse', as described in Algorithm 1. The proposed algorithm reduces the loss of low priority customers, by giving a small delay to processing their requests rather than rejecting them, thus it keeps low priority customers on the system. The algorithm gives a small delay to processing "PC_browse" requests rather than rejecting them. The algorithm works as follows:

- If the buffer of Mobile_buy request is not full, then process the first Mobile_buy request.
- If the buffer of Mobile_buy request is not empty, then wait until it becomes empty then process the first PC_buy request.
- If the buffers of Mobile and PC buy requests are not empty, then wait until they become empty then process the first Mobile_browse request.
- If the buffers of Mobile and PC buy requests and Mobile_browse are not empty, then wait until they become empty then process the first PC_browse request.

Algorithm 1. Priority scheduling Mechanism Algorithm

```
if (priority of arriving request== highest)
    {
    if (Mobile_ buy_buffer not full)
                    Process this request;
            else
                    Drop this request;
    } // End if
else if (priority of arriving request== 2)
    {
        if (PC_buy_buffer not full)
        {       while    ! ( Mobile_buy_buffer is empty)
                        {wait;}
                            process this request;
    }//End if
                else
                    Drop this request;
    }//End else if
else if (priority of arriving request== 3)
    {
    if (Mobile_browse_buffer not full)
    {        while (!(Mobile_ buy_buffer is empty)||( !(PC_buy_buffer is empty))
                            {wait;}
                        Process this request;

    }//End if
    else
                    Drop this request;
    }//End else if
else if(priority of arriving request== lowest)
    {
    if (PC_browse_buffer not full)
        {      while (!(Mobile_ buy_buffer is empty)||( !(PC_buy_buffer is empty)||( !(Mo-
bile_browse_buffer is empty))
                        {wait;}
                        Process this request;

    }//End if
    else
                    Drop this request;
    }//End else if
```

As seen in algorithm 1 there is a busy waiting for low priority requests inside each handler to avoid lost connection and keep the client on the website. However, with algorithm 1, the response time will increase therefore, it could be useful to add operation timed out scenario or run the additional processes to serve clients simultaneously.

4   Development of the PSM System

This section describes the prototype implementation of the proposed approach. We have implemented the proposed approach as a Java-based prototype system which is developed using the Java active object model [10]. The prototype system simulates the provisioning of m-commerce or e-commerce services and processes different types of clients requests (browse and buy) both from PC clients as well as from Mobile clients. The system randomly generates a number of requests of a particular type. The system is implemented using JCreator LE 4.00 on Microsoft Windows XP. TCP connection is used between the components of the system in order to ensure reliable communication and to avoid loss of messages.

The main components of the prototype system are explained as follows (see Figure 2):

Mobile Clients: The mobile client receives a link from the web server which is used to connect it to a dedicated handler. After the client has sent a number of fixed browse, or buy, requests, it informs the Handler that it has finished its requests.

PC Clients: The PC client receives a link from the web server which is used to connect it to a dedicated handler. After the client has sent a number of fixed browse, or buy, requests, it informs the Handler that it has finished its requests.

Gatekeeper (GK): This component deals with admission control and handles the initial client requests. When a client connects to the Gatekeeper, a fresh action is passed to both the client and a new instance of the Handler, allowing these components to interact with each other.

Handler: The handler passes links from each client to the appropriate virtual buffer for classification and processing. In other words, an instance of this component is created for each client that connects to the system. It starts by receiving requests from a mobile client and terminates when the client has finished submitting requests. It passes links to the appropriate counter (specified below) which checks to see whether there is any space to accommodate the client's request. If there is space, the request is processed, the counter decremented, and the results are passed to the client. If there is no space, the request is rejected and the client is informed accordingly. The handler then waits to process the next request

Scheduler: The scheduler deals with the thread priorities that are created for each client, access to the processor and processers may be added here.

Counter: A number of components keep a record of the number of each type of request that is currently handled.

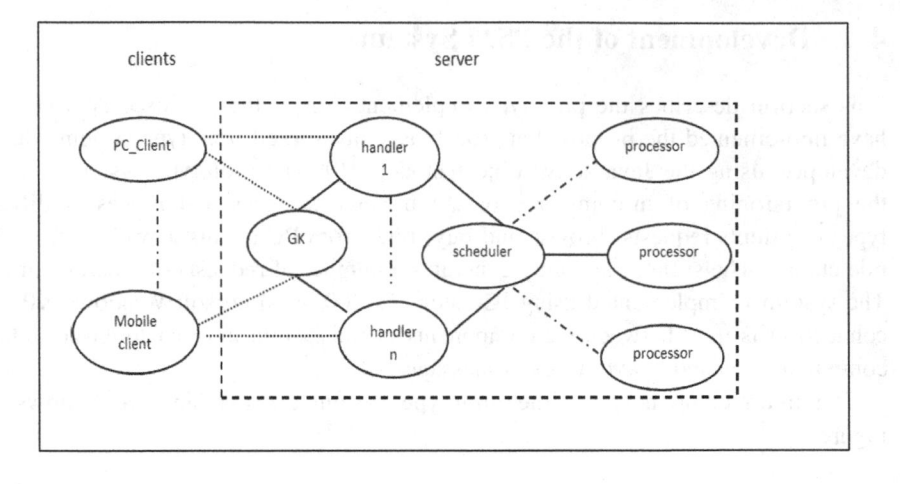

Fig. 2. Main components of PSM

5   Evaluation

Based on the prototype system we conduct various experiments in order to evaluate the performance and reliability of the proposed PSM approach. Our evaluation concerns the server side processing of m-commerce requests. That is, by efficiently processing m-commerce requests will improve the performance and consequently the reliability of m-commerce requests. Performance evaluation of the wireless networks or the individual mobile devices is beyond the scope of this work.

Experimental Setup: In the experimentation, the buffer capacity is set such that it can hold a maximum of 100 requests – i.e., the maximum value of the Counter goes to 100, but this can be easily increased. The service time for each type of request is chosen randomly (through exponential distribution) with a mean of 1ms. We use the thread's priority in order to allocate different priorities to different requests. For example, MAX_PRIORITY is assigned to buy requests (say, from mobile clients), and MIN_PRIORITY to PC requests (which are classified as low priority). In order to measure the response time and dropped requests, we build Report component in our system and also include facility for average computation on client's side.

We calculate average response time, dropped requests and throughput. Observed response time as seen by the client side can give clear information about server performance. When the server is 100% utilized, we can show that the protocol gives best value by completing most of the highest priority Mobile_buy requests.

Each server uses multiple threads where each connection is assigned to a dedicated handler thread so by varying the number of these connections, we can vary the load on the server. Moreover, different arrival rates can be produced by changing the number of clients or changing the waiting time.

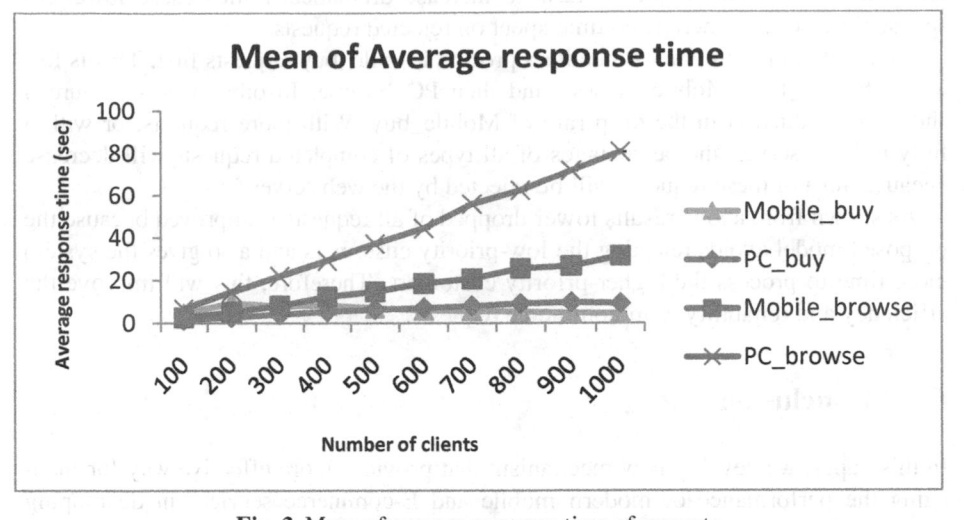

Fig. 3. Mean of average response time of requests

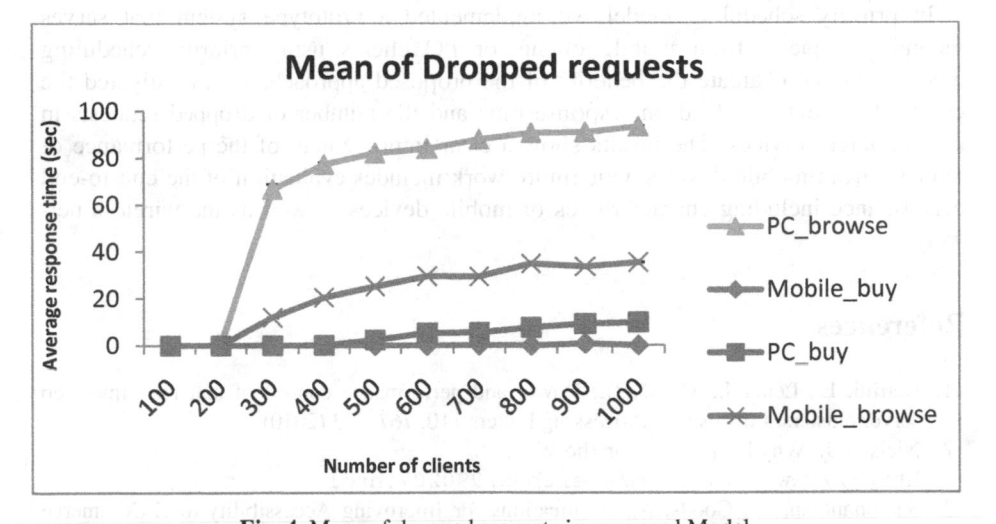

Fig. 4. Mean of dropped requests in proposed Model

Figure 3 shows the average response time of all types of request that are served by the web server. It is clear that the proposed PSM approach significantly reduces the response time of high priority requests such as Mobile_buy and PC_buy requests. Response times are low for small numbers of clients, whereas larger numbers of clients (PC and mobile) produce a heavy load on the web server, resulting in a slightly increased average response time for high-priority requests because the web server processes most "Mobile_buy" requests. Average response times (in Figure 3) are compatible with the dropped requests (in Figure 4) at the same point of 300 clients the dropped "PC_browse" requests starts to increase dramatically thus cause lower response time because there is no time spent on rejected requests.

As shown in Figure 4 most handlers process Mobile_buy requests first. This is followed by PC_buy, Mobile_browse and then PC_browse. In other words, Figure 4 shows the reduction in the drop rate of Mobile_buy. With more requests, or with a fully-utilized server, the percentages of all types of completed requests will decrease because most of these requests will be rejected by the web server.

As shown from above results lower dropped of all requests is approved because the proposed model avoids rejecting the low-priority customers and also gives the system more time to process the higher-priority customers. Therefore, this will improve the efficiency and reliability of m-commerce requests.

6   Conclusion

In this paper, we develop new mechanism that provides more effective way for managing the performance of modern mobile and E-commerce services in developing countries. We proposed admission control and priority scheduling model that include web server with the aim of improving the performance of mobile services.

In priority scheduling model we implemented a prototype system that serves incoming requests from mobile clients or PC clients using priority scheduling mechanism. To evaluate the benefits of the proposed approach, we investigated the effect of the extreme load on response time and the number of dropped requests in m-commerce services. The results show a clear improvement of the performance of requests from mobile devices. Our future work includes evaluation of the end-to-end performance including characteristics of mobile devices as well as the wireless networks.

References

1. Bertini, L., Leite, J., Mossé, D.: Power and performance control of soft real-time web server clusters. Information Processing Letters 110, 767–773 (2010)
2. Nielsen, J.: Why People Shop on the Web,
   http://www.useit.com/alertbox/990207.html
3. Sambhanthan, A., Goods, A.: Implications for Improving Accessibility to E-Commerce Websites in Developing Countries -A Study of Hotel Websites. eprint arXiv:1302.5198 (2013)
4. Ghandeharizadeh, S., Yab, J., Barahmand, S.: COSAR-CQN: An Application Transparent Approach to Cache Consistency. In: The Twenty First International Conference on Software Engineering and Data Engineering, LA,California, June 27-29 (2012)
5. Jilly, K., Juiz, C., Thomas, N., Puigjaner, R.: Adaptive admission control algorithm in a QoS-aware Web system. Information Sciences 199, 58–77 (2012)
6. Zhang, Z., Wang, H.P., Liu, J.T., Hu, Y.F.: Performance Analysis and Optimization of Network Server Based on Node Cache, Computer Engineering, 1, 003. In: Proceedings of the Fifth IEEE Symposium on Computers and Communications, ISCC 2000, pp. 359–363 (2000)

7. Chollette, C.C., et al.: A queue scheduling approach to quality of service support in Diff-Serv networks using fuzzy logic. In: 2012 International Conference on Computer and Communication Engineering (ICCCE). IEEE (2012)
8. Kaszo, M., Legany, C.: Analyzing Customer Behavior Model Graph (CBMG) using Markov Chains. In: The 11th International Conference on Intelligent Engineering Systems (INES 2007), Budapest, Hungary, 29 June -1 July (2007)
9. Milner, R.: Communicating and Mobile systems: the π-Calculus. Cambridge University Press (1999)
10. Wellings, A.J.: Concurrent and Real-Time Programming in Java. Wiley, University of York (2004)
11. Crovella, M., Frangioso, R., Harchol-Balter, M.: Connection scheduling in web servers. In: Second Symposium of Internet Technologies and System (USITS 1999), Boulder, CO,USA, October 11-14, vol. 2, ACM (1999)
12. Rawat, M., Kshemkayani, A.: SWIFT: Scheduling in web servers for fast response time. In: Second IEEE International Symposium on Network Computing and Applications (NCA 2003), Cambridge, MA, USA, April 16-18, pp. 51–58 (2003)
13. Rahman, M.M.: Barriers to M-commerce Adoption in Developing Countries – A Qualitative Study among the Stakeholders of Bangladesh. The International Technology Management Review 3(2), 80–91 (2013)
14. Hyun, M.Y., Lee, S., Hu, C.: Mobile Mediated Virtual Experience in Tourism:Concept, Typology and Applications. Journal of Vacation Marketing 15(2), 149–164 (2009)
15. Smith, A.: Exploring m-commerce in terms of viability growth and challenges. International Journal of Mobile Communication 4(6), 682–703 (2006)
16. Hossain, M.S., Khandanker, M.R.A.: Implementation challenges of mobile commerce in developing countries - Bangladesh perspective. In: 14th International Conference on Computer and Information Technology (ICCIT), Dhaka, Bangladesh, December 22-24, pp. 399–404 (2011)
17. Aleid, F.A., Rogerson, S., Fairweather, B.: A consumers' perspective on E-commerce: practical solutions to encourage consumers' adoption of e-commerce in developing countries - A Saudi Arabian empirical study. In: 2010 IEEE International Conference on Advanced Management Science (ICAMS 2010), Chengdu, China, July 9-11, pp. 373–377 (2010)
18. Aleid, F.A., Rogerson, S., Fairweather, B.: A suppliers' perspective on e-commerce: Suppliers responses to consumers' perspectives on e-commerce adoption in developing countries — A Saudi Arabian empirical study. In: Fifth International Conference on Digital Information Management (ICDIM 2010), Thunder Bay, Canada, pp. 379–383 (2010)
19. Younas, M., Awan, I., Chao, K.-M.: Network-centric strategy for mobile transactions. International Journal of Interconnection Networks (JOIN) 5(3), 329–350 (2004)
20. Awan, I.: Mobility management for m-commerce requests in wireless cellular networks. Information Systems Frontiers 8(4), 285–295
21. Nafea, I., Younas, M., Holton, R., Awan, I.: A priority-based admission control scheme for commercial web servers. International Journal of Parallel Programming, doi:10.1007/s10766-013-0290-5

A Selective Predictive Subscriber Mobility Using the Closest Criterion

Fatma Abdennadher and Maher Ben Jemaa

ReDCAD Laboratory,
National School of Engineers of Sfax,
University of Sfax, B.P. 1173, 3038 Sfax, Tunisia
fatmaabdennadher@gmail.com, maher.benjemaa@enis.rnu.tn

Abstract. Mobility support is among the most defying topics into publish/subscribe systems. In fact, the mobility of the subscriber causes message loss, an increase in the latency and in the overhead. We resort to the proactive caching by defining a procedure for selecting the candidates brokers for being the caching points. We define a metric named threshold, and we select the brokers which have the values of weight superior to this metric. Added to that, we extend our approach by the select closest criterion for minimizing the delay of transfer. So, we select the closest caching point for the transfer of messages in the cases of a handoff to a non caching point. Hence, we have succeed to minimize the buffering costs and the delay of transfer.

Keywords: Mobility, Publish/Subscribe, Prediction, Mobile Computing.

1   Introduction

Nowadays the popularity of the mobile devices is growing in a quick manner proportionally to the increase of our need to access information through these devices. The mobility of the user has increased the need on receiving information wherever he is connected to. In fact, the mobility of the user includes nomadic scenarios when roaming from home to office. In these cases, the user disconnects from one broker and reconnects to another one. This disconnection can be occurred also in an involuntary way due to the limited resources. So, when the disconnected users reconnect, they await to receive the disseminated data during their disconnection. This imposes the need of a middleware infrastructure that covers a scalable and flexible communication model, to accommodate with the dynamic characteristic of the mobile computing.

In particular, the dissemination of information, in recent years, such as traffic information, electronic auctions and stock trading has been played by the paradigm of publish/subscribe (pub/sub) systems [1–3]. In fact, the pub/sub paradigm is composed of three components. Hence, we find the subscriber which consumes its interest from the event produced by the publisher and the matching is assured by the brokers. So, the pub/sub system is notified about the existence

I. Awan et al. (Eds.): MobiWis 2014, LNCS 8640, pp. 126–136, 2014.

of specific events by the publisher. On the other side, subscriptions are emitted by subscribers to describe their concern about a certain set of events. When a new event is received, the broker insures the matching of this event versus the set of subscriptions. Then, the event is delivered to all concerned subscribers. The decoupling in time, space, and synchronization between the interacting parties represents the main advantage of this paradigm. Hence, this advantage helps in the management of applications characterized by frequent disconnection and movement of subscribers. In the majority of the actual middleware systems, the optimization is elaborated for fixed networks. So, there is a great need to extend these systems to manage the mobility of the subscriber.

Our work proposes a selective predictive approach while minimizing the buffering cost and the delay of transfer of cached publications. This is elaborated by the application of a dynamic selection of the most probably next visited brokers that are devoted to be the caching points. Our experimental results are effective for different pub/sub systems extended to support the mobility of the subscriber.

When looking in the literature, we have found three categories of approaches for the management of mobile subscribers in pub/sub networks: The first category is the durable based subscriptions[4, 5], the second category is the reactive approaches [6, 7, 10, 11], and the third category is the proactive approaches [12–14].

Our paper is organized as follows: We give an overview of the related works in section 2. Then, we describe our approach in section 3. Next, we examine the results of our experimentation in Section 4. Lastly, we conclude this paper in Section 5.

2   Related Work

This section summarizes the categories of approaches dealing with the mobility of the subscriber into three classes according to the manner and the time of recuperating the messages issued during the disconnection of the subscriber.

2.1   Durable Subscription

The authors in [4] proposed an approach in which each broker plays the role of a persistent buffer for the received notifications and then sends them to interested subscribers. These notifications are characterized by a validity period that induces their remove when it expires. The drawback of this approach is the overload on the broker network by increasing the consumption of memory and the processing time. Added to that, the process of buffering is very costly. So, it induces an increase in the overhead. Hence, the performance of the system will be degraded. Besides, this approach risks the loss of messages for long interval disconnection. This can be caused by the limited space of buffers or the expiration of validity period of notifications. Also, this approach suffers from the duplication of messages.

Another durable approach was implemented in the Elvin system [5] for the management of disconnected operation. A proxy component was added to buffer the events during the disconnection of the subscriber. This component plays the role of a normal subscriber for the event server and a server for the subscriber. Hence, the subscriber connects to the proxy component to recuperate the correspondent events. The drawback of this work is its limitation to disconnected operation. Hence the mobility of the subscriber between brokers is not managed. Hence, when the subscriber disconnects, it is obligated to reconnect to its old proxy. In a consequence, the network is overloaded and the performance is affected.

2.2 Reactive Subscriber Mobility

In [6, 7], the authors proposed an approach to treat the mobility of the subscriber from one broker to another by analyzing the performance of a pub/sub system based on JMS [8, 9]. They use a handoff manager component that is associated with each broker to treat the mobility of the subscriber. The subscribers are required to store the address of the old broker. When their reconnection occurs, they connect to the handoff manager of the new broker. In consequence, this handoff manager contacts the handoff manager of the old broker. The integration of the handoff manager with the broker causes additional overload. Hence, the support of frequent disconnection and connection is difficult to hold. Added to that, the authors of this approach do not evaluate the overhead cost of their strategy.

Another reactive approach was established in [10]. The authors defined a component named mediator which buffers the interested events during the disconnection of the mobile subscriber. Hence, the mobile subscriber upon its reconnection recuperates all its missed messages from this mediator. This approach suffers from the lack of clarity of its implementation. Added to that, it is characterized by its lack of scalability as it does not permit the interconnection of multiple mediators in an arbitrary topology.

The authors in [11] elaborated another reactive approach. The main idea consists on keeping a virtual counterpart at the last broker to which the subscriber connected. When the movement of the subscriber is detected by the new broker, the relocation process starts. Hence, the junction broker between the new and the old brokers is found. So, all buffered events will be recuperated from the old broker through the junction. The drawback is the use of the junction that can lead to a complication of the algorithm and an increase in the handoff latency. Added to that, there is the risk of the overload on the junction broker.

2.3 Proactive Mobility Management

The main advantage of the proactive approaches is the minimization of delay on forwarding the messages to the subscriber upon its reconnection issued during its disconnection. In fact, the delay is a critical metric in streaming and real-time applications. So, this reduce in terms of delay is offered at the cost of increasing the buffer space.

A proactive approach is described in [12, 13] that exploits the future locations of the subscriber by caching the needed data before the reconnection of the subscriber. Hence, per-subscriber caching is implemented at potential future locations. The authors limit their description to the high level. Added to that, they do not consider the mobility prediction. In addition, there is the risk of an overload occurring in the hosted broker. This is due to the fact of caching similar interest in the same broker. Furthermore, this approach does not consider permanent and long interval disconnections.

In [14] another proactive approach is presented. The basic idea is the use of the neighbor graph that collects the next possible brokers where the mobile subscriber will move. So, the activation of the subscriptions in the set of the neighbor graph is done during the disconnection of the mobile subscriber. The construction of the neighbor graph is occurring when the mobile subscriber reconnects to a new broker and when there is a request of transferring the context. This strategy risks leading to a high overhead. In fact, once the broker is visited by the mobile subscriber, it will be a caching point for this subscriber regardless of its probability to be visited again. So, there will be a very high number of wasting resources.

3 Proposed Approach

Nowadays, the movements of real users can be characterized by a repeated behavioral patterns. Indeed, if we observe these movements, then we can remark that it would be a high probability that the subscriber will visit the locations that have been visited many times by the same subscriber. Hence, it would be very useful to profit from these measurements for the improvement of mobility management.

This section shortly describes our procedure that is classified into the proactive approaches. Its main advantage is the minimization of wasting resources and the reduction in the delay of transfer. This is assured by selecting only the most probable brokers to be visited as caching points.

The prediction[15] of mobility is an efficient strategy to improve the performance in the system. The basic idea is the use of the past and actual states. Hence, the future states are estimated before some time in accordance to the previous states occurred previously.

Our objective is the anticipation of the future movements during runtime. Hence, the monitoring phase imports the useful information for precise prediction. Thus, we supervise the mobility of the subscriber and we examine the correspondent values of weights to anticipate future mobility models.

The caching points are selected according to their values of weights that should be higher or equal than the threshold value that is computed in a dynamic manner. The core idea of our selection tends to minimize the transfer latency while reducing the caching cost by updating the threshold value. By assuming that the subscriber S performs Y_{ij} movements from broker B_i to broker B_j, so the weight of movement is equivalent to the following formula where S(i) is the set of caching points for broker B_i:

$$W_{ij} = \frac{Y_{ij}}{\sum\limits_{k \ in \ S(i)} Y_{ik}}. \tag{1}$$

Algorithm 1. SelectClosest(c, b_i, b_j)

c: client, b_i: old broker, b_j: new broker,
d_{min}: minimal-distance$(b_k; b_j)_{b_k \in Selected-Neighbor-Set(b_i) \cup \{b_i\}}$;
d_{min}=distance $(b_i; b_j)$;
if bi receives a Notify message from bj **then**
   | **for** $b_k \in$ Selected-Neighbor-Set(b_i) **do**
   | | Update-Weight($b_i; b_k$) ;
   | **end**
   | **if** $(b_j \notin$ Selected-Neighbor-Set(b_i)) **then**
   | | **for** $b_k \in$ Selected-Neighbor-Set(b_i) **do**
   | | | **if** $(distance$ $(b_k; b_j) < d_{min})$ **then**
   | | | | d_{min}=distance $(b_k; b_j)$;
   | | | | $b_{closest(b_j)} = b_k$;
   | | | **end**
   | | **end**
   | | **if** $b_{closest(b_j)}! = null$ **then**
   | | | Forward-Subscriptions-Publications($c; b_{closest(b_j)}; b_j$);
   | | **end**
   | | **else**
   | | | Forward-Subscriptions-Publications($c; b_i; b_j$);
   | | **end**
   | **end**
   | **for** $b_k \in$ Selected-Neighbor-Set(b_i) $\setminus \{b_j\} \cup \{b_i\}$ **do**
   | | **if** $(b_k \notin$ Selected-Neighbor-Set(b_j)) $\|$ $(b_k \in$
   | | Selected-Neighbor-Set(b_j)$\&(w_{jk} < w_{th(j)}))$ **then**
   | | | delete-sub-pub($c; b_k$) ;
   | | **end**
   | | **if** $(b_k \in$ Selected-Neighbor-Set(b_j))$\&(w_{jk} >= w_{th(j)}))$ **then**
   | | | neighbor-subscribing($c; b_k$) ;
   | | **end**
   | **end**
   | **for** $b_k \in$ Selected-Neighbor-set(b_j) **do**
   | | **if** $b_k \notin$ Selected-Neighbor-set $(b_i)\&(w_{jk} >= w_{th(j)})$ **then**
   | | | neighbor-subscribing($c; b_k$) ;
   | | **end**
   | **end**
end

The proactive approaches cited before select the caching points without taking account of their probabilities to be the next station for the mobile subscriber. Thus, the previous approaches are exposed to suffer from high overhead. This risk is increased when there are a high number of subscribers and in a consequence resulting in an increased number of subscriptions or the subscribers move quickly. Furthermore, we tend to improve the previous proactive schemes by defining the concept of weight. This value expresses the probability of the movement of the subscriber from the broker to which it is connected to the possible brokers that it may connect to after disconnecting from its actual broker. Hence, the selected caching points are those presenting a weight value equal or greater than the threshold value. The weight of different brokers are computed according to the mobility patterns. Thus, the weight threshold of broker B_i can be defined by the below formula where N is the cardinal of S(i):

$$W_{th(i)} = \frac{1}{N} \, . \tag{2}$$

The threshold value for each broker is updated dynamically in accordance to the movement of the subscriber between the different brokers. The caching points begin storing the publications matching the content of the subscriptions of the disconnected subscriber under the demand of the old broker. When the old broker receives the acknowledgment from its set of caching points, it delivers to them the received publications during the lap of time that the caching points spent to activate their store. Hence, the subscriber recuperates all its messages from its new broker when it is a caching point. The caching process is stopped when the subscriber reconnects. This stop is occurred under the demand of the old broker that is notified by the new broker.

In our approach, we tend to minimize the overload induced by the process of caching through selecting only the most visited brokers. Our approach is generic as it is not limited to a specific subscription knowledge. Moreover, we do not limit our strategy to a specific topology.

Algorithm 1 describes the procedure for our proposed approach. Our calculation of weights is updated dynamically according to the mobility patterns of the mobile subscriber. Hence, the caching points are changing perpetually. Indeed, when the subscriber disconnects from one broker and reconnects to another broker, the correspondent weights of the old broker are updated. Added to that, the set of caching points is changed corresponding to the new broker. Consequently, the caching points that are not common between the old and the new brokers are deactivated. Hence, we compute accurately the threshold value in the aim of selecting the most probable caching points. We have added an optimization to our approach that we named the closest criterion. In fact, we resort to the closest criterion when the new broker visited by the mobile subscriber is not included in the caching points of the old broker. Indeed, if the mobile subscriber faces such a situation, the old broker will forward to it the published messages during its disconnection. Consequently, this results in a high delay of transfer especially when the old broker and the new broker are far from each other. So, when we apply the closest criterion, the mobile subscriber is served by the closest caching

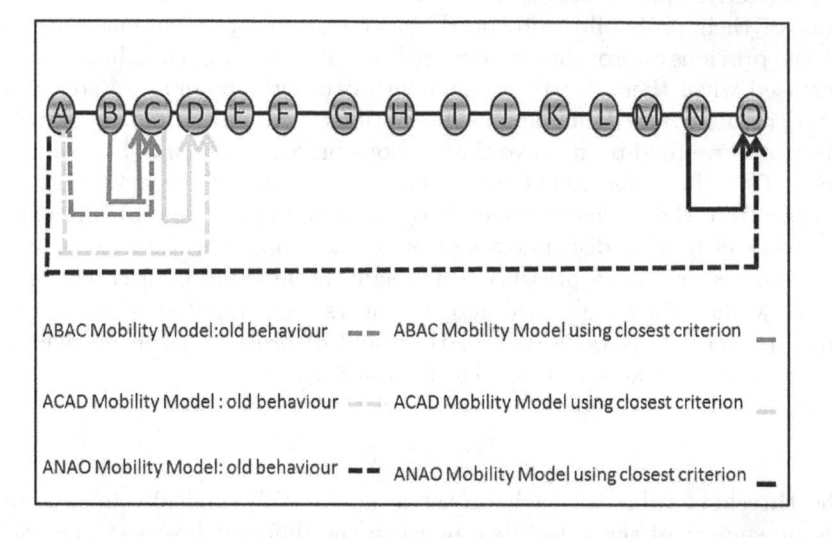

Fig. 1. Select Closest Criterion under different Mobility Models

point. Hence, in such a situation the closest broker to the new broker into the caching points of the old broker, will deliver the cached publications.

Fig. 1 represents the topology of brokers that we have. In this example, the subscriber follows three mobility models such as *(ANAO)*. Hence, when the subscriber connects to broker O, it recuperates the messages from broker N through the closest criterion. Thus, we gain the distance of thirteen brokers that have a significant improvement in the minimization of the delay of transfer.

4 Experimentation

We examine the adequacy of our proposed approach using a prototype implementation. We present evaluation results that investigate system performance with the proposed solution consisting of adding the closest criterion. We compared our approach to the proactive strategy cited in [14] for the forwarding of messages when the new broker is not a caching point. We consider the delay as a metric for the evaluation of the performance of our approach. This metric is defined as the difference between the time of reconnection and the time of reception of published messages during the disconnection. We realized all our experiments with one client roaming between fifteen brokers. When the mobile client connects, it subscribes to specific contents, then it disconnects. So, the risk here is the forward of publications matching the contents demanded by the client is occurring during the period of the disconnection. Hence, if such publications are forwarded, the mobile client will recuperate them upon its reconnection. For demonstrating the purpose of this paper, we propose the metric of delay of publications' reception by the mobile client upon its reconnection. Indeed, we have noted that when the new broker visited by the mobile client is not a neighbor for the old broker, this forward can lead to an increase in the delay, especially when the new broker is far from the old broker. This is completely logic, as the forward of publications will be done by the old broker, when the new broker is not selected as a caching point.

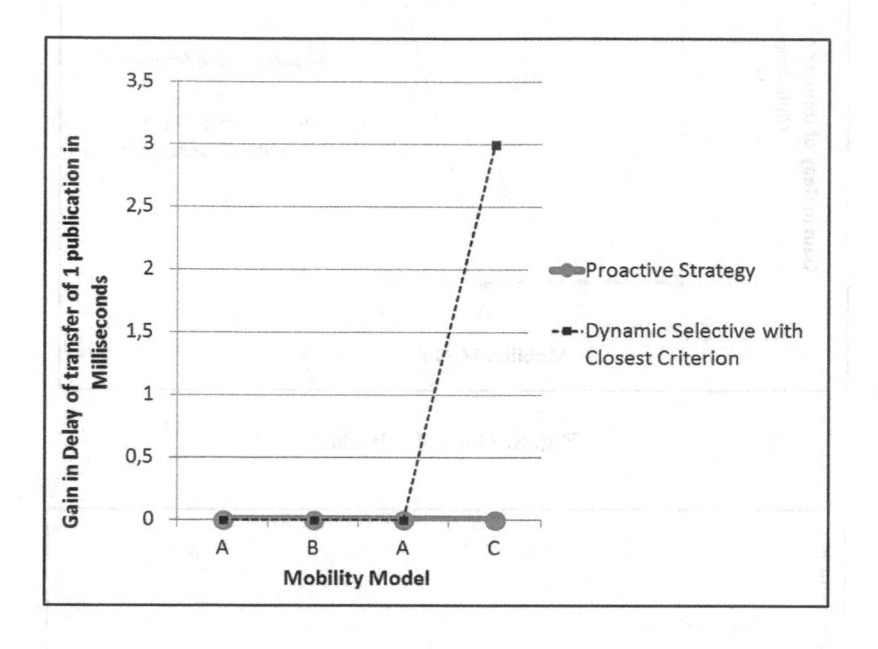

Fig. 2. Gain of 1 Broker

Fig. 2 and Fig. 3 show that the gain in delay is increasing proportionally to the gain of distance between brokers. Hence, by considering that we have the topology mentioned in Fig. 1. So, with *(ABAC)* as a mobility model, that means that the client connects to A, then B, next A, later C, thus, the broker C is not yet selected as a neighbor for caching when the mobile client connects to it. Thus, with the proactive approach, the recuperation of publications will be insured by broker A. In contrast, when we applied the closest criterion, this will be assured by broker B. As the movement from broker A to broker B has been dynamically saved and in a consequence broker B is selected as a caching point. Hence, we gain 3 milliseconds in the transfer delay of 1 publication. Similarly, when the mobile client moves according to *(ACAD)* as a mobility model, we gain 5 milliseconds in the delay of transfer of 1 publication when the mobile client reconnects to broker D. The best gain is offered when the mobile client follows *(ANAO)* as a mobility model and connects to broker O, so it gains the distance of thirteen brokers.

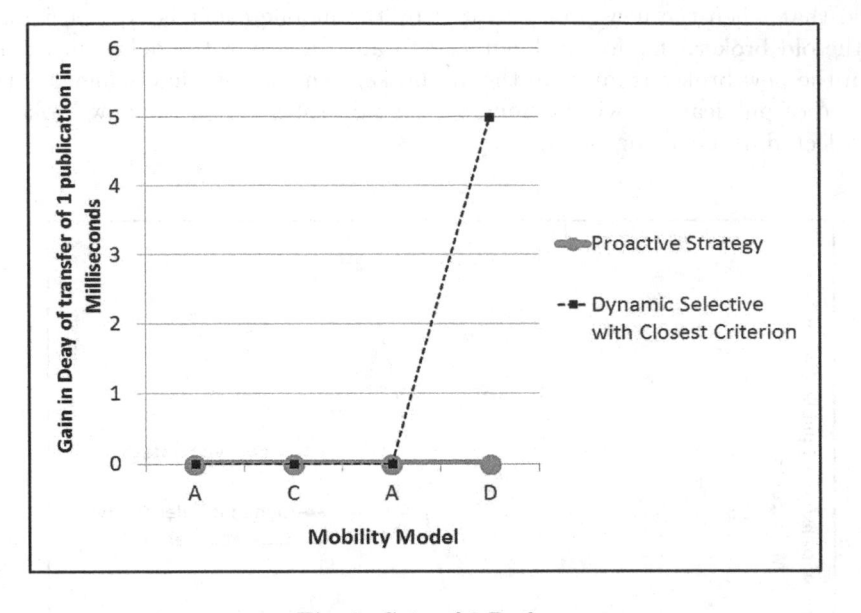

Fig. 3. Gain of 2 Brokers

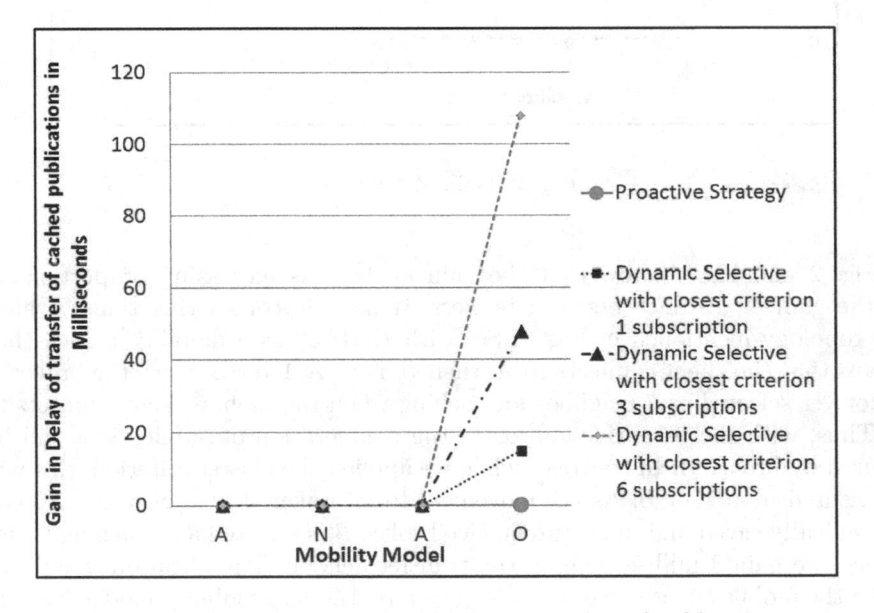

Fig. 4. Gain of 13 Brokers with different number of publications

Fig. 4 shows that the gain of delay increases proportionally to the increase in the number of forwarded publications. In this experimentation, the application of the select closest criterion permits to gain the distance of thirteen brokers as we have *(ANAO)* as a mobility model. Hence, when we have 1 buffered message, the select closest criterion permits to gain 15 milliseconds. When we have 3 buffered messages, we gain 48 milliseconds. So, the most gain is obtained when we have 6 buffered messages, which is 108 milliseconds.

5   Conclusion

This paper represents our work for supporting the mobility of the subscriber in pub/sub networks through the use of a predictive selective approach in the aim of minimizing the buffering cost and the handoff delay. In fact, we select only a subset of caching points. The selection is based on the most probable brokers to be visited. Added to that, we have added the select closest criterion to minimize the delay of transfer. We examined the capacity of our suggested approach through the use of a prototype implementation. We explored the results of this evaluation that examine its performance when comparing it to the standard proactive scheme. The experimental results demonstrated that our approach ensures a gain in the transfer delay compared to the proactive approach. In our future work, we plan to consider other metrics for the amelioration of the performance of our approach.

References

1. Huang, Y., Garcia-Molina, H.: Publish/Subscribe Tree Construction in Wireless Ad-Hoc Networks. In: Chen, M.-S., Chrysanthis, P.K., Sloman, M., Zaslavsky, A. (eds.) MDM 2003. LNCS, vol. 2574, pp. 122–140. Springer, Heidelberg (2003)
2. Huang, Y., Garcia-Molina, H.: Publish/Subscribe in a Mobile Environment. Wireless Networks, pp. 643–652. Springer, New York (2004)
3. Eugster, P.T., Guerraoui, R., Sventek, J.: Distributed asynchronous collections: Abstractions for publish/subscribe interaction. In: Bertino, E. (ed.) ECOOP 2000. LNCS, vol. 1850, pp. 252–276. Springer, Heidelberg (2000)
4. Podnar, I., Lovrek, I.: Supporting Mobility with Persistent Notifications in Publish/Subscribe Systems. In: Proceedings of the 3rd International Workshop on Distributed Event-based Systems (DEBS 2004), Edinburgh, Scotland, UK, pp. 80–85. ACM Press (2004)
5. Sutton, P., Arkins, R., Segall, B.: Supporting Disconnectedness-Transparent Information Delivery for Mobile and Invisible Computing. In: Proceedings of the 1st International Symposium on Cluster Computing and the Grid (CCGRID 2001), pp. 277–285. IEEE Computer Society, Washington, DC (2001)
6. Farooq, U., Parsons, E., Majumdar, S.: Performance of Publish/Subscribe Middleware in Mobile Wireless Networks. In: Proceedings of the 4th International Workshop on Software and Performance (WOSP 2004), Redwood City, California, pp. 278–289. ACM (2004)
7. Farooq, U., Majumdar, S., Parsons, E.: High Performance Middleware for Mobile Wireless Networks. Mobile Information Systems Journal 3(2), 107–132 (2007)
8. Sun Microsystems.: Java Message Service Specification 1.1. Technical Report, Sun Microsystems (2002)
9. Hapner, M., Burridge, R., Sharma, R., Fialli, J., Stout, K.: Java Message Service. Sun Microsystems Inc. (2002)

10. Bacon, J., Moody, K., Bates, J., Hayton, R., Ma, C., McNeil, A., Seidel, O., Spiteri, M.: Generic Support for Distributed Applications. IEEE Computer 33(3), 68–77 (2000)
11. Fiege, L., Gartner, F.C., Kasten, O., Zeidler, A.: Supporting Mobility in Content-based Publish/Subscribe Middleware. In: Endler, M., Schmidt, D.C. (eds.) Middleware 2003. LNCS, vol. 2672, pp. 103–122. Springer, Heidelberg (2003)
12. Cilia, M., Fiege, L., Haul, C., Zeidler, A., Buchmann, A.P.: Looking into the Past: Enhancing Mobile Publish/Subscribe Middleware. In: The 2nd international Workshop on Distributed Event-Based Systems (DEBS 2003), pp. 1–8. ACM (2003)
13. Fiege, L., Zeidler, A., Gartner, F.C., Handurukande, S.B.: Dealing with Uncertainty in Mobile Publish/Subscribe Middleware. In: 1st International Workshop on Middleware for Pervasive and Ad-Hoc Computing, pp. 60–67. PUC-Rio (2003)
14. Gaddah, A., Kunz, T.: A Pro-Active Mobility Management Scheme for Pub/-Sub Systems using Neighborhood Graph. In: The 2009 International Conference on Wireless Communications and Mobile Computing: Connecting the World Wirelessly, pp. 1–6. ACM (2009)
15. Kwon, S., Park, H., Lee, K.: A novel mobility prediction algorithm based on user movement history in wireless networks. In: Baik, D.-K. (ed.) AsiaSim 2004. LNCS (LNAI), vol. 3398, pp. 419–428. Springer, Heidelberg (2005)

Towards an Automated Safety Suit for Industrial Service

Markus Aleksy[1] and Thomas Scholl[2]

[1] ABB Corporate Research
Industrial Software Systems Program
Wallstadter Str. 59, 68526 Ladenburg, Germany
markus.aleksy@de.abb.com
[2] ABB AG
Group Function Quality & Sustainability
Kallstadter Strasse 1, 68309 Mannheim, Germany
thomas.scholl@de.abb.com

Abstract. Wearable and mobile computing technologies enable new types of safety-related applications due to augmentation of sensing and computational devices, thus introducing new - non-intrusive interaction styles. Wearable sensor technologies provide the mobile worker with the opportunity to measure information about the environment as well as his own condition. Mobile devices enable accessing, processing, visualizing, alarming, and communicating information without being constrained to a single location. In this paper, we present an automated safety vest that follows an non-intrusive and modular design. It can sense various environmental and health conditions and is controlled by a mobile application running on a smart phone. The modular design of the wearable sensors makes it easy to integrate it with existing safety equipment, such as a high visibility vest.

1 Introduction

Occupational Health and Safety (OHS) is a business issue that is important for any kind of companies for multiple reasons. First of all, each company has to ensure that all workers and sub-contractors remain safe all the time. Moreover, reducing employee injury rates and illness related costs will give a competitive advantage by saving related costs as well as due to increasing productivity.

The International Labour Organization (ILO) and the World Health Organization (WHO) give a common definition on the OHS objectives:

> *"The main focus in occupational health is on three different objectives: (i) the maintenance and promotion of workers' health and working capacity; (ii) the improvement of working environment and work to become conducive to safety and health and (iii) development of work organizations and working cultures in a direction which supports health and safety at work and in doing so also promotes a positive social climate and smooth operation and may enhance productivity of the undertaking"* [3].

Safety is becoming more important due to various reasons. The increasing complexity of industrial plants introduces a source of new hazards. Moreover, executing service

I. Awan et al. (Eds.): MobiWis 2014, LNCS 8640, pp. 137–144, 2014.

activities in confined spaces which are not intended for human occupancy is another challenge due to the fact that they may have an atmosphere containing harmful levels of contaminant. Additionally, performing service activities in rural areas aside frequently used traffic routes may lead to emergencies that are difficult to detect. Generally speaking, supporting lone workers operating in industrial environment should be considered with respect to what extent their safety can be improved. Here, utilizing wearable and mobile technologies can provide some benefit.

2   Motivation

Advances in mobile computing and sensor technologies facilitate innovative solutions in the form of mobile applications. Mobile devices, such as smart phones and tablets provide the mobile worker with the opportunity to create, access, process, store, and communicate information on the move. In addition, sensor technologies enable us to measure information about the environment and provide that data to a mobile device for closer inspection.

A wearable system that collects environmental data and monitors the wearer's health conditions would introduce a new dimension of service personnel's safety support. Basically, various personal health parameters can be measured [5], e.g. the heart- or pulse rate, tiredness, consciousness, cognitive load / stress level. Moreover, similar approaches has been suggested to support different domains, such as providing assistance to firefighters [6]. That way, a wearable computing system that automatically senses the environment as well as the personal health of the worker can be also utilized in industrial environment. In addition, extending it with a computational unit, such as a smart phone, would enable data analysis and the opportunity to automatically detect emergency situations. Thereafter, the system would be able to contact a remote control center self-acting, i.e., without any additional user interaction. Such a system can cover situations where a worker is losing consciousness at the same time.

3   Wearable Computing

The vision of wearable computing is providing an unrestricted system that shows right information at the right time and supports sharing of context with others. Wearable computing is a excellent example of the combination of mobile computing and sensors. It makes the computer invisible in our daily lives as it is embedded into clothing or everyday items, such as eyeglasses. The characteristics used to describe wearable computing include hands-free use, always on, and sensors. This means that wearable devices are always on and working, sensing, and acting [4]. Wearable devices can range from commercial off-the-shelf products, such as smart watches up to specialized solutions that incorporate sensors into clothing. The corresponding technological components include input devices (e.g. wrist-worn keyboards), output devices (such as HMD's), context sharing systems (e.g. video camera), and context sensing systems (e.g. acceleration sensors or image processing).

Wearable computing was assumed to make a breakthrough in the industry a decade ago [7]. However, equipment costs and technical reliability were some of the obstacles for wide-spread practical applications in the past. Nowadays, we can witness that the maturity of wearable devices is increasing and approaching a state, where it can be considered to be utilized in industrial applications.

Wearable devices can increase the situation awareness of field personnel in plants by providing the needed and accurate information on the move. In addition, mobile technologies can help field technicians to ensure safe working environment. The presented automated safety vest was developed to increase the safety of field workers in an non-intrusive way. Wearing a high-visibility vest is often required while servicing a plant. Moreover, many of the service workers are already equipped with a mobile phone. Thus, adding some features, such as sensors and feedback devices into the vest as well as operating it via a mobile (smart)phone would realize improved safety system without necessarily introducing new safety-related devices.

4 Overview of the Wearable System

The wearable system consists of two major components: An automated safety vest and a smart phone.

4.1 Automated Safety Vest

Sensing the environmental conditions of the worker as well as monitoring his health is a key success factor to realize an enhanced safety system. We used an off-the-shelf high visibility vest as a foundation for our prototype. The vest is supplemented by various sensors and actuators. In our prototype, we utilized a heart beat sensor, a body temperature sensor, a carbon monoxide sensor, and an environmental temperature & humidity sensor. Besides sensors and communication components, additional components were included into the vest, such as an emergency button, speaker, and vibrator. The emergency button enables instant emergency calls. The speaker and vibrator help to alarm the worker that the measured environmental conditions exceeded the preset levels. Figure 1 presents the original design of the automated safety vest.

4.2 Smart Phone

The mobile device – an off-the-shelf smart phone – collects the measured values and acts as the control center of the vest. Service staff is usually equipped with a cell phone. Thus, replacing it with a smart phone enables new opportunities. Smart phones include additional sensors, such as an accelerometer, magnetometer, and global positioning system (GPS). They may help to collect additional information, such as gathering the location of the mobile worker. Moreover, they include various communication components, such as mobile networks, wireless local area networks (WLANs), Bluetooth, etc. that enable wireless communication. Ruggedized smart phones that provide a scratch-resistant display, water-resistance, and are dust-proof are available on the market starting from around 200 US$. Thus, replacing a regular cell phone with a ruggedized smart phone is related to relatively low investments.

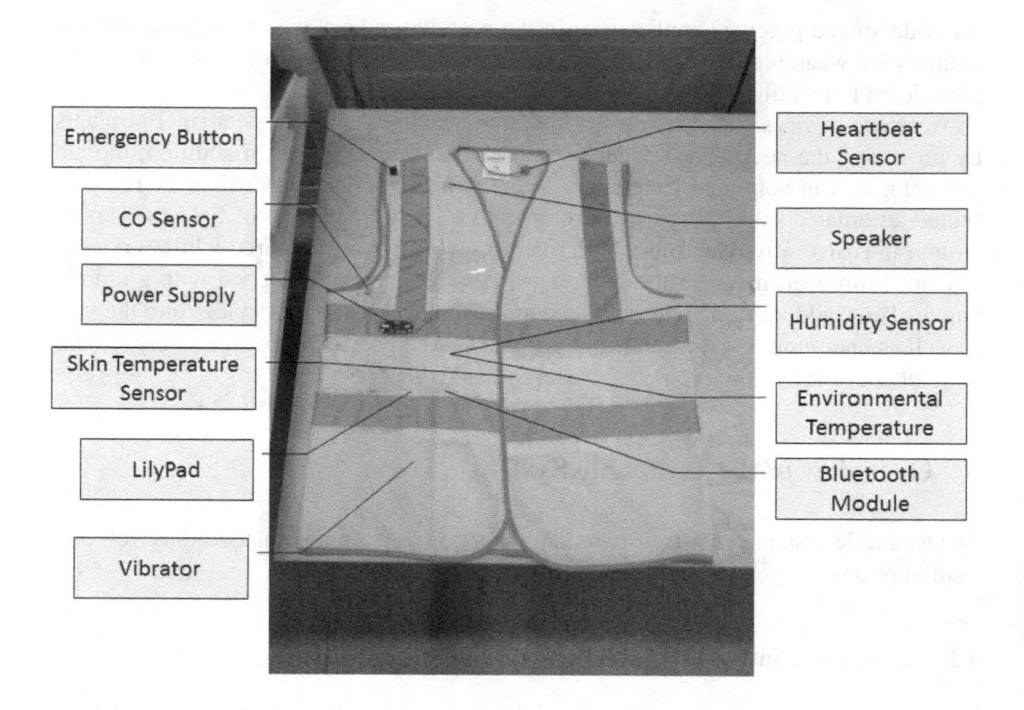

Fig. 1. Automated safety vest

The purpose of the mobile application is to collect sensor data and to display alerts and notifications when anomalous conditions are detected. In a first step, some user preferences have to be specified to ensure that the automated safety vest will perform the proper actions in case of unusual situations. The alert preferences include time-out specification, alert actions, and contact information, such as e-mail address and phone number. Additionally, thresholds for utilized sensors have to be set up. The main screen of the application presents real time data transferred from the safety suit via Bluetooth (cf. Figure 2). It allows the user to monitor his vital signs and sensor data in a graphical manner. In an emergency case the system can automatically send messages including the last GPS coordinates of the user's location to a supervisor or/and a control center.

5   Improvements

The original design of the automated safety was evaluated in real-world service environment. Here, several suggestions for improvement were collected, such as loose integration between the computing part and the vest or extending the power supply. The modified automated safety vest incorporates several improvements compared to the first version (cf. [2]). From software perspective, we were able to reduce the cycle time and improve the accuracy of the pulse rate. Furthermore, several hardware-related improvements were implemented that will be presented in the next sections.

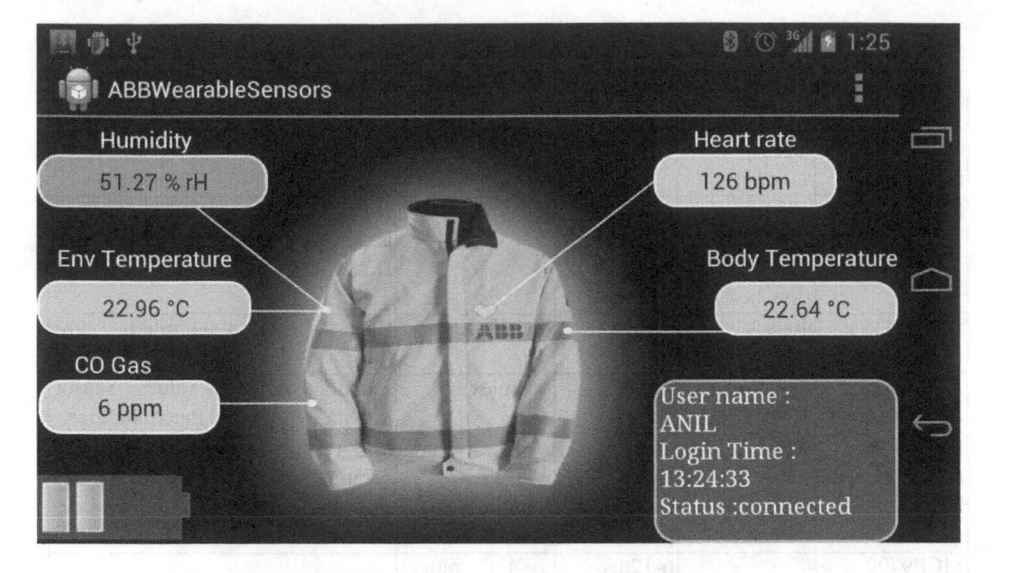

Fig. 2. Main screen of the mobile app presenting wearable sensor data

5.1 Power Supply

The LilyPad power supply was improved. In a first step, we analyzed various sensors with regard to their power consumption and accurateness (cf. Table 1). The largest power consumer is the carbon monoxide sensor with approximately 150mA. In addition, the Bluetooth module consumes up to 300mA (peak), although the average is less than 50mA. Thus, the old battery was replaced. The new battery ensures sufficient power supply for at least 5 hours.

5.2 Body Temperature Sensor

We evaluated three temperature sensors: TMP36, TMP37, and the LilyPad temperature board (MCP9700). TMP37 seemed to be the most suitable sensor. However, all of the listed sensors are equipped with analogue outputs. This means that even small changes in voltage were reflected in the measured temperature. This was the case when the heater of the CO sensor was started. Therefore, it was replaced by a Dallas DS18B20 sensor with a digital output.

5.3 Acceleration Sensor

It turned out that the value range of the ADXL335 sensor ($\pm$ 3g) was too limited to enable reliable fall detection. Thus, it was replaced by an ADXL345 sensor which provides a measuring range of $\pm$ 16g and very good resolution. Moreover, the sensor already includes additional internal algorithms, e.g., a fall detection algorithm. In case a fall is detected, this information is stored locally on the sensor. This capability has

Table 1. Overview of the analyzed sensors

Sensor	Power consumption		Accurateness	Remarks
	Measured	Data sheet		
TMP37 (body temperature)	26uA	<50uA	±2°C	Works fine.
MQ-7 (CO)	145mA (high heat) 45mA (low heat)	150mA (high heat) 42mA (low heat)	unknown	High power consumption leads to heating. Sensor has to be calibrated. Data sheet is vague.
ADXL335 (acceleration)	400uA	350uA	complex	Range of values too limited.
ADXL345 (acceleration)	-	max. 140uA	complex	Extended range of values. Sensor provides additional functionalities.
SHT15 (env. temp. and humidity)	1uA sleep 550uA transmit	1uA sleep 600uA transmit	temp.: < ±0.5°C hum.: < ±2%	Low response rate. Measured temperature seems to be too high.
MCP9700 (temperature)	-	6-12uA	± 4°C, range: 0°C-70°C	
HIH-4030 (humidity)	-	200uA	0-59%RH: ±5%RH 60-100%RH: ±8%RH	Requires non condensing environment.
TGS3870 (CO)	-	11-120mW avg. 38mW	30-900ppm	
Vibe board	-	75-85mA		Vibration board.
LilyPad Buzzer	-	110mA		Washing will damage the buzzer.
Bluetooth Mate Gold	avg. 50mA max. 300mA	avg. 25mA conn: 30mA	-	Power consumption depends on various factors, such as signal strength. Range: 106 m (open air).

the advantage that the sensor values do not have to be read out every few milliseconds. Moreover, the sensor data is transmitted digitally.

5.4 Housing

The new prototype was encased in a plastic half-shell housing (cf. Figure 3). That way, it can be easily incorporated with a safety vest, e.g. by inserting it into the breast pocket of the safety vest (see Figure 4). This approach provides the benefit that the prototype can be readily attached to and detached from the vest. However, utilizing the new developed housing resulted in increased heat generation. Thus, the data sampled by the ambient temperature sensor did not provide reliable values anymore. The measured temperature deviated around 10 degrees Celsius from the actual temperature. We decided to move the SHT15 sensor into a separate enclosure. The corresponding enclosure is shown in front of the breast pocket (cf. Fig. 4).

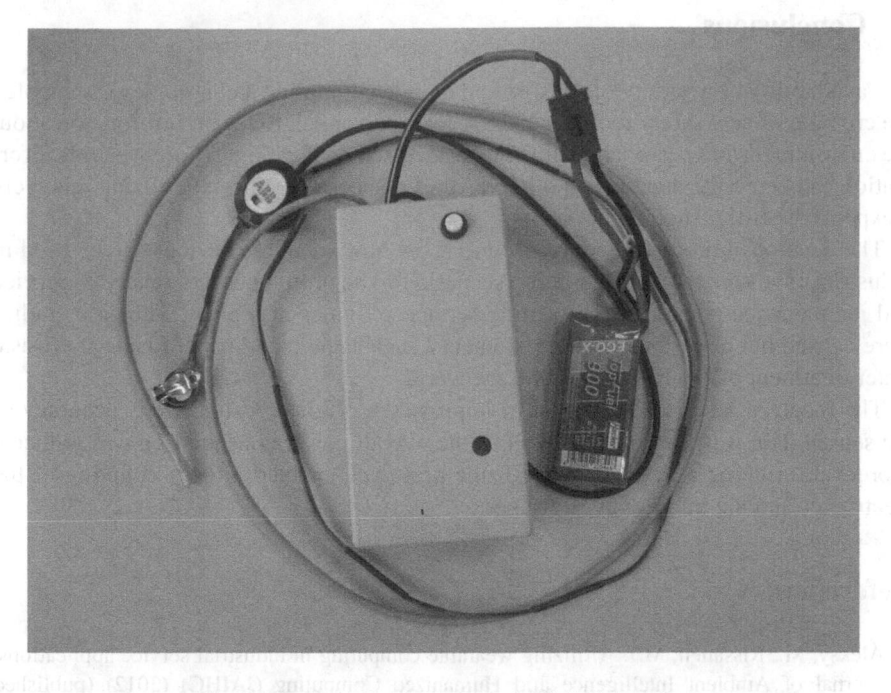

Fig. 3. The prototype in a plastic half-shell housing

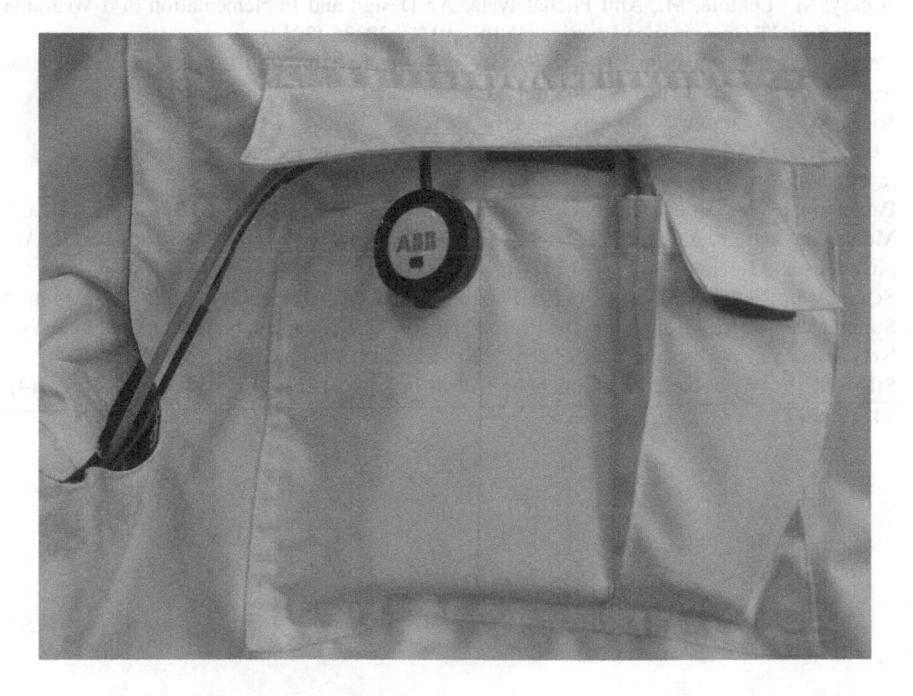

Fig. 4. The prototype located in the breast pocket of a safety vest

6 Conclusions

The availability of a variety of sensors and mobile computing technologies has enabled the creation of new safety tools for field service personnel. Relevant information about the environment and personal health can be accessed on the move. Moreover, this information can be easily shared with others. All of this can be achieved utilizing relatively inexpensive off-the-shelf components.

The developed prototypes were used to show how wearable devices can be used in industrial environments. The common scenario for the prototypes was related to service and maintenance personnel performing service activities at a plant. The case studies were carried out in various business domains, such as pulp and paper plants and waste water treatment plants located around the world.

The received feedback was used to improve the original design. Here, accuracy of the sensed data was improved as well as the overall power consumption was reduced. Moreover, utilizing a new housing for the prototype enabled a loose coupling of the electronics and the traditional safety vest.

References

1. Aleksy, M., Rissanen, M.J.: Utilizing wearable computing in industrial service applications. Journal of Ambient Intelligence and Humanized Computing (JAIHC) (2012) (published online)
2. Aleksy, M., Lehtola, M., Anil Puchakayala, A.: Design and Implementation of a Wearable Safety Suit. IT Convergence Practice (INPRA) 1(1), 28–36 (2013)
3. Coppeé, G.H.: Occupational Health Services and Practice. In: Stellman, J.M. (ed.) Encyclopedia of Occupational Health and Safety. International Labor Organization (2011)
4. Kieffner, T.: Wearable Computers: An Overview,
   http://misnt.indstate.edu/harper/Wearable_Computers.html
   (accessed February 13, 2014)
5. Pantelopoulos, A., Bourbakis, N.G.: A Survey on Wearable Sensor-Based Systems for Health Monitoring and Prognosis. IEEE Transactions on Systems, Man, and Cybernetics-Part C: Applications and Reviews 40(1), 1–12 (2010)
6. Scholz, M., Riedel, T., Decker, C.: A Flexible Architecture for a Robust Indoor Navigation Support Device for Firefighters. In: Proceedings of the Seventh International Conference on Networked Sensing Systems (INSS 2010), Kassel, Germany, pp. 227–232 (June 2010)
7. Stanford, V.: Wearable computing goes live in industry. IEEE Pervasive Computing 1(4), 14–19 (2002)

SmartARM: Smartphone Based Activity Recognition and Monitoring System for Heart Failure Patients

Umer Fareed

Department of Electrical, Electronics, and Telecommunications Engineering and Naval
Architecture, University of Genoa,
Via dell 'Opera Pia 13, 16145, Genoa, Italy
umer.fareed@edu.unige.it

Abstract. With recent advancements in the medical field, activity monitoring applications that are proficient in measuring health-related data have become common. These devices are capable of transmitting information wirelessly and can be used in conjunction with smart phones to pass on data content to devices with similar operating capability. Motion sensor embedded smartphones provide users information about their own physical activity in an understandable format that may be used for a variety of applications. In this paper, I introduce the design and implementation of a health activity monitoring and diagnostic system suitable for heart failure patients. The main objective of this work is to collect data from external sensors that measure patient's vital signs and predict future events by observing these physical readings of the heart patient.

Keywords: Activity recognition, smart phone, remote health monitoring, health device profile.

1   Introduction

Heart failure (HF) is among the leading cause of deaths around the world for adults over 65 years of age [1]. The exact causes of heart failure are difficult to analyze due to challenges in diagnosis and treatment of older patients. Almost, 25% of the patients who suffer a heart attack are re-hospitalized within a month and half of them are certain to be readmitted within 6 months. This unplanned readmission not only surges the treatment expenses liable on the national healthcare system but also increases the total medical expenditure of the hospital by 20-25% annually [2].

To economize the costs associated with HF patient treatment, an evidence-based care system is needed that can improve the quality of medical care provided to heart failure patients during their stay at the hospital. In such a situation, a scalable remote health monitoring system that has the ability to collect, store, and process large amount of data gathered from the sensors in an active and legible manner is the likely choice. Moreover, there exists a need of performing intelligent analysis on the gathered data. In simple words, the system should be capable enough to extrapolate useful information or prognosticate patterns from the analyzed data. The collected

I. Awan et al. (Eds.): MobiWis 2014, LNCS 8640, pp. 145–152, 2014.
© Springer International Publishing Switzerland 2014

information is used to keep a check on patient condition wherein alarming for a continuous degradation or improvement in patient health.

However, current health monitoring systems lack advanced diagnostic capabilities as they lack efficient transmission of data for a timely response and a direct connection between the patient and the facilitator for effective recommendation adhering to the patient condition. My proposed solution is an end-to-end system that covers data collection and storage aspects of remote monitoring as well as performs data analytics. Smartphone as the core of the activity recognition and monitoring system plays the role of a communication hub to transport data received by external sensors as well as of a sensor to detect physical events and process these quantities. It also offers an administrative portal and a query based feedback system that allows the medical staff to keep a check on patient daily routine. I expect my system to accurately predict the worsening of HF symptoms in patients by performing statistical analysis on real data collected from a medical center.

The remainder of this paper is organized as follows. Section 2 describes some of the related work in the area of activity recognition and monitoring. Section 3 explains in detail the architecture of the proposed activity monitoring system. Section 4 describes the experimental setup and possible results. Section 5 concludes the paper.

2   Related Work

Use of activity recognition for health monitoring has become an interestingly popular area of research in the last decade. We see many efforts put forward for a number of application areas conforming to activity monitoring. Wearable accelerometer based body sensors capable of inferring human mobility levels are an example of small size sensors with high level of accuracy. We observe a large use of these on-body sensors placed at different parts of the body [3] for accurately determining physical activities of the subject ([4-7]). Other related works are dependent on the positioning of sensors and specific laboratory conditions but lack accuracy [8] when used at diverse positions and different circumstances.

The major drawbacks with use of these multiple wearable sensors is the uneasiness of handling numerous wires attached to the body and the feeling of the irritation that comes from wearing sensors for a long duration. A few works also illustrate the lessening of the use of wearable sensors to a single tri-axial accelerometer for activity recognition but also show a drastic drop in accuracy as compared to use of multiple wearable sensors [9]. However using a single sensor is more preferable and convenient in real world scenarios and especially in cases where the patients are old. Also, use of single sensor would result in fewer signals thus reducing computational power.

I also review the proposed work for telemonitoring solutions adapted in the recent past for improvements in HF patient readmission rates or death [10-12]. These proposals for HF patients suffer limitations as they require trained technicians to attach sensors to a patient's body and are reactive when HF patient symptoms are already worsened. Also, they consider weight factor and symptoms that do not serve as accurate and responsive measures for the early prediction of heart failure [13].

3   System Architecture

The proposed Activity Recognition and Monitoring System (SmartARM) is a three-tier, end-to-end remote monitoring system that includes extensive hardware and software components designed and developed to provide standard health activity monitoring procedures. The overall system architecture is summarized in Figure 1.

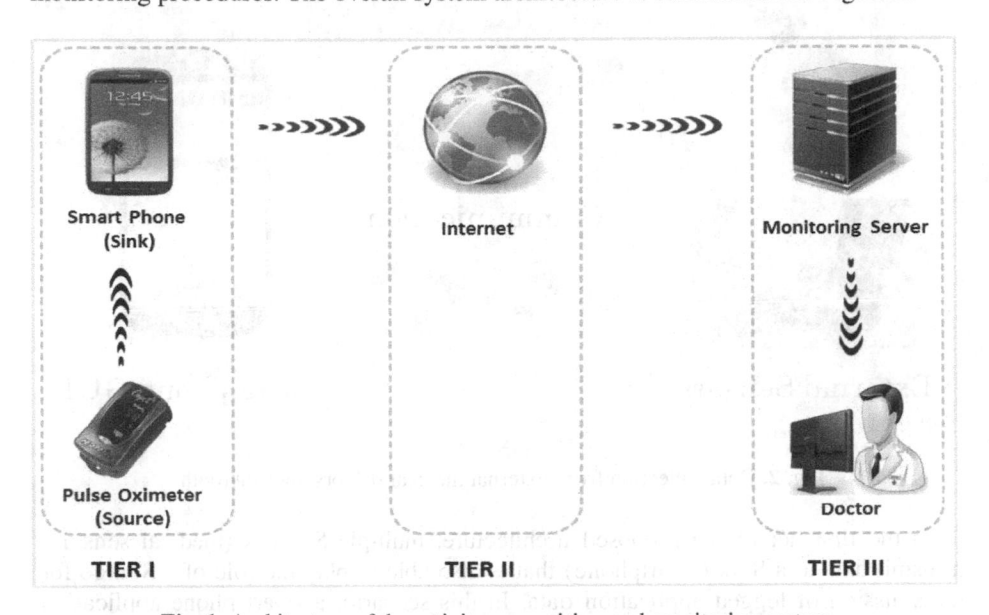

Fig. 1. Architecture of the activity recognition and monitoring system

The first tier consists of a data collection framework, which is formed from a set of external sensing devices that measure various bodily statistics such as weight, fat percentage, water saturation, blood pressure, cardiac frequency, blood oxygen saturation and body movements. The data from these sensors is collected, processed and relayed via a smartphone-based gateway to the storage server that constitutes the second tier of the SmartARM architecture. This large amount of data is stored and indexed using a scalable database and is easily accessible using a web interface. The third tier includes an analytic engine that is used for reasoning purpose to generate statistical data models and predicting outcomes based on various machine learning and data mining algorithms. In the following sections, I describe the design and working of these components of the activity recognition & monitoring system briefly.

3.1   Data Collection with Smartphone

For the data collection, I use an Android smartphone as a central hub for receiving patient physical measurements from the external sensors and communicating them to the web-server as shown in figure 2. All the sensing devices that I am using are Bluetooth enabled and work with the Bluetooth Health Device Profile (HDP). HDP defines the profile that is used for connecting application data Source devices such as weight scales, glucose meters, thermometers, and pulse-oximeters to application data Sink devices such as mobile phones, laptops and desktop computers [14]. HDP depends upon MCAP as its transport protocol and references Data Exchange Specifications to define the data-layer [15].

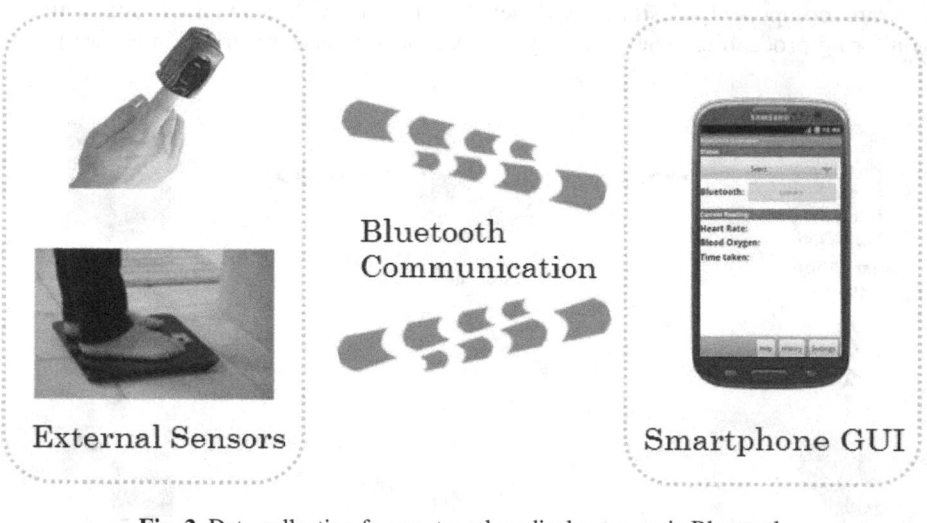

Fig. 2. Data collection from external medical sensors via Bluetooth

In the first tier of the proposed architecture, multiple Sources (medical sensors) transmit data to a Sink (smartphone) that is also able to play the role of a Source for transmission of logged application data. In this scenario, a smart phone application acts as a Sink for the external sensors used by the patient and as a Source for a storage server at the remote site where the patient data is stored. This data is then routed to a doctor through a reliable media (Internet, mobile phone network) via medical server application at the hospital site as shown in figure 1.

SmartARM architecture has GUI support for both the web and smartphone application wherein different options to check patients' weight, water saturation, cardiac frequency, fat percentage and oxygen saturation are available. The interfaces for application are designed in a simple, clear, and communicative way so that patients and doctor do not have to worry about the underlying software architecture and operating system. Patient data is made available in the form of graphs and tables for view.

SmartARM smartphone App is compatible with any device running Android OS version 2.0 or above and operated with HDP Bluetooth profile to avoid any compatibility issue with different vendor external sensors. For Bluetooth communication between phone and external sensing device, a pairing session is required. After pairing, both devices share a link key that can be used for authentication and encryption purposes for secure data communication. Once a control channel is established for communication, no more pairing is needed in the future. Smart phone receives external data through the Data Channel which is capable of periodic or batch transmissions as well as it can be kept open for an indefinite period of time for streaming data transmission.

To suit our needs, I have configured data channels as streaming data channel for streaming application data from pulse oximeters and reliable data channel for weight scale. For example, a pulse oximeter (Source) is used to measure oxygen saturation. After determining the reading, the Source searches for and discovers the Sink device that is to receive its data. The Source initiates a connection for data channel and the recorded data is transferred. Data received by the smartphone is then displayed to the user through the Android app GUI.

Smartphone app is designed to be user friendly and with simple choice options that reflect choosing a corresponding device for recording measurements. The user is provided with the option to select a weighing scale and given a brief instruction to record a reading. After the patient selects the option for the desired measurement, a Bluetooth connection with the selected device is established and a reading is recorded that is displayed to the user. User can take multiple measurements and is also provided with the option to view history of the measurements recorded earlier.

3.2   Data Storage

The next step after data collection is to store and manage the data in a way that it can be easily accessed with the android phone and the web application. For data storage and access we need a highly scalable data storage that can handle growing storage needs as well as provides secure transition and storage of data through encrypted access mechanisms. We can either choose a public cloud data storage for storage of data as these clouds are securely managed and are reliable for data transfer or opt for a relational database management system to store structured data such as sensor readings, events and data observations along with individual patient details for daily monitoring as shown in figure 3.

In order to process the data for real time analysis and transmission of data from the smart phone to the remote web server for displaying the user data, I use a central storage and a relational database to manage data queries. This client-server interaction is achieved through PHP scripting and MySQL database queries are used to send and retrieve information from the server. For making connection to PHP scripts, I use HTTP POST request methods to post data from the client. In my design, the client is Android device and on server side there is a combination of PHP script and web services. We post patient data periodically to the web server whenever there is query from server side for the updated data.

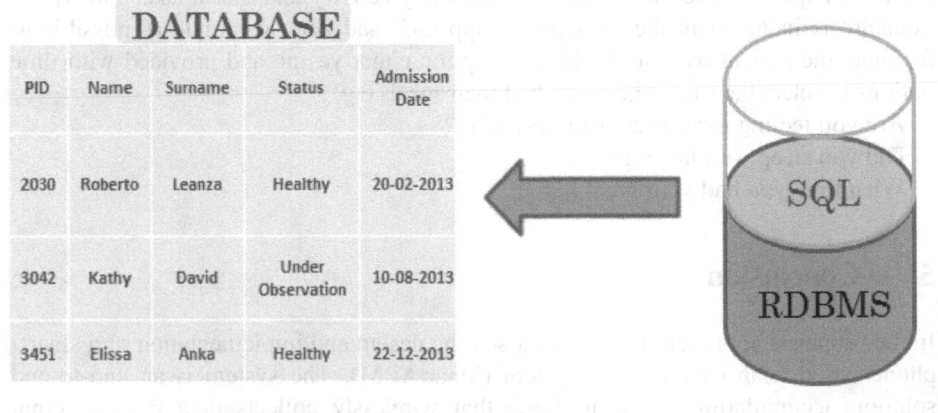

Fig. 3. SQL database for storing and managing patient data

3.3   Data Analytics

The major strength of SmartARM over other activity monitoring systems is in the analytics engine. The large amount of patient data is a key resource that needs to be processed and analyzed for knowledge extraction. The analytics engine uses a set of data mining tools and techniques that can be applied to this processed data to discover hidden patterns and generate multiple statistical models for data classification, clustering and association. These models can then be used for both diagnostic and predictive purposes that enable support for cost-savings and decision making. With this diagnosis, it is highly likely a possibility to be able to predict the worsening of HF patient symptoms before the patient is re-hospitalized.

Initially, during data collection phase, the analytics engine work in offline mode wherein the data is downloaded and analyzed using various learning and classification techniques. Once a strong diagnostic model is generated and validated, it can be uploaded to the server for real time data diagnostics and predictions. For real time execution, different classification algorithms; Naïve Bayes Classifier (NBC), Nearest Neighbor (kNN) and Decision Tree (C4.5) are used to optimize the model. This classification helps to detect any pattern that is inconsistent with the daily measurements and could trigger an alarm about the HF patient worsening condition.

4   Experimental Setup

We expect clinical data from a private hospital in the coming months for experimental setup. The plan is to analyze HF patient's daily weight, water saturation, fat percentage, cardiac frequency and oxygen saturation measurements for duration of two months for a group of 10 patients. We ask the patients to use the external sensors at least once in a day. The time for recording the reading is left free to the patient as a single reading in a day is adequate for analysis. The patients under observation are to be given a tutorial about the use of weighing scale and pulse-oximeters and the presence of smartphone near the external devices.

We also encourage the patients to participate in a daily questionnaire by responding to few questions to get an idea of their daily activity and diet intake. This questionnaire is included in the smartphone app GUI and kept as simple as possible to facilitate the patient by just checking an option either yes/no and provided with time options to select the time when they had their meals e.g.

Are you feeling more tired than yesterday?

Did you sleep well last night?

What time you had your breakfast?

5   Conclusion

In the proposed approach, I have discussed the design and implementation of a smartphone based health monitoring system (SmartARM). The system is an end-to-end solution accumulating (a) smartphone that wirelessly collects data from external sensor devices, (b) a scalable database for data storage and access by the web interface and (c) an analytics engine for diagnostic prediction using machine learning and data mining algorithms. The system architecture promises optimal performance in terms of computational and energy efficacy as it uses smartphone as the core that not only plays the role of a central hub to convey data received from external sensors but also of a sensor with the ability to measure and process physical measurements allied to the patient health.

I expect SmartARM to predict better prognosis as compared to the daily weight change metric predictors used by the other health monitoring systems as it also considers cardiac frequency, fat percentage and oxygen saturation measurements for the decision. Its functioning could be further enhanced with integration of multiple sensor nodes appropriate for other daily physical activities. The initial medical results from the experimental phase with real patients expected in next 1-2 months would be vital for the performance evaluation of the monitoring system.

Acknowledgment. This work is supported in part by the Erasmus Mundus Joint Doctorate in Interactive and Cognitive Environments, which is funded by the Education, Audiovisual & Culture Executive Agency under the FPA no 2010-0012.

References

1. Lloyd-Jones, D., Adams, R.J., Brown, T.M., Carnethon, M.S., Dai, G., Simone, D. F.T.B., Ford, E., Furie, K., Gillespie, C.: Executive summary: heart disease and stroke statistics— 2010 update. American Heart Association. Circulation 121 (2010)
2. Jencks, S.F., Williams, M.V., Coleman, E.A.: Rehospitalizations among patients in the Medicare fee-for-service program. NE. J. Med. 360, 1418–1428 (2009)
3. Bao, L., Intille, S.: Activity recognition from user-annotated acceleration data. In: Ferscha, A., Mattern, F. (eds.) PERVASIVE 2004. LNCS, vol. 3001, pp. 1–17. Springer, Heidelberg (2004)
4. Lukowicz, P., Junker, H., Stäger, M., von Büren, T., Tröster, G.: WearNET: A distributed multi-sensor system for context aware wearables. In: Borriello, G., Holmquist, L.E. (eds.) UbiComp 2002. LNCS, vol. 2498, pp. 361–370. Springer, Heidelberg (2002)
5. Huỳnh, T., Blanke, U., Schiele, B.: Scalable recognition of daily activities with wearable sensors. In: Hightower, J., Schiele, B., Strang, T. (eds.) LoCA 2007. LNCS, vol. 4718, pp. 50–67. Springer, Heidelberg (2007)
6. Atallah, L., Lo, B., King, R., Guang-Zhong, Y.: Sensor Placement for Activity Detection using Wearable Accelerometers. In: International Conference on Body Sensor Networks, pp. 24–29. IEEE Xplore (2010)
7. Mathie, M., Coster, A., Lovell, N., Celler, B., Lord, S., Tiedemann, A.: A pilot study of long-term monitoring of human movements in the home using accelerometry. J. Telemed. Telecare 10(3), 144–151 (2004)
8. Bussmann, J., Martens, W., Tulen, J., Schasfoort, F., van den Berg-Emons, H., Stam, H.: Measuring daily behavior using ambulatory accelerometry: the activity monitor. J. Behav. Res. Methods 33(3), 349–356 (2001)

9. Karantonis, D., Narayanan, M., Mathie, M., Lovell, N., Celler, B.: Implementation of a real-time human movement classifier using a triaxial accelerometer for ambulatory monitoring. IEEE Trans. on Info. Tech. in Biomedicine 10(1), 156–167 (2006)

10. Mortara, A., Pinna, G.D., Johnson, P., Maestri, R., Capomolla, S., La Rovere, M.T., Ponikowski, P., Tavazzi, L.: Home telemonitoring in heart failure patients: the HHH study (home or hospital in heart failure). E. J. H. F. 11, 312–318 (2009)

11. Desai, A.S.: Home Monitoring Heart Failure Care Does Not Improve Patient Outcomes: Looking Beyond Telephone-Based Disease Management. American Heart Association. Circulation 125, 828–836 (2012)

12. Chaudhry, S.I., Phillips, C.O., Stewart, S.S., Riegel, B., Jerant, A.F., Krumholz, H.M.: Telemonitoring in Patients with Heart Failure: A Systematic Review. J. Card. Fail. 13(1), 56–62 (2007)

13. Ideal Life (2011), http://www.ideallifeonline.com

14. Health Device Profile, http://www.bluetooth.com/Specifications/HDP_SPEC_V10.pdf

15. ARS Software Bluetooth HDP, http://www.ars2000.com/Bluetooth_HDP.pdf

SARA: Singapore's Automated Responsive Assistant, A Multimodal Dialogue System for Touristic Information

Andreea I. Niculescu, Ridong Jiang, Seokhwan Kim, Kheng Hui Yeo,
Luis F. D'Haro, Arthur Niswar, and Rafael E. Banchs

Institute for Infocomm Research, 1 Fusionopolis Way, Singapore 138632
{andreea-n,rjiang,kims,yeokh,luisdhe,aniswar,
rembanchs}@i2r.a-star.edu.sg
http://hlt.i2r.a-star.edu.sg/staff/

Abstract. In this paper we describe SARA, a multimodal dialogue system offering touristic assistance for visitors coming to Singapore. The system is implemented as an Android mobile phone application and provides information about local attractions, restaurants, sightseeing, direction and transportation services. SARA is able to detect the user's location on a map by using a GPS integrated module and accordingly can provide real-time orientation and direction help. To communicate with SARA users can use speech, text or scanned QR code. Input/output modalities for SARA include natural language in form of speech or text. A short video about the main features of our Android application can be seen at: http://vimeo.com/91620644. Currently, the system supports only English, but we are working towards a multi-lingual input/output support. For test purposes we also created a web version of SARA that can be tested for Chinese and English text input/output at: http://iris.i2r.a-star.edu.sg/StatTour/.

Keywords: multi-modal dialogue system, mobile application, tourist information system, natural language interaction.

1 Introduction

The tourism industry is considered to be one of the biggest economic sectors generating an estimated eleven percent of the global domestic product [1]. Traditionally, tourists rely on using static information such as book guides, printed maps, and informative flyer material to locate points of interest. This way of getting to know a new place is considered to be useful although the source of information might be outdated.

Given the grow of the tourism sector and the prevalent usage of smart phones nowadays, the ICT industry has started to focus on creating tools to help travelers to orient and move smoothly in new environments [2]. Such tools include interactive maps, reservation and automatic check-in systems, personalized recommendation applications, travel guide assistants, etc.

I. Awan et al. (Eds.): MobiWis 2014, LNCS 8640, pp. 153–164, 2014.
© Springer International Publishing Switzerland 2014

1.1   Local Context

According to the Singapore Tourism Board the number of tourists coming to Singapore is yearly increasing [3]. In 2013, the total number of tourists hit a new record: 15.5 million people came to visit the island, which represents the highest tourist rate in the past decade. This increasing amount of visitors requires additional information resources in terms of accommodation, board, food and beverage, transportation and touristic guidance.

In this context, SARA was built as a response to the growing demand for personal touristic assistance and offers a comfortable solution for those who want to explore the city by themselves and have no human guide around.

Currently, there are several other local touristic applications available at Google Play Android application store, such as *Your Singapore Guide*, *Your Singapore Navigation*, *Singapore Guide* etc., that provide information for tourists. However, these applications have a lower degree of interactivity, in the sense that they support neither speech input/output modalities nor question & answering (QA) style of interaction as SARA does, presenting the information as any other descriptive internet web page.

1.2   Related Work

Generally, most of the applications concerning touristic guidance offer services in terms of either navigation or exploration. Applications meant for navigation include examples such as *Siri*, *Google Maps navigation*, *Sygic*, etc. On the other hand, applications offering exploration services, which present descriptive information for the user to read, include examples such as *Wikihood*, *Triposo*, *Your Singapore Guide*, etc. No doubt, these applications provide highly valuable information and help; but, for the users, navigation and exploration make more sense if performed simultaneously, i.e. without having to switch between applications [10]. Therefore, there is a need of creating a tool which can handle both of these categories.

Additionally, users need an application that does not distract them from their current task – which is walking on the street, looking around etc. In this sense, it is important to mention that most of the current applications offering navigation and exploration services use visual information displayed on the mobile phone screen. To address this problem many natural language systems were developed. Examples include pedestrian navigation systems [4] [5] [6] [7] [8] [9] [10], city guidance systems [11] [12] and QA systems [13].

Our system SARA complements the work mentioned above reuniting navigation and exploration in a single application that combines visual information with speech to create a more natural way of interaction. In the future, the system will also support multi-lingual services – at the moment still under development – which represents an additional feature that distinguishes SARA from all the other applications.

2   System Architecture

SARA is based on a client-server architecture, as presented in figure 1: the client mobile application communicates with the server using a JSON Object based protocol.

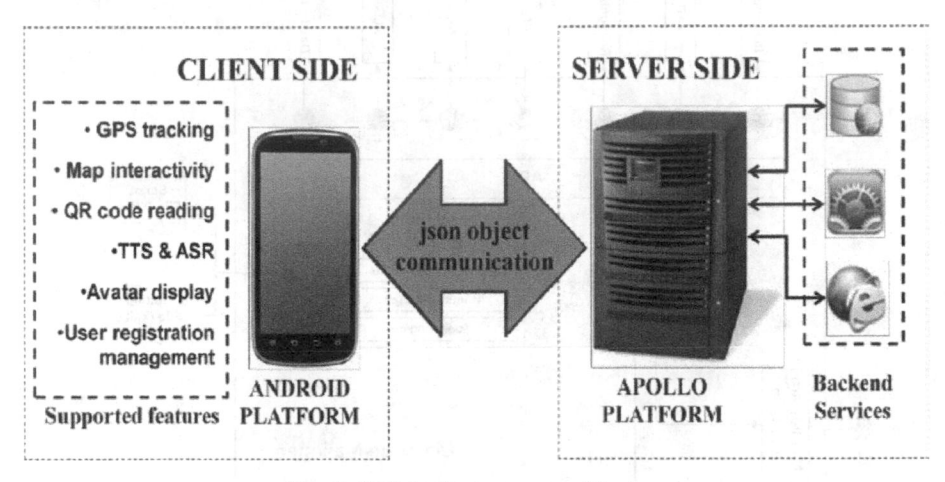

Fig. 1. SARA client-server architecture

2.1   Server Side

On the server side, SARA uses a hybrid approach to natural language understanding (NLU) and dialogue topic tracking [14]. The components transform the recognition output passed from the native Android's speech recognizer into a semantic representation using rules and statistical models. The models were trained by using data collected for the Singapore touristic domain. A total of 40 hours of human-human dialogue data for English and Chinese was collected. The dialogues include sequences of questions asked by visitors and answers containing explanations provided by tour guides. The dialogues were manually annotated on three levels of semantics: words, utterances, and dialogue segments.

The dialogue manager (DM) implemented in SARA incorporates two different strategies: a rule-based approach using a set of manually defined heuristics for determining proper system actions to each input; and an example-based method using an index filled with input-response pairs collected from Wikipedia articles related to Singapore. For each user input the most similar example in the index is selected based on cosine similarities between term vectors with TF-IDF weights [15]. While the rule-based approach is mostly used for handling goal-oriented scenarios, the example-based approach focuses more on general question answering scenarios [16].

Finally, the natural language generation component uses a template-based approach [17] to generate an appropriate response to the user query. Once generated, the response is then passed to the native Android's text to speech engine.

SARA's main components are linked together by using APOLLO [18]. As shown in figure 2, APOLLO is a component-pluggable dialogue platform that allows the interconnection and control of the different interdependent components used in the implementation of the system, such as:

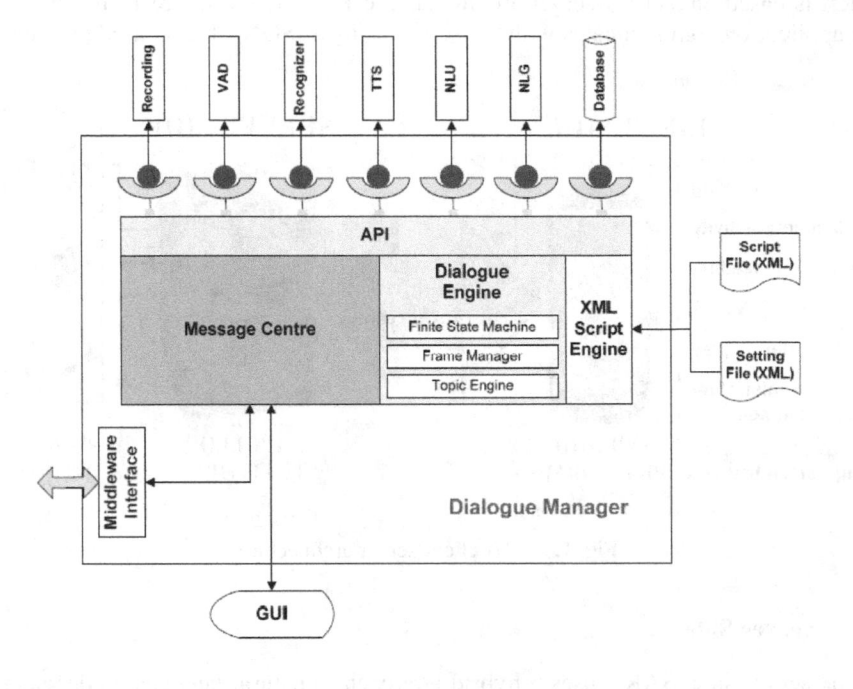

Fig. 2. APOLLO dialogue platform: basic architecture

- *Dialogue components*, which include the main components of dialogue engines, such as automatic speech recognition, natural language understanding, natural language generation and speech synthesis among others.

- *Input/output components*, which provide the means for integrating different input and output utilities including speech, text, image and video into the platform

- *Backend components*, which allow for the integration of different information sources, such as databases, web crawlers and browsers, rule and inference engines, as well as the different user profiles, short and long term memory contents stored by the system.

- *Task manager components*, which include all individual dialogue management engines that coexist within the platform in a concurrent manner

Apart from specifically designed plugins, the platform also allows socket communication using TCP-IP protocols. The component interconnection within the platform, as well as the information flow control can be programmed by using the platform's XML-based scripting meta-language.

2.2   Client Side

On the client-side, SARA has nine software modules that enable different system functionalities. Below, we describe briefly each of these modules:

- *User registration and management.* This module is responsible for user registration and log-in. When the application is used for first time, the module creates a user profile containing the person's name and email. For sub-sequential logins the system retains the user's credentials, i.e. the user doesn't need to re-input the password and email address. To update or modify his/her profile the user can access a set-up page directly from the application.

- *Map display and interactivity module.* This module is responsible for displaying the current user location – assuming the GPS is enabled – as well as other locations of interest retrieved by the system. The map is able to display routes as computed by the API and to link map locations to URL addresses provided by the server.

- *GPS tracking module.* This module uses all on-phone necessary resources to determine the exact location of the user. Position coordinates are communicated to the served-based information services for geo-localization purposes. If the user chooses not to enable GPS/location tracking module, the system provides relevant answers without taking the geographic context into consideration.

- *On-phone speech capabilities.* This module exploits the Android's native ASR and TTS resources to convert speech to text and text to speech.

- *Avatar display module.* This module uses image functionalities to display an avatar on the phone screen (see figure 3). The avatar responds to instructions and commands provided by the system performing different activities, such as thinking, smiling, searching, answering, asking questions, etc. The avatar is accompanied by a text bubble in which textual and hyper-textual information is provided to the user.

- *QR code reader module.* This module is responsible for scanning and reading QR codes. System generated QR codes are identified by a specific prefix that the application knows. For non-system generated QR codes, i.e. any other QR code that does not belong to the SARA platform, the mobile application is able to decode and execute the corresponding default action: display the text, browse the corresponding URL, etc.

- *Integration with phone call and SMS.* This module uses on-phone capabilities to support basic functionalities, such as placing a phone call or sending an SMS.

- *Internet browsing module.* This module uses Android resources to display the contents of URLs provided by the server-based information system or the QR code reader. It has browsing capabilities in the sense that once an URL has been displayed, the user can click on any link and start navigating in the Internet.

- *Client-server communication module.* This module is responsible for sending and receiving all necessary information between the client (mobile application) and the server-based information system (APOLLO). It uses a JSON Object based protocol to interchange variable information between the server and the client.

3   User Interface Design

As shown in figure 3, the application has two main screens: a login screen and a dashboard/home screen. The dashboard screen contains a user input field, an avatar display and four navigation option buttons related to:

Fig. 3. SARA mobile app: main screens

- An interactive map in which users can see locations of interest and get directions.
- A web browser that, when available, opens a webpage relevant to the query.
- A picture gallery, where pictures related to the query are stored and displayed.
- A scanner that offers users with the possibility of scanning either generic or specific system generated QR codes.

By tapping on the buttons the user can navigate at any moment into one of the four specific function screens presented in figure 4.

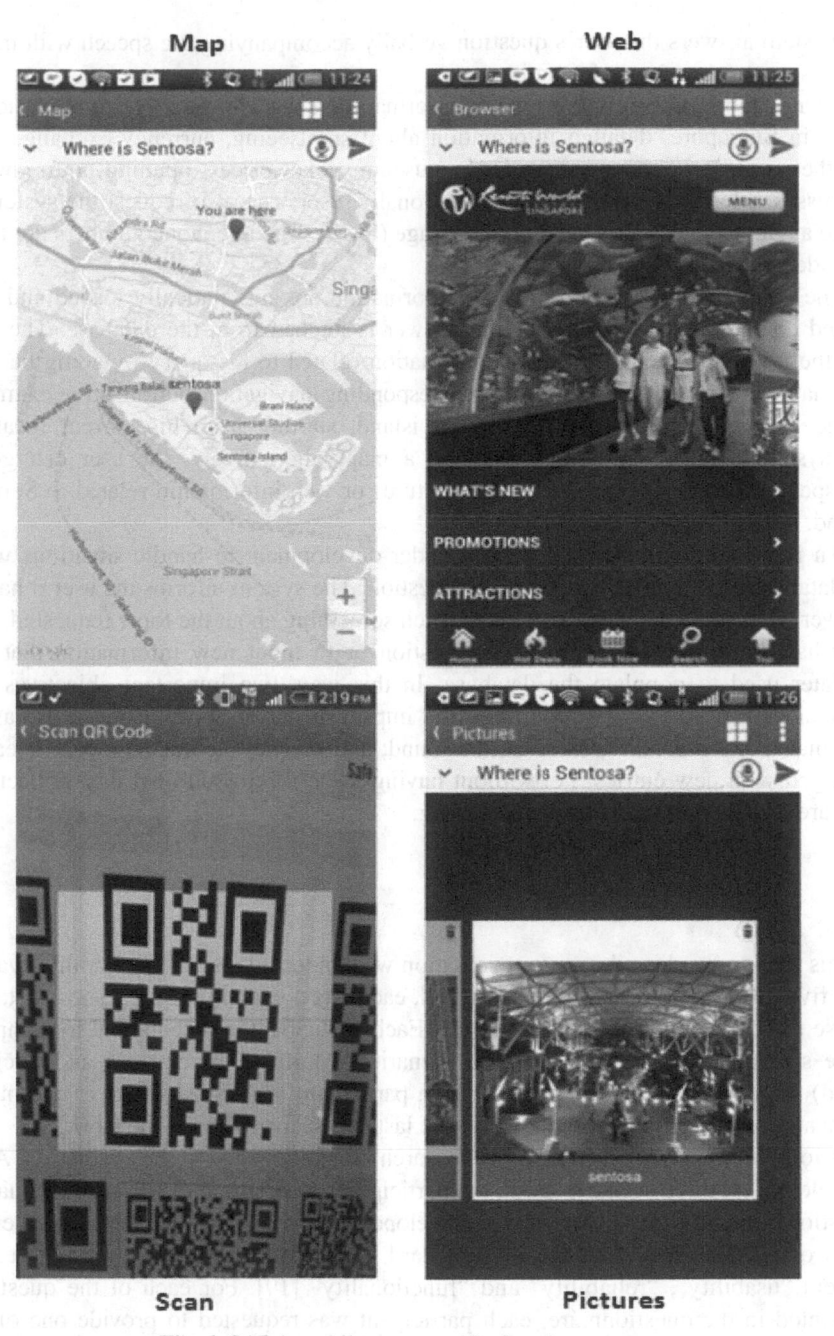

Fig. 4. SARA mobile app: specific function screens

The interaction style with the system is multimodal: users can talk or type the question and receive information from SARA in spoken, written and graphical form, i.e.

the system answers the user's question verbally accompanying the speech with maps, images or web browser information.

Users can request different type of information, such as how to get to a particular place in Singapore, detailed information about sightseeing, currency exchange rate, weather, restaurant recommendations, museum, ticket prices, opening hours, hotels addresses, telephone numbers, etc. Additionally, users can also request the system to place a telephone call or send a text message (SMS). The telephone numbers are to be provided by the server.

The maps, images or web browser information are automatically loaded and presented on the output screen once the answer is fetched from the database. The user has the option to check additional information related to his query by going back to the main screen and tapping on the corresponding navigation button – for example, if the user asks how to go to Sentosa island, starting from his current location, the system explains directions showing a map; alternatively, the user can go to the specific function screens to check pictures or web information related to Sentosa island.

An interesting strategy is currently under development to handle situations when no database records match a particular question. The system informs the user it has no answer and asks if the user can help to teach something about the topic requested. The user has the option to rephrase the question or to input new information that can be later used to populate the database. In this way, two important objectives can be achieved: first, through rephrasing the impact of out-of-vocabulary words can be eliminated and thus, an answer can be found; and second, the database can be easily enlarged with new entries, i.e. without having to perform additional data collections that are usually costly and time consuming.

4   System Evaluation

In this section we describe a user evaluation we conducted on SARA. For this evaluation five different use cases were designed, each one containing several specific tasks. These use cases are presented in table 1. Each participant was requested to complete three scenarios. Since the first three scenarios (Marina Bay, Sentosa and Orchard Road) are conceptually very similar, each participant was asked to select one out of these and additionally to complete also the last two scenarios from the table.

A total of 10 participants from our research lab participated in the evaluation. After completing all three scenario tasks, the participants were asked to fill in an evaluation questionnaire. The questionnaire was developed in accordance with the recommendations of the ISO/IEC 9126 quality standard model and, accordingly, it focuses on system "usability", "reliability" and "functionality" [19]. For each of the questions presented in the questionnaire, each participant was requested to provide one of the following five categorical scores: strongly agree (SA), agree (A), neutral (N), disagree (D), or strongly disagree (SD).

Table 1. Five use cases for Singapore touristic agent evaluation

User scenario	Specific Objectives
Marina Bay	Find a convenient MRT station to reach the Marina Bay area
	Find a suitable place for having lunch
	Ask for places of interest in the Marina Bay area
	Select one place of interest and ask questions about it (including location)
Sentosa	Find and select transportation options to Sentosa
	Ask for places of interest in Sentosa
	Select one place of interest and ask questions about it (including location)
	Find a suitable place for having dinner
Orchard Road	Find a convenient MRT station to reach Orchard Road
	Ask for shopping centres in Orchard Road and select one to go
	Ask for a hotel conveniently located near the shopping centre you selected
	Find a suitable place for having dinner
Moving around Singapore	Ask for directions on how to go to the zoo
	Ask for information related to the zoo
	Find a suitable place for having lunch in some central Singapore area
	Find directions on how to reach that area
	Ask information about museums in Singapore
General Information	Ask about the type of weather in Singapore
	Ask information about the languages spoken in Singapore
	Find out information about the currency and exchange rates in Singapore
	Find out when was Singapore founded and who was the founder
	Ask about places of interest to visit in Singapore
	Select two places of interest and find about their locations

Based on the interaction results for each considered scenario we computed the objective completion rate, as the percentage of the specific objectives completed with respect to the total number of objectives in the task. Figure 5 summarizes the objective completion rates for the first scenarios (Marina Bay, Sentosa and Orchard Road), the second scenario (Moving around Singapore) and the third scenario (General Information).

As seen in figure 5, scenario 3 (General Information) achieved the best performance with an objective completion rate of 60%. In contrast, scenario 2 (Moving around Singapore) achieved the worst performance in terms of objective completion rate: 33%. Here, the most common errors reported by the users – which were later confirmed by the dialogue session logs – were related to the proper identification of venues and venue directions. This information is of fundamental importance for fine tuning and improving the system performance for future release.

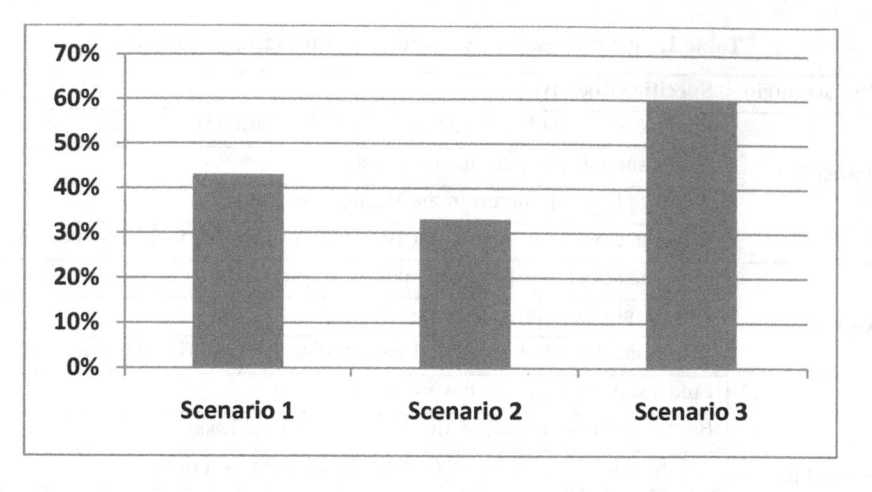

Fig. 5. Objective completion rates for the evaluated scenarios

The results of the subjective evaluation on the user experience are presented in figure 6. As seen from the figure, the highest percentages were achieved for user "agreeing" (SA+A) on statements concerning the usability, reliability and functionality of the system. On the other hand, it is also important to notice that there are visible "disagreement" statements (D+SD) percentage bars concerning the usability and reliability of the system. These negative results were caused in particular by scenarios when venues and directions were not properly identified by the system.

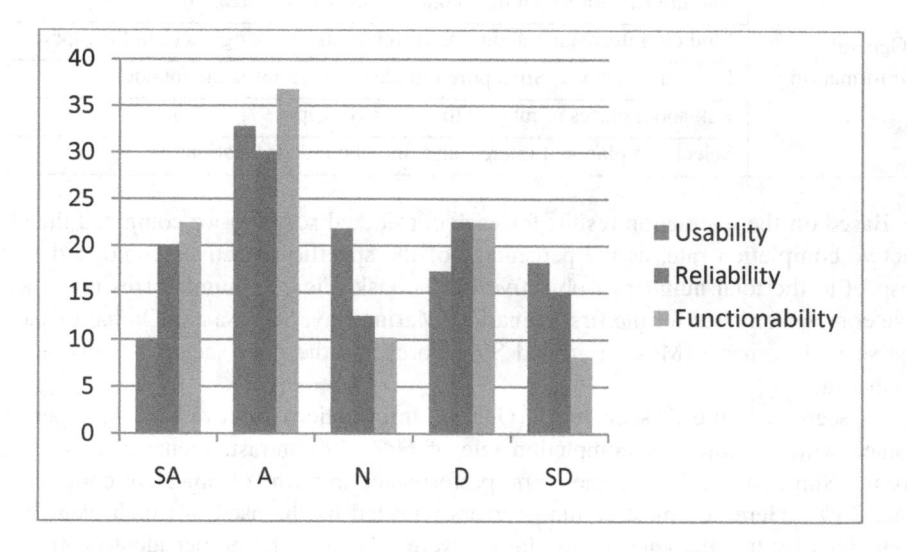

Fig. 6. Results of the subjective evaluation on user experience

5 Conclusions and Future Work

In this paper we presented SARA, an automatic touristic information system for the city of Singapore, which combines general QAs about Singapore's touristic spots and task-oriented dialogues for hospitality and transportation services. The system is currently implemented as Android application and as web-based system.

Our first evaluation round showed that our system needs several improvements before it can reach the level of a successful commercial application. The information collected during the evaluation provided valuable feed-back on system performance and user experience. As such, our next goal is to work towards the improvements suggested by our test participants.

Additionally, we are planning to extend the system with multilingual capabilities – at the moment, the mobile application supports only English, while the web system can be used for both English and Chinese.

Another improvement planned concerns with error handling strategies for misspelled venues, either for incorrectly typed user inputs or out-of-vocabulary misrecognized speech inputs. In the future, the system will be able to provide alternative options in cases when, for example, users misspell the name of a venue.

We also plan to create an iOS and Windows mobile version of the application, improve the usability of current user interface, enlarge the database coverage with additional touristic information, and integrate it with our digital receptionist and restaurant recommendation systems.

Finally, we plan to conduct a second system evaluation by engaging real users to interact with the system. The result of this evaluation study will ultimately help us to improve future versions of SARA regarding both, performance and user experience.

Acknowledgments. We are grateful to the developer team from Extentia Information Technology for the help provided concerning the development of the UI interface and video demo. Also, we would like to thank to all test users for the effort they put in participating in our evaluation study.

References

1. Kabassi, K.: Personalizing recommendations for tourists. Telematics and Informatics 27(1), 51–66 (2010)
2. Wium, M.: Design and Evaluation of a Personalized Mobile Tourist Application. Master Thesis. Norwegian University of Science and Technology (2010)
3. Singapore Tourist Board, http://www.stb.gov.sg/
4. Malaka, R., Zipf, A.: Deep Map – challenging IT research in the framework of a tourist information system. In: Information and Communication Technologies in Tourism 2000, pp. 15–27. Springer (2000)
5. Raubal, M., Winter, S.: Enriching way finding instructions with local landmarks. In: Egenhofer, M., Mark, D.M. (eds.) GIScience 2002. LNCS, vol. 2478, pp. 243–259. Springer, Heidelberg (2002)

6. Dale, R., Geldof, S., Prost, J.: CORAL: Using Natural Language Generation for Navigational Assistance. In: Proceedings of ACSC 2003, Australia, (2003)
7. Bartie, P., Mackaness, W.: D3.1.2 - The Space-Book City Model. Technical report, The SPACEBOOKProject (FP7/2011-2014 grant agreement no.270019) (2013)
8. Shroder, C.J., Mackaness, W., Gittings, B.: Giving the Right Route Directions: The Requirements for Pedestrian Navigation Systems. Transactions in GIS, 419–438 (2011)
9. Dethlefs, N., Cuayahuitl, H.: Hierarchical Reinforcement Learning and Hidden Markov Models for Task-Oriented Natural Language Generation. In: Proc. of ACL (2011)
10. Janarthanam, S., Lemon, O., Bartie, P., Dalmas, T., Dickinson, A., Liu, X., Mackaness, W., Webber, B.: Evaluating a city exploration dialogue system combining question-answering and pedestrian navigation. In: Proc. ACL (2013)
11. Ko, J., Murase, F., Mitamura, T., Nyberg, E., Tateishi, M., Akahori, I., Hataoka, N.: CAMMIA: A Context-Aware Spoken Dialog System for Mobile Environments. In: IEEE ASRU Workshop (2005)
12. Kashioka, H., Misu, T., Mizukami, E., Shiga, Y., Kayama, K., Hori, C., Kawai, H.: Multimodal Dialog System for Kyoto Sightseeing Guide. In: Asia-Pacific Signal and Information Processing Association Annual Summit and Conference (2011)
13. Webb, N., Webber, B.: Special Issue on Interactive Question Answering: Introduction. Natural Language Engineering 15(1), 1–8 (2009)
14. Kim, S., Banchs, R.E., Li, H.: Wikipedia-based Kernels for Dialogue Topic Tracking. In: Proceedings of ICASSP (2014)
15. Banchs, R.E., Li, H.: IRIS: a chat-oriented dialogue system based on the vector space model. In: Proceedings of the ACL 2012 System Demonstrations, pp. 37–42. Association for Computational Linguistics (2012)
16. Xue, X., Jeon, J., Croft, W.: Retrieval models for question and answer archives. In: Proceedings of the 31st Annual International ACM SIGIR Conference on Research and Development in Information Retrieval, pp. 475–482 (2008)
17. Becker, T.: Practical Template-Based Natural Language Generation with TAG. In: Proceedings of the Sixth International Workshop on Tree Adjoining Grammar and Related Frameworks (TAG+6), pp. 101–104 (2002)
18. Jiang, R.D., Tan, Y.K., Limbu, D.K., Li, H.: Component pluggable dialogue framework and its application to social robots. In: Proc. Int'l Workshop on Spoken Language Dialog Systems (2012)
19. ISO/IEC 9126 quality standard model,
http://www.iso.org/iso/iso_catalogue/catalogue_tc/catalogue_detail.htm?csnumber=39752

mSWB: Towards a Mobile Semantic Web Browser

Tamás Matuszka[1,2], Gergő Gombos[1], and Attila Kiss[1]

[1] Eötvös Loránd University, Budapest, Hungary
{tomintt,ggombos,kiss}@inf.elte.hu
[2] Inter-University Centre for Telecommunications and Informatics, Debrecen, Hungary

Abstract. An enormous amount of information stored in semantic format has become available nowadays. In order to browse this huge data, the development of different browsers has become necessary. Today, many browsers available, but these are typically desktop applications. Vast knowledge bases have been created by means of linking the different public datasets. The efficient query of these data is a difficult problem. The currently available browsers typically do not allow browsing over the federated datasets, generally displaying only the information of a specified dataset. In this paper a mobile semantic web information system is presented, which allows smartphones to browse federated semantic datasets. In addition, the details of data integrator middleware and the Android-based client and the evaluation are described.

Keywords: Mobile Semantic Web, Linked Open Data, Semantic Browser, Mobile Software System.

1 Introduction

The vision of Semantic Web comes from Tim Berners-Lee. One of the main objectives of Semantic Web is that vast information available on the Web can be recognized by computers, so it will be comprehensible to computers. Nowadays, the vast majority of information available on Internet is unstructured, found in text format (PDF, Word, etc.). This solution is suitable for humans because it is well readable, but this makes the automated processing difficult. Semantic Web is intended that this knowledge will be machine-processable. The Semantic Web has two basic ideas: the first one is the metadata assignment of resources and the second one is the inference to the content of documents based on these metadata [2]. Semantic Web is based on different technologies. The Resource Description Framework (RDF) is responsible for describing the resources [10]. RDF uses a simple conceptual description of the information: our knowledge is represented as statements in the form of subject-predicate-object (or entity-attribute-value). These expressions are known as triples in RDF terminology. This way our data can be seen as a directed graph, where a statement is an edge labeled with the predicate, pointing from the subjects node to the objects node. SPARQL [14] is an RDF query language that is able to retrieve and manipulate data stored in RDF format. It is similar to SQL query language. SPARQL formulates the queries as

I. Awan et al. (Eds.): MobiWis 2014, LNCS 8640, pp. 165–175, 2014.

graph patterns, thus the query results can be calculated by matching the pattern against the data graph. Ontologies can be used to describe the hierarchy of complex conceptual systems, and to carry out knowledge inference. It defines the concepts and the relations, rules and restrictions among them.

Nowadays, there are numerous databases which contain theoretical and experimental results of various scientific experiments in the field of computer science, biology, chemistry, etc. in semantically represented format. There is quite a complex collection of these kinds of data maintained by the Linked Data Community. The essence of Linked Data shortly is to interconnect different data sources on the Web using links. Thus, additional facts can be found by using inferences and a deeper knowledge base can be obtained than before. According to the Linked Data principles, the data should be represented by URIs, which are deferenceable (by means of HTTP URIs). These URIs contain useful information (typically in RDF format). In addition, other URIs are also included in the information that allows to explore the information between the datasets [5]. In order to browse semantically represented datasets, specific applications had to be developed, called semantic browsers. Today, due to the enormous size of semantically represented data, several semantic browsers have been developed [1], [3], [6]. These browsers can be divided into two categories in terms of data display: the first one is the visual, and the second one is the text category. The text browsers typically provide table view and human-readable labels are used for displaying. In contrast, the visual browsers visualize the RDF graph and the relations among the data. Typically, with a few exceptions, these browsers are not native mobile applications. Due to the proliferation of smartphones, there is increasing demand towards the mobile Semantic Web.

In this paper a Linked Data-driven mobile semantic web browser is presented whose novelty is, contrary to current trends that enables the mobile browsing of Linked Data. The details of the middleware that is responsible for federated query executing and result providing through web services are described. In addition, the functions of Android-based client are showed. The system allows the users to browse over federated datasets. The client finds the list of resources for the desired keyword, and allows displaying, filtering the associated data. Furthermore, due to the interconnectivity, the total federated dataset will become browsable.

The rest of the paper is organized as follows. After the introductory Section 1, we present some applications that are similar to our system in Section 2. Thereafter, we outline the preliminary definitions in Section 3. Then, the details of our system are described in Section 4. Section 5 demonstrates the obtained results and the evaluation of the system. Finally, the conclusion and the future plans are described in Section 6.

2   Related Work

Berners-Lee et al. present an RDF browser and editor, namely Tabulator in [3]. Tabulator allows to traverse an open web of RDF resources. According to the authors, Tabulator is a user-friendly browser, which enables navigation through RDF links via a website or Firefox add-on. The browser provides different displaying of data: in addition to conventional tabular view, map view and time-line view are also provided by Tabulator.

Bizer and Gau have implemented the Disco Hyperdata Browser which provides simple navigation through Semantic Web [6]. The browsers renders all data belonging to the given resource on an HTML website. The resources may contain hyperlinks, with its help the browser can navigate among resources. The browser dynamically collects the data during the navigation among the resources by means of dereferencing of URIs.

Tummarello et al. describe the Sig.ma system in [17] which is a service and end user application at the same time. The Web of Data can be handled as an integrated information dataset by means of the Sig.ma. Large scale Semantic Web indexing, logic reasoning, data aggregation heuristics were used by the system in order to information enriching. The thus obtained data can be used as embeddable mashup, as machine processable service as well as data browsing service. The integrated information given by keyword-based search contains the name of data source. In addition, navigation among the resources is provided by Sig.ma.

According to Seeliger and Paulheim, the existing semantic browsers only display the facts without any logical grouping or use of the semantics. The main idea of our work is to organize the semantically-related facts into groups. For example, in case of a company, there are facts about the company structure (departments, president, etc.), the product (name, description), the services, the employees, and so on. This logically grouping works automatically. The similarity was measured by WordNet [12]. Afterwards, the weighted facts were clustered into groups. The name of thus obtained groups were named after the common WordNet ancestor. If it is not possible, the name of the most common used fact was used as the name of the group [15].

Micsik et al. show the LODMilla semantic browser in [11] which is able to navigate through arbitrary data sources. The application is based on the visualization of RDF graph and the relation among the semantically represented data. LODMilla's visualization is rendered on HTML website. The user is able to open new resources (a new node of graph will appear on the canvas), to search in open resources, to search for new resources, save/share/load the given session as a new URI. The implementation of undo-redo operations contribute to the web browsing experience as well.

DBpedia Mobile [1] is a location-sensitive semantic application, which enables its users to browse linked data on their mobile devices by navigating a map. The objects on the map are displayed using icons based on the YAGO categories [16]. By clicking on these icons, we can access DBpedia (which stores the knowldege of Wikipedia in semantically represented format) descriptions and Flickr[1] photos can be accessed for the selected object. The user can use filters for a search, and the results can be browsed using a detailed view, which displays

---

[1] https://www.flickr.com

information about the object using multiple data sources. DBpedia Mobile is an application designed exclusively for one particular data set, while our browser is general-purpose, and supports arbitrary data sets.

3   Preliminaries

As we mentioned in the introduction, the Semantic Web [2] provides various techniques to manage the data available on the Internet. This section gives insight into the basic concepts of Semantic Web that are necessary for under-standing what our system is capable of and how it works. The main technologies that are used in our system are the following: Resource Description Framework (RDF), RDF Schema (RDFS), SPARQL query language, Web Ontology Language (OWL). In the formal discussion we follow the concepts and notations intro-duced in [13].

The Resource Description Framework is a description language, where the information is represented by RDF triples. Informally an RDF triple consists of a subject, a predicate, and an object; or alternatively it consists of an entity, a property, and the value of that property of the described entity. This represen-tation form is similar to natural language sentences. For example the sentence *'Eötvös Loránd University is located in Budapest.'* can be translated into the triple *(Eötvös Loránd University, location, Budapest)*. Three kinds of terms are distin-guished: IRIs represent entities (e.g. *http://dbpedia.org/resource/ELTE*) or relations (e.g. *http://dbpedia.org/ontology/location*); literals can only occur as value of a prop-erty; blank nodes are the terms that do not represent real world entities, they just help to construct complex values, for example, mail addresses which consist of multiple parts such as postal code, city, street and number. Below is the formal definition of RDF triples (Definition 1).

Definition 1. *Let I, B, and L (IRIs, Blank Nodes, Literals) be pairwise disjoint sets. An RDF triple is a $(v_1, v_2, v_3) \in (I \cup B) \times I \times (I \cup B \cup L)$, where v_1 is the subject, v_2 is the predicate and v_3 is the object. A finite set of RDF triples is called an RDF graph or RDF dataset.*

The RDF Schema is a data-modeling vocabulary built on the top of RDF for defining concepts, properties and constraints which are essential for organizing the knowledge represented by triples. The Web Ontology Language also enables us to define concept and property hierarchies, however, it is a computational logic-based language. Therefore logical constraints and rules can be expressed in order to verify the consistency of that knowledge or to make implicit knowledge explicit. The formal definition of an ontology is presented in Definition 2, based on [18].

Definition 2. *An ontology is a structure $O := (C, \leq_C, P, \sigma)$, where C and P are two disjoint sets. The elements of C and P are called* classes *and* properties, *respectively. A partial order $\leq_C$ on C is called class hierarchy and a function $\sigma: P \to C \times C$ is a signature of a property. For a property $p \in P$, its domain and its range can be defined in* *the following: $dom(p) := \pi_1(\sigma(p))$ and $range(p) := \pi_2(\sigma(p))$, where π is the projection operation. Let $c_1, c_2 \in C$ be two classes; if $c_1 \leq_C c_2$, then c_1 is a subclass of c_2 and c_2 is a superclass of c_1.*

SPARQL is a query language for retrieving and manipulating RDF data. It is an SQL-like declarative language; the queries are based on pattern matching, where the patterns are in the form of triples, though they can contain variables as well. Most of the keywords and their meanings are the same, such as *SE-LECT, WHERE, LIMIT*. However, there are some new keywords in SPARQL, for example, *OPTIONAL* means optional pattern matching, or *FILTER* that defines constraints for the variables. Definition 3 gives the abstract syntax of the filter conditions and Definition 4 presents the abstract syntax of the SPARQL expressions.

Definition 3. *Let V be the set of distinct variables over $(I \cup B \cup L)$. The variables are distinguished by a question mark. Let $?X, ?Y \in V$ be variables and $c, d \in (L \cup I)$ be a literal and an IRI constant, respectively. We define the filter conditions recursively as follows. The $?X = c$, $?X =?Y$, $c = d$, $bound(?X)$, $isIRI(?X)$, $isLiteral(?X)$, and $isBlank(?X)$ are atomic filter conditions. Thereafter, if R_1, R_2 are filter conditions, then $\neg R_1$, $R_1 \wedge R_2$ and $R_1 \vee R_2$ are filter conditions as well.*

Definition 4. *A SPARQL expression is built up recursively in the following way:*

1. *the triple $t \in (I \cup V) \times (I \cup V) \times (L \cup I \cup V)$ is a SPARQL expression,*
2. *if Q_1, Q_2 are SPARQL expressions, and R is a filter condition, then Q_1 FILTER R, Q_1 UNION Q_2, Q_1 OPT Q_2, and Q_1 AND Q_2 are SPARQL expressions as well.*

The discussion of formal semantics of SPARQL is out of the scope of this paper. Set and multiset semantics are described in [13].

4   System

The details of the implemented system is described in the next section. We discuss the data integrator and provider middleware and give a formal model using Abstract State Machine as well. In addition, the features of the client are also presented.

4.1   Formal Model for the Federated Middleware

Our mobile semantic browser is based on a federated middleware which can handle more endpoints at the same time. The federated system is described by ASM (Abstract State Machine) model. The ASMs represent a mathematically well-founded framework for system design and analysis [7]. It is introduced by Gurevich [9]. The ASM algebra is made up of universes, functions, and rules. The universes include the entities. The functions provide the link between the universes. The rules are transaction steps and they have condition to activate. The ASM has a ground model that is a base of the system functions, this model is presented in [8]. That model will be refined now. The model describes the expected requirements of the system.

4.2   Model for Semantic Browser Federated System

The ground model uses four universes (FEDERATED, QUERY, ENDPOINT, REQUEST and RESULT). The system (FEDERATED) receives a query (QUERY) and runs this query on the appropriate endpoints (ENDPOINT) by means of requests (REQUEST). The semantic browser must gather information about a particular URI. Therefore, the QUERY actually has a URI or STRING type in the refined model. The URI is a particular entity, whereas the STRING is a simple text (or keyword) for which we want URIs as a result. Since the universe of ground model has not changed, therefore, no need to change the function neither. In order to distinguish the type of queries (STRING or URI), the following two function have been defined: $isIRI : QUERY \rightarrow \{true, false\}$ and $isString : QUERY \rightarrow \{true, false\}$. These functions are needed in order to send the queries to the appropriate endpoint. If the query is an URI, then it requires a SPARQL endpoint, while, if it is a string, the request is directed to the faceted search (provided by DBpedia server). In addition, we need to know whether the endpoints are able to answer the request or not. In order to answer this question, the following functions are defined: $canIRI : ENDPOINT \rightarrow \{true, false\}$ and $canString : ENDPOINT \rightarrow \{true, false\}$. The before mentioned properties have been set to each endpoint in the initial step.

The rules will change because the refined system will run the queries that are specifically required for the semantic browser. Four rules were defined in the ground model. The first rule formulates the QUERY request in the federated system. If the system is waiting for a query, then it will receive it. The second rule makes REQUEST based on the QUERY and sends it to the ENDPOINT-s. In the refined system, the sending of the request to the appropriate endpoint depends on the type of the request. If the type of request is STRING, then this request will be sent only to those endpoints which are able to process it. Consequently, the URI requests also will be sent only to the appropriate endpoints. Therefore, the rule is changed to:

```
if  fstate(f) = start_req && fworkingOn(f) = q  then
    do  forall  e ∈ ENDPOINT
            if  isIRI(q)&&canIRI(e)||isString(q)&&canString(e)
                if  estate(e) = waiting  then
                    EXTEND REQUEST by req with
                        reqQuery(req) := q
                        eworkingOn(e) := req
                        estate(e) := running
                        rres(req) := undef
                    endextend
                endif
            endif
            fstate(f) = running
    enddo
endif
```

The third rule of ground model formulates the occurring of the events. In an endpoint occurs either a *timeout* or a *finish* event which fits in the refined model as well. This rule takes the given result to the QUERY's result in case of the occurring the event. The last rule describes the final state of the system. When each endpoint has completed running due to some event, the system will be resetting. This rule also does not need to change in the refined system.

4.3   Implemented Middleware

The middleware provides a web service that is accessible via REST API. The Jena[2] framework was used for running semantic queries by the middleware. If the system receives a keyword-based request for URI, then it will be sent to faceted search (for example, http://dbpedia.org/fct), and the result will be a list of the corresponding URIs. In other case, when the system receives a URI, then it will produce a simple SPARQL query which returns with the corresponding properties and objects. The middleware runs the queries in parallel on the different endpoints, thereby increasing the efficiency of availability. Since some endpoints might be overloaded or just not available, the response time may increase. For this reason, it was necessary to apply a time limit that is four second currently. This is the time that is not too much, the system will not be slow; and not too short, the endpoints could response within this time limit in a normal case. The given, distinct result is converted and sent to the client by the middleware. The prefixes was extracted from the result and sent to the client during the conversion. The URIs was shortened by prefixes as well. This method helps to decrease the size of the transmitted data.

4.4   Client

The functions of the client application will be discussed in the next section. As we mentioned before, the middleware provides the data via web services and the client is based on this data. The prototype of the client an Android-based application. The tests were made on a Samsung GT-I5500 smartphone which includes Android 2.2 operation system.

After the application started, the client offers a search box that allows the users to search for resources based on the keyword. Arbitrary keyword can be used during the browsing, this can be seen on Figure 1(a). The query response will be a list that includes resources corresponding to keyword provided by DBpedia. One or more resources can belong to one keyword, thus the user can select the correct one from this list, which is shown on Figure 1(b).

The next activity contains all properties and objects corresponding to the selected resource in a table view, this solution can be viewed on Figure 2(a). Since a huge amount of data can correspond to a resource, thus the displaying of this information happens in dynamic way. When the user has reached the bottom of the table, several new row will load into the table view automatically.

---

[2] https://jena.apache.org/

In order to enhance the user experience, the prefixed versions of the URIs will appear in the table instead of the full URIs. The resources may contain URIs that linki to images as well. In this case, the client application downloads the image automatically and displays the resized picture in the table view. The image can be seen in the original size in a new activity by clicking on its thumbnail.

 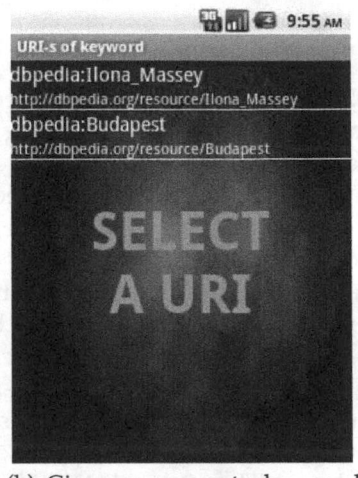

(a) Keyword-based search   (b) Given resources to keyword 'Budapest'

Fig. 1. Activities of client application

A resource may include properties that store geographical location as well. In that case, the client application automatically extracts the longitude and latitude coordinates corresponding to the given entities based on the *geo:lat* and *geo:long*

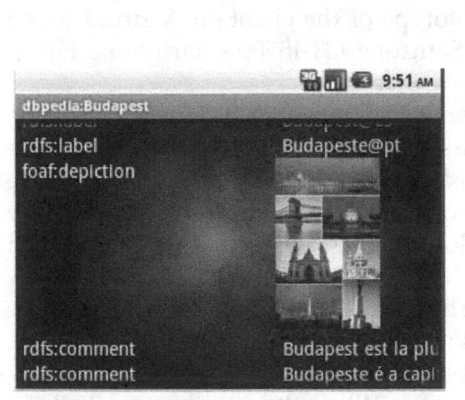 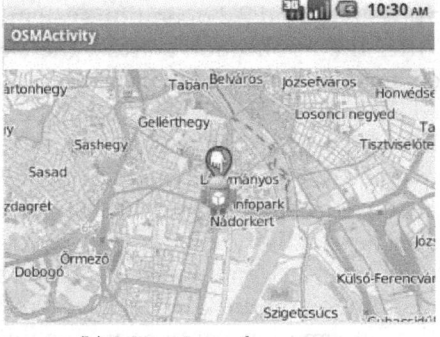

(a) Table view of a resource   (b) Map view of a resource

Fig. 2. Different views of a resource

properties. This resource can be displayed on a map view with the help of 'Show on map' function that is located in the local menu. This solution can be viewed on Figure 2(b). The user can navigate through all URI elements of the table view. In this way, our application allows the data discovery among the different data sources. Since a resource may contain numerous properties, it is possible that the user cannot find immediately the sought property. To avoid of this, we have implemented a new search box, where the user can filter the name of the corresponding properties. In addition, undo-redo functions were developed to provide the web browsing similar experience.

5   Results and Evaluation

The evaluation of system is based on three aspects. The first one is the number of properties corresponding to a given resource. We have examined the number of result obtained from DBpedia, and the federated query returned by our system. Thereafter, we made the run-time analysis, based on the sequential and parallel execution.

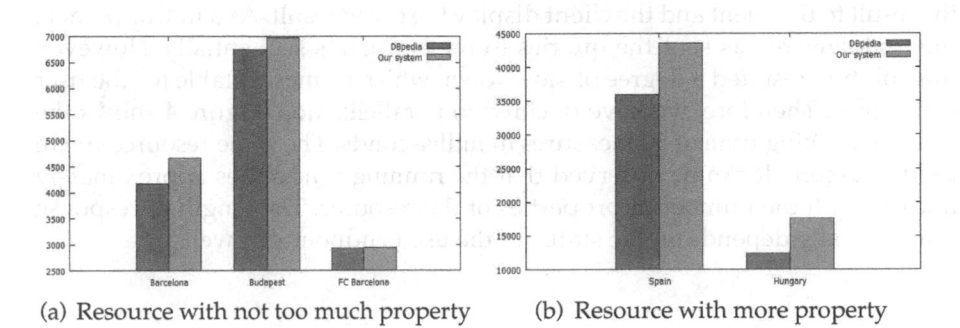

(a) Resource with not too much property   (b) Resource with more property

Fig. 3. Number of properties

The number of properties corresponding the given keywords can be seen on Figure 3. We wanted to know, how much more result are available after our federated query, as if we are used only the DBpedia. Nine different data sources were used besides DBpedia. However, the number of data sources can be expanded easily. Figure 3(a) shows the results in that case, when the number of belonging properties are not too much. It can be observed that there is significant difference between the number of DBpedia results and our system's result. Figure 3(b) depicts the case, when the resource has a large amount of properties. Here can be observed more significant difference between the number of the properties. On the basis of the two figures we concluded that there is an increase in the number of properties belonging to a resource. Nevertheless, most of the data comes from the DBpedia.

Thereafter, we measured the running time of the system. In this case, the running time is the elapsed time between the middleware received a URI, sends

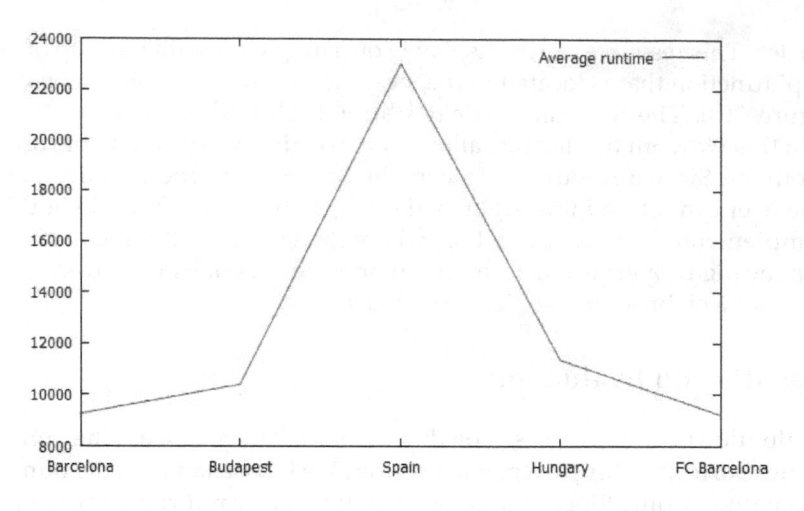

Fig. 4. Average runtime

the result to the client and the client display the given result. As a first approach, the middleware has sent the queries to the endpoints sequentially. However, this solution resulted a degree of slowdown, which is unacceptable for the user experience. Therefore, we have decided to parallelization. Figure 4 shows the average running time of 50 measures in milliseconds. The same resources were used as before. It can be observed that the running time scales approximately linearly with the number of properties of the resource. The length of response time typically depends on the status of the used endpoints as well.

6   Conclusion

In this paper, a Linked Data-driven mobile semantic browser was presented that is able to navigate through arbitrary data sources, in contrast to the most existing solutions, which use specific data sources. The formal model of the middleware was described. In addition, we have developed a prototype based on the formal model. The implemented middleware is responsible for running the federated query, integrating the resulted data after query and providing data to the client through REST web services. Furthermore, we described the client application, which has several features. For example, the user can navigate through the resources after keyword-based search by means of native Android application. The result of browsing can be viewed in a table view as well as map view.

In the future, we would like to organize the semantically related properties of a resource into groups. In this way, the user experience can be increased. We are intending to decrease the response time of the middleware as well. In order to validate the work we have carried out, a more in-depth investigation into measuring the performance of the middleware is needed.

Acknowledgments. This work was partially supported by the European Union and the European Social Fund through project FuturICT.hu (grant no.: TAMOP-4.2.2.C-11/1/KONV-2012-0013) and TAMOP-4.2.2.C-11/1/KONV-2012-0001 supported by the European Union, co-financed by the European Social Fund.

References

1. Becker, C., Bizer, C.: DBpedia Mobile: A Location-Enabled Linked Data Browser. In: 1st Workshop about Linked Data on the Web (2008)
2. Berners-Lee, T., Hendler, J., Lassila, O.: The semantic web. Scientific American 284(5), 28–37 (2001)
3. Berners-Lee, T., Chen, Y., Chilton, L., Connolly, D., Dhanaraj, R., Hollenbach, J., Lerer, A., Sheets, D.: Tabulator: Exploring and analyzing linked data on the semantic web. In: Proceedings of the 3rd International Semantic Web User Interaction Workshop (2006)
4. Bizer, C., Lehmann, J., Kobilarov, G., Auer, S., Becker, C., Cyganiak, R., Hellmann, S.: DBpedia-A crystallization point for the Web of Data. Web Semantics: Science, Services and Agents on the World Wide Web 7(3), 154–165 (2009)
5. Bizer, C., Heath, T., Berners-Lee, T.: Linked data-the story so far. International Journal on Semantic Web and Information Systems 5(3), 1–22 (2009)
6. Bizer, C., Gau, T.: Disco-hyperdata browser (2008)
7. Börger, E.: High level system design and analysis using abstract state machines. In: Hutter, D., Traverso, P. (eds.) FM-Trends 1998. LNCS, vol. 1641, pp. 1–43. Springer, Heidelberg (1999)
8. Gombos, G., Kiss, A.: SPARQL query writing with recommendations based on datasets. In: Yamamoto, S. (ed.) HCI 2014, Part I. LNCS, vol. 8521, pp. 310–319. Springer, Heidelberg (2014)
9. Gurevich, Y.: Evolving algebras: An attempt to discover semantics. Current Trends in Theoretical Computer Science, pp. 266–292 (1993)
10. Lassila, O., Swick, R.R.: Resource Description Framework (RDF) Schema Specification, http://www.w3.org/TR/rdf-schema
11. Micsik, A., Tóth, Z., Turbucz, S.: LODmilla: shared visualization of Linked Open Data. In: Bolikowski, Ł., Casarosa, V., Goodale, P., Houssos, N., Manghi, P., Schirrwagen, J. (eds.) TPDL 2013. CCIS, vol. 416, pp. 89–100. Springer, Heidelberg (2014)
12. Miller, G.A.: WordNet: a lexical database for English. Communications of the ACM 38(11), 39–41 (1995)
13. Pérez, J., Arenas, M., Gutierrez, C.: Semantics and Complexity of SPARQL. In: Cruz, I., Decker, S., Allemang, D., Preist, C., Schwabe, D., Mika, P., Uschold, M., Aroyo, L.M. (eds.) ISWC 2006. LNCS, vol. 4273, pp. 30–43. Springer, Heidelberg (2006)
14. Prud'hommeaux, E., Seaborne, A.: SPARQL Query Language for RDF, http://www.w3.org/TR/rdf-sparql-query/
15. Seeliger, A., Paulheim, H.: A Semantic Browser for Linked Open Data. In: Proc. International Semantic Web Conference ISWC (2012)
16. Suchanek, F.M., Kasneci, G., Weikum, G.: Yago: a core of semantic knowledge. In: Proceedings of the 16th International Conference on World Wide Web, pp. 697–706. ACM (2007)
17. Tummarello, G., Cyganiak, R., Catasta, M., Danielczyk, S., Delbru, R., Decker, S.: Sigma: Live views on the Web of Data. Web Semantics: Science, Services and Agents on the World Wide Web 8(4), 355–364 (2010)
18. Volz, R., Kleb, J., Mueller, W.: Towards Ontology-based Disambiguation of Geographical Identifiers. In: I3 (2007)

Extending the Interaction Flow Modeling Language (IFML) for Model Driven Development of Mobile Applications Front End

Marco Brambilla[1], Andrea Mauri[1], and Eric Umuhoza[1,2]

[1] Politecnico di Milano. Dipartimento di Elettronica, Informazione e Bioingegneria
Piazza L. Da Vinci 32. I-20133 Milan, Italy
{marco.brambilla,andrea.mauri,eric.umuhoza}@polimi.it
[2] AtlanMod team, Ecole des Mines de Nantes
4, rue Alfred Kastler 44307 Nantes Cedex 3, France
eric.umuhoza@mines-nantes.fr

Abstract. Front-end design of mobile applications is a complex and multidisciplinary task, where many perspectives intersect and the user experience must be perfectly tailored to the application objectives. However, development of mobile user interactions is still largely a manual task, which yields to high risks of errors, inconsistencies and inefficiencies. In this paper we propose a model-driven approach to mobile application development based on the IFML standard. We propose an extension of the Interaction Flow Modeling Language tailored to mobile applications and we describe our implementation experience that comprises the development of automatic code generators for cross-platform mobile applications based on HTML5, CSS and JavaScript optimized for the Apache Cordova framework. We show the approach at work on a popular mobile application, we report on the application of the approach on an industrial application development project and we provide a productivity comparison with traditional approaches.

1 Introduction

Front-end design is a complex and multidisciplinary task, where many perspectives intersect. Front-end becomes even more crucial in mobile applications, where the user experience must be perfectly tailored to the application objectives. However, development of mobile user interactions is still largely a manual task, which yields to high risks of errors, inconsistencies and inefficiencies. Several researches have applied model-driven techniques to the specification of software application interfaces and user interaction in broad sense. Among them, we can cite the ones focusing on Web interfaces (W2000 (HDM) [2], OO-HDM [16], WebDSL [7], OOH-Method [8], WebML [5], RUX-Model [11] and HERA [20]). Furthermore some approaches apply model driven techniques for multi-device UI modeling such as IFML [4], TERESA [3], MARIA [14], MBUE [13], UsiXML [19] and UCP [15].

I. Awan et al. (Eds.): MobiWis 2014, LNCS 8640, pp. 176–191, 2014.

However, none of them specifically address the needs of mobile applications development. Therefore, in mobile applications, front-end development continues to be a costly and inefficient process, where manual coding is the predominant development approach, reuse of design artifacts is low, and cross-platform portability remains difficult. The availability of a platform-independent user interaction modeling language can bring several benefits to the development process of mobile application front-ends, as it improves the development process, by fostering the separation of concerns in the user interaction design, thus granting the maximum efficiency to all the different developer roles; it enables the communication of interface and interaction design to non-technical stakeholders, permitting early validation of requirements.

In this paper we propose a model-driven approach to mobile application development based on the OMG standard language called Interaction Flow Modeling Language (IFML). We propose an extension of the IFML modeling language tailored to mobile applications and we describe our implementation experience that comprises the development of automatic code generators for cross-platform mobile applications based on HTML5, CSS and JavaScript optimized for the Apache Cordova framework. We show the approach at work on a running example based on a popular existing application, and we report on one of our experiences in developing industrial mobile applications,with a short summary on the productivity comparison with traditional approaches.

The paper is organized as follows: Section 2 reviews the related work; Section 3 summarizes the core features of the IFML language; Section 4 presents our extensions to IFML tailored to mobile application development; Section 5 shows a running example; Section 6 describes our implementation and our industrial experience (including a comparison to traditional approaches); and Section 7 concludes.

2   Related Work

This work is related to a large corpus of researches that address conceptual modeling of software applications. Among the ones mainly focusing on the Web we can cite: (i) The Web Modelling Language (WebML) [5], defined as a conceptual model for data-intensive Web applications and conceived as a high level, implementation-independent conceptual model accompanied by the associated design environment, called WebRatio [1]; (ii) W2000 (formerly HDM) [2] which introduced a notion of model-based design, clearly separating the activities of authoring in-the-large (hypertext schema design) and authoring in-the-small (page and content production); (iii) OO-HDM [17], a UML-based approach for modeling and implementing Web application interfaces; (iv) Araneus [12], a modeling proposal for Web applications that allows one to represent the hypertext organization, with nested relations and inter-page links; (v) Web Application Extension for UML (WAE) [6], a UML extension for describing Web application interfaces and the client-server interactions; (vi) WebDSL [7], a domain-specific language consisting of a core language with constructs to define entities, pages

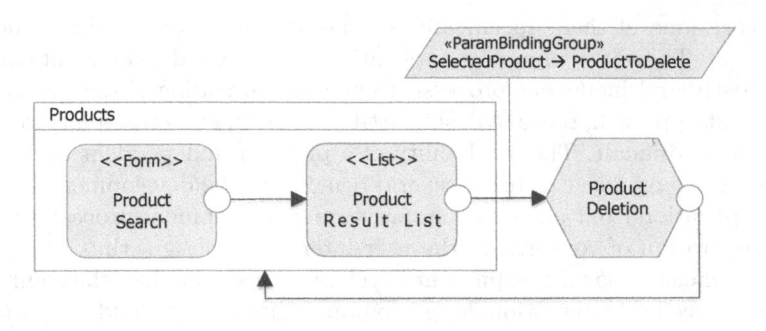

Fig. 1. IFML example: product search, listing and deletion

and business logic, plus extensions; (vii) OO-HMETHOD [8], based on UML interaction diagrams; (viii) Hera [20], a model-driven design approach and specification framework focusing on the development of context-dependent or personalized Web information system. More traditional methods for user interface design use state machines (in different flavours) as the underlying formalism, such as Jacob [9], Leung et al. [10] and StateWebCharts [21]. Other recent proposals in the Web Engineering field represent the RIA foundations (e.g., Urbieta [18]) by extending existing Web engineering approaches. Commercial vendors are proposing tools for Web and mobile development, such as IBM WorkLight, Mendix and Outsystems.

Some researches apply model based approaches for multi-device user interface development. Among them we can cite: (i) TERESA(Transformation Environment for inteRactivE Systems representations)[3], based on a so-called *One Model, Many Interfaces* approach to support model based GUI development for multiple devices from the same ConcurTaskTree (CTT) model; (ii) MARIA [14], another approach based on CTT; (iii) MBUE(Model Based Useware Engineering); (iv) UsiXML (USer Interface eXtended Markup Language) [19] and (v) Unified Communication Platform (UCP).

3   The Interaction Flow Modeling Language (IFML)

The Interaction Flow Modeling Language (IFML) supports the platform independent description of graphical user interfaces for applications accessed or deployed on such systems as desktop computers, laptop computers, PDAs, mobile phones, and tablets. An IFML model supports the following design perspectives: (1) The *view structure specification*, which consists of the definition of view containers, their nesting relationships, their visibility, and their reachability; (2) The *view content specification*, which consists of the definition of view components, i.e., content and data entry elements contained within view containers; (3) The *events specification*, which consists of the definition of events that may affect the state of the user interface. Events can be produced by the user's interaction, by the application, or by an external system; (4) The *event transition specification*, which consists of the definition of the effect of an event on the user interface;

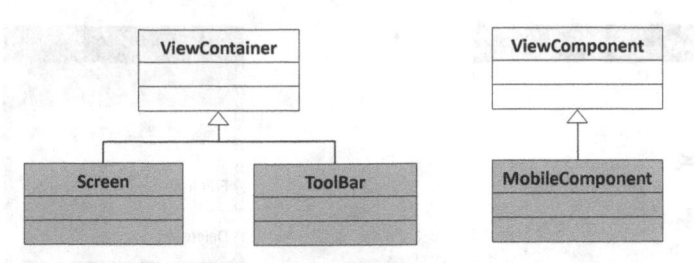

Fig. 2. IFML mobile extension: Screen,ToolBar and mobileComponent

(5) The *parameter binding specification*, which consists of the definition of the input-output dependencies between view components and between view components and actions; and (6) The reference to *actions* triggered by the user's events. The effect of an event is represented by an *interaction flow* connection, which connects the event to the view container or component affected by the event. The interaction flow expresses a change of state of the user interface: the occurrence of the event causes a transition of state that produces a change in the user interface.

Figure 1 shows a simple example of IFML model where the user can search for a product by entering some criteria in the Product Search Form. The matching items are shown in a list. The selection of one item causes a delete action to be triggered on it. When the deletion is completed, the updated list of products is displayed again.

IFML concepts can be stereotyped to describe more precise behaviours. For instance, one could define specific stereotypes for describing web pages (a specific kind of view container); forms, lists and details (specific kinds of view component); submission or selection events; and so on.

4   Extending IFML for Mobile Apps

Mobile applications have rich interfaces that resemble on a smaller scale those of full-fledged desktop applications, possibly with additional complexity of the interaction patterns, at the purpose of exploiting at best the limited space available. This aspect, together with mobility and availability of sensors, such as camera and GPS, introduce features that are best captured by providing mobile-specific extensions of a platform-independent modeling language like IFML.

The proposed extensions come from extensive modeling experience on mobile applications using the IFML standard, which covered both modeling of several existing mobile applications (including *CamScanner*, *Instagram*, *iPhone Gallery*, *Twitter*, *RedLaser* and many others) and design and implementation of new mobile applications for industrial customers (as reported in Section 6).

The IFML standard as described in Section 3 does not cover the mobile-specific aspects. In the next paragraphs, we describe the IFML extensions allowing the modeling of mobile application. Those extensions will address both the

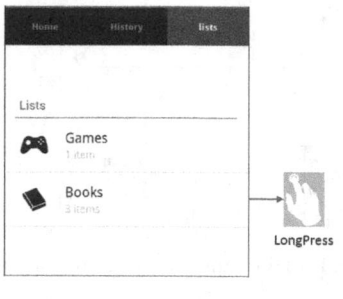 

Fig. 3. IFML mobile extension: Example of the *LongPress* event

components of the user interface and the events. In our experiments, we identified three categories of mobile events: (i) events generated by the interaction of the user such as *tap and hold, swipe,* etc.; (ii) events triggered by the mobile device features such as sensors, battery, etc.; and (iii) finally events triggered by user actions related to the device components such as taking a photo, recording a video or using the microphone.

4.1   IFML Mobile Extension: Containers and Components

In this section we describe the concepts added in order to model the components that characterized the mobile context (as shown in Figure 2). A new class called *Screen* has been defined to represent the screen of a mobile application. Since the screen is the main container of a mobile application, it extends the core class *ViewContainer* of the IFML standard. The class *ToolBar* represents a particular subcontainer of the screen. It may contain other containers and may have on its boundary a list of events. It extends the core class *ViewContainer* of IFML standard.

A characteristic trait of mobile interfaces is the utilization of predefined View-Containers devoted to specific functionalities(including *Notifications* area and *Settings* panel). These system level containers provide economy of space and enforce a consistent usage of common features. The *MobileSystem* stereotype has been defined to distinguish these special ViewContainers. A ViewContainer stereotyped as *MobileSystem* denotes a fixed region of the interface, managed by mobile operating system or by another interface framework in a cross-application way. The class *MobileComponent* denotes the particular mobile view component such as buttons, images, icons etc. A MobileComponent is subject to user events,described next. The *MobileSystem* stereotype can be applied also to View-Components to highlight that the interface uses the components built-in in the system(as shown in Figure 7).

4.2   IFML Mobile Extension: MobileContext

The Context assumes a particular relevance in mobile applications, which must exploit all the available information to deliver the most efficient interface. There-

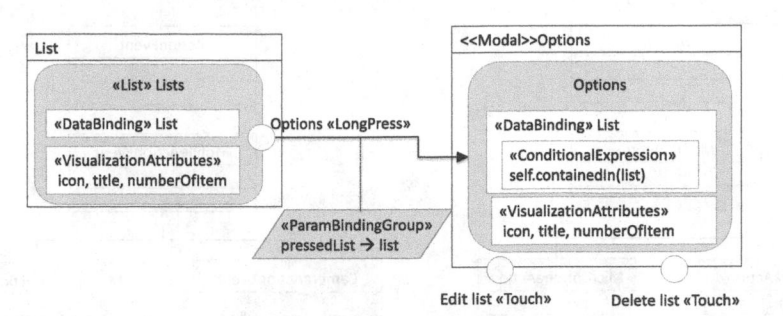

Fig. 4. IFML Mobile extension: Example of *LongPress* event used to display options of a pressed list

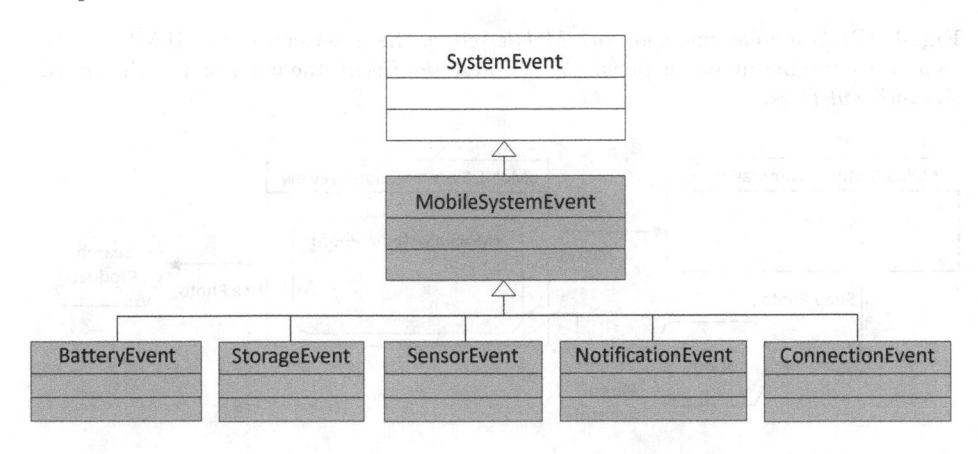

Fig. 5. IFML mobile extension: Mobile system events

fore, the context must gather all the dimensions that characterize the user's intent, the capacity of the access device and of the communication network, and the environment surrounding the user. A new class *MobileContext* extending the *Context* has been defined to express the mobile contextual features.

4.3   IFML Mobile Extension: Events

In this section we describe the new event types that are defined within IFML for the mobile context. First, a new class *MobileUserEvent* allowing the modeling of the mobile user events have been defined. *MobileUserEvent* extends the core class *ViewElementEvent* of the IFML standard. The following classes extend MobileUserEvent for modeling the specific mobile user events: *DragDrop*; *DoubleTap*; *Swipe*; *Pinch*; *Spread*; *Touch*; *LongPress*; *Scroll*; and *Shake*. Each class represents an event related to the gesture which triggers it.

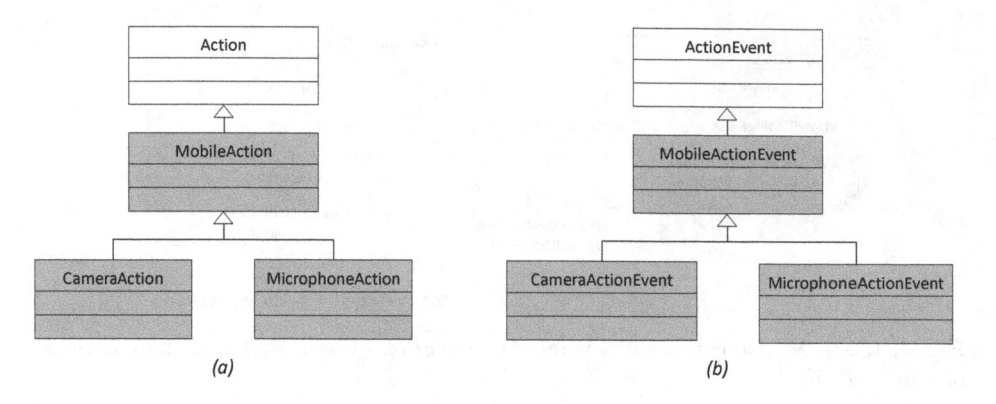

Fig. 6. IFML mobile extension:*(a)* *MobileAction*, the extension of the IFML *Action* to address specific mobile actions. *(b)* *MobileActionEvent*, the extension of the IFML *ActionEvent* class.

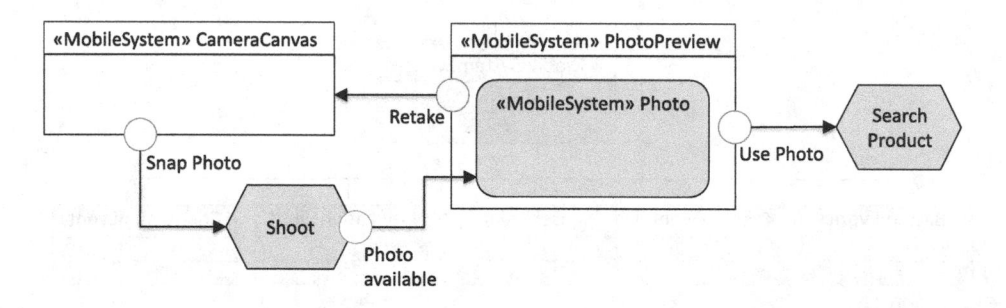

Fig. 7. IFML Mobile extension: Example of usage of MobileAction(*Shoot*), MobileActionEvent(*Photo available*) and *MobileSystem* streotype

The screens in Figure 3 show an example of the usage of the *LongPress* gesture allowing the user to manage the selected list. Figure 4 shows a fragment of IFML model for lists management. When a user performs the *LongPress* gesture on one element of the list a pop up containing information of the selected element is shown allowing her to edit or delete the list.

A new class *MobileSystemEvent* extending *SystemEvent* has been defined to express the mobile system events. The following classes extend *MobileSystemEvent* for specific system events.

- *BatteryEvent*,describing the events related to the state of the battery.
- *StorageEvent*,describing the events related to the archiving capacity.
- *NotificationEvent*,grouping the events related to the generic notifications handled by the operating system.
- *ConnectionEvent*,describing the events related to the connection state of the device.

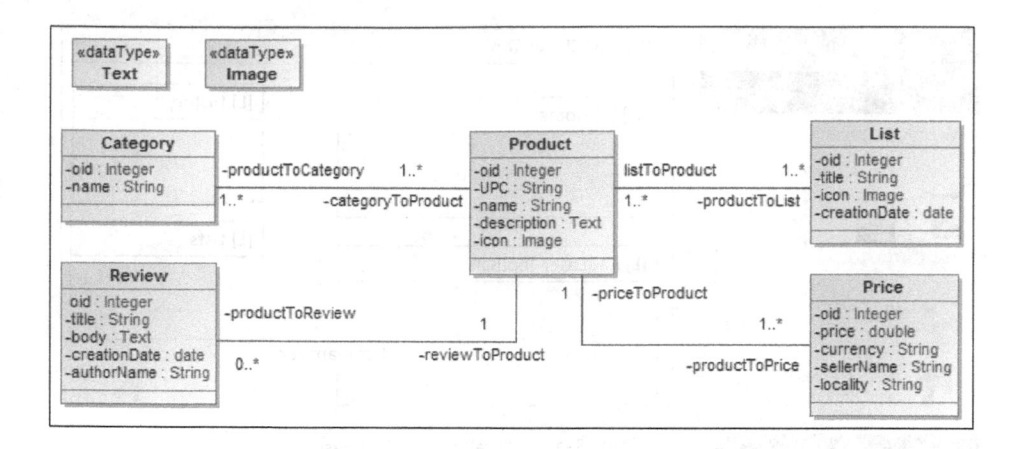

Fig. 8. Domain model of the RedLaser mobile app

– *SensorEvent*, defining events related to the sensors of the device. The *SensorEvent* extends ExternalEvent IFML core class. The most commonly used sensors are proximity sensor, motion sensor, magnetometer sensor,Gyroscope and position sensor. The classes *PositionEvent, MotionEvent, AccelerationEvent, ProximityEvent* and *RotationEvent* extend the *SensorEvent* to represent the events related to the specific sensors.

MobileActionEvent class has been defined to model the events triggered by a mobile action. Among mobile actions, we have actions related to the photo camera such as the *Shoot* action and actions related to microphone as reported in Figure 6. Figure 7 shows example of such events. A user takes a photo with the device's photo camera and the application displays the product corresponding to the taken photo if any. Once the photo is available, a screen asking the user if he wants to use or retake the photo is displayed. The *photo available* event is associated to the action *shoot.*

5   Case Study: The RedLaser Example

To demonstrate the applicability and the expressive power of the proposed extensions, this section exemplifies their use by modeling some of the functions of RedLaser[1], a shopping app available for iPhone, Windows Phone and Android. Figure 8 shows the data model of the RedLaser application. In RedLaser the *products* are organized in *categories*. Each product has one or more *prices*. A user can create a *list* of the products he likes. The application allows the user to *review* a product.

---

[1] http://redlaser.com/

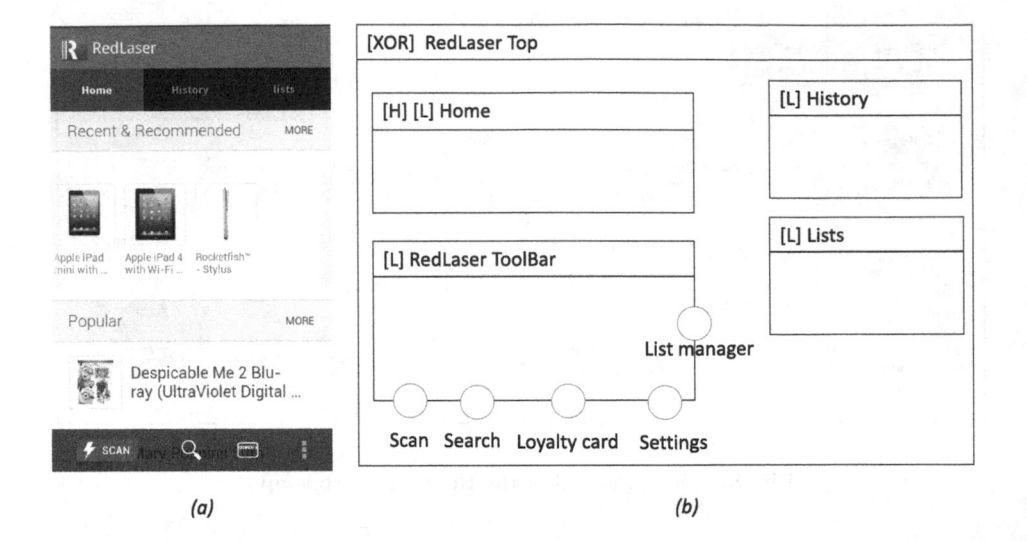

Fig. 9. Case study: *(a)* the home screen of RedLaser application; *(b)*IFML model showing logical organization of RedLaser application

The RedLaser user interface consists of a top level container, which is logically divided into three alternative sub containers one containing the recent and popular products, the second one containing the history of the application and the last one allowing the user to save its favorites(as shown in Figure 9).

The IFML model of the top screen comprises the *ToolBar* of the app and three screens in alternative. (1) *Home*. Is the default screen accessed when the user starts the app; (2) *History*. It contains the log of the application; and (3) *Lists*. It allows the user to save its favorite products.

Product searching. The app allows the user to search a product in four different ways:(1) keyword search; (2) Photo based searching. The input of the searching system is a picture taken through the camera of the device; (3) Voice based searching; and (4) Barcode search.Figure 10 shows the screens allowing the searching of a product. Figure 11 shows a piece of IFML model for Keyword-Search and a voice based searching. The user can use the *product selection* event associated to each product on the lists of retrieved products to see its details as shown on the Figure 12.

Figure13 shows a piece of IFML model of the product overview. This model shows also the usage of the *swipe* user event to navigate among the sub screens of overview.

6   Implementation Experience

Besides the formal definition of the mobile extensions to the IFML language, our research included the implementation of a complete prototype model editor in

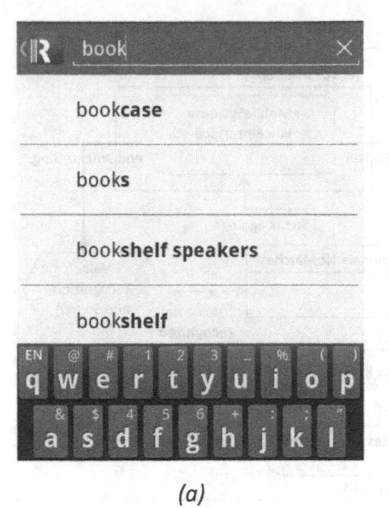
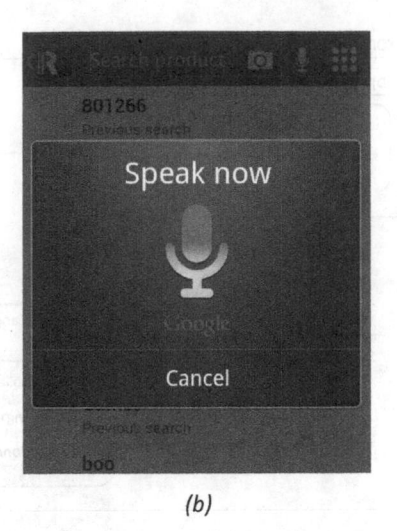

(a)   *(b)*

Fig. 10. Case study:UI for product searching. *(a)* Shows the user interface for *keyword based* search; *(b)* Shows the interface allowing the user to interact with the device's microphone in *voice based* search.

Eclipse, a code generator tailored to cross-platform mobile development, a few exemplary models built by reverse-engineering existing mobile applications, and some industrial developments for actual customers.

6.1 Modeling Tool

A snapshot of the modeling interface is shown in Figure 15. The tool has been implemented using the Obeo Sirius framework (http://www.eclipse.org/sirius/) and will be released as opensource Eclipse Project, and will benefit from the contribution of the community of MDE developers.

6.2 Code Generator

Regarding the mobile applications generation, our architecture is based on Apache Cordova (an open-source cross-platform framework for mobile development), specifically on the Adobe PhoneGap distribution. The idea is to generate HTML5, CSS3 and JavaScript code out of mobile-specific IFML models, wrap it in the Cordova container and then send the zip folder containing the whole code to the Build PhoneGap online platform in order to get the Android application file (apk) and the iOS application file (ipa). The architecture is shown in the figure 14. The mobile application generation is available at two levels: (i) starting only from the domain model (a ER diagram describing the data model underlying the app); or (ii) starting from the IFML model. So the generator analyses the input model of the application, serialized as an XML file (XMI) with all the information about the application data and interactionand produces all the

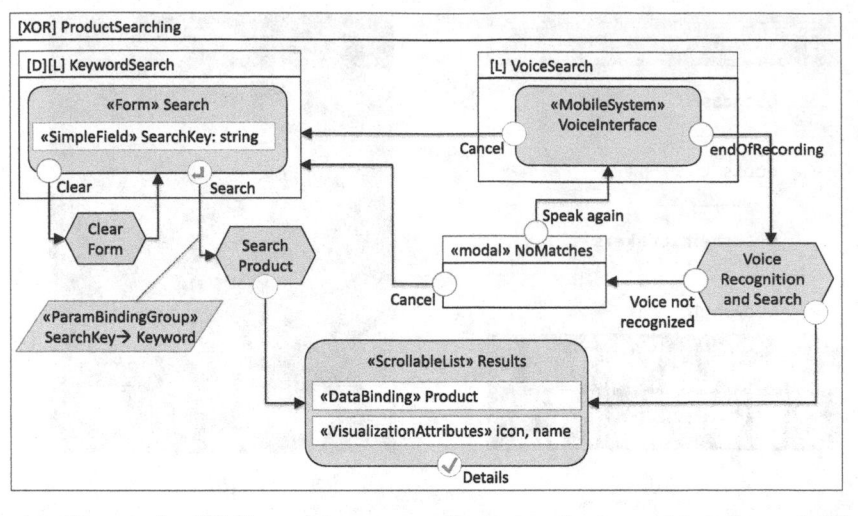

Fig. 11. Case study: IFML model corresponding to product searching shown in Figure 10. The model consists of input forms allowing the user to enter the keyword, Search Product actions and scrollable lists displaying the retrieved products.

JavaScript and html files needed to run the mobile application. Our attention has been focused on the client side, since the server side consists of a traditional REST service, for which code generators are already available within WebRatio starting from IFML diagrams. The look and feel of the generated applications is based on a basic CSS3 file, which includes general rules for mobile interaction patterns. Eventually, if needed, it is possible to add other custom generation rules. In order to implement our prototype we used Groovy (a scripting language consisting of a simplified Java syntax, eventually converted in actual Java) and ANT as generation engine. The ANT file provides all the required libraries for the generation, including Groovy and Dom4j for the model analysis and Jaxen, an open source XPath library. Moreover it provides some libraries required for the generated applications, like Backbone.js, Require.js, jQuery, Handlebars, Underscore.js and Spin.js. The ANT engine launches a main Groovy file, which in turn starts some Groovy templates in order to generate JavaScript and Html files.

Within this implementation work, we have also designed the metamodel of a few platforms (HTML 5, Java Swing, and the new Microsoft .Net WPF) and we have defined the mappings from the IFML abstract concepts to the platform-specific concepts of the three cases mentioned above.

6.3   Industrial Experience

The approach has been put at work on some industrial cases already. We report here on one of those cases, for which we also have some quantitative effort comparison with traditional development approaches. In the discussed scenario,

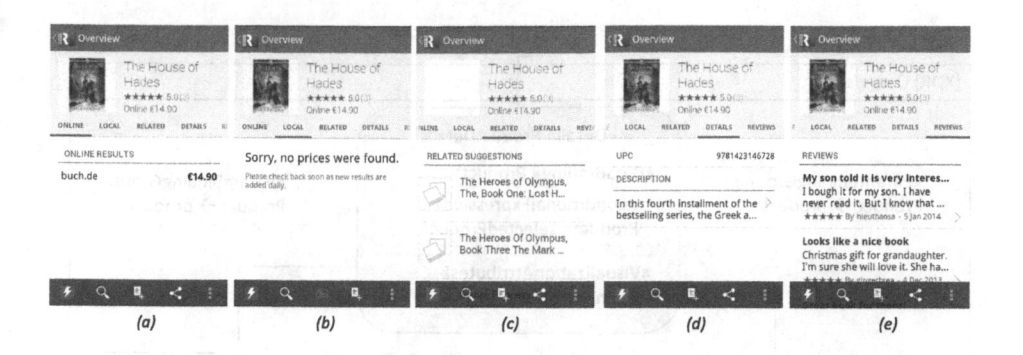

Fig. 12. *(a)*This screen shows the a list of the prices available *online* for the selected product. It is the default screen of *product overview*; *(b)*The *local* is accessed from the *online* and *related* screens by using *SwipeRight* and *SwipeLeft* gestures respectively; *(c)* Shows the list of other product *related* to the selected one. *(d)* Displays the details of the selected product; *(d)* Contains a list of *reviews* related to the selected product.

the customer is a wholesale distributor of products for mechanical work-shops and tire repairers, with tens of thousands of different products in stock, for the whole European market. Products span from tires, to bolts, to large mechanical appliances for workshops such as gantry cranes.

The customer requested a mobile application to be deployed on tablets and cell phones (but to be used mainly on tablets) for its field agents, i.e., salesman that are assigned some geographical areas and go to customers for selling the goods. Requirements included: the need of the app to run completely offline; the need of periodic or upon-request synchronization of the product catalog with the centralized copy of the data (including product information, photos, and technical sheets); dynamic calculation of prices based on the customer profile; and the possibility of defining custom versions of the catalog for specific types of customers.

The development of the application was performed by three teams of professional software developers, one focusing on the sever-side implementation of the REST services for managing the access to the centralized catalog data; one implementing the client-side of the mobile application manually; and one implementing it with our approach. Each team was composed by 2 developers, highly skilled for the respective technical needs. Both teams addressing the client side targeted cross-platform development through PhoneGap, with the same client-side architecture, JS libraries and functional and visual requirements.

The initial requirements specification implied 4 man-days of work (including discussions with the customer). The server-side development was performed using the Web Service modeling features of the WebRatio Platform. This resulted in a development effort of 9 man-days. On the client side, a common effort has been reported on the definition of the graphical styling of the app, which had to be extensively discussed and agreed upon with the customer. That part of the

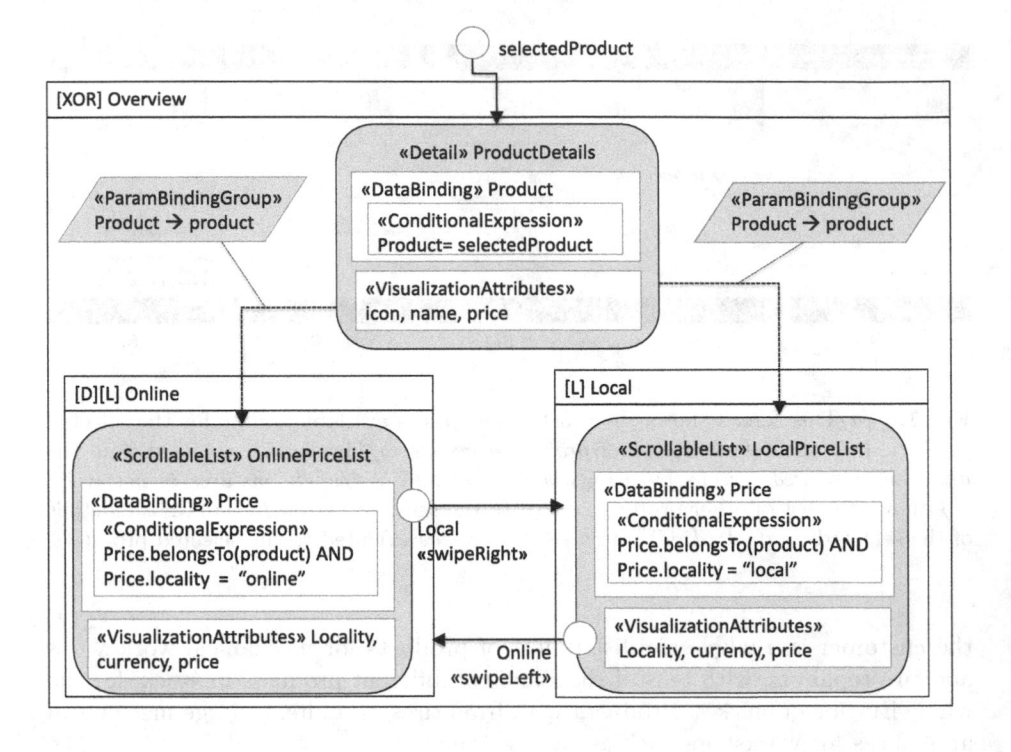

Fig. 13. Case study: IFML model corresponding to *Online* and *Local* tabs of product overview shown in figure 12. It consists of *ProductDetail* ViewComponent and two alternative lists of prices. The default one for online prices and the second displaying the local prices of the selected product.

work accounted for 5 man-days. Finally, the client-side software development efforts have been:

- **manual development: 21 man-days**, organized as: 2 man-days on graphical style implementation and application to the code, 12 man-days on app structure and user interaction development, 7 man-days on client-server interaction and push notification implementation;
- **model-driven development: 11 man days**, organized as: 1 man-day on graphical styling, 7 man-days on app structure design, and 3 man-days on client-server interaction design.

Furthermore, both client-side teams reported a testing period of 2 weeks. Thus, on the core mobile app development the model driven approach allowed to save 48% of the effort. Considering the total cost of analysis and development, this reduces the development cost of 21% overall.

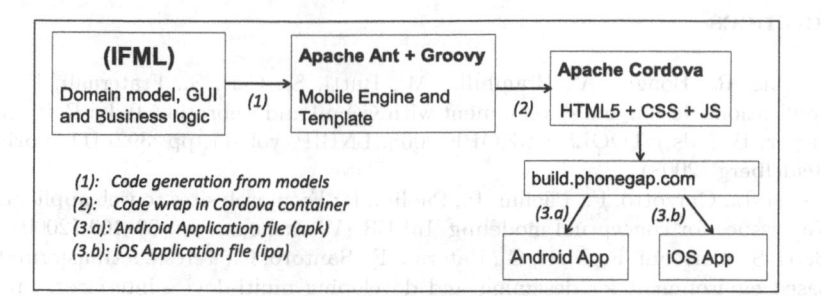

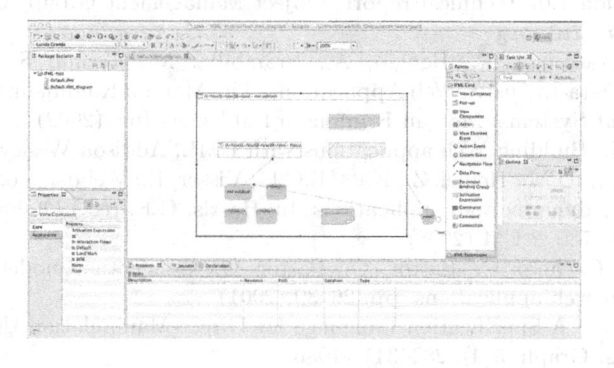

Fig. 14. Architecture for cross-platform mobile development followed in this research

Fig. 15. Snapshot of the opensource IFML modeling tool developed in this research

A thorough comparison hasn't been possible on the other industrial cases because of the high cost of manual development of the applications. However, productivity in the other cases has been at the same levels.

7 Conclusions

In this paper we presented a mobile extension of OMG's standard IFML (Interaction Flow Modeling Language) for mobile application development. Our modeling of exemplary existing apps shows that the language is expressive enough to cover all the typical development needs on mobile. Furthermore, industrial experiences gave positive feedback on the applicability, effectiveness and efficiency of the approach. Future works will cover the implementation of more refined code generators and the study of design patterns for model-driven mobile applications design.

Acknowledgement. This work was partially funded by the AutoMobile EU 7th FP SME Research project (http://automobile.webratio.com).

References

1. Acerbis, R., Bongio, A., Brambilla, M., Butti, S., Ceri, S., Fraternali, P.: Web applications design and development with webml and webratio 5.0. In: Paige, R.F., Meyer, B. (eds.) TOOLS EUROPE 2008. LNBIP, vol. 11, pp. 392–411. Springer, Heidelberg (2008)
2. Baresi, L., Garzotto, F., Paolini, P., Paolini, P.: From web sites to web applications: New issues for conceptual modeling. In: ER (Workshops), pp. 89–100 (2000)
3. Berti, S., Correani, F., Mori, G., Paternò, F., Santoro, C.: Teresa: a transformation-based environment for designing and developing multi-device interfaces. In: CHI Extended Abstracts, pp. 793–794 (2004)
4. Brambilla, M., Fraternali, P., et al.: The interaction flow modeling language (ifml), version 1.0. Technical report, Object Management Group (OMG) (2014), http://www.ifml.org
5. Ceri, S., Fraternali, P., Bongio, A., Brambilla, M., Comai, S., Matera, M.: Designing Data-Intensive Web Applications. The Morgan Kaufmann Series in Data Management Systems. Morgan Kaufmann Publishers Inc. (2002)
6. Conallen, J.: Building Web applications with UML. Addison Wesley (2002)
7. Groenewegen, D.M., Hemel, Z., Kats, L.C.L., Visser, E.: Webdsl: a domain-specific language for dynamic web applications. In: Harris, G.E. (ed.) OOPSLA Companion, pp. 779–780. ACM (2008)
8. Gómez, J., Cachero, C., Pastor, O., Pastor, O.: Conceptual modeling of device-independent web applications, pp. 26–39 (2001)
9. Jacob, R.J.K.: A Specification Language for Direct-Manipulation User Interfaces. ACM Trans. Graph. 5(4), 283–317 (1986)
10. Leung, K.R.P.H., Hui, L.C.K., Yiu, S.M., Tang, R.W.M.: Modeling Navigation by Statechart. In: Proc. COMPSAC 2000, pp. 41–47 (2000)
11. Linaje, M., Preciado, J.C., Sánchez-Figueroa, F.: A Method for Model Based Design of Rich Internet Application Interactive User Interfaces. In: Proceedings of International Conference on Web Engineering, Como, Italy, July 16-20, pp. 226–241 (2007)
12. Mecca, G., Merialdo, P., Atzeni, P., Crescenzi, V., Crescenzi, V.: The (short) araneus guide to web-site development. In: WebDB (Informal Proceedings), pp. 13–18 (1999)
13. Meixner, G., Seissler, M., Breiner, K.: Model-driven useware engineering. In: Hussmann, H., Meixner, G., Zuehlke, D. (eds.) Model-Driven Development of Advanced User Interfaces. SCI, vol. 340, pp. 1–26. Springer, Heidelberg (2011)
14. Paternò, F., Santoro, C., Spano, L.D.: Maria: A universal, declarative, multiple abstraction-level language for service-oriented applications in ubiquitous environments. ACM Trans. Comput.-Hum. Interact. 16(4) (2009)
15. Raneburger, D., Popp, R., Kavaldjian, S., Kaindl, H., Falb, J.: Optimized GUI generation for small screens. In: Hussmann, H., Meixner, G., Zuehlke, D. (eds.) Model-Driven Development of Advanced User Interfaces. SCI, vol. 340, pp. 107–122. Springer, Heidelberg (2011)
16. Schwabe, D., Rossi, G., Barbosa, S.D.J.: Systematic Hypermedia Application Design with OOHDM. In: Proc. Hypertext 1996, pp. 116–128 (1996)
17. Schwabe, D., Rossi, G., Rossi, G.: The object-oriented hypermedia design model, pp. 45–46 (1995)

18. Urbieta, M., Rossi, G., Ginzburg, J., Schwabe, D.: Designing the Interface of Rich Internet Applications. In: Proc. LA-WEB 2007, pp. 144–153 (2007)
19. Vanderdonckt, J.: A MDA-compliant environment for developing user interfaces of information systems. In: Pastor, Ó., Falcão e Cunha, J. (eds.) CAiSE 2005. LNCS, vol. 3520, pp. 16–31. Springer, Heidelberg (2005)
20. Vdovják, R., Frăsincar, F., Houben, G.-J., Barna, P.: Engineering Semantic Web Information Systems in Hera. Journal of Web Engineering 1(1-2), 3–26 (2003)
21. Winckler, M., Palanque, P.: StateWebCharts: A Formal Description Technique Dedicated to Navigation Modelling of Web Applications. In: Jorge, J.A., Jardim Nunes, N., Falcão e Cunha, J. (eds.) DSV-IS 2003. LNCS, vol. 2844, pp. 61–76. Springer, Heidelberg (2003)

Software Quality Testing Model for Mobile Application

Zhenyu Liu, Yun Hu, and Lizhi Cai

Shanghai Key Laboratory of Computer Software Testing and Evaluation
Shanghai Development Center of Computer Software Technology, Shanghai, China
{lzy,clz,huy}@ssc.stn.sh.cn

Abstract. With the rapid development of the network technology, intelligent device and mobile applications has been the developed fastly. The mobile device will increasingly widely used even replace the traditional computer, the application test for mobile Internet was put on the agenda. From this paper, the characteristics of mobile applications are analyzed. The paper proposed quality model and quality attributes corresponding to testing requirements for mobile applications under mobile Internet. Also relevant properties testing techniques and methods is given to pay attention during the test from different test view, which indicating that the quality of the final model could be effective for mobile applications.

1   Introduction

With the popularity of mobile Internet, smart devices and mobile applications has been the rapid development of mobile Internet community as a whole has become a hot topic of common concern. Mobile Internet communications and the Internet will combine into one community in recent years. Mobile communications and the Internet to become the world's fastest growing and largest potential market followed by mobile Internet applications are also colorful, entertainment, business and information services into a variety of applications to start people's lives. Based on the portability of a mobile device, mobile applications has feature: cross-platform, lightweight and Web-based. The mobile applications integrated voice, message, video, content type, personal information management, location-based services, e-commerce, games and the so on [1].

In the 1980s, people began to use the traditional PC computer. Nowadays, mobile devices will increasingly widely used replace the traditional PC and bring the information age into mobile platform. Mobile operating system, such as Android, iOS, and Windows Phone, will exceed and even replace Windows, Linux and other traditional desktop operation system. In the next years, the use of personal computer users will focus on the mobile device, while the application of traditional desktop operating system will be transferred to the operating system for more mobile devices. Currently smartphones holdings increased rapidly year by year, just like iPhone and Android already known. According to reports, Android is the second most popular mobile OS, surpassing BlackBerry and iPhone OS [2][3].

I. Awan et al. (Eds.): MobiWis 2014, LNCS 8640, pp. 192–204, 2014.
© Springer International Publishing Switzerland 2014

A variety of applications, games, entertainment and operating experience are more intelligent, smart phones can be consider to have been changing the way people life slowly. Future mobile phones will surely bring people into intelligent direction. So testing requirements is increasingly urgent.

During software testing for mobile applications, there are many problem faced especially. In the one hand, whether it is industry led by the independent development of the operating system or application software openly, competitive environment will result in the speed and quality and more inclined to speed. On the other hand, smart mobile devices and laptop computers are already become the world's most popular electronic products. The rapidly change of features and performance, involving payments, privacy and other applications have been conducted on the use of mobile phones. The life of people has been gradually transferred from the PC to the mobile device. However, the current research on testing technology of mobile software is relatively slow.

Currently, there are many research on the mobile device testing, but have not made the software test is based on the quality of the model from the perspective of the application. This paper described for the black-box testing mobile applications and analyzed various quality elements in test. According to the quality model, the elements of the mobile device proposed quality testing should be tested. And then some characters which gives is need to choose in the test design and test execute.

The rest of the paper is structured as follows. Section 2 discusses mobile test quality model and also makes comparison between traditional software and mobile applications. Section 3 introduces the test technology how test can be performed with the quality model. Section 4 discusses related work and Section 5 summarizes paper with further work.

2   Test Quality Model

The current development of the computer has been bring into the era of mobile Internet, smart phones, tablet PCs, including television have become a kind of the people's intelligence device. The social, navigation, payment and other applications in the mobile Internet era is increasingly prevalent.

Software testing in mobile Internet technology has also inherited the traditional method of communication networks and Internet software testing. At the same time, the mobile technology is not simple traditional software due to diverse devices and applications. More technical requirements are also considered in the mobile Internet.

Relative to the flourishing consumer market for enterprise-class user needs a lot of attention becomes deserted, not only in the upper layer application services in the operating system level of the mobile device but also in resource consumption. Therefore, it is necessary to give a complete quality assessment regardless of the kind of mobile devices, which is not only conducive to the development of mobile Internet applications, but will also further improve the mobile application testing techniques.

According to the characteristics of software features included in each of the features, test model and related test methods for each child characteristics are given.

2.1   Difference with Traditional Software

Mobile Internet applications and traditional applications still have a lot of different. The differences between these two types of software are:

- Software used in device: Traditional applications use primarily in front of a computer, and mobile applications are used anywhere with hand.
- Operation in software: Traditional primarily with the mouse, and mobile applications primarily through the fingers to complete the operation.

The mobile application software has one of the biggest feature is the user experience, which is placed unprecedented importance. For smart phones, tablet device and other mobile intelligent device. The whole operation of various actions behavior are to operate by hand touch, thus requiring the user experience will be much higher than conventional applications. Traditional desktop application software is mainly done simply by a mouse click button operation. But at the mobile application, the user experience will always be the first thing to be considered the hand operation compared to the mouse operation[4][5].

2.2   Problem in Mobile Software

The following limitations and problem faced by the mobile applications about the current mobile device testing:

- Test management level is not high. The software industry and other industries, which the need for advanced enterprise management skills will play out and support a number of test management tool to some extent. It is important that the guiding ideology of the kind of management is quite lacking from the view of the observation.
- Technical support is not enough. The current mobile Internet software testing technology development is relatively slow. Therefore, the safety testing, performance testing and compatibility tests have no more good solutions.
- Test engineers overall technical level is not enough. These three aspects are a direct result of the overall level of professional quality testing industry personnel is difficult to improve.

With the popularity of mobile Internet, mobile phones and other smart device are getting faster. The number of mobile users continues to rise with the rapid development of mobile applications. From the mobile applications, the development and test requirements of mobile applications are concerned the standards of quality based on software elements. Mobile device testing problems faced:

1. Three intelligent device platform differences

Combined with a variety of underlying middleware, middleware business, communication middleware support for applications in smart device operating system, applications can be divided into two types of local applications and web applications [6].

2. Mobile application testing complex factors

Traditional mobile testing methods are violent, crazy and very troublesome.

- Up to 1.02 billion global mobile web users.
- 74% of people will not tolerate more than 5s page load time.
- Gartner predicts that by 2014 over 90% of enterprise applications will support intelligent device[7].

2.3   Quality Model for Mobile Application

In this paper, the quality of the model is proposed from ISO/IEC 9126 from the perspective of the quality of the model [8]. Each model elements and sub-elements of design of mobile application testing should follow.

Function
Basic functional test is a software function. Functional quality characteristics are given. Two categories of mobile applications should be considered: stand-alone client, network support clients.

Table 1. Function

Character	Descrption	Applicable
Suitability	Ability of software products provides a set of functions suitable for the specified tasks and user objectives.	Yes
Accuracy	Software products provide the ability to correct or consistent with the desired result or effect accuracy.	Yes
Interoperability	Each data on different platforms differences, whether data can be shared across different platforms.	Yes
Security	Security capability on mobile intelligent device can be realized. It is possible to prevent security threats techniques.	Yes

Reliability
Reliability in the mobile device is actually software stability during operation. The mobile device and its performance, stability evaluation of the application will be important factors for widespread use. With the increasing number of users, the reliability is a dynamic quality character in quality model, which affected performance of server and network, also affecting the end user eventually. Reliability refers to the software product's ability to maintain the level of required performance when used under specified conditions. So whether the level of performance capability to maintain, mobile applications is need to pay more attention.

Table 2. Reliability

Character	Descrption	Applicable
Maturity	Software product to avoid failure caused by the ability of the software failure. Mobile applications to a variety of situations that may arise, the exception for evaluation. As for network anomalies, server downtime or appear to error information, such as 404,502 in the circumstances.	Yes
Fault tolerance	In the case of a failure, software or its specified fault violation occurs, the software product's ability to maintain the required level of performance.	Yes
Recoverability	In the case of failure occurs, the level of performance required software products rebuild and restore capabilities directly affected the data.	Yes

Usability

When used under specified conditions, the software product should to be understood, to learn, easy to use and the ability to attract users.

These features are obvious in the mobile application especially because the operations of mobile application are very user friendly. Many people are making the consideration for good ease of use. Ease of use of mobile devices to a large extent is the user function is convenient, fast main evaluation methods.

Ease of use can also be referred to as user experience. According to definition, user experience testing is test before the product delivered to the customer in a series of user-experience perspective, such as the friendly interface, smooth operation and the function meets the user requirements. Therefore, table 3 gives the user experience tests with following aspects.

Table 3. Usability

Character	Descrption	Applicable
Understandability	Software product enables users to understand how the software is suitable and the ability to be able to software for specific tasks and conditions of use . Easier to understand the elements in the user interface. In many situations: some aspects of functionality, reliability and ease of use also affect the efficiency.	Yes
Learnability	Function can be better used if provided ability of learning. Software products enables users to learn the how to use application properly.	Yes
Operability	Software product enables users to operate and control its ability to move the client adds new operations, such as multi-point operation, sliding operation, which do not included in legacy applications.	Yes

Table 3. (*continued*)

Attractiveness	Software product 's ability to attract users . Related to software designed to make itself more attractive for the user attributes, such as the use of color and graphical design feature. In fact, many download mobile applications are a lot of factors determined by the use of a stage, the user may uninstall or remove the application artificially, rather than reaching the end of the software life cycle.	Yes

Efficiency

The browser-based applications of different mobile device is client-side policy for local application, which is similar to the traditional Client / Server model.

Table 4. Efficiency

Character	Descrption	Applicable
Time	Under specified conditions, the software product to perform its functions, provide appropriate response and processing times and throughput capacity.	Yes
Resources utilization	CPU and memory resources are traditional resource evaluation methods in the mobile device	Yes

Maintainability

The software product may be modified capability. Modifications may include correcting, improving or software environment, requirements and functional specifications to adapt to change. Maintenance capability is available for each application to be considered. For the user level, maintainability is an inherent property. After maintenance existing user information will be changed and mode of operation are able to meet customer demand.

Table 5. Maintainability

Character	Descrption	Applicable
Analyzability	Software product defects or diagnostic software to identify the cause of failure or the ability to be modified.	Yes
Changeability	Software product ability to enable the ability to specify the changes can be implemented.	Yes
Stability	Software products ability to avoid defects caused due to a software modification.	Yes
Testability	Software products have been modified so that the ability of the software can be confirmed	No

Portability

On one hand, mobile applications consist of many data. In applications, there are similar or close functions. On the one hand, a lot of maintenance work provides new features in these applications.

Table 6. Portability

Character	Descrption	Applicable
Adaptability	Applicability of different language	Yes
Installability	Software products to be installed in the specified environment capabilities.	Yes
Coexistence	Software products in the public environment with other independent software and its ability to share common resources.	Yes
Replaceability	Multiple platforms. There is the two levels concept, one is portability within same platform, the other is portability between different platforms. For that applications cannot communicate across multiple platforms, the ability of eeplaceability meaning that the application can only be installed on iOS applications but also support the Android platform for same mobile applications	Yes

3   Test Method

These tests mentioned above are based on the different needs created. Each test has a different demand, in fact, the facing problem of mobile application test and web application test currently is similar with the rapid growth of mobile application. The traditional testing methods are not very suitable for these applications.

With the development of mobile applications, mobile devices can not only make voice calls, send messages, but also has the function of the Internet link, games and other classical application in traditional computer, such as office, reader and so on. At the same time, such as NFC, gravity sensor, GPS and other devices or components integrated in the mobile device, the mobile device is not merely a simple mobile telephone. The modern mobile phone has ability in communication, entertainment, do office work and other functions in one smart device.

Currently, in the field of mobile devices, the larger the market share of device operating system are Apple iOS, Google Android, HP WebOS, Microsoft Window Phone and BlackBerry QNX. The mobile device already has good processing ability, memory, storage media and the operating system is a complete mobile system.

- Operating system: from technical architecture perspective, operating system is different, the use of traditional software are currently based on the Windows platform. However, the operating system of mobile phone is not a single mainstream operating systems, such as mentioned Android, iOS , etc., even if the same

Android system, there are different versions of the operating system differences, such as Android 2.1 or Android 2.3

- Network: the traditional mobile applications may be concerned about the field of communication, such as the use of the network. There are rarely involved in traditional applications for the application is concerned. Compared to traditional software and UI interface, the distinction with network is large in mobile device.
- Software approach: In their software usage, traditional software using Client/Server or Brower/Server hybrid mode, there is a difference with mobile system using Client/Server mode.

3.1   Test Element Category

Generally, the mobile application is not suitable for use traditional idea for software testing. Mobile application device, from iOS to Android, has same test aspects from functional testing to non-functional test, such as security test and performance test.

Test types of mobile applications involving functional testing, performance testing, security testing, stability testing, usability testing, reliability testing, compatibility testing. Numerous mobile applications and their rapid response to market enhance user feelings, as well as the convenience of a mobile device used to test the quality and responsiveness of a higher demand.

Table 7. Mobile Test Category

Test element	Coverd character
Function	Suitability
	Accuracy
	Analyzability
	Changeability
Interface	Interoperability
Security	Security
Usability	Understandability
	Learnability
	Operability
	Attractiveness
Reability	Maturity
	Fault tolerance
	Recoverability
	Stability
Performance	Time
Resouce	Resources utilization
Compatibilty	Installability
	Adaptability
	Coexistence
	Replaceability

3.2   Test Technology

Function

In mobile applications, interfaces, and processes are part of suitability in mobile application test. Conventional software mouse operation has not yet appeared in mobile applications. Therefore the mobile device gestures become test goal in the function when interface menu has disappeared.

Accuracy is a software program to achieve the functions noted in the correct elements.

- Position: Enter a valid input and expect the software to complete some of the provisions of the act in accordance with the instructions
- Reverse: Enter an invalid input and expect the software to give a reasonable error

Interface

Users rely on mobile applications for any kinds of requirements increasingly. Here interface means the user interface between the application and its corresponding server.

Interface testing is the primary way for server communication and client mobile applications, which tablet device uses different standard protocols completely through the interface. Many data transfers in interface are dependent on custom protocols, which protocols process have to solve fault tolerance requirements, for example, protocol transmission errors, protocol processing error. Therefore, whether there is sufficient fault tolerance to ensure the effectiveness in these interfaces. A common interface should be verified from functionality to reliability support in a mobile application test.

Stability is that service control ability whether running or standby in background, especially involving under DNS, the service provider space situation. Domestic service providers often a well-known large-scale DNS name resolution failure. Under circumstances, test could request background API just like 404 code error. The API interact data should be a fixed format such as JSON and XML and parsing errors will inevitably occur when an exception is thrown. The processing for anomalies may cause the program does not work.

Security

Security capability on mobile intelligent device is important to prevent potential security threats techniques. As we known, the ability of software product is to protect information and data, which cannot read or modify the information and data by unauthorized persons or systems, rather than refuse to authorized persons or systems access to information and data. At present, the security mechanism is very weak in mobile device. The security problem occurs everywhere, especially in the new generation of 4G and other mobile networks. The mobile phone users are more susceptible to viruses, malware and adware attacks, cell phone privacy leak, flow consumption rates. These series of security issues will become more prominent gradually.

WiFi, two-dimensional code, mobile providers are new technology with rapid development in many mobile applications. The security tests in smartphone include:

- Privacy protection, also known as the privacy and security
- Transaction security of information transmission
- LBS geographic information services for various mobile applications will gradually combine portable personal privacy information and become common more and more.
- Impact of malicious programs in the mobile network environment, the malicious program may take many forms, such as the way advertising program.
- Program exist the back door.

Reliability
According to statistics data, wireless traffic in the intelligent mobile device are more than 10 times caused by non-intelligent mobile phone. In the United States, Britain, Germany, Japan, operators have appeared signaling communication network paralysis caused by network storm.

Mobile applications affect the reliability of three levels of meanings:

- Server: the number of users is small when mobile application has just released, but the number of users will be increased gradually with more customers installing applications. Therefore, how to quickly respond to customer needs goals is an ultimate issue when the ability of server beyond the maximum performance. However, performance may increase the number of users greatly and eventually lead to other problems, such as reliability problems.
- Network: Different from traditional LAN, mobile applications using a wireless LAN network, such as WiFi or 3G network, there are some the reliability of an impact, for example, instability of the network, signal coverage, the switched signal.
- Client capability: The ability to deal with different applications clients will have an impact on reliability.

There are some relation between reliability and compatibility, which the reliability also needs to be tested on multiple platforms.

For different mobile phone systems also need pay attention. Specifically, the Android system firmware 1.5, 1.6 and 2.0 above are to be tested separately. Because Android 1.5,1.6 and above SDK has achieved a lot of inconsistencies since compatibility a big problem. In the absence of special solution, the tester will find that program will collapse (resource files and API issues) in Android 1.6 when the programs could running well in Android 1.5 .

For iOS system, we should consider the test difference in addition to iOS3, iOS4 and iOS5. We just want to say as much as possible cautious testing as harsh. As for long audit cycle in App store, you cannot fix the issue in a very short period of time in the App store when a serious system error found during testing. Then the end user will need to tolerate the weak or bring your application not use by user to some extent.

Performance
The current environment of mobile applications, the phone's performance will need the relatively high cost of network traffic comparable to the desktop computer a decade ago. Due to the battery standby time is shorter, the performance of the phone

result in the bottleneck. The current mobile software development must face two issues. The one is how to make the software less memory and the other is less traffic transmission. These aspects will improve the stable performance. In actual projects, common performance testing tasks consists of defining performance objectives, establish performance benchmarks, system tuning and compare the results with previous run automated performance tests for each release version. Performance testing for the mobile applications should be tested both server side and client side.

The main factor in application efficiency of mobile applications consists of:

- mobile device processing application performance
- data transmission over the network
- processing time

Performance bottlenecks in hardware generally refers to the problem of CPU, RAM issues, which divided into server hardware bottlenecks, network bottlenecks, server operating system bottlenecks (configuration or parameters), middleware bottlenecks (configuration, database, web server, etc.) , applications bottleneck (SQL statements, database design, business logic , algorithms, etc.) .

- System software bottleneck: refers to an application server, web server software applications, or further a database system.
- Application bottleneck: refers to developers of new procedures should be developed.
- Operating systems bottleneck: for traditional software, generally refers to windows / unix / linux operating systems. For mobile device, the main target are these operating systems: iOS, Android, WindowsPhone. Different operating systems use different technology as the principle is different.
- Network devices bottleneck: refers to the firewall, dynamic load balancing, switches and other network equipment.

Resource Cost

Energy resources of resources cost in the mobile device is different from the traditional client, which based on continuous power supply. However, the power of the mobile device is limited and the factors influence the power consumption is very complicated.

To measure the energy cost in smartphones consists of:

- Energy cost of an NRA (Video / Web Browsing)
- Energy cost of a parameter (Volume, Brightness)
- Energy cost across smartphones (iPhone, BB)
- Energy cost across networks (3G, WiFi, Bluetooth)

Compatibility

Compatibility test is vital test purpose in the mobile test. The mobile applications in market are much larger than the desktop computing. The current situation is that the majority of applications developed to merely meet market requirements.

There is no economically practical way to support the platform. There is no clear market leader when there will be hundreds of different platforms. The software allows developers to support one platform may be very easy, but not so easy to support so many different platforms. Even supports mainstream mobile manufactures should consider the high cost problem, which is not simply unrealistic thing. How to solve the contradiction between the growing testing platform and high cost of the test project is critical issue.

4   Related Works

The number of applications on the App store and Google Play has collectively reached over a billion. Most of the prior work on verification of mobile applications has focused on model-based testing, test automation, and privacy protection[9].

Model-based testing is a testing methodology where the system under test   is described with a formal model. In [10] presents experiences in model-based graphical user interface testing of Android applications.   The test automation is help test applications using application model-based [11] .

Test automation also use tools to help to improve the efficiency, In Android SDK, these is a monkey testing tool (Monkey) for sending pseudorandom user events, such as key presses and screen taps to the device. The Monkey tool is useful in testing the stability of applications [12][13] .

However, considering the large number of mobile applications, it is important for users to understand how mobile applications are using sensitive information and resources on their devices. In test for privacy leaks, TaintDroid [14], PiOS [15] and AppScanner [16] are works that take advantage of dynamic and static analysis of mobile applications.

5   Conclusion and Future Works

In this article we focus on ensuring the quality character of mobile applications running on the mobile platform. The paper proposed the quality model for mobile applications. The character in quality model covered the classical the quality character and be organized in category.

With the fast development of mobile hardware and improvement of user experience in mobile device, the new features will be more diverse in the future, such as faster data processing speed, more long-lasting battery life, larger screen and more brilliant clarity in new mobile devices. Especially various sensors are greatly improves high-tech applications in mobile devices. The transition from manual testing to automate testing with automation test tools will be the future work.

Acknowledgements. The work is supported by Shanghai STCSM Program under Grant No. 12QB1402300, Shanghai STCSM Program under Grant No. 13XD1421800 and Shanghai STCSM Program under Grant No. 13511505303.

References

1. Nuccini, H., Di Francesco, A., Esposito, P.: Software Testing of Mobile Applications: Challenges and Future Research Directions. In: 7th International Workshop on Automation of Software Test, pp. 29–35. IEEE Press, New Jersey (2012)
2. Takala, T., Katara, M., Harty, J.: Experiences of System-Level Model-Based GUI Testing of an Android Application. In: 4th IEEE International Conference on Software Testing, Verification and Validation, pp. 377–386. IEEE Press, New York (2011)
3. Chaudhuri, A.: Language-based security on android. In: 4th Workshop on Programming Languages and Analysis for Security, pp. 1–7. ACM Press, New York (2009)
4. Myers, G.J.: The Art of Software Testing. John Wiley & Sons, Inc., New Jersey (2004)
5. Wasserman, A.I.: Software Engineering Issues for Mobile Application Development. In: The FSE/SDP Workshop on Future of Software Engineering Research, FoSER 2010, pp. 397–400 (2010)
6. Berardinelli, L., Cortellessa, V., Di Marco, A.: Performance Modeling and Analysis of Context-Aware Mobile Software Systems. In: Rosenblum, D.S., Taentzer, G. (eds.) FASE 2010. LNCS, vol. 6013, pp. 353–367. Springer, Heidelberg (2010)
7. Gartner, http://www.gartner.com/technology/home.jsp
8. ISO/IEC 9126: Information technology-Software product evaluation-Quality characteristics and guidelines for their use. Standard (2006)
9. Cui, Q., Hu, Y.: Internationalized Software Testing. Electric Industry Press (2006)
10. Chen, G., Kotz, D.: A Survey of Context-Aware Mobile Computing Research. Technical report (2000)
11. Hu, C., Neamtiu, I.: Automating GUI Testing for Android Applications. In: 6th International Workshop on Automation of Software Test, pp. 77–83. IEEE Press, New York (2011)
12. UI/Application Exerciser Monkey, http://developers.androidcn.com/guide/developing/tools/monkey.html
13. Jiang, B., Long, X., Gao, X.: MobileTest: A Tool Supporting Automatic Black Box Test for Software on Smart Mobile Devices. In: 2nd International Workshop on Automation of Software Test, pp. 38–44. IEEE Press, New Jersey (2007)
14. Enck, W., Gilbert, P., Chun, B.G., Cox, L.P., Jung, J., McDaniel, P., Sheth, A.N.: Taintdroid: An Information-Flow Tracking System for Realtime Privacy Monitoring on Smartphones. In: 9th USENIX Symposium on Operating Systems Design and Implementation, pp. 1–6 (2010)
15. Egele, M., Kruegel, C., Kirda, E., Vigna, G.: PiOS: Detecting Privacy Leaks in iOS Applications. In: The Network and Distributed System Security Symposium (2011)
16. Amini, S., Lin, J., Hong, J.I., Lindqvist, J., Zhang, J.: Mobile Application Evaluation Using Automation and Crowdsourcing. In: PETools: Workshop on Privacy Enhancing Tools (2013)

Defining Relevant Software Quality Characteristics from Publishing Policies of Mobile App Stores

Luis Corral, Alberto Sillitti, and Giancarlo Succi

Free University of Bozen-Bolzano
Piazza Domenicani 3, 39100 Bolzano-Bozen, Italy
{luis.corral,alberto.sillitti,giancarlo.succi}@unibz.it

Abstract. Publishing a product in a mobile app store implies a process that makes a software product accessible to millions of users. Developers require the means to evaluate the quality of the mobile software product from a viewpoint that considers the mobile business, users, target platforms and app stores. In this paper, we surveyed the publishing guidelines of six major app stores to identify the most important software quality requirements set upon mobile apps. We leveraged the ISO/IEC 25010 quality standard as a mechanism to assure the fulfillment of the quality requirements from the mobile app stores, and we defined an association between such requirements and the characteristics of the quality standard. Finally, we introduced a Mobile App Quality Model, which aims to provide a reference to assure the development of mobile-specific, market-compliant mobile software applications.

Keywords: App, Market, Mobile, Quality, QFD, Software, Standard, Store.

1 Introduction

The introduction of high-end mobile devices with increasing computing capabilities, and the growing availability of mobile data networks have boosted the development and distribution of software applications (best known as "apps"). Today, software developers are able to create mobile applications and expose them to a great number of users through different distribution channels. With such a rich potential, mobile application markets ("app stores") evolved to offer an efficient software delivery platform that provides developers with a powerful way to showcase their products, and offers users a vast display window to search and acquire mobile apps.

Offering a product in an app store makes a software product easily accessible to millions of users. This easiness raises an important concern about trusting the quality of a given product to be installed and used in a personal communication device. To keep up with a standard quality level, major app stores rely on product development policies and publishing guidelines that every product must observe to be included in the market. Customers evaluate and review the products as well, making their ratings and comments publicly available in the store front-end. These processes help in providing a trustworthy guide for potential customers; however, to judge accurately the quality of a mobile application, it is necessary to have a reference that permit to compare the application from an objective and reliable point of view.

I. Awan et al. (Eds.): MobiWis 2014, LNCS 8640, pp. 205–217, 2014.

In this paper, we identified the most relevant quality requirements set upon mobile apps by surveying the publishing guidelines of six major application stores. With the results of this survey, we implemented a Quality Function Deployment to associate these quality requirements with the quality characteristics of the ISO/IEC 25010 software quality standard. After this analysis, we defined a standard-based, mobile-specific software quality model. Our approach aims to contribute on the quality assurance of the mobile software product, providing a reference to guarantee the quality assessment of mobile software applications from a market-aware perspective.

The rest of the paper is organized as follows: Section 2 introduces app stores and their quality requirements; Section 3 extracts and summarizes software quality requirements from the publishing guidelines of six major app stores; Section 4 covers the ISO/IEC 25010 software quality standard; Section 5 implements a Quality Function Deployment to associate the requirements from app stores and the quality characteristics from ISO/IEC 25010; Section 6 introduces a software quality model for mobile applications based on the most relevant quality requirements from application stores. Section 7 closes this work with a summary, future research and conclusions.

2   Mobile Application Stores

The ability to produce applications able to be installed, utilized and managed in a mobile phone opened a big market opportunity previously bounded to telephone manufacturers and carrier companies [1]. In an effort to facilitate and promote the distribution of applications targeted to the same operating system, the "App Store Model" [2, 3] is an approach in which a mobile software platform offers the necessary infrastructure for developers and users to respectively offer and obtain software products. Developers utilize the app store as a high-profile platform to showcase their products to millions of potential customers, paying an entrance fee and giving to the store a percentage of the profit generated by each sale. On the other hand, users access an application delivery platform, search for the desired application, pay for it (if required), download it, and install it in their smart device [4, 5]. The App Store Model was popularized by Apple through the iOS App Store for the iPhone product family. Since then, this model has been the trendsetter for similar software delivery platforms that manage the distribution of mobile software apps [6, 7, 8].

App stores are the premier channel for the dissemination of mobile software products, hosting thousands of apps and reporting millions of downloads. This relevance makes app stores a precious source of information to determine trends about app usage, mobile business and general mobile app economy [9]. The quality of the products in app is normally regulated by market policies and is judged by customer's reviews and ratings. Mobile app stores pose several requirements that a product must meet to be included in their catalogues. Under this rationale, app stores' guidelines represent the minimum quality expectations for a mobile app to enter into service. Publishing policies are highly influential for developers, since the lack of compliance may cause the rejection or exclusion of the product from the app store.

In addition to the quality criteria of app store policies, some research works have explored assorted means to assess the quality of mobile applications in a quantitative fashion. Dantas et al. proposed a mechanism to evaluate quantitatively the quality the mobile software product [10]; Spriestersbach and Springer identified a group of quality characteristics of mobile web applications [11]; Mantoro outlined a proposal of incorporating quality metrics for context-aware applications based on the ISO 9126 standard [12], and Marinho and Resende introduced a relationship between mobile quality factors with development guidelines and best practices [13,14].

This body of research suggests the need of identifying the most relevant attributes of mobile applications and customizing general-purpose product quality strategies to suit the needs of the mobile environment [14]. Our effort picks up from this approach, aiming to develop a standard quality reference to evaluate mobile applications. To accomplish this goal, we need to identify the requirements that drive the quality of the mobile software product with a market-aware perspective, setting these requirements as high-level goals, and introducing the means to assure such goals systematically.

3   Quality Requirements from Mobile Application Stores

To start our analysis, we retrieved the publishing guidelines from six major application stores, selected to cover comprehensively the major mobile operating platforms and the most important distribution channels. The publishing guidelines can be retrieved from each application store website:

- *Android OS:* Google Play[1], Amazon Appstore[2], Nook Apps[3],
- *Apple iOS:* iOS App Store[4],
- *Microsoft Windows Phone:* Windows Phone Store[5], and
- *Blackberry OS:* Blackberry World[6].

Our analysis is based on the contents of the publishing guidelines as of September, 2013. We acknowledge that the application markets reserve the right to revise and change their policies with relative frequency, which may bring as consequence that some of the analyzed concepts or policies could vary slightly.

First, we focused on reading analytically the app store policies to identify all the requirements that do not focus on the quality of the software product; for example, those concerning about payments, revenues, and the terms and conditions under which developers should use the app store. Since none of these clauses represent characteristics intrinsic to the software product, they were not included in our review. Then, once we set aside the non-product characteristics, we studied the rest of the requirements to ensure that they can be categorized as development guidelines, that is, requirements

---

[1] https://play.google.com/about/android-developer-policies.html
[2] https://developer.amazon.com/help/faq.html
[3] https://nookdeveloper.zendesk.com/entries/
21247706-nook-apps-developer-policy
[4] https://developer.apple.com/appstore/resources/approval/
guidelines.html
[5] http://msdn.microsoft.com/en-US/library/windowsphone/develop/
hh184843(v=vs.105)
[6] http://developer.blackberry.com/java/documentation/
bp_intro_1984355_11.html

that can be put on practice while analyzing, designing, coding and testing the application. For a better organization, we used Google's Android OS quality taxonomy[7] to group the requirements: Performance, Responsiveness, Seamlessness, Functionality, Energy Management, Security, Visual Design and Content. After extracting the quality requirements, we conducted a comparative analysis of them to minimize overlapping or duplicity on them (for instance, requirements expressed in different words but referring to the same concept). Once we summarized and classified the requirements, we analyzed each group of requirements to extract commonalities and eliminate duplicates. After the list was consolidated, we calculated the frequency count for each requirement to see how many app stores consider it as part of their publishing conditions. The results of the summary are shown in Table 1.

Table 1. Summary and frequency of quality requirements of major mobile application stores

	Google Play	Amazon Appstore	Nook Apps	iOS Store	Windows Phone	Blackberry World	Frequency
1. Performance							
1.1 Optimize Code	x					x	2
1.2 Perform as per device capabilities	x		x		x		3
1.3 Sustain network slowness	x					x	2
1.4 Minimize data usage						x	1
2. Responsiveness							
2.1 Fixed seconds for app response or launch	x		x		x		3
2.2 Indicators to know the status of the app			x			x	2
2.3 Use of contextual menus						x	1
3. Seamlessness							
3.1 No crashes	x		x	x	x		4
3.2 Reduce input errors	x					x	2
3.3 No bugs				x			1
3.4 No reboots				x			1
3.5 Assure stable sessions			x		x		2
3.6 Improve user experience						x	1
3.7 High app scalability						x	1
4. Functionality							
4.1 App should perform as advertised		x		x	x		3
4.2 No hidden features				x			1
4.3 Provision of added value			x	x			2
4.4 No "beta/lite" applications			x	x			2
4.5 Full functionality of device's hardware					x		1
4.6 Priority on phone functionality	x		x		x		3
5. Energy management							
5.1 Avoid battery drains	x		x	x	x	x	5
5.2 Avoid stay awake			x				1
5.3 Practices for energy saving					x		1

---

[7] http://developer.android.com/guide/practices/index.html

Table 1. (*continued*)

6. Security								
6.1 Permission management	X					X		2
6.2 Credential management	X					X		2
6.3 Controlled use of external storage	X		X					2
6.4 Not to risk customer data		X		X	X	X		4
6.5 Utilize hardware with official APIs		X	X	X				3
6.6 No damages to devices				X	X			2
6.7 Follow a privacy policy					X			1
6.8 Encryption						X		1
7. Visual Design								
7.1 Icon guidelines	X	X	X	X				4
7.2 Support layouts, icons, sizes	X	X	X	X				4
7.3 Follow design guidelines	X			X	X	X		4
7.4 Ads in compliance with policy				X	X			2
7.5 Utilization of an official GUI						X		1
8. Content								
8.1 No offensive content	X	X	X	X	X			5
8.2 Not to promote illegal acts	X	X		X	X			4
8.3 No malware	X				X			2
8.4 No advertisement		X						1
8.5 No reference to other stores		X	X					2
8.6 Package size limit				X	X			2
8.7 Respect content ratings				X		X		2
8.8 Region-specific restrictions					X			1

4   Software Quality Characteristics: ISO/IEC 25010

We propose that app store policies can be met by ensuring a group of standardized quality characteristics. To this end, it is necessary to describe a relationship between the identified market requirements with a family of quality characteristics from a suitable software standard. We revisited a software product quality standard of the ISO series. Given the evolution of ISO/IEC 9126 towards ISO/IEC 25010 [15], we selected the latter, updating the discussion to the most recent version. Our selection was based on the dissemination and applicability of the standard. Other software quality standards were dismissed since they were specific, or of very narrow applicability.

We analyzed the quality characteristics and sub-characteristics of ISO/IEC 25010 to identify those applicable to the mobile software product in the app market context. ISO/IEC 25010 defines a software quality model that can be analyzed in two orthogonal dimensions: developer's viewpoint (Internal and External quality, Table 2) and customer's viewpoint (Quality in Use, Table 3), making it suitable for app store policies that consider both perspectives.

Table 2. Product Quality Model: Internal and External Quality

Quality Characteristics	Quality Sub-Characteristics
1. Functional suitability	Completeness, Correctness, Appropriateness
2. ?Performance efficiency	Time behavior, Resource utilization, Capacity
3. Compatibility	Coexistence, Interoperability
4. Usability	Appropriateness recognizability, Learnability, Operability, User-error protection, User interface aesthetics, Accessibility
5. Reliability	Maturity, Availability, Fault tolerance, Recoverability
6. Security	Confidentiality, Integrity, Non-repudiation, Accountability, Authenticity
7. Maintaintability	Modularity, Reusability, Analyzability, Modifiability, Testability
8. Portability	Adaptability, Installability, Replaceability

Table 3. Product Quality Model: Quality in Use

Quality Characteristics	Quality Sub-Characteristics
1. Effectiveness	Effectiveness
2. Efficiency	Efficiency
3. Satisfaction	Usefulness, Trust, Pleasure, Comfort.
4. Freedom from risk	Economic risk mitigation, Health and safety risk mitigation, Environmental risk mitigation
5. Context coverage	Context completeness, Flexibility

ISO/IEC 25010 does not include a definition of the detailed software quality attributes, leaving them open to suit the needs of each specific software product. Our approach benefits from this flexibility, as it opens the door to adapt this quality model to the requirements from any particular scope, like, in this case, the mobile app domain. Moreover, the attributes can be related to metrics, permitting a quantitative way to measure the quality of the product and deliver relevant information about it, which can be later used to feedback the development and assurance processes [16].

5   Associating ISO/IEC 25010 with Mobile Quality Requirements

After isolating the quality requirements from mobile app stores and examining the quality characteristics of ISO/IEC 25010, we need to describe a sustained association between them. To reach this goal, we considered the implementation of principles of customer-driven engineering, which allows to assure the design quality of the product based on characteristics implicitly and explicitly desired by the customer. This approach was implemented using the Quality Function Deployment (QFD) [17]. The QFD helps to translate customer needs into technical characteristics [18].

In the scope of software development, the QFD has been previously discussed as a suitable way to manage and process software requirements [19, 20, 21, 22]. Since the quality requirements from the different app stores reflect the needs of the customer, the target device and the execution environment, a QFD facilitates the consolidation of these requirements, and provides the tools to organize and rank them.

Our Quality Function Deployment has the goal of providing a quantitative relationship between the mobile app store quality requirements and the ISO/IEC 25010 quality characteristics. After that, we rank the relationships defined by the QFD to build a quality model identifying the characteristics that are most relevant to the major mobile app stores. To guarantee the accuracy of the QFD, we developed it using the Nominal Group Technique with a team formed by two university full professors specialized in Software Engineering, two graduate students researching on Software Engineering, and three staff members of three software companies specialized on the development of mobile applications. The QFD was conducted based on the methodology proposed by [23], which establishes a series of 5 steps:

Step 1. Customer Requirements: The initial step is the elicitation of the customer requirements; that is, to gather information about what are the characteristics that the product should have. We obtained this information from Table 1, extracting the 44 requirements taken from the stores, and classifying them as the "Demanded Quality".

Step 2. Customer Importance Ratings: We need to rate the importance of each requirement, as this number will be used later in a relationship matrix. We scaled the importance from 1 to 6, based on the frequency that each requirement may have on the six analyzed app stores. Said this, the minimum value is 1, for those requirements that appear only in one app store, and the maximum possible level of importance is 6, for those requirements that are considered by all the six analyzed app stores. We called this value the Demanded Quality Weight (DQW). In addition, it was calculated the Demanded Quality Relative Weight (DQRW), which indicates the overall importance of the quality requirement relative to the weights of all other quality requirements. The DQRW is given by the quotient of the DQW divided by the sum of the weights of all other DQW. The computed values of DQW and DQRW are shown in Table 4.

Table 4. Demanded Quality Weight and Demanded Quality Relative Weight

Demanded Quality Requirement from Application Markets	Demanded Quality Weight	Demanded Quality Relative Weight
1.1 Optimize Code	2	2.08%
1.2 Perform in compliance with device capabilities	3	3.13%
1.3 Sustain network slowness	2	2.08%
1.4 Minimize data usage	1	1.04%
2.1 Fixed seconds for app response/launch	3	3.13%
2.2 Indicators to know the status of the app	2	2.08%
2.3 Use of contextual menus	1	1.04%
3.1 No crashes	4	4.17%
3.2 Reduce input errors	2	2.08%

Table 4. (*continued*)

3.3 No bugs	1	1.04%
3.4 No reboots	1	1.04%
3.5 Assure stable sessions	2	2.08%
3.6 Improve user experience	1	1.04%
3.7 High app scalability	1	1.04%
4.1 Perform as advertised	3	3.13%
4.2 No hidden features	1	1.04%
4.3 Provision of added value	2	2.08%
4.4 No "beta/lite" applications	2	2.08%
4.5 Full functionality of HW	1	1.04%
4.6 Highest priority on telephony functions	3	3.13%
5.1 Avoid battery drains	5	5.21%
5.2 Avoid stay awake	1	1.04%
5.3 Best practices for energy	1	1.04%
6.1 Permission management	2	2.08%
6.2 Credential management	2	2.08%
6.3 Controlled use of storage	2	2.08%
6.4 Not to risk customer data	4	4.17%
6.5 Use HW with official APIs	3	3.13%
6.6 No damages to devices	2	2.08%
6.7 Follow a privacy policy	1	1.04%
6.8 Encryption	1	1.04%
7.1 Icon guidelines	4	4.17%
7.2 Support resolutions, icons	4	4.17%
7.3 Follow design guidelines	4	4.17%
7.4 Ads compliant with policy	2	2.08%
7.5 Utilize official GUI APIs	1	1.04%
8.1 No offensive content	5	5.21%
8.2 No illegal activities	4	4.17%
8.3 No malware	2	2.08%
8.4 No advertisement	1	1.04%
8.5 No reference other stores	2	2.08%
8.6 Package size limit	2	2.08%
8.7 Respect content ratings	2	2.08%
8.8 Region-specific restrictions	1	1.04%

Step 3. Quality Characteristics: The Quality Characteristics describe the product in terms of attributes that may be measured. In our QFD, the Quality Characteristics were taken from the 42 quality sub-characteristics of our selected standard, ISO/IEC 25010 (column "Quality sub-characteristic" of Tables 2 and 3), since they describe with the highest granularity available the traits that the developer should consider towards assuring the quality of the software product.

Step 4. Relationship Matrix: The relationship matrix determines the interaction between the Demanded Quality and the Quality Characteristics, that is, the relationship between the customer needs and the instruments at hand to monitor them. In accordance to ISO/IEC 25010, we executed a separate relationship analysis for the Internal/External Quality characteristics and for the Quality in Use characteristics. The QFD requires the calculation of a Relationship Value (RV) that describes the association between the demanded quality requirements and the quality characteristics. We calculated the RV according to our methodology [23], which recommends scaling the value in three levels: 9 for a strong relationship, 3 for a moderate relationship, 1 for a weak relationship (0 represents no relationship). Page limitations do not allow us to include the relationship matrix here, but it is available in the project's website[8].

Step 5. Quality Characteristic Importance Ratings: The association between the Demanded Quality and the Quality Characteristics allows the calculation of parameters that denote the relevance of each quality requirement. We obtained the Quality Characteristic Weight (QCW), which indicates the overall importance of the quality characteristic. It is given by the sum of all Relationship Values between each Demanded Quality Requirement and the analyzed Quality Characteristic, multiplied by their corresponding Demanded Quality Relative Weight. Then, we calculated the Quality Characteristic Relative Weight (QCRW), which indicates the weight of the quality characteristic relative to the weights of other characteristics. It is obtained by the quotient of the Quality Characteristic Weight divided by the sum of all other Quality Characteristic Weights. With this value at hand, we can rank the Quality Characteristics by importance. This analysis is discussed in detail in Section 6.

6   Creation of the Mobile App Quality Model

The association between the quality requirements and the quality characteristics that address them allows us to outline a Mobile App Quality Model. This Quality Model leverages a general-purpose quality model (ISO/IEC 25010) specializing it to the needs of the mobile product, in the context of the mobile application business. This implies that the model should focus on the characteristics that deliver more value to the quality requirements of the app stores and dismisses the less relevant quality characteristics.

To assess the importance of the quality sub-characteristics, we appraised the value of their Relative Weights. To do the selection, we defined a threshold, i.e., a minimum Relative Weight (QCRW) that each sub-characteristic must exceed to be included in the final model. Every sub-characteristic with a QCRW lower than the threshold value was dismissed. To guarantee a high level of confidence in the model, we kept the sub-characteristics that lead to a potential level of accomplishment of more than 90% based on the total sum of their Relative Weights. For Internal/External Quality, the threshold was therefore set in 2%, and 8% for Quality in Use. The selected Internal/External Quality sub-characteristics of the Mobile App Quality Model are shown in Table 5, and the selected sub-characteristics of the Mobile App Quality in Use Model in Table 6.

---

[8] http://www.inf.unibz.it/~lcorralvelazquez/qfd.html

Table 5. Mobile App Quality Model: Selected Internal/External Quality Sub-Characteristics

Internal/External Quality Sub-characteristics	Relative Weight
1.1 Functional completeness	6.18%
1.2 Functional correctness	6.32%
1.3 Functional appropriateness	8.22%
2.1 Time behavior	3.36%
2.2 Resource utilization	5.70%
2.3 Capacity	3.51%
3.1 Co-existence	2.60%
3.2 Interoperability	2.52%
4.1 Appropriateness recognizability	7.42%
4.2 Learnability	3.07%
4.3 Operability	4.75%
4.5 User interface aesthetics	5.59%
4.6 Accessibility	2.27%
5.1 Maturity	3.33%
6.1 Confidentiality	4.28%
6.2 Integrity	4.46%
6.3 Non-repudiation	8.00%
6.4 Accountability	6.14%
6.5 Authenticity	3.65%
Sum of Total Weights (Confidence)	**91.37%**

Table 6. Mobile App Quality Model: Selected Quality in Use Sub-Characteristics

Quality in Use Sub-characteristics	Relative Weight
1. Effectiveness	9.54%
2. Efficiency	9.54%
3.1 Usefulness	10.15%
3.2 Trust	15.70%
3.3 Pleasure	11.61%
3.4 Comfort	10.06%
4.1 Economic risk mitigation	8.60%
4.2 Health and safety risk mitigation	8.04%
5. Context completeness	11.51%
Sum of Total Weights (Confidence)	**94.74%**

From the development point of view, it is clear that application markets concentrate on showcasing products that are functional and do not present any flaw and shall not lead to any malfunction in the mobile system. Development-oriented characteristics such as modularity, reusability, analyzability, etc. have the lowest relevance. From the user point of view, it is noticeable that the majority of the Quality in Use sub-characteristics are relevant to the publishing policies of the app stores.

The Mobile App Quality Model reflects this trait: Tables 5 and 6 show that 12 Internal/External quality sub-characteristics and 2 Quality in Use sub-characteristics were dismissed, reducing the Mobile App Quality Model to 19 Internal/External quality sub-characteristics (Table 7) and 9 Quality in Use sub-characteristics (Table 8). The quality model was simplified, but it keeps a high level of confidence to meet the requirements of the publishing policies of the analyzed app stores.

Table 7. Mobile App Quality Model: Development-Oriented Quality Characteristics

Quality Characteristics	Quality Sub-Characteristic
1. Functional Suitability	Completeness, correctness, appropriateness
2. Performance Efficiency	Time behavior, Resource utilization, Capacity
3. Compatibility	Coexistence, Interoperability
4. Usability	Appropriateness recognizability, Learnability, Operability, User interface aesthetics, Accessibility
5. Reliability	Maturity
6. Security	Confidentiality, Integrity, Non-repudiation, Accountability, Authenticity

Table 8. Mobile App Quality Model: User-Oriented Quality Characteristics

Quality Characteristics	Quality Sub-Characteristic
1. Effectiveness	Effectiveness
2. Efficiency	Efficiency
3. Satisfaction	Usefulness, Trust, Pleasure, comfort.
4. Freedom from risk	Economic risk mitigation, Health and safety risk mitigation
5. Context coverage	Context coverage

The Mobile App Quality Model does not include a description of the detailed quality attributes, leaving them open to fit the specific needs of the vast variety of mobile apps. From these custom quality attributes, one may define the metrics that help on the quantitative analysis of the goals set by the quality characteristics. The Mobile App Quality Model facilitates the definition of parameters to evaluate the quality of the mobile software product with respect to such requirements. Finally, the total sums of the Relative Weights of the selected characteristics denote a high level of confidence of our Model with respect of what is actually required by the major mobile app stores.

7   Conclusions

After identifying and prioritizing the most relevant quality characteristics and defining the Mobile App Quality Model, it is necessary to conduct an experiment to implement the model and test its applicability and usefulness in a real-world scenario. We plan to conduct an evaluation of a set of Open Source mobile applications [24], since selecting Open Source products guarantees access to the source code to perform the Internal/External Quality analysis, and we will evaluate the product metrics made available by the corresponding app store (e.g., number of downloads, user ratings and comments) to evaluate the Quality in Use model.

In this paper, we reviewed and compared the publishing guidelines of six of the major mobile app stores that serve the most important mobile operating platforms. We extracted the product quality requirements from their publishing policies and organized them in categories to find commonalities, differences and key factors. We leveraged the quality model of ISO/IEC 25010 to outline a relationship between the app store quality policies with the standard's quality characteristics, as an effective way to assure the fulfillment of the app market demands. Utilizing the Quality Function Deployment methodology, we associated the quality requirements from the mobile app stores with the quality characteristics of ISO/IEC 25010, and we ranked this association to define a mobile-specific, standard-based software quality reference.

To succeed in the mobile software market, developers require the means to measure the quality of their mobile software products from a point of view that considers the particularities of the mobile environment and the mobile business. Identifying the most relevant software quality characteristics from the major mobile app stores, and organizing them in a Mobile App Quality Model aims to contribute on the improvement of the assurance processes that guarantee the production and delivery of mobile-specific, market compliant mobile software applications.

References

1. Kimbler, K.: App store strategies for service providers. In: Proceedings of the 14th International Conference on Intelligence in Next Generation Networks, pp. 1–5 (2010)
2. Hammershoj, A., Sapuppo, A., Tadayoni, R.: Challenges for mobile application development. In: The 14th Int. Conf. on Intelligence in Next Generation Networks, pp. 1–8 (2010)
3. Rao, B., Jimenez, B.: A comparative analysis of digital innovation ecosystems. In: Proc. of the 2011 Technology Management in the Energy Smart World, pp. 1–12 (2011)
4. Goul, M., Marjanovic, O., Baxley, S., Vezecky, K.: Managing the enterprise business intelligence app store: Sentiment analysis supported requirements engineering. In: Proc. of the 45th Hawaii International Conference on System Sciences, pp. 4168–4177 (2012)
5. Hall, C.: Getting Features and Functionality from Enterprise App Stores. Cutter IT Journal, 1554–5946 (2013) ISSN: 1554-5946
6. Gonçalves, V., Walravens, N., Ballon, P.: How about an App Store? Enablers and constraints in platform strategies for mobile network operators. In: Proceedings of the 9th International Conference on Mobile Business, pp. 66–73 (2010)
7. Tuunainen, V.K., Tuunanen, T., Piispanen, J.: Mobile service platforms: Comparing Nokia OVI and Apple App Store with the IISIn Model. In: Proceedings of the 10th International Conference Mobile Business, pp. 74–83 (2011)
8. Cortimiglia, M.N., Ghezzi, A., Renga, F.: Mobile applications and their delivery platforms. IT Professional 13(5), 51–56 (2011)
9. D'Heureuse, N., et al.: What's app? A wide-scale measurement study of smart phone markets. ACM Mobile Computing and Communications Review 16(2), 16–27 (2012)
10. Dantas, V.L.L., Marinho, F.G., da Costa, A.L., Andrade, R.M.C.: Testing requirements for mobile applications. In: Proceedings of the 24th International Symposium on Computer and Information Sciences, pp. 555–560 (2009)

11. Spriestersbach, A., Springer, T.: Quality attributes in mobile web application development. In: Bomarius, F., Iida, H. (eds.) PROFES 2004. LNCS, vol. 3009, pp. 120–130. Springer, Heidelberg (2004)
12. Mantoro, T.: Metrics Evaluation for Context-Aware Computing. In: Proc. of the 7th International Conference on Advances in Mobile Computing & Multimedia, pp. 574–578 (2009)
13. Marinho, E.H., Resende, R.F.: Quality factors in development best practices for mobile applications. In: Proceedings of the 12th International Conference on Computational Science and its Applications, vol. IV, pp. 632–345 (2012)
14. Corral, L., Georgiev, A.B., Sillitti, A., Succi, G.: Method Reallocation to Reduce Energy Consumption: An implementation in Android OS. In: Proc. of the 29th Symposium on Applied Computing. ACM (2014)
15. International Organization for Standardization, International Standard ISO/IEC FDIS 25010: Systems and software engineering — Systems and software Quality Requirements and Evaluation (SQuaRE) System and software quality models. © ISO/IEC (2010)
16. Ministry of Economy, Trade and Industry, Japan, Software Metrics Advanced Project. Product Quality Metrics Working Group. Investigative Report on Measure for System/Software Product Quality Requirement Definition and Evaluation (2011)
17. Akao, Y.: Development history of Quality Function Deployment. The customer driven approach to Quality planning and deployment. Asian Productivity Organization (1994)
18. Myint, S.: A framework of an intelligent quality function deployment (IQFD) for discrete assembly environment. Computers & Industrial Eng. 45(2), 269–283 (2003)
19. Karlsson, J.: Managing software requirements using Quality Function Deployment. Software Quality Journal 6(4), 311–326 (1997)
20. Ramires, J., Antunes, P., Respício, A.: Software requirements negotiation using the software Quality Function Deployment. In: Fukś, H., Lukosch, S., Salgado, A.C. (eds.) CRIWG 2005. LNCS, vol. 3706, pp. 308–324. Springer, Heidelberg (2005)
21. Kivinen, T.: Applying QFD to improve the requirements and project management in small-scale project. Master Thesis. University of Tampere, Finland (2008)
22. Xiong, W., Wang, X.T.: Software requirements management using QFD: A process perspective. In: Proc. of the Int. Symp. on Comput. Intelligence and Design, pp. 295–299 (2008)
23. Creative Industries Research Institute, Quality Function Deployment. Auckland University of Technology (2007)
24. Georgiev, A.B., Sillitti, A., Succi, G.: Open Source Mobile Virtual Machines: An Energy Assessment of Dalvik vs. ART. In: Corral, L., Sillitti, A., Succi, G., Vlasenko, J., Wasserman, A.I. (eds.) OSS 2014. IFIP AICT, vol. 427, pp. 93–102. Springer, Heidelberg (2014)

Securing Business Data on Android Smartphones

Mohamed Ali El-Serngawy and Chamseddine Talhi

Dept. Software Engineering and IT
École de technologie supérieure
Montréal, Canada
Mohamed.elserngawy.1@ens.etsmtl.ca,
chamseddine.talhi@etsmtl.ca

Abstract. In this paper, we study the security of Enterprise Business data on Android Smartphone. The contribution of the paper is threefold: (1) identifying the main business case scenarios of using Smart phones for business activities and the associated security issues, (2) evaluating the risks associated with the identified scenarios under the current Android security architecture, and (3) investigating academic and industrial efforts proposed to secure business solutions on Android Smart phones. The third contribution has been given special attention to identify the possible alternatives and discuss their viability.

Keywords: Smartphone, Android, security architecture, threat vectors, risk analysis, Enterprise security.

1   Introduction

Recently, the wide use of Smart phones encourages organizations to adopt them in their enterprise solutions and use them to access their intra networks. In fact smart phones have many benefits that could help improve enterprise solutions, like mobility behavior which can be used to allow immediate access to key customer data or feed the decision makers with real time information or provide quick feedback response. Therefore mobility can improve operational effectiveness and visibility across value chain, reducing operational cost of an organization, and enhancing decision making. However when organizations start integrating smart phones to their enterprise solutions, they face many management and security issues. First, the diversity of smartphone platforms is challenging the portability of the solution on various devices, especially for "bring your own device" BYOD approaches. Second, the high mobility characterizing smart phones make them easy to stolen which make organization data confidentiality under risk. Third the increasing number of mobile applications vulnerabilities discovered almost every day make any mobile enterprise solution under high potential security risks. Android is one of the leading platforms adopted by smart phones industry and it has 87% of the current used smart phones in the world [30]. In fact, by the mid of 2013 Android applications store "Google Play" [42] has more than 850,000 applications with more than 40 billion download [17]. Therefore, we will focus on Android platform with enterprise solutions in this paper. We will classify the uses of the smart phones applications with the enterprise

I. Awan et al. (Eds.): MobiWis 2014, LNCS 8640, pp. 218–232, 2014.

solutions, then we will argue the security risks and vulnerabilities for Android platform, and at the end we will explore and evaluate the current proposed solutions to manage the security risks we defined for Android platform uses in Enterprise.

This paper is organized as follows. In section 2 we present a new taxonomy for smart phone enterprise applications, Section 3 contains private data definitions of smart phone users, applications vulnerabilities and our classification of security risks in Android platform. In section 4, we will explore the current proposed solutions to manage security risks. Section 5 presents example of current industry solutions and section 6 contains our conclusion.

2 Taxonomy of Enterprise Mobile Applications and Their Security

We focus on Android platform in this paper; however the taxonomy we propose could fit on all smart phone platforms. We adapted the enterprise mobile applications taxonomy proposed in [3]. While the taxonomy in [3] addresses the issue of developing enterprise mobile applications; our taxonomy is security-driven. In fact, for each category of mobile applications, we discussed the main business scenarios and identified the associated security risks depending on data confidentiality and business data transactions point of view. The result presented in figure 1, a bottom-up five-layer classification where lower layers represent applications with lower security risks and upper layers represent applications with higher security risks and these layers are overlapped in the security risks. These layers are the following:

- **Public Broadcast Applications:** These applications usually broadcast static information contents or general public services for a wide group of users, like company flyers, information about university campus, emergency exits, etc. This kind of applications usually produce public data with limited or without data transactions which mean low security risks in terms of data confidentiality.

- **Information Applications:** These applications are used to present products, offers, events, etc. thus they usually have heavy data transactions between end users and the enterprise solution. In terms of data confidentiality these applications could be used to capture the end users private data like interest search words, GPS coordinates, network provider, etc. From the company' side, the end user has accessibility to feed the enterprise solution with valuable data, for example the integrity of users' feedback can be altered which could affect the validity and efficiency of its processes. Those both sides of data confidentiality make the system with high security risks to control and manage.

- **E-Finance Applications:** Applications with electronic money transaction could be a special kind of the previous category "information application". Indeed, the enterprise solution has another actor to interact with rather than the end user, for example a financial mediator should be integrated with the system to complete the money transaction operation. In terms of data confidentiality the system has the same security risks as "information application", however it has new actor to interact with, which adds new security risks to manage and control.

- **Data Operation Applications:** These applications are designed to achieve complex business scenarios for which any data operation should be performed between internal trusted users like employees and their company systems in the company intra network, for example applications allowing employees to submit their timesheets and tasks. In case of "BYOD model" where employees are allowed to use their own smartphone, these applications can represent a source security threats for the enterprise systems. Indeed the enterprise solutions should have ability to isolate and secure their own data transaction from the employee personal use, which is not easy to achieve as we will see later in this paper. In terms of data confidentiality the company data could be exposed through employee device, which means high security risks to manage and control.

- **Collaborative Applications:** These applications could be considered as a special kind of the previous category "Data Operations" however, they are designed for collaborative purpose between trusted users, like for example video conference services, instance file sharing applications, etc. In terms of data confidentiality the system has the same high security risks as the previous category but with more complex scenarios to manage.

In terms of business transaction security risks, the first three categories could be fit under B2C "Business to Consumer" [55] model and the last two categories could be fit under B2E "Business to Employee" [55] model, we will specify the main security risks at the end of Section 3 after reviewing the Android platform vulnerabilities and possible attacks.

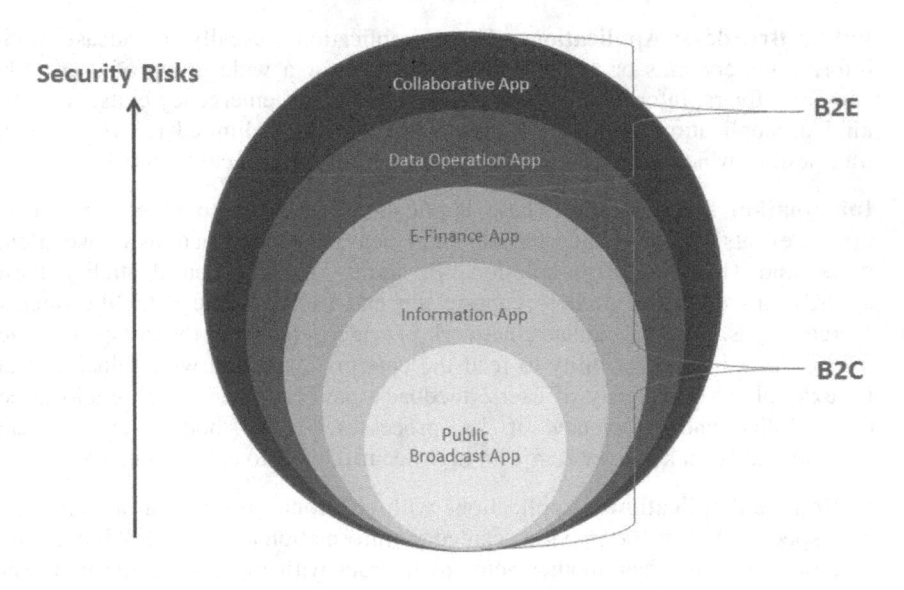

Fig. 1. Taxonomy of Enterprise mobile Apps and their security risks

3   Private Data and Android Vulnerabilities

The high number of malwares detected for Android OS everyday shows that there are high vulnerabilities in Android Security architecture & development environment. In this section, we will explore the vulnerabilities of Android applications that have impact on the security risks in the enterprise systems. In the following we will present private data on Smartphone, the main attacks threatening them and in the end we de- fine the main security risks.

3.1   Smart Phone Privacy Issues

- *Smartphone Identification.* Smartphone identifier could be phone number, inter-national mobile equipment identity number (IMEI), International Mobile Sub-scriber Identity (IMSI) or SIM Card Serial Number (ICCID). Many applications use one of these unique identifiers to access their networks or check user identity. In real scenarios, these unique identifiers are bundled with username and password to create unique user identification in many applications. Consequently, accessing these unique identifiers facilitates attacking users' privacy since they are reused in other applications.

- *Physical Location.* There are many applications providing Location Base Ser- vices LBS [20] like map navigation, nearest services identification, location shar- ing in social networks. While the presence of these applications on the device is legitimate and justified, they cannot be trusted when the device is running enter- prise applications. In fact, these applications can track the user physical location and thus may threaten enterprise privacy and even the physical safety of the user. For example, "consider a rural mobile accountant agent who uses an enterprise application to record transactions as he goes around customers and distribute money. Typically, any third-party application that has the required Android per- missions would have access to the location information. However, when the ac- countant agent is running the enterprise application, location information be- comes enterprise sensitive data", and thus should be accessible only to enterprise applications. This is very important to protect the physical security of the ac- countant agent.

- *External Storage.* Any data stored in the external memory storage is accessible to any other application having the permissions required to access external storage. In fact, the permissions of the majority of files stored in external storage are de- fined as RW or not encrypted, thus any application can access them or even modi- fy them!

- *Super User Access.* Rooting Android means granting the user full privilege to control the Android OS; known as root or super user access [18]. The goal of rooting Smartphones is to overcome limitations that carrier and hardware manufacture put on the device. However the problem with rooted phones is that any malware successes to gain the root user privilege will get full control of the

Android OS. With root permissions, malware is able to access any application folder in internal memory, user contact list, control the hardware function like Wi-Fi, Bluetooth, GPS, etc. All these malicious activities could happen without notifying the user.

3.2   Main Attacks

After specifying the user private data, we will explore the possible attacks that could target them.

- *Privilege Escalation.* Android OS use IPC mechanism to let applications communicate with each other's. The authors of [47] investigate the permission leakage of IPC mechanism, the problem happens when "the application with less permission is not restricted to access components of a more permission application". In other words, Android's security architecture does not ensure that a caller application is assigned at least the same permissions as a callee application or component". For example, if we have an application Ax having only a permission to access the user contacts list and there are another application Bx having a permission to access the internet and GPS functions, through the IPC mechanism Ax could use a component of Bx to send the user contacts list to third party server through Internet.

- *Root Kit Attack.* Rootkit is software used by an attacker to gain root-level access to the Android OS. Rootkits allow hackers to administratively control the Smartphone, which means executing files, hiding processes, accessing logs, monitoring user activities, and even changing the Smartphone settings like GPS, Wifi, etc. Rootkits infect the Smartphone by installing themselves as loaded kernel modules LKM and thus, are loaded each time the operating system is booted. The author of [6] shows that there is a way to hook the system_call_table through/dev/kmem access technique in Android which makes the attacker able to inject his malicious code. The rooting attack in [59] shows an E-Finance service appli- cation that stores the public authentication certificate into internal saving struc- ture in the SdCard. The rooting attack makes it possible to acquire manager's au- thority and get access to every system file. Therefore, the attacker succeeds to get this authority and become able to expose the public authentication certificate of E-Finance service in order to use it later for E-finance transactions.

3.3   Main Security Risks

After exploring the vulnerabilities that could affect the mobile applications, we list our understanding of the security risks we could have in Table 1:

Table 1. List of main security risks

1- Mobile Client Applications Security Risks
• Attacker can decompile the executable file of mobile applications and perform reverse engineering to get sensitive information from the source code.
• Many applications could have the same permission to access system resources at the same time.
• Unencrypted data & weak cryptographic implementation of application sensitive data on external and internal data storages can lead to malicious transactions.
2- Middleware Application Security Risks
• Middleware applications where internal communications with system processes and outer communication with servers components like http web services, an adversary may spoof request/response messages.
• Shared middleware applications with global access or undefined permission set will be vulnerable to malwares.
3- Network & Communication Security Risks
• Insecure communications channels may lead to lose data or man in the middle attacks.
4- Device stolen or lost case Risks
• Un-authorized user is able to misuse data on device.

4   Security Solutions from Academia

After we specify the main security risks that enterprise solutions should deal with, the following table lists the proposed functions that should be provided to cover these security risks.

Table 2. List of proposed function to cover security risks

1- Policy Management:
- The enterprise solution should have ability to enforce and validate a security policy to any smartphone communicating with it.
- Fully controlling the smartphone while it is communicating with the enterprise solution and releasing this control once disconnected.
2- Data Isolation:
- Enterprise solution should provide data isolation between its own stored data and other personal data of the user.
3- Data Encryption:
- Provide encryption function for data and commands.
4- Secure Communication:
- Establishing secure communication parameters between smartphone and the enterprise solution are required.
5- Easy Integration:
- Ensuring smooth integration with the existing systems.

Table 2. (*continued*)

6- **Performance and Overhead:**
-    Introducing as less overhead as possible security solutions on the smartphone and on the enterprise solution architecture.

In the following, we will explore the most common ideas of solutions proposed in related work to overcome these security risks.

4.1   Trust Droid [64]

Trust Droid is a proposed solution to provide data isolation and applications policy management at different layers of Android software stack. Trust Droid assumes that the enterprise networks are trusted and the employee is trusted too, however, smartphones are generally not trusted because employees are prone to security critical errors, such as installing malware or disabling security features. The main idea of Trust Droid is to classify the applications into three predefined categories; or "Colouring them" as mentioned by the authors [64]. The first category gathers pre-installed system applications like the content providers and services, the second category is trusted third party applications provided by the enterprise systems, and the third category is dedicated to untrusted third party applications like any other application installed by the employee for personal use. This classification is performed by checking the application certificate at installation time. Based on this classification, each application will run under its category's policy where untrusted applications cannot access resources or communicate with applications belonging to the trusted category. Trust Droid provides mandatory access control MAC [7] for each category domain to control files accessing and sharing. In addition, Trust Droid provides a firewall to control network sockets and internet protocol; the firewall rules are based on the policy of each category.

Evaluation: from security perspective Trust Droid could be vulnerable to runtime attacks like buffer overflow because the TCB model of Trust Droid assumes that the low level system layer is secure. In addition, if an adversary identifies vulnerabilities in one of these pre-installed applications, he could break the domain isolation and get access to data belonging to trust applications. Trust Droid has other weaknesses in managing enterprise dynamic data, for example it cannot prevent an enterprise application from uploading personal files, also managing categories policy limited to application development phase, and it cannot be updated after installation which limits the evolution of the solution over time. From performance perspective, based on section 5.2 of [64], Trust Droid introduces acceptable performance overhead. Finally, there is no data encryption functionality to be managed by the solution.

4.2   Unified Security Enhancement Framework [5]

Authors of [5] propose a unified and effective kernel-level framework to secure the Android OS by introducing three mechanisms: first is Root Privilege Protection (RPP) which keeps track of a list of trusted programs with root privileges, second is Resource Misuse Protection (RMP) which keeps track of important system resources that are vital in the Android OS and finally Private Data Protection (PDP) which disallows trusted programs to access sensitive data through enforcing the least privilege principle in the permission-based access control.

Evaluation: from security perspective the framework was evaluated by conducting three experiments based on three malicious behaviors, first one is trying to gain root access, second one is changing system resources like configuration files which is always target by attacker, last one is trying to access user private data like contact list. The framework succeeded to prevent all these attacks; however the framework just narrows the threats attacks possibilities because any malicious application installed by super user can inherit all root access, and for RMP, the mechanism restriction related to phone configuration itself which cannot be modified by any application and this is not the case in enterprise applications which need more flexibility to prevent conflicts between applications. The system doesn't have remote management capabilities for installed applications, and for performance perspective section 5 in [5] shows that related to monitoring files and system calls from framework component the system increase the overhead by almost 25% average than normal Android OS.

4.3   Polite Policy Framework [48]

The proposed idea of polite policy framework is to control applications behavior at execution time. Indeed, developers use a modified API to provision security at the build phase of the application itself, which enables polite framework to achieve fine grained policy control as well as be easily adopted in the mobile application develop- ment life cycle. Policies are dynamically fetched from an enterprise policy server at run time which gives the enterprise administrators high management capabilities. When an enterprise application starts, the system creates a parallel thread that moni- tors the phone state and stops or kills the application if the enterprise policies are not met. The advantage in this solution is that the enterprise policy is enforced only on enterprise applications executions time; thus, the personal use of the device will not be affected.

Evaluation: from security perspective, the solution has two types of policies; first is API level policy, which manages the device resources like GPS, Wi-Fi, etc. and the second is application level policy, which manages the data flow. Also Polite framework gives the developer data encryption functionalities to secure enterprise data and perform remote device wipe functionality for device stolen case, however this good policy classification doesn't prevent system component itself to be exploited under root access attack or privilege escalation attack. Another weak point is that the enterprise application itself is responsible for the communication with policy server and policy enforcement! That will make policy conflict between enterprise applications and it could increase threats on policy server. Overall the system could be the easiest in integration process implementation. From performance perspective, section VI- c [48] shows that polite framework takes 6% more time than normal native library command execution.

4.4   CRêPE [45]

CRêPE is a solution for Enforcing Fine-Grained Context-Related Policies on Android. It acts as a security mechanism in addition to the standard Android security and allows users and other predefined trusted parties to define context-related policies which can be installed, updated, and applied at runtime. These policies can be applied in a fine-grained manner, e.g. for each application. The context-related policy consists of two different types of policies:

- Access control policy: access rules that use the XACML standard [42].
- Obligation policy: specifies the actions that should be done, like activate or disable a system resource like GPS, Wifi, camera or start and stop applications.

The system component manages policies check at all android stack layers: application layer, framework layer, and kernel layer. Moreover, the user is able to manage poli- cies rules, i.e., "create, update and delete" locally form the device (through GUI ap- plications) or remotely via SMS message, Bluetooth and QR-code using public key infrastructure PKI schema.

Evaluation: from security perspective, CRêPE extends the permission check mechanism in android OS by adding further checks to the current active CRêPE policy, this approach can be considered as prevention of privilege escalation attacks. Also CRêPE has CRePEIPTables component which is working in the kernel level as firewall to filter the network access. However there are two weaknesses in this solution; first defining the policy depends on the user orientation of security needs which is not enough to secure the device; second CRêPE protects the communication between its components by PKI system using X.509 certificates stored as root authority, a rooting attack as described in [59] could expose the authentication certificate and the system will be vulnerable to any income message. From performance perspective, Section VI-B in [45] shows that policy activation and deactivation overhead is influenced by the number of conflict rules defined in the policy, but the overall efficiency overhead could be acceptable.

4.5   SE for Android [25]

Android has a Linux Kernel OS and thus, relies on the Linux discretionary access control (DAC) [51] to implement the permission model of Android security architecture. Indeed, Android uses DAC in two ways:

- Sandboxing technique to provide data and code execution isolation between applications [15].
- Authorizing applications to access system resources like Wifi, GPS, etc.

Security Enhanced Linux (SE Linux) [24] was originally developed as a Mandatory Access Control (MAC) [7] mechanism for Linux. The goal of MAC is to allow the OS constraining the ability of a subject or initiator to access or generally perform some sorts of operation on an object or target depending on a wide set of rules. In [54].

SE Linux and a middleware MAC are integrated to Android OS to overcome the shortage of Android DAC mechanisms.

Evaluation: from security perspective; authors of [24] evaluate SE Android by investigating previously published malwares and vulnerabilities. Regarding root exploits malwares. SE Android was able to prevent some of applied rootkits like Ginger Master [29] and Zimperlich [9], however SE Android was not able to prevent others like KillingInTheNameOf and psneuter exploits [10]. Regarding the application layer vulnerabilities, SE Android provides an effective means of preventing applications from performing privilege escalation attacks and unauthorized data sharing through kernel interfaces. However, SE Android has some limitations that should be considered. First, the effectiveness of its security depends on the defined policy which means SE Android cannot mitigate anything not defined in the policy rules. Second, SE Android was not able to mitigate Kernel level vulnerabilities applied by rootkits. Third, SE Android cannot protect against threats originating from shared hardware resources, for example actions performed by a baseband processor or a network card [24]. For performance and efficiency the SE-Android overhead was negligible compared with normal Android OS.

4.6   L4Android [19][50]

L4Android is a microkernel derived from L4Linux [20] which is created by adding the required code by Android to L4Linux. L4Android divides the OS kernel functions into small components, each component implements one basic service and is equipped with only permissions needed for its correct operation. The goal of L4Android is to run Android in a virtual machine on the top of the microkernel, thus we can run two An- droid OS as virtual machine one is for private use and the other for business purpose. *Evaluation*: from security perspective, virtualization provides high domain data isola- tion between business partition and personal partition as long as the business partition is not infected. For policy management perspective, the enterprise system may still need to apply such policies for the business partition in case of multiple enterprise applications. From performance perspective, L4Android has more execution time than the normal Android and related to [21] it has performance issues with graphic driver components. There are many hypervisor developed to achieve the same domain data isolation technique like Xen [39], KVM [32] and Code Zero [11]. Overall, virtualization could be good technique to provide secure environment and data isolation; however the power efficiency, performance and implementation coast will be barriers to apply it.

4.7   Improving Security with OS-Level Virtualization [58]

Linux Containers (LXC) [21] is a lightweight OS level virtualization that isolates processes and resources without the need to provide instruction interpretation mechanisms and other complexities of full virtualization like hypervisor virtualization mechanism. Authors of [63] provides user pace containers to isolate and control the resources of single applications or groups of applications running on top of one kernel for Android OS. This typically includes a unique hostname, process identifiers (PIDs), inter-process communications (IPCs), a file system, and network resources. *Evaluation*: from security perspective, the major advantage of this virtualization tech- nique compared to system virtualization is that the isolation layer – the kernel – has full control over all resources and can directly interfere with all processing layers and in all subsystems, this allows fine grained policy enforcement for system calls and integrity measurements of sensitive application groups at runtime. Also the system has a remote management component in the kernel level so it is isolated from Android user space and encryption functionality could be integrated at the device level for a whole file system or at a per-file basis. from performance perspective in section-9 at [63] the evaluation test shows that negligible performance overhead happen compared with the original Android OS performance.

4.8   Matrix of Proposed Solutions and Suggested Functions

In this matrix we relate the proposed solutions feature with the suggested functions to cover security risks. We used three symbols: (-) mean this function is weak or

Table 3. Matrix of proposed solutions and suggested Functions

	Policy Manageme	Data Isolatio	Data Encryptio	Secure Communicati	Easy Integratio	Performance & Overhead
Trust Droid	+	*	-	*	+	-
Security enhancement framework	-	+	-	+	-	+
Polite Policy Framework	*	+	*	-	*	+
CRêPE	*	*	-	*	+	+
SE-Android	*	+	-	+	+	+
L4Android	+	*	-	-	-	+
OS-Level Virtualization	+	*	-	+	+	*

does not exist, (*) mean this function has good implementation, (+) mean this function needs more enhancement.

5   Security Solutions from Industry

Many smartphone manufacture, telecommunication providers and security solution companies start collaborate together to provide a complete secure solutions for managing smartphone in Enterprise systems using the same ideas as we presented in section 4. Samsung, one of these smartphone manufactures, provides a complete solution for secure smartphone management in enterprise system named KNOX. KNOX [44] is an Android based solution built on the integration between hardware layer using Trust Zone (TZ) technology [29] with software layer using SE for Android and Android Containers technology. The advantage of using TZ technology is partitioning the memory and CPU resources into a "secure" and "normal" world, which allow TZ- based Integrity Measurement Architecture (TIMA) to continuously monitor the integrity of the Linux kernel. TIMA runs in the secure-world and cannot be disabled, while the SE for Android Linux kernel runs in the "normal" world. The Android Container provides isolation between the enterprise programs operation environment and other programs operation environment like the OS level virtualization solution we discussed in section 4. Finally, the system has data encryption function that allows enterprise IT administrators to encrypt data on the entire device and has virtual private network (VPN) support to establish secure communications.

There are other companies providing secure enterprise mobile solutions like VMware [38] and TrendMicro [37], however all these solutions still new in the industry and need times to be evaluated.

6   Conclusion

In this paper we proposed a security driven taxonomy for enterprise mobile applications, then we identified the user private data on smartphones, possible attacks and applications vulnerabilities on Android. We defined the security risks and proposed security functions to cover these risks, and then we surveyed the current proposed solutions ideas and validate them with our proposed functions. Finally, we presented Knox as real industry solution from Samsung. We come with matter of fact that there is shortage between the old security models which applied now in the enterprise systems and the new era of smartphones and tablets platforms. Therefore, industries need more flexible and secure models to be integrated to their enterprise systems.

References

1. Amiya, K.: Empirical study of the robustness of inters process communication in android, Purdue university
2. Osterman, A.: Research White Paper Published October 2012, "The Need for IT to Get in Front of the BYOD Problem"
3. Unhelkar, B., Murugesan, S.: The Enterprise Mobile Applications Development Framework. IT Professional 12(3), 33–39 (2010)
4. Bravo, P., Garcia, D.F.: Proactive Detection of Kernel-Mode Rootkits. In: 2011 Sixth International Conference on Availability, Reliability and Security (ARES), August 22-26, pp. 515–520 (2011)
5. Lee, C., Kim, J., Cho, S.-J., Choi, J., Park, Y.: Unified security enhancement framework for the Android operating system. Springer Science+Business Media, New York (2013)
6. You, D.-H., Noh, B.-N.: System Security Research Center, Chonnam National University. Android platform based linux kernel rootkit.
7. Bae, H., Kim, S.-W., Yoo, C.: Graduate School of Convergence IT, Korea University, Seoul, Republic of Korea. Building the Android platform security mechanism using Trust Zone.
8. http://archive09.linux.com/feature/113941
9. http://c-skills.blogspot.ca/2011/02/zimperlich-sources.html
10. http://cve.mitre.org/cgi-bin/cvename.cgi?name=CVE-2011-1149
11. http://cve.mitre.org/cgi-bin/cvename.cgi?name=CVE-2011-1717
12. http://dev.b-labs.com/
13. http://developer.android.com/guide/components/index.html
14. http://developer.android.com/guide/components/intents-filters.html
15. http://developer.android.com/guide/components/processes-and-threads.html
16. http://developer.android.com/training/articles/security-tips.html
17. http://en.wikipedia.org/wiki/Google_Play
18. http://home.mcafee.com/VirusInfo/VirusProfile.aspx?key=554488
19. http://l4android.org/
20. http://l4linux.org/
21. http://linuxcontainers.org/
22. http://old.nabble.com/L4Android-performance-issue-td34125968.html
23. http://reviews.cnet.com/8301-19736_7-57578709-251/hack-your-android-like-a-pro-rooting-and-roms-explained/
24. http://selinuxproject.org/page/Main_Page
25. http://selinuxproject.org/page/SEAndroid
26. http://source.android.com/tech/security/#the-application-sandbox
27. http://tomoyo.sourceforge.jp/
28. http://www.adtpulse.com/home/how-pulse-works/mobile
29. http://www.arm.com/products/processors/technologies/trustzone/index.php
30. http://www.businesswire.com/news/home/20130214005415/en/Android-iOS-Combinid

31. http://www.csc.ncsu.edu/faculty/jiang/GingerMaster/
32. http://www.linux-kvm.org/page/Main_Page
33. http://www.ok-labs.com/geektv/watch/mobile-virtualization-security-delivered
34. http://www.ok-labs.com/products/ok-android
35. http://www.samsung.com/ca/business-images/resource/case-study/2012/11/EBT_1208_EBTsource_MobileSecurity_Whitepaper_WP-0-1.pdf
36. http://www.tldp.org/LDP/tlk/ipc/ipc.html
37. http://www.trendmicro.com/us/enterprise/product-security/mobile-security/
38. http://www.vmware.com/mobile-secure-desktop/
39. http://www.xen.org/products/xenhyp.html
40. https://code.google.com/p/seek-for-android/wiki/AndroidContainer
41. https://labs.mwrinfosecurity.com/tools/drozer/
42. https://play.google.com/store
43. https://www.oasis-pen.org/committees/tc_home.php?wg_abbrev=xacml
44. https://www.samsungknox.com/overview/enterprise-it
45. CRêPE: A System for Enforcing Fine-Grained Context-Related Policies on Android. IEEE Transactions on Information Forensics and Security 7(5) (October 2012)
46. Park, J., Sandhu, R.: The UCONABC usage control model. ACM Trans. Inf. Syst. Secur. 7, 128–174 (2004)
47. Boutet, J.: SANS Institute InfoSec Reading Room, Malicious Android Applications: Risks and Exploitation
48. Kumar, U., Kodeswaran, P., Nandakumar, V., Kapoor, S.: Polite: A policy framework for building managed mobile apps. In: Military Communications Conference, MILCOM 2012, October 29, November 1, pp. 1–6 (2012)
49. Davi, L., Dmitrienko, A., Sadeghi, A.-R., Winandy, M.: System Security Lab,Ruhr-University Bochum, Germany "Privacy Esclation Attack on An- droid"
50. Lange, M., Liebergeld, S., Lackorzynski, A., Warg, A., Danisevskis, J., Nordholz, J.C.: Security in Telecommunications, TU Berlin, Germany "Hotmobile, Demo: L4Android Security Framework on the Samsung Galaxy S2" (2012)
51. Lange, M.: Steffen Liebergeld Universität Berlin and Deutsche Telekom Laboratories L4Android: A Generic Operating System Framework for Secure Smart phones
52. Zhao, M., Ge, F., Zhang, T., Yuan, Z.: Institute of Command and Automation, PLA University of Science and technology, Nanjing, China "AntiMalDroid: An Efficient SVM-Based Malware Detection Framework for Android"
53. Kodeswaran, P., Nandakumar, V., Kapoor, S.: Securing Enterprise data on smart phone using run time information flow control. In: 2012 IEEE 13th international Conference on Mobile Data Management (2012)
54. Fehrenbach, P.: Android Vulnerability Analysis with Mercury Framework, http://it-securityguard.com/Pentest_09_2012.pdf
55. Dornbusch, P., Ller, M.M., Buttermann, A.: It- Security in Global Corporate Networks (February 4 2003)
56. Samarati, P., de Vimercati, S.C.: Access Control: Policies, Models, and Mechanisms. In: Focardi, R., Gorrieri, R. (eds.) FOSAD 2000. LNCS, vol. 2171, pp. 137–196. Springer, Heidelberg (2001)

57. Hay, R.: IBM Rational Application Security Research Group, "Opera Mobile Cache Poisoning XAS" (September 2011)
58. Wessel, S., Stumpf, F., Herdt, I., Eckert, C.: Fraunhofer Research Institution AISEC, Munich, Germany "Improving Mobile Device Security with Operating System-Level Virtualization"
59. Zhong, S., Li, L., Liu, Y.G., Yang, Y.R.: Computer Science Department Yale University, Department of Computer Sciences The University of Texas Austin, "Privacy-Preserving Location-based Services for Mobile Users in Wireless Net- works"
60. Smalley, S., Craig, R.: Trusted Systems Research National Security Agency "Security Enhanced (SE) Android: Bringing Flexible MAC to Android"
61. Sven Bugiel technische university Darmstadt Practical lightweight domain isolation on Android,
62. Hayes, T.: Mitigating Signaling Based Attacks on Smart phones Collin Mulliner, Steffen Liebergeld, Matthias Lange, and Jean-Pierre Seifert Technische Universität Berlin and Deutsche Telekom Laboratories
63. TE-ENWEll, ALBERT B. JENGl, Department of Computer Science and Information Engineering, National Taiwan University "Android privacy"
64. Kumar, U.: A policy framework for building managed mobile App. In: Kodeswaran, P., Vikrant, S. (eds.) IBM Research India, University of Florida,
65. Jun-Jang, W.: Sik-Whan, Hyung-Woo, Hong-ill, Jeomg-Nyeo: Hanshin University & knowledge base information security & software research Lab "Rooting Attack Detection Method on the Android based Smart Phone"
66. Zhang, X., Seifert, J.-P., Acıiçmez, O.: SEIP: Simple and efficient integrity protection for open mobile platforms. In: Soriano, M., Qing, S., López, J. (eds.) ICICS 2010. LNCS, vol. 6476, pp. 107–125. Springer, Heidelberg (2010)
67. http://resources.idgenterprise.com/original/AST-0038025_ Aujas_White_paper__Mitigating_Security_Risk_in_USSD_Apr11_.pdf

Simulation of the Best Ranking Algorithms for an App Store

Luisanna Cocco, Katiuscia Mannaro, Giulio Concas, and Michele Marchesi

Department of Electric and Electronic Engineering, University of Cagliari, Piazza D'Armi, 09123 Cagliari, Italy

Abstract. The world of mobile applications is relatively young. However, it has already grown and will continue to expand in the future. Consequently, an increasing number of mobile application stores provide new ways for the users of downloading mobile applications and for the developers of submitting new applications. Millions of consumers look for mobile applications to download - i.e. games, maps, movie, e-mails and so on. This extraordinary new world represents an exceptional challenge for application developers who want to earn and obtain new business opportunities. Our research work focused on studying, analyzing and modeling the best strategies that should be adopted in a mobile application store in order to maximize efficiency and profit. We propose a model that simulates a complex system of mobile applications, developers, and users, all together interacting in an application mobile store. Here the developers build and upload mobile applications to the mobile applications store and the users browse the store and download only the mobile applications that arouse their attention.

Keywords: App Store, Mobile Apps, Agent Simulation Model.

1 Introduction

During the last two decades, mobile devices experienced an exceptional growth. From the earliest devices that combined functions of the mobile phones with the ones of the Personal Digital Assistant, we have arrived to devices that support/display streaming video, surf the web, download movies, read email, game or listen to music, and more.

We have observed a growth as never seen before in mobile technology, in particular as regards the capabilities and variety of mobile devices, but also as regards the number of users that approached to the mobile technology world.

Indeed, every day millions of people use tablets and smarthphones both for work and for pleasure. Our life has been influenced irrevocably by the mobile technologies, and consequently, by the world of mobile applications (apps).

In the past few years, tablets and smarthphones became the main communication and entertainment devices for millions of people. Millions of consumers look for mobile applications to download - i.e. games, maps, movie, e-mails and so on. So, mobile technology represents an interesting field to investigate in order to

I. Awan et al. (Eds.): MobiWis 2014, LNCS 8640, pp. 233–247, 2014.

find the best strategies for delivering and developing its applications [12]. Indeed, this extraordinary new world represents an exceptional challenge for application developers who want to earn and obtain new business opportunities.

Our research work focused on studying, analyzing and modeling the best strategies that should be adopted in a mobile application store in order to maximize efficiency and profit. In this paper we propose a model that simulates a complex system of mobile applications, developers, and users, all together interacting in an application mobile store (apps store). Generally the developers build and upload mobile applications to the mobile applications store and the users browse the store and download the mobile applications that arouse their attention. Our work aims to delineate the strategies that a developer should follow in order to be a successful developer, since being a successful developer pays, also declared also in [2], [4], [14] and [7]. Our model follows and complements the research activity carried out by Lim et al. in [10], [9] and [11], in which the developers' successfull strategies are investigated. In particular we modified the behaviour of the agents and introduced some additional features for the apps. We start by examining some research works in literature and introducing the original model. We continue by showing our proposed model and in order to enhance our contribution we present our results. We suggest some strategies derived from discussed findings. In conclusion we summarize the findings and discuss the remaining issues.

2   Related Work

Despite the market of mobile devices and mobile app stores are growing, there are few studies that focus on the apps' popularity or income strategies that an app store should adopt. Mostly studies deal with mobile ecosystem security and privacy. Grace et al. [6] focus on potential privacy and security risks posed by embedded or in-app advertisement libraries available on smartphone platforms. In [1], a generic security architecture for the Android OS is proposed in order to instantiate different security solutions. In [3], the authors try to understand user attitudes toward security and privacy for smartphones and how they may differ from attitudes toward more traditional computing systems to direct and build an effective, secure mobile ecosystem. In [15], the rise of mobile applications and why code signing certificates is analyzed. This is because it is essential to protect the whole mobile apps ecosystem.

However to our knowledge there are some studies about apps downloads and their usage. For instance, Bohmer et al.[19] developed a mobile app to collect mobile app usage information from over 4,100 users of Android devices. Petsas et al. [13] monitored and analyzed four popular third-party Android app marketplaces in order to better understand how download patterns, or popularity trends and development strategies in the mobile app ecosystem. This paper focuses on measuring, analyzing, and modeling the app popularity distribution, and explores how pricing and revenue strategies affect app popularity and developers income. Chen and Cheng in [20] developed an evaluation framework to construct mobile value-added services. Their study used survey forms to collect feedback from 35 industry and research institution experts and scholars. They present the finding on the mobile value-added services strategy and the results can be used as guides for players in the mobile communications industry to review, improve, and enhance their service and strategy. In [21] the authors explore the question which platform type an operator should adopt if he wants to play a meaningful role in the mobile service domain. The paper describes advantages and disadvantages of different platform types and lists some core competences an operator should have, or develop, in order to successful adopt a certain platform type. In [22] the authors describe the implications that different market and technology trends have on the mobile application development market. In their paper they take a developers perspective in order to explore how the identified trends will impact the mobile application development markets. Finally in [10], the authors investigate what strategies a developer should use to be a successful developer. For this aim they proposed the AppEco model, the first Artificial Life model of a mobile application ecosystem. The same authors in [9] use AppEco to investigate common publicity strategies adopted by developers and their effects on app downloads. Moreover in [11] they use AppEco to investigate how optimally to organize the app store content in Apple's iOS App Store. Our research work starts from this AppEco model.

3   An Introduction to the Original Model

In this section, we describe the model from which our research work stems. Our model is an evolution of the AppEco model. AppEco is an Articial Life simulation of the mobile ecosystem developed by Lim and Bentley [9]. In AppEco the developers build and upload apps to the app store and the users browse the store, modeled through two Charts. One chart is called *New App Chart* and the other *Top App Chart*. The users are modeled as random users and so they download the apps in a random way.

3.1   App Store

The App Store is modeled using two Chart: Top and New App Chart. The Top App Chart shows the apps' ranking depending on the number of downloads of the apps, whereas the New App Chart shows the apps' ranking depending on time instant in which the apps are uploaded in the app store. Over time, both charts are updated.

The Top App Chart is updated with four ranking algorithms:

- Weighted 4-day Downloads (W4),
- Weighted 7-day Downloads (W7);
- Current Downloads (Cur) and
- Cumulative Downloads (Cum).

These four algorithms associate to every app a specific score according to a specific function defined in the work [10]. The apps are inserted in the Top Apps Chart in order of decreasing score.

The four algorithms are the following:

1. the Weighted 4-day Downloads algorithm, in which the function that computes the app's score is the following:

$$score = 8D_1 + 5D_2 + 5D_3 + 3D_4;$$

2. the Weighted 7-day Downloads algorithm, in which the function that computes the app's score is the following:

$$score = 4D_1 + 3D_2 + 2D_3 + D_4 + D_5 + D_6 + D_7$$

where D_n indicates the number of downloads received by the app on the $n - th$ days before the current day.
3. the Current Download Algorithm in which the app's score is the total number of downloads received by the app on the previous day;
4. the Cumulative Download algorithm, in which the app's score is the total number of downloads received by the app since it was uploaded.

As regards updating the New App Chart, each new app has a probability $P_{OnNewChart}$ of appearing on the New App Chart. The size of this chart is limited and is equal to $N_{MaxNewChart}$. Consequently, only a limited number of new apps can be selected to appear in this chart. These apps are extracted in a random way. When the apps list is smaller than size of the chart, then the oldest apps appear in the lowest positions of the chart. Over time, the oldest apps are not listed anymore.

3.2   Mobile Applications

Each app is modelled through a *feature matrix* that identifies it uniquely.

This matrix has ten rows and ten columns (100 cells). Each cell defines a particular features that the app has got. So if a cell has a value equal to one, then the app offers that particular feature. On the contrary, if a cell has a value equal to zero, then the app does not offer that feature. The probability of a cell to be equal to one is P_{Feat}.

In addition to the feature matrix, every app is associated to a particular characteristic. An app can be or not be infectious with a probability $P_{Infectious}$. If an user downloads an infectious app then he recommends it to his friends, who in turn will download that app.

A good example of infectious app is WhatsApp Messenger, the most popular mobile application that allows the users to exchange messages. Of course the user that likes using WhatsApp Messenger needs his friends install this app in their mobile devices.

3.3   Agents: Developers and Users

In the App Ecosystem [10] the developers create apps by adopting four kind of strategies.

The *Innovator Strategy*, in which the developers create their app in a random way. The cells have got unitary value with probability equal to P_{Feat}.

The *Milker Strategy*, in which the developers adopt the previous strategy when they create their first app, whereas for creating their next apps they copy the features of their own lastest app, modifying its unitary cells in a random way.

The *Optimizer Strategy*, in which the developers adopt the Innovator strategy when they create their first app, whereas for creating their next apps they copy the features of their own best app modifying its unitary cells in a random way.

The *Copycat Strategy*, in which the developers copy the features of an app extracted in a random way from the Top App Chart.

The results shown in their work established that no strategy can guarantee a winner. They can only give some guidelines to follow in order to be a successful developer. In the case of Innovator, Milker and Copycat strategies, the developers can be successful or not. This depends on luck and it do not follow any reasoning able to guide them towards the success. Only in the case of Optimizer Strategy, the developers create their apps in order to satisfy the needs of the customers. Indeed, they develop their app modifying their own best app, their most downloaded app. As regards the developer behaviour, the App Ecosystem [10] assumes that each developer takes a fixed number of days to build an app. This number, called *devDuration*, is defined for each developer at the moment in which the simulation starts. In addition, to each developer is associated a state. The developers can be active or inactive. At initial time all the developers are active but over time they can become inactive with a probabiliy $P_{Inactive}$.

With regard to the users, a *preference matrix* is associated to them and it uniquely identifies them. Also for this agent, the matrix has ten rows and ten columns. Each cell can be equal to 1 with probability P_{Pref}. A cell with unitary value means the user desires the feature represented by that cell. There is a correspondence among cells in the preference matrix and cells in the feature matrix. Indeed, for example a cell set to one in position (2,2) both in the preference matrix of an user and in the feature matrix of a particular app implies that the app offers the feature desired by the user.

Further, an attribute called *numFriends* is associated to each user. This attribute is needed to represent the number of friends to whom a user recommend an infectious app. This number is a random number with power law distribution in the range $[0, 150]$. The upper limit of this range derives from the Dunbar number [5]. According to Dunbar, a person is only able to manage relationships with at most 150 friends. Each user cannot browse the app store every day. Therefore, a number of days between each browsing of the app store is associated to each user. This number, called *daysBtwBrowse*, is defined at the start of the simulation. Finally, as regards the user and developer population, we underline that over time the number of users and developers varies following an expression that stems from the ecology literature [8]:

$$pop_t = MinPop + \frac{MaxPop - MinPop}{1 + e^{St-D}} \tag{1}$$

This expression is a sigmoid growth function where S determines the slope of the growth curve, D shifts the curve from left to right, $MinPop$ is the minimum population, $maxPop$ is the maximum population, reached in the end of the simulation.

4   The Proposed Model

Up to now, we have described the Artificial Life Simulation of Mobile App Ecosystem proposed by Lim and Bentley [11], [10]. In order to make this model more realistic, we modified the behaviour of the agents and introduced some additional features for the apps. Our model differs from the Lim's and Bentley's model for the following features. The shop front of the app store is modeled by two charts as in the AppEco model. These charts are called New Apps Chart and Top Apps Chart. When the simulation starts the New Apps Chart is filled in a random way. Whereas in next simulation steps each new app has a probability $P_{OnNewChart}$ of appearing on this Chart. At initial time, Top Apps Chart is empty. Afterwards, it is filled ranking the apps by the algorithms proposed by Lim and Bentley (**Weighted 4-day Downloads**, **Weighted 7-day Downloads**, **Current Downloads** and **Cumulative Downloads**).

In addition to these algorithms we introduce the following three algorithms:

1. **Last Month Downloads** (LM) in which the app's score is the total number of downloads received by the app in the previous month,
2. **Last Two Month Downloads** (LTM) in which the app's score is the total number of downloads received by the app in the previous two months,
3. **Last Year Downloads** (LY) in which the app's score is the total number of downloads received by the app in the previous year.

These algorithms were proposed to study the behaviour of the simulating model in response to the top app ranking algorithms different from those proposed in [11]. As regards the app creation strategies, the developers create their apps adopting the *Evolutionary* or the *Random Strategy*. The former strategy establishes that the developers create their apps modyfing their own best app. The best app of a developer is his app having the highest number of download. So the developers create their apps in order to satisfy the needs of the customers, and then trying to forecast the app demand. The latter strategy establishes that the developers create their apps building the feature matrix in a random way, and so the developer's success depends on luck. To model the behaviour of the app users in a way as realistic as possible, we consider an app store in which four typologies of users interact:

1. **Random Users** download the apps in a random way,
2. **Herd Follower Users** download the more downloaded apps,
3. **Stingy Users** download the free apps,

4. **Sensible Users** download the apps which have the lowest price and the highest star number.

A category, a price and a number of stars (user's preferences) are associated to each app. This influences the attention of users for a specific app as happens in reality. Each user browses the New App Chart and the Top App Chart, and conducts a specific search among these apps. This search returns a random number of apps, between $[Key_{Min}, Key_{Max}]$, to visit and download. The user downloads an app only if it arouses his interest. Let us analyze in detail the behaviour of the four typologies of users.

1. The first type, **Random Users**, visit a random number of apps, N, between $[Key_{Min}, Key_{Max}]$. They download the apps not yet downloaded. Then apps visited N are extracted both from the New App Chart and the Top App Chart in a random way.
2. The second type, **Herd Follower Users**, sort the apps in descending order according to the number of downloads of the apps. These users visit the first N apps having the highest number of download. They download the apps
   - not yet downloaded,
   - whose category arouses their attention, and
   - whose feature matrix matches with their preference matrix.
   Also in this case, N is a random number of apps between $[Key_{Min}, Key_{Max}]$.
3. The third type, **Stingy Users**, download only free apps, choosing them among the free apps in the New App Chart and the Top App Chart. The downloaded apps must not be downloaded yet and must belong to the category that arouses the attention of the user.
   The apps to download are N, N being a random number of apps between $[Key_{Min}, Key_{Max}]$.
   When in the New App and in the Top App Chart there are N free apps, all of them are downloaded.
   Otherwise, when in the New App Chart and in the Top App Chart there are M apps ($M < N$), then only the M free apps can be downloaded.
4. Finally, the last type of users, **Sensible Users** download the apps with the lowest price and the highest star number. These users sort the apps in ascending order according to their price. They visit the first N apps having the lowest price. Among these apps they choose the apps
   - not downloaded yet,
   - whose category arouses their attention, and
   - whose feature matrix matches their preference matrix.
   Again, N is a random number of apps between $[Key_{Min}, Key_{Max}]$.

In order to investigate the response of the model to different initial setting, we set the price and the category of the apps following two different configuration: **Random Setting** and **Real Setting**. Instead, in both the configurations the number of stars is associated to each app in a random way.

In the first configuration we set the values of the different app characteristics and the purchase preferences of the users in a random way.

Table 1. App Price, count of application submissions and most popular apps

Price	Percentage	App Category	Submission Number per Month
Free	61.63%		
$ 0.99	18.70 %	Games	1064
$ 1.99	7.7 %	No-Games	2470
$ 2.99	4.13 %	**Most Popular**	Percentage
$ 3.99	1.84 %	Games	18.44%
> $ 3.99	6 %	No-Games	81.56%

In the second configuration we set the values of the different app characteristics in a real way, following the data reported in the web site "148apps.biz" ([16], [17] and [18]).

The used data are shown in the tables 1. Note that, for simplicity the apps are divided into only two groups: games and no-games.

5   Results

In order to highlight what app creation strategies and what top app chart ranking algorithms allow the developers, and in general, the app store to achieve the success, we implemented it in Java Code.

Contrary to Lim and Bentley's work ([11]), our aim is not to calibrate the model in order to match the behaviour of a real app store. We aim to propose a model as realistic as possible, which can be used to analyze and study the best ranking methods and app creation strategies in app stores. In particular, one of our goals is to investigate what are the best ranking algorithms of apps in the Top Apps Chart, and the best rate of app change of the New Apps Chart when in the market there are users having different app purchase preferences and apps having different characteristics.

For this purpose, we computed the average download-to-browse (D-B) ratio and run different simulation blocks over a time span of 700 days.

For evaluating the model robustness, we implemented the Monte Carlo method running each simulation block 50 times.

The average download-to-browse (D-B) ratio is defined as in [11], and hence as the total number of apps downloaded divided by the total number of apps browsed.

Therefore, for example, a D-B ratio of 0.4 means that for every ten apps the user browses, four apps are downloaded. A D-B ratio equal to 1 means that the user downloads immediately all the apps he/she browses.

We organized different simulation blocks in order to study the market response to

- different app creation strategies,
- different ranking algorithms of the apps in the Top App Chart,
- different probabilities $P_{OnNewChart}$: 0.1, 0.01, 0.001 and 0.0001.

The simulation blocks runs are three.

The first and second blocks study a market in which the price and the categories of the apps and the purchase preferences of the users are set in a random way. They were run once for each $P_{OnNewChart}$ and for each probability they were run once for each top app ranking algorithm. We run the first block with $P_{OnNewChart}$ equal to 0.1 seven times, choosing for each time a different top app ranking algorithms ($W4$ or $W7$ or Cur or Cum or LM or LTM or LY).

In the first block the developers adopt the evolutionary app creation strategy, whereas in the second block the developers adopt the random app creation strategy.

Finally, in the third block the model is calibrated using the Real Setting, and so it studies a market in which the price and the categories of the apps and the purchase preferences of the users follow a strategy that should be closer to the real ones. In this block the developers adopt the evolutionary app creation strategy. This block was run once for each $P_{OnNewChart}$ and for each $P_{OnNewChart}$ once for each top app ranking algorithm.

In the following table we report some of the parameter values adopted in these three simulation blocks. These values are extracted by some Lim and Bentley's works [11] and [10].

In this work, the authors aimed to calibrate the simulation to match the behaviour of a real app store. For this reason, they used Apple's iOS App Store because it is the oldest and most established app store and extracted the data in Table 2.

Table 2. Parameter value of the proposed model

$[Pop_{minUser}, Pop_{maxUser}]$	[1500,40000]	$[dev_{min}, dev_{max}]$	[1,180]
D_{User}	-4	P_{Pref}	0.4
S_{User}	-0.0038	P_{Feat}	0.04
$[Pop_{minDev}, Pop_{maxDev}]$	[1000,120000]	$P_{infectious}$	0.0001
D_{Dev}	-4	$N_{MaxNewChart}$	40
S_{Dev}	-0.005	$N_{MaxTopChart}$	50
$N_{initApp}$	500	$P_{Inactive}$	0.0027
$[bro_{min}, bro_{max}]$	[1,360]	$[Key_{min}, Key_{max}]$	[0,50]
$P_{OnNewChart}$	0.001		

5.1 First Simulation Block

The first simulation block entails a model in which the developers create their app following the app creation evolutionary strategy, whereas the values of the app characteristics and the purchase preferences of the users are set adopting the Random Setting configuration.

The obtained results running the first simulation block match the results reported in [11]. The highest D-B ratios occur when the probability of a new app of appearing on the New App Chart is higher. In particular, the orders of magnitude of D-B ratio vary from 10^{-3} to 10^{-1}, while the probability $P_{OnNewChart}$ varies from 0.0001 to 0.1.

In Table 3 we can observe that the highest D-B ratio is 0.1007. It is extracted from the simulation set run with $P_{OnNewChart}$ 0.1. Lowest value of D-B ratio is 0.0068, extracted from the simulation set run with $P_{OnNewChart}$ 0.0001.

Table 3. First Simulation Block: Average and Standard Deviation of the D-B ratio at timestep T=700

$P_{OnNewChart}$	App Ranking Alghoritm	Avg. D-B ratio	Std. Deviation
0.1	Cumulative Downloads	**0.1007**	0.0098
	Current Downloads	0.1006	0.0110
	Weighted 7-day Downloads	0.0994	0.0128
	Weighted 4-day Downloads	0.0992	0.0119
0.01	Current Downloads	0.1005	0.0113
	Weighted 7-day Downloads	0.1000	0.0120
	Weighted 4-day Downloads	0.0986	0.0118
	Cumulative Downloads	0.0983	0.0133
0.001	Weighted 7-day Downloads	0.0086	0.0046
	Weighted 4-day Downloads	0.0080	0.0052
	Cumulative Downloads	0.0078	0.0053
	Current Downloads	0.0070	0.0039
0.0001	Cumulative Downloads	0.0078	0.0044
	Weighted 4-day Downloads	0.0075	0.0040
	Current Downloads	0.0072	0.0036
	Weighted 7-day Downloads	**0.0068**	0.0037

Table 4. First Simulation Block: Average and Standard Deviation of the D-B ratio at timestep T=700 for the new proposed algorithms

$P_{OnNewChart}$	App Ranking Alghoritm	Avg. D-B ratio	Std. Deviation
0.1	Last Two Month Downloads	0.1008	0.0108
	Last Year Downloads	0.1001	0.0095
	Last Month Downloads	0.0953	0.0109
0.01	Last Month Downloads	0.0978	0.0119
	Last Two Months Downloads	0.0970	0.0132
	Last Year Downloads	0.0964	0.0091
0.001	Last Month Downloads	0.0082	0.0048
	Last Two Months Downloads	0.0081	0.0050
	Last Year Downloads	0.0080	0.0046
0.0001	Last Year Downloads	0.0089	0.0057
	Last Two Months Downloads	0.0086	0.0053
	Last Month Downloads	0.0075	0.0044

As regards the top app ranking algorithms, the algorithms updating more quickly the Top App Chart do not guarantee the highest D-B ratio over time for each $P_{OnNewChart}$. This is in contrast with the results of Lim and Bentley in which this trend is true for all the values of the $P_{OnNewChart}$.

Indeed, only when the probability $P_{OnNewChart}$ is equal to 0.01 the **Weighted 4-day Downloads, Weighted 7-day Downloads (W7)**, and **Current Downloads (Cur)** algorithms guarantee the highest D-B ratios over time.

Consequently, in this specific case, the algorithm that guarantees the lowest values of the D-B ratio is the **Cumulative Downloads** algorithm.

Instead, as regards the new algorithms proposed (Last Month Downloads, Last Two Month Downloads and Last Year Downloads algorithms) the consideration just described is not valid. So, it is not true that the algorithm updating more quickly the Top App chart guarantee the highest D-B ratios (see Table 4).

Whereas for they is true the particular trend described at the beginning of this section for the probability $P_{OnNewChart}$. These simulation sets confirm that the highest D-B ratios are associated with the highest probabilities of each new app of appearing on the New App Chart.

5.2   Second Simulation Block

In order to evaluate the influence of the Evolutionary App Creation Strategy on the D-B ratio, we run a second simulation block. In this set the developers adopt the Random App Creation Strategy. The values of the app characteristics and the purchase preferences of the users are set adopting the Random Setting.

In this case, the highest D-B ratios are associated with neither the highest probabilities of each new app of appearing on the New App Chart, nor the app ranking algorithms that update the Top App Chart more quickly.

As shown in Table 5 no particular advantage can be obtained by increasing of the probability $P_{OnNewChart}$ or modifying the top app ranking algorithms.

Comparing the results obtained in the first and in this second block, we can observed that the App Creation Strategy adopted by the developers influence the value of the D-B ratios. Hence, in the market in which the users interact with different purchase preferences the App Creation Strategy adopted by the developers influence the D-B ratios. Lim and Bentley in work [11] reported a different result. Indeed, they refer that the app creation strategies do not influence the D-B ratio.

5.3   Third Simulation Block

In the third simulation block, the developers create their app following the app creation evolutionary strategy and the values of the app characteristics and the purchase preferences of the users are set adopting the Real Setting configuration (see Tables 1).

This is because, it is necessary to evaluate the robustness of the model and the validity of the considerations done when the app parameter configuration varies.

We assume that 30% of the submitted apps by the developers are Games, whereas the remaining 70% are not Games. In addition, we supposed that 61.6% of the apps is free, 18.7% costs \$0.99, 7.7% costs \$1.99, 4.13% costs \$2.99, and the remaining costs about from \$3.99 and \$10.

Table 5. Second Simulation Block: Average and Standard Deviation of the D-B ratio at timestep T=700

$P_{OnNewChart}$	App Ranking Alghoritm	Avg. D-B ratio	Std. Deviation
	Cumulative Downloads	0.0100	0.0047
0.1	Weighted 4-day Downloads	0.0099	0.0043
	Weighted 7-day Downloads	0.0098	0.0042
	Current Downloads	0.0093	0.0041
	Weighted 7-day Downloads	0.0094	0.0042
0.01	Current Downloads	0.0090	0.0039
	Cumulative Downloads	0.0086	0.0037
	Weighted 4-day Downloads	0.0084	0.0040
	Cumulative Downloads	0.0090	0.0054
0.001	Weighted 4-day Downloads	0.0085	0.0045
	Weighted 7-day Downloads	0.0081	0.0038
	Current Downloads	0.0072	0.0037
	Cumulative Downloads	0.0094	0.0056
0.0001	Current Downloads	0.0094	0.0058
	Weighted 7-day Downloads	0.0087	0.0049
	Weighted 4-day Downloads	0.0085	0.0042

We set the purchase preferences of the users according to the data shown in Table 1, ref.[16], [17] and [18].

The results shown in Table 6 highlight that the Real Setting configuration for the app characteristics and for the purchase preferences of the users does not change the general tendency of the first simulation set.

Table 6. Third Simulation Block: Average and Standard Deviation of the D-B ratio at timestep T=700

$P_{OnNewChart}$	App Ranking Alghoritm	Avg. D-B ratio	Std. Deviation
	Cumulative Downloads	0.0122	0.0041
0.1	Current Downloads	0.0125	0.0042
	Weighted 7-day Downloads	0.0128	0.0041
	Weighted 4-day Downloads	0.0118	0.0040
	Current Downloads	**0.0135**	0.0049
0.01	Weighted 7-day Downloads	0.0132	0.0039
	Weighted 4-day Downloads	0.0114	0.0038
	Cumulative Downloads	0.0120	0.0037
	Weighted 7-day Downloads	0.0075	0.0042
0.001	Weighted 4-day Downloads	0.0076	0.0049
	Cumulative Downloads	0.0076	0.0045
	Current Downloads	0.0076	0.0051
	Cumulative Downloads	0.0078	0.0044
0.0001	Weighted 4-day Downloads	0.0079	0.0051
	Current Downloads	0.0067	0.0038
	Weighted 7-day Downloads	**0.0066**	0.0041

Indeed, the lowest D-B ratios are associated with the $P_{OnNewChart}$ equal to 0.0001, and the highest D-B ratio is associated with $P_{OnNewChart}$ equal to 0.01 and with Current Download algorithm. Therefore, the highest D-B ratios are associated with the highest probabilities of each new app of appearing on the New App Chart.

In addition, when the probability of each new app of appearing on the New App Chart is equal to 0.01 the algorithms that guarantee the highest D-B ratios are the app ranking algorithms that prevent the oldest apps appearing and staying on the Top App Chart for a long time.

In general, we can conclude that adopting the app creation evolutionary strategy and setting high values for the probability $P_{OnNewChart}$ guarantee a higher efficiency of an app store.

On the contrary, both updating the Top App Chart very quickly and very slowly implies mechanisms that can reduce the efficiency of the app store, and hence, the D-B ratio values.

Probably, this happens because in the first case the users interface with many new apps for too short period of time, whereas, in the second case they interface with the same apps for a too long period of time. In these two cases, no app is able to reach a number of downloads comparable to that obtained when $P_{OnNewChart}$ is equal to 0.01.

6   Conclusions

During the last two decades, we have observed an exceptional growth in mobile technology, in particular as regards the capabilities and variety of mobile devices, but also as regards the number of users that approached to the mobile technology world.

Every day millions of people use tablets and smarthphones, both for work and for pleasure. Their life has been influenced irrevocably by the world of mobile technology, and consequently, by the world of mobile apps.

The world of mobile apps is relatively young, but it has already grown and will continue to expand in the future. This extraordinary new world represents an exceptional challenge for developers willing to create new mobile apps to earn money and at the same time to help the people to be more productive or simply to have fun. In order to analyse and study the best strategy that an app store should adopt for maximizing its efficiency and its profit, we proposed a simulation model. In this model developers build and upload apps to the app store and the users browse the store in order to download the apps following their purchase preferences.

The results highlighted that the highest D-B ratios are associated with the highest probabilities of each new app of appearing on the New App Chart ($P_{OnNewChart}$). In addition, when the probability of each new app of appearing on the New App Chart, $P_{OnNewChart}$, is equal to 0.01 the highest D-B ratios are guaranteed by the app ranking algorithms that update the Top App Chart more quickly. In a market in which the customers do not download the apps in a random way but following their preferences, the app creation strategies adopted by the developers are relevant. Indeed, the app creation strategies influence the efficiency of the app store, and hence the number of downloaded apps (D-B ratio). Our results suggest that the developers should create their apps in order to satisfy the needs of the customers, and hence they should try to forecast the app demand. In addition, they should investigate on the rate and on the mechanisms with which the Charts are updated. The model presented in this work represents a valid model to analyse the app market and the best strategies that guarantee the success of the app stores and the developers.

References

1. Bugiel, S., Heuser, S., Sadeghi, A.-R.: Flexible and fine-grained mandatory access control on android for diverse security and privacy policies. In: Proceedings of the 22Nd USENIX Conference on Security, SEC 2013, pp. 131–146. USENIX Association, Berkeley (2013)
2. Chen, B.X.: Coder's half-million-dollar baby proves iphone gold rush is still on (February 12, 2009),
http://www.wired.com/gadgetlab/2009/02/shootis-iphone/
3. Chin, E., Felt, A.P., Sekar, V., Wagner, D.: Measuring user confidence in smartphone security and privacy. In: Proceedings of the Eighth Symposium on Usable Privacy and Security, SOUPS 2012, pp. 1:11:16. ACM, New York (2012)
4. Dredge, S.: Angry birds bags 6.5m christmas day downloads. the guardian (2012),
http://www.theguardian.com/
5. Dunbar, R.I.M.: Neocortex size as a constraint on group size in primate. Journal of Human Evolution (1992)
6. Grace, M.C., Zhou, W., Jiang, X., Sadeghi, A.-R.: Unsafe exposure analysis of mobile in-app advertisements. In: Proceedings of the Fifth ACM Conference on Security and Privacy in Wireless and Mobile Networks, WISEC 2012, pp. 101–112. ACM, New York (2012)
7. Jansen, S., Finkelstein, A., Brinkkemper, S.: A sense of community: A research agenda for software ecosystems. In: ICSE Companion, pp. 187–190. IEEE (2009)
8. Kingsland, S.E.: Modeling nature: Episodes in the history of population ecology. University of Chicago Press (1995)
9. Lim, S.L., Bentley, P.J.: App epidemics: Modelling the effects of publicity in a mobile app ecosystem. In: ALIFE (2012a)
10. Lim, S.L., Bentley, P.J.: How to be a successful app developer: Lessons from the simulation of an app ecosystem. SIGEVOlution 6(1), 2–15 (2012b)
11. Lim, S.L., Bentley, P.J.: Investigating app store ranking algorithms using a simulation of mobile app ecosystems. In: IEEE Congress on Evolutionary Computation, pp. 2672–2679 (2013)
12. Monarchmedia, I.: White Paper. Mobile App Development: Methods, Marketplaces, and Monetization. Monarch Media, Inc., Santa Cruz, CA 95060 (2012)
13. Petsas, T., Papadogiannakis, A., Polychronakis, M., Markatos, E.P., Karagiannis, T.: Rise of the planet of the apps: A systematic study of the mobile app ecosystem. In: Proceedings of the 2013 Conference on Internet Measurement Conference, IMC 2013, pp. 277–290. ACM, New York (2013)
14. Baghdassarian, S.: C. M. Gartner says worldwide mobile application store revenue forecast to surpass $15 billion in 2011,
http://www.gartner.com/newsroom/id/1529214/ (January 26, 2011)
15. Symantec, White paper. Securing the rise of the mobile apps market: Code signing and mobile application development. Symantec Corporation (2013)
16. 148Apps.biz iOS development news and information for the community, by the community, App Store Metrics, http://148apps.biz/app-store-metrics/ (January 14, 2014)

17. 148Apps.biz iOS development news and information for the community, by the community, Application Price Distribution, http://148apps.biz/app-store-metrics/?mpage=appprice (January 14, 2014)
18. 148Apps.biz iOS development news and information for the community, by the community, Application Category Distribution, http://148apps.biz/app-store-metrics/?mpage=catcount (January 2014)
19. Bohmer, M., Hecht, B., Schoning, J., Kruger, A., Bauer, G.: Falling asleep with Angry Birds, Facebook and Kindle: a large scale study on mobile application usage. In: MobileHCI 2011, pp. 47–56 (2011)
20. Chen, P.-T., Cheng, J.Z.: Unlocking the promise of mobile value-added services by applying new collaborative business models. Technological Forecasting And Social Change 77(4), 678–693 (2010)
21. Gonçalves, V., Walravens, N., Ballon, P.: How about an App Store? Enablers and Constraints in Platform Strategies for Mobile Network Operators. In: The Ninth International Conference on Mobile Business and Ninth Global Mobility Roundtable (ICMB-GMR), pp. 66–73 (2010)
22. Holzer, A., Ondrus, J.: Mobile application market: A developer's perspective. Telematics and Informatics 28(1), 22–31 (2010)

Evaluating Usability of Cross-Platform Smartphone Applications

Gebremariam Mesfin[1], Gheorghita Ghinea[2,3], Dida Midekso[1], and Tor-Morten Grønli[3]

[1] Addis Ababa University,
Addis Ababa, Ethiopia
mesfin.assres@gmail.com, mideksod@yahoo.com
[2] Brunel University,
London, UK
george.ghinea@brunel.ac.uk
[3] Norwegian School of IT,
Oslo, Norway
tmg@nith.no

Abstract. The computing power of smartphones is increasing as time goes. However, the proliferation of multiple different types of operating platforms affected interoperable smartphone applications development. Thus, the cross-platform development tools are coined.

Literature showed that smartphone applications developed with the native platforms have better user experience than the cross-platform counterparts. However, comparative evaluation of usability of cross-platform applications on the deployment platforms is not studied yet.

In this work, we evaluated usability of a crossword puzzle developed with PhoneGap on Android, Windows Phone, and BlackBerry. The evaluation was conducted focusing on the developer's adaptation effort to native platforms and the end users.

Thus, we observed that usability of the cross-platform crossword puzzle is unaffected on the respective native platforms and the SDKs require only minimal configuration effort. In addition, we observed the prospect of HTML5 and related web technologies as our future work towards evaluating and enhancing usability in composing REST-based services for smartphone applications.

Keywords: Usability, PhoneGap, Android, Windows Phone, BlackBerry, Cross-platform applications.

1 Introduction

It is well known that smartphones are playing a very important role in people's life. They are used in education, healthcare, business, etc. Smartphones may be described as kinds of mobile phones with increased capabilities such as touch screen, intelligence and alertness, though there is no agreed definition of a smartphone in the literature. However, the specific question that needs to be answered for a specific application is how smart the smartphone is?

I. Awan et al. (Eds.): MobiWis 2014, LNCS 8640, pp. 248–260, 2014.

For the purpose of this study, we consider the smartphone features as described in [1] and hence we define smartphones as mobile phones that are capable of accessing the Internet and are equipped with mobile operating systems such as Apple's iOS, Google's Android, Microsoft's Windows Phone, and BlackBerry and software can be installed on.

On top of the operating system, smartphones are equipped with software development kits (SDKs) that enhance the characteristics of smartphone application software and configurations such as reusability, and interoperability.

Smartphone applications can broadly be categorized into native and cross-platform based on the software development environments they are produced from.

The native applications belong to one category of smartphone applications that are written and developed for specific operating system. Jobe [2] describes native applications to have unhindered access to device hardware and support all user interface and interactions available in the respective mobile operating environment.

Cross-platform applications, on the other hand, can be dedicated mobile web applications, generic mobile web applications (also called mobile websites), and hybrid applications [2]. They are implemented based on a web browser, and the fundamental web technologies are HTML5, JavaScript, and Cascading Style Sheet (CSS).

— *Dedicated mobile web applications* - are designed to mimic the native applications of the host operating system but they execute on a web browser.
— *Generic mobile web applications* - correspond to mobile versions of websites.
— *Hybrid applications* - are a combination of both mobile web and native applications developed with standard web languages, but typically have access to the native device APIs and hardware and they are typically distributed through 'App stores'.

In terms of productivity and time to market, cross-platform smartphone applications are preferred to native ones. However, cross-platform smartphone applications are challenged by the limitation in user experience when deployed on native platforms. In this work, we evaluate the usability of such applications on their respective deployment operating platforms.

This paper is structured as follows. Smartphone application development and cross-platform development tools are discussed in sections 2 and 3 respectively. Concrete comparison of usability of cross-platform applications is presented in section 4. In Section 5 we discuss our findings and eventually, we draw our conclusions in Section 6.

2   Smartphone Application Development

In this section we consider the native and cross-platform application development in some depth. In addition, we consider the Sun Microsystems's Java ME separately as it contains such set of runtime environments and APIs developed for a wide range of resource constrained devices including the Smartphone.

2.1   Java ME

Java ME is designed to use smaller virtual machines and APIs to create content for the severe restrictions on computational power, battery life, memory, and network bandwidth of the devices. It is a platform, a collection of technologies and specifications, that are designed for high-end and low-end consumer devices and smartcards through its CDC, CLDC, and Java card APIs configurations respectively.

According to the description given in [3] and the context given in our study, the CDC represents the smartphone domain. The CLDC and Java card APIs are thus beyond the scope of this review. Isakow et al. [3] noted that the CDC targets larger devices with more capabilities like the smartphones and newer CDC applications are written like the Java SE systems but with a subset of APIs available in Java SE.

In the CDC configuration, a device stack is situated on top of the smartphone hardware and operating system but beneath the smartphone applications. The stack contains the configuration information, device profile and personal profile layers.

The configuration layer is a Java runtime environment for a family of devices consisting of a JVM to execute Java byte code, the native code that serves as an interface to the underlying system, and a set of core Java runtime classes.

An example of device profile is the Foundation Profile (FP) that adds additional Java SE classes to the CDC configuration which helps as a foundation for building other profiles. The Personal Profile (PP) provides Java ME specification for the devices that need a high degree of Internet connectivity and web fidelity.

Similar software layering and configuration approaches are also provided by other smartphone application platforms such as the Windows Phone, Android, and iOS, and the cross-platform Smartphone application development environments [4].

2.2   Native Applications

The native applications are written and developed for specific operating system such as Windows Phone, Android, BlackBerry, iOS and Firefox OS. In the following paragraphs, we provide brief information on these operating systems and their corresponding integrated development environments [2].

Windows Phone

Windows Phone is one of the operating systems for smartphones. In the latest versions of Windows Phone, smartphone applications are written in managed code by frameworks that support multiple languages such as c# from the Microsoft.NET environment.

Windows Phone is primarily built with the Windows Phone SDK. Where Silverlight is an add-on for powerful, engaging interfaces and XNA for 2D or 3D games and development is done on Visual Studio. Programs created for Windows Phone are packaged into XAP files, which is the Silverlight application package [4].

Android
Android is one of the leading operating systems for smartphones. It is based on the Linux kernel and developed as an open source system platform. In addition to the operating system, Android provides development environment to write managed code with Google's Java libraries, and the Dalvik Virtual Machine for the smartphone applications to run on [24].

The development environment enables to use 2D and 3D graphic libraries, a customized SQL engine for persistent storage, and 3G, 4G and WLAN network capabilities [4]. Eclipse and IntelliJ IDEA are software development tools for Android.

BlackBerry
BlackBerry is a proprietary mobile operating system developed by BlackBerry Limited for its BlackBerry line of smartphone and tablet handheld devices. It is based on the QNX operating system, which is popular in industrial computers and used in many car computers.

BlackBerry 10 operating system uses an innovative combination of gestures and touches for navigation and control. Details on the system architecture of BlackBerry 10 can be found on the BlackBerry developer site [23]. Eclipse is one of the software development tools used to develop BlackBerry applications.

Apple iOS
iOS is an operating system (architecture shown in Fig. 3) for many Apple's devices including iPhone and its applications are written in an object-oriented programming language called Objective-C - which is an extension of the C language, and using a library called Cocoa Touch.

Development for iOS requires a computer or a VMware running Mac OS. Xcode is the most commonly used integrated development environment to write iOS applications. It includes an editor, analysis tool, iOS simulator, and the SDK [4, 5].

Firefox OS
Firefox OS corresponds to a new approach for smartphone operating systems based on web technologies, namely, HTML5, JavaScript and Web APIs. Grønli et al. [4] described this new approach in such a way that it brings open Web APIs to communicate directly with the smartphone hardware and provides a direct link to the web-based application marketplace. In general, the native development environments are good at exploiting each device's capabilities. However, they lack cross-platform compatibility.

3   Cross-Platform Development Tools

The smartphone operating systems are so rich in libraries and built-in features. However, they still face the heat of the market to match customer's high expectations because their basic architecture and support of programming languages is different.

Literature such as in [6] describe that the proliferation of a fragmented smartphone market with multiple operating platforms makes the development of native mobile applications a challenging and costly endeavor. To alleviate this situation, the literature and industry envisions cross-platform development approaches.

The essence of cross-platform environments is a subset of the software development environments aiming at building platform independent applications. Cross-platform application development environments work based on the general principle of *"write once, and run everywhere"*. In the smartphone application development, Dalmasso et al. [7] described the general architecture of the cross platform mobile application development tools as shown in Fig. 1.

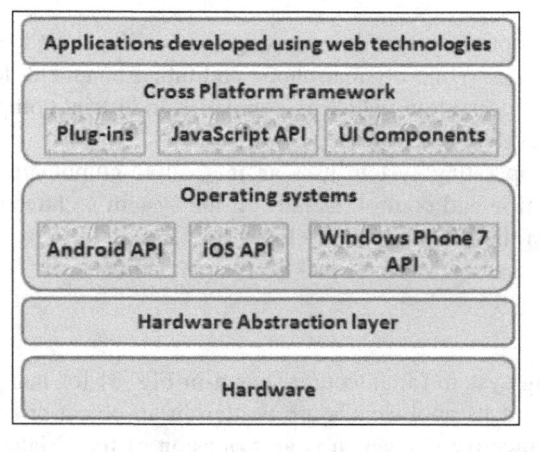

Fig. 1. General architecture of cross platform mobile application development tools

However, as pointed out in [6], the diverse hardware and software platforms inevitably make portability a hassle for mobile-application developers. Portability primarily depends on runtime support and the feasibility of achieving identical look-and-feel and functionality across platforms. There are several attempts of implementations of cross-platform smartphone application development environments. For example Java ME supports cross-platform development through configurations and profiles. Gavalas and Economou [8] describe a configuration as the minimum Java VM features and library set for devices with similar processing and memory limitations, user interface requirements, and connection capabilities, while a profile comprises libraries specialized in the unique characteristics of a particular device class.

Grønli et al. [4] investigated the strengths and weaknesses of the mobile application development ecosystem and pointed out that the developer support has been improved the performance of developer tools through provision of higher level abstraction of performance-critical third party libraries. However, according to Grønli et al., cross-platform development environments like the Firefox OS are being challenged by the different implementations, immature platform support, variety of devices, and variety of browsers while the platform specific ones like Windows Phone, iPhone, and Android are benefiting from being tightly integrated with their respective operating system. The work by Grønli et al. [4] showed that there is better integration between the development environment and deployment devices on the platform specific ones than that of the cross-platform environment. This indicates that the cross-platform application development still is in its early stages.

Literature such as in [6,7, 8] showed that cross-platform development tools are flourishing aiming at addressing user experience, stability of framework, ease of updating, cost of development for multiple platforms, and the time to market of an application. When realized, the interests of many developers would be satisfied in terms of releasing applications for major mobile platforms such as iOS and Android and provide a consistent user experience across the platforms with minimal or no change to the original code.

PhoneGap, Rhomobile, JQuery Mobile, and Xamarin are some of the cross-platform mobile application development tools available. We provide a quick overview of these tools as follows.

PhoneGap

PhoneGap is an open source cross-platform smartphone application development tool developed by Adobe System Inc under Apache license. It provides a decent toolbox for building native mobile applications using only HTML5, JavaScript and CSS [7], [9]. PhoneGap is quite popular among users mainly because of its flexibility, straightforward architecture and ease of use. Its architecture is mainly composed of Web application, PhoneGap, and the operating system along with native APIs (See Fig. 2).

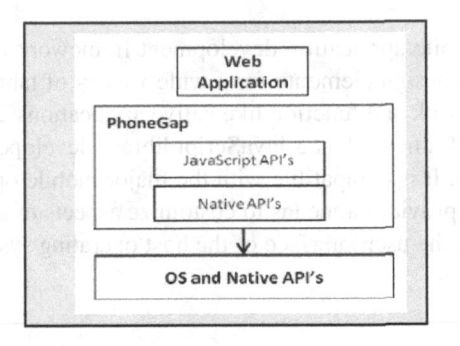

Fig. 2. Interfacing Layers of the PhoneGap Architecture

Palmieri et al. [9] explained that PhoneGap is a "wrapper" that allows developers to enclose applications written in known programming languages into native applications. That is, applications developed using PhoneGap are neither purely web-based and nor purely native and thus some layout rendering is done via web-view instead of the native language of the operating system, and there is lack of support of HTML in some functions. PhoneGap does not provide its own IDE to develop applications, but developers have to write the source code with an IDE and port their code into other IDEs such as the Eclipse for Android and XCode for iOS. Thus far, PhoneGap permits the creation of applications for Windows Phone, Android, iOS, Bada, Black-Berry, Symbian, and WebOS operating systems.

RhoMobile

RhoMobile is another cross-platform mobile application development tool developed by Motorola solutions Inc that is used to build application for iOS, Android, Black-Berry, Windows Phone, and Symbian [9]. It is an open source Ruby-based mobile development environment used to develop enterprise applications and data on a single source code across the different operating systems listed above.

The RhoMobile suite provides an IDE called RhoStudio. Alternatively, it offers the possibility to write applications with any other IDE which supports HTML, HTML5, CSS, JavaScript and Ruby such as Eclipse, Visual Studio, Netbeans, and IntelliJ. RhoMobile uses the Model View Controller (MVC) pattern to develop mobile applications.

Applications developed with RhoMobile are compiled into Java bytecode to be executed on BlackBerry, or compiled into Ruby bytecode to be executed on all other operating systems that are running on real or virtual devices.The RhoMobile architecture is composed of Controller, HTML templates, source adapter, RhoStudio (or any other editor), Ruby executor, device capability such as the APIs for camera and GPS, object relational mapper (ORM) called Rhom which provides an interface to interact with the SQLite database, a RhoSync client, and RhoSync server.

jQuery Mobile

jQuery Mobile is a mobile application development framework that enables and supports touch events and design elements for a wide variety of tablets and smartphones in order to make them look and function like native applications[2].

The jQuery Mobile framework is a JavaScript library developed and maintained by a project called jQuery. It is compatible with the major mobile operating systems and desktop browsers, and provides a means to customize aspects of the user interface and CSS in order to imitate the user interface of the host operating system.

Sencha Touch

Sencha Touch 2.0 is another powerful yet a complex cross-platform mobile application development framework. Its SDK tools provide access to a subset of phone native API such as camera, notification, connection, and orientation [25]. In addition, Sencha Touch offers the possibility to build native packaging deployable on iOS and Android application markets.

In summary, the cross-platform development tools such as the above noted ones leverage device capabilities with the help of JavaScript APIs and generate the HTML code for presentation.

4   Comparison of Usability of Cross-Platform Application

In this study we employ literature review to frame the research setting, and usability technique to evaluate usability of the smartphone application developed with Phone-Gap as a cross-platform development tool. PhoneGap is chosen because it is the most widespread and for technical convenience of the researchers to work with the Eclipse IDE on the Windows platform, and Visual Studio.

Usability is defined by the ISO [16] on its guidance on usability as the extent to which a product can be used by specified users to achieve specified goals with effectiveness, efficiency and satisfaction in a specified context of use.

Based on the above definition, Carol Barnum [17] underscored the need to consider the target group of users (not all users) for a particular product; the specific design goals of a product are identical with the goals of its users; and users use the application in a certain environment (context) and it is essential that the application is designed to be used under those terms.

In this research, a crossword puzzle is developed with draggable alphabets, target drop slots on a table, and list of clues as shown on Fig 4. The puzzle was initially developed in [21] with HTML5, JavaScript, and CSS and has been modified to fit into our context of use. The basic features of the puzzle used for the evaluation are text, image, hovering, drag, drop, button, navigation, platform configuration, and the SDK used.

Our evaluation process consisted of the following four phases:

1. First, the HTML5 based crossword puzzle is developed as a general web application and tested with a smartphone web browser (the Opera Classic) as a mobile web.
2. Then, for the Android platform, we setup the Android SDK on the Eclipse IDE. In addition the PhoneGap plug-ins - cordova.js, cordova.jar, and the config.xml files incorporated; the android manifest tweaked, and more.
3. After that, the Windows Phone development environment was setup on Visual Studio 2010 Express for Windows Phone. We used PhoneGap plug-ins from Cordova for Windows Phone (namely, PhoneGap Custom and PhoneGap Starter); Google's JavaScript plug-in; and other custom plug-ins.
4. Finally, a development environment for BlackBerry was setup with PhoneGap-blackberry, and JavaScript plug-ins.

In this study, usability evaluation is conducted from the viewpoint of both the developer who does the development and adaptation to the native platforms and the end users who actually play the game.

The developer viewpoint is framed under the developer-tools usability theme [20] that is the ease to use of the tool to develop applications for multiple platforms. Specifically, for the interest of time, we just considered the efforts exerted by the developer to adapt to the Android, Windows Phone, and BlackBerry native platforms in terms of lines of code.

The end user viewpoint, on the other hand, is part of the classical usability evaluation as described in Jacob Nielsen [18]. Jacob Nielsen described in his book entitled

Usability Engineering usability as a set of attributes of a user interface; namely; learnability, efficiency, memorability, errors and satisfaction.

The descriptions of usability presented above are full of subjectivity and evaluation with these attributes is highly biased. Thus, ten general principles of user interface design are coined as heuristics and a description of each is provided [17, 18].

In a similar context, a ten point usability measurement tool called system usability scale is presented in [19]. Jeff Sauro [19] describes this tool to be technology independent and has since been tested on hardware, consumer software, websites, cellphones, IVRs and even the yellow-pages.

As the system usability scale tool has become an industry standard [19], we used it to evaluate the usability of the crossword puzzle on Android, Windows Phone, and BlackBerry devices. The system usability scale is a five point Likert scale with the ten questions as shown on Table 1 below.

Table 1. Questions in the System's Usability Scale Tool

No	Questions
1	I think that I would like to use this system frequently.
2	I found the system unnecessarily complex.
3	I thought the system was easy to use.
4	I think that I would need the support of a technical person to be able to use this system.
5	I found the various functions in this system were well integrated.
6	I thought there was too much inconsistency in this system.
7	I would imagine that most people would learn to use this system very quickly.
8	I found the system very cumbersome to use.
9	I felt very confident using the system.
10	I needed to learn a lot of things before I could get going with this system.

Nine users participated in the evaluation of the crossword puzzle in three groups and played on each of the three operating platforms. Each user was briefly introduced about the puzzle, asked to play, and respond to the questions. Accordingly, a summary of their responses on the usability of cross-platform crossword puzzle on the three different operating platforms is shown in Table 2.

Table 2. Summary of Responses on Usability of the Crossword Puzzle

Question numbers	Response	Number of respondents for		
		Android	Windows Phone	BlackBerry
1,5	Very high	2	3	1
1,5	High	1	-	2
3,7,9	High	3	3	3
2,8,	Low	3	3	3
4,6,10	Low	3	2	3
4,6,10	Very low	-	1	-

The Android version of the puzzle has been tested on a real Samsung Galaxy Ace device. However, the usability evaluation result shown in Table 2 is based on the tests on the respective device emulators.

5   Discussion

As described earlier in the previous section, our discussion of results is based on both the developer and the end user viewpoints.

With the developer viewpoint, we considered the efforts required by the developer [20] to adapt to the Android, Windows Phone, and BlackBerry platforms with respect to the text, image, hovering, dragging, dropping, button click, navigation, platform configuration, and the SDK features of the crossword puzzle and the development platform.

Initially the puzzle was developed with HTML5, CSS3, and JavaScript but targeting the desktop browser. The same source code was also accessed as a mobile web with only limited usage difference such as hovering needs long touch in mobile web as opposed to the point-and-hold on the desktop browser.

However, the same source code was deployed on the Android platform as a cross-platform app with PhoneGap and the hovering, dragging, and dropping features were lost completely.

The source code has been debugged by applying fairly large number of JavaScript lines of code and plug-ins to make it compatible with the Android platform and the puzzle's behavior was preserved as shown in Fig. 3.

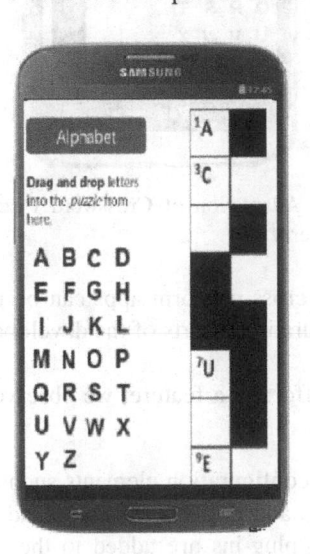

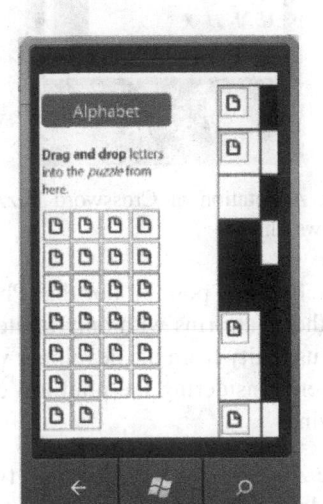

Fig. 3. The Crossword Puzzle on Android Platform

Fig. 4. Distortion of Crossword Puzzle on Windows Phone

The same source code that correctly run on the Android platform with its Phone-Gap plug-in has been deployed on the Windows Phone and BlackBerry platforms with their respective PhoneGap plug-ins and all the features of crossword puzzle worked correctly without any adaptation efforts to maintain those features except that a few SDK configuration efforts have been made.

For example, among the SDK configuration requirements we encountered that im-ages disappeared both from the alphabet pallet and the puzzle board (see Fig. 4) when deploying on the Windows Phone.

The 'build action' file property of all images is converted from 'resource' into 'content' and the app was rebuilt into the proper features as shown in Fig. 5. The crossword puzzle source code which was tweaked to make it compatible with the Android platform was deployed on the BlackBerry platform (See Fig. 6) with the proper PhoneGap configuration and it showed no observable behavioral change.

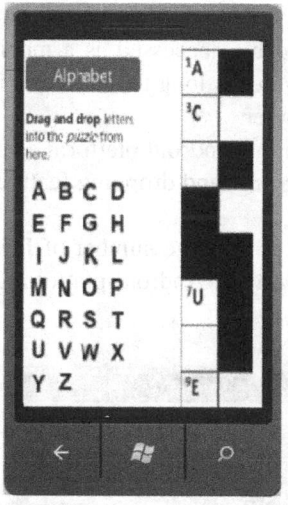 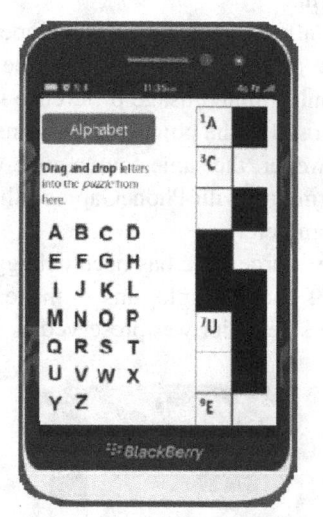

Fig. 5. Adaptation of Crossword Puzzle for Windows Phone   **Fig. 6.** Adaptation of Crossword Puzzle for BlackBerry

Our findings pointed out that PhoneGap based cross-platform apps can be ported into other platforms with only limited SDK configuration efforts of the developer and hence usability from the developer viewpoint.

When considering the platform configuration effort as a feature, we observed the following:

— The Android platform required tweaking of the configuration elements such as the cordova.js, cordova.jar, config.xml, and the android manifest. In addition, Google's JavaScript plug-in, and other custom plug-ins are added to the source code.
— The PhoneGap Custom and Starter, Google's JavaScript plug-in, and other custom plug-ins for Windows Phone; and

— The PhoneGap-blackberry, editing the configuration file, and adding JavaScript plug-ins for the BlackBerry.

Thus, we found out that the Windows Phone is easier to configure because the minimal configuration effort required to run the crossword puzzle is less than the Android and BlackBerry platforms.

The result of usability evaluation from the end user viewpoint (Table 2 above) also indicated that the usability of the cross-platform app remains an affected across the individual platforms when ignoring the impact of the form factor of each device. The Windows Phone version, however, is found to be more usable than the other two versions.

6   Conclusion

It is observable that the cross platform mobile application development frameworks are benefiting developers to build applications for multiple platforms. However, there is a little doubt on the behavior of the resulting cross-platform applications (in terms of usability from the viewpoint of the developer as well as the end user) on the native platforms.

Usability of the resulting applications from the developer viewpoint is seen in terms of the effort required in lines of code, and platform configuration to adapt into the respective native platforms. For the end user, on the other hand, we applied ten questions usability questionnaire.

Our finding showed that the usability of cross-platform smartphone applications remains an affected when deployed on the respective native platforms. In addition, we observed that the cross-platform development tools such as PhoneGap require only minimal configuration effort to deploy the cross-platform app to the specific platforms. HTML5 and related web technologies together with cross-platform tools would offer considerable opportunities to enhance usability of developer tools.

Thus, our future work will consider the usability of existing REST-based service to compose cross-platform smartphone applications. In addition, the prospect of HTML5 and related technologies will be explored to enhance usability in the composition of REST web services (towards developing an end-user mash-up tool) for smartphone applications.

References

1. Cassavoy, L.: What Makes a Smartphone Smart?, http://cellphones.about.com/od/smartphonebasics/a/what_is_smart.htm (accessed on July 23, 2013)
2. Jobe, W.: Native Apps vs. Mobile Web Apps, iJIM 2013 (2013)
3. Isakow, A., Shi, H.: Review of J2ME and J2ME-based Mobile Applications. International Journal of Computer Science and Network Security (IJCSNS) 8(2) (2008)
4. Grønli, T.-M., Hansen, J., Ghinea, G., Younas, M.: Mobile Application Platform Heterogeneity: Android vs Windows Phone vs iOS vs Firefox OS (Submitted 2013)

5. https://developer.apple.com/xcode/ (accessed: January 20, 2013)
6. Heitkötter, H., Hanschke, S., Majchrzak, T.A.: Evaluating Cross-Platform Development Approaches for Mobile Applications. In: Cordeiro, J., Krempels, K.-H. (eds.) WEBIST 2012. LNBIP, vol. 140, pp. 120–138. Springer, Heidelberg (2013)
7. Dalmasso, I., Datta, S.K., Bonnet, C., Nikaein, N.: Survey, Comparison and Evaluation of Cross Platform Mobile Application Development Tools. In: IEEE 2013 (2013)
8. Gavalas, D., Economou, D.: Development Platforms for Mobile Applications: Status and Trends. In: IEEE 2011 (2011)
9. Palmieri, M., Singh, I., Cicchetti, A.: Comparison of Cross-Platform Mobile Development Tools. In: IEEE 2012 (2012)
10. Heitkötter, H., Hanschke, S., Majchrzak, T.A.: Evaluating Cross-Platform Development Approaches for Mobile Applications. In: Cordeiro, J., Krempels, K.-H. (eds.) WEBIST 2012. LNBIP, vol. 140, pp. 120–138. Springer, Heidelberg (2013)
11. Hang, F., Zhao, L.: HyperMash: A Heterogeneous Service Composition Approach for Better Support of the End Users. In: IEEE 2013 (2013)
12. Andreas, S., Krusche, S.: Evaluation of cross-platform frameworks for mobile applications. In: Proceedings of the 1st European Workshop on Mobile Engineering 2013 (2013)
13. Wargo, J.M.: PhoneGap Essentials: Building Cross-platform Mobile Apps. Addison Wesley (2012)
14. Marino, E., Spini, F., Paoluzzi, A., Minuti, F., Rosina, M., Bottaro, A.: HTML5 Visual Composition of REST-like Web Services. In: IEEE 2013 (2013)
15. Holzinger, A., Treitler, P., Slany, W.: Making Apps Useable on Multiple Different Mobile Platforms: On Interoperability for Business Application Development on Smartphones. In: Quirchmayr, G., Basl, J., You, I., Xu, L., Weippl, E. (eds.) CD-ARES 2012. LNCS, vol. 7465, pp. 176–189. Springer, Heidelberg (2012)
16. Guidance on Usability: ISO 9241-1, International Organization for Standardization1998 (1998)
17. Barnum, C.: Usability Testing Essentials. Elsevier (2011)
18. Nielsen, J.: Usability Engineering. Academic Press, Orlando (1993)
19. Sauro, J.: Quantitative Usability, Statistics, and Six Sigma: Measuring Usability (2014), http://www.measuringusability.com/sus.php (accessed on February 18, 2014)
20. Faulring, A., Myers, B.A., Oren, Y., Rotenberg, K.: A Case Study of Using HCI Methods to Improve Tools for Programmers. In: IEEE 2012 (2012)
21. GitHub, Inc. (US), https://github.com (accessed on February 15, 2014)
22. Zibran, M.F.: What Makes APIs Difficult to Use. International Journal of Computer Science and Network Security (2008)
23. System Architecture of BlackBerry 10, https://developer.blackberry.com/native/documentation/core/com.qnx.doc.neutrino.sys_arch/topic/about.html (accessed on March 2014)
24. Android Architecture (accessed from the Embedded Linux Wiki), http://elinux.org/Android_Architecture (March 2014)
25. Dalmasso, I., Datta, S.K., Bonnet, C., Nikaein, N.: Survey, Comparison and Evaluation of Cross Platform Mobile Application Development Tools. In: IEEE 2013 (2013)

Analysis of B2C Mobile Application Characteristics and Quality Factors Based on ISO 25010 Quality Model

Ekrem Yildiz[1], Semih Bilgen[2], Gul Tokdemir[3], Nergiz E. Cagiltay[4], and Y. Nasuh Erturan[5]

[1] Department of Information Sciences, METU, Ankara, Turkey
ekrem.yildiz@live.com
[2] Electrical Engineering Department - METU, Ankara, Turkey
bilgen@metu.edu.tr
[3] Department of Computer Engineering, Cankaya University, Ankara, Turkey
gtokdemir@cankaya.edu.tr
[4] Department of Software Engineering, Atılım University, Ankara, Turkey
nergiz@atilim.edu.tr
[5] Department of Medical Informatics - METU, Ankara, Turkey
nasuherturan@gmail.com

Abstract. The number of mobile applications in mobile market has rapidly increased as new technology and new devices are emerging at remarkable speed which shows mobile applications have an important role in every field of our life. Among those, even some of the mobile applications have a long time life as end-users use those effectively, some of them fail to do so that prevents the companies to reach from their aim. The main reason of that problem results from the quality of the mobile applications. Although there are some methods and metrics to analyze the quality of mobile applications, they have lack of criteria since they are mostly based on ISO 9126 quality model factors which are invalid anymore. This study aims to analyze both mobile commerce applications' characteristics and quality factors and sub-factors based on ISO 25010 product quality model. Accordingly a quality model is proposed by analysis performed by a group of experts from the mobile software development area. The results of this study aims to help developing more qualified and effective mobile applications from developer perspective.

Keywords: Software quality model, Mobile Application quality model, ISO 25010.

1   Introduction

The mobile application technology is rapidly expanding in every fields of our life with the help of advances in technology. According to Gartner Group, which is a market research firm, 428 million mobile devices were sold worldwide in the first quarter 2011, which is a 19% increase from the previous year [1]. Furthermore, Gartner predicts that over 185 billion mobile applications will be downloaded by the end of year 2014 [1]. It

I. Awan et al. (Eds.): MobiWis 2014, LNCS 8640, pp. 261–274, 2014.
© Springer International Publishing Switzerland 2014

is so obvious from these statistical evidences that mobile phone is important for our lives so is the mobile application.

The rapid growth rate in this field has significantly brought out the need of mobile application development. Therefore, mobile application development area, which is almost new, brings many opportunities for both enterprises and individual developers [2]. Demands on software quality increased rapidly with the rapid growth of mobile applications [3]. The applications are expected to be stable, quick and have good user interface [4]. In order to provide these requirements, software developer, designer, tester and quality member should be interested in the characteristics of mobile applications and assure the typical quality of them. Therefore, it is necessary to study the mobile software product quality requirements to provide analysis framework that will increase the application quality as developers will have a broader perspective for this issue. Furthermore, stakeholders will have a chance to analyze the quality of the mobile applications.

In this research study, we intend to use ISO 25010 quality model to identify acceptance criteria, analyze and evaluate a specific application domain which is business to customer (b2c) mobile application. As mobile application quality studies are mostly based on ISO 9126 quality model, which is not valid anymore, providing new quality criteria from ISO 25010 quality model makes this study important.

The rest of this paper is structured as follows; firstly, literature review was conducted to analyze software quality practices, mobile application quality practices, and b2c mobile application quality practices. After that, the approach for this study was given that shows the choosing base model for this study. In next section, Garofalaki et al. study was discussed to use characteristics of b2c mobile applications. Later, online survey was conducted with experts who have computer science background. In section 4, results were discussed. Finally, conclusion and future works are given.

2   Literature Review

Considering the mobile application is a new area, most of the quality studies about mobile application are based on the software quality models. The following sections explore well-known quality studies which are McCall and ISO software quality model. After that, both mobile application and b2c mobile application quality practices are presented.

2.1   McCall Software Quality Model

McCall's study which proposed a framework for the measurement of software quality has a major contribution to software quality model area [5]. It was developed by the US air-force electronic system decision (ESD), the Rome air development center (RADC), and general electric (GE), with the aim of improving the quality of software products [6]. McCall specified that software characteristics should relate directly to mission requirements and serve to define a variety of quality factors: maintainability, reliability, flexibility, correctness, testability, portability, reusability, efficiency, usability, integrity, and interoperability [5]. Those eleven quality factors are grouped into three dimensions which are product operations, product revisions, and product transition. The relationship between quality characteristics and metrics is the one of the major contributions of this model [6]. However, functionality of the software products does not take into consideration by this model.

2.2   ISO 25010 (SQUARE) Software Quality Model

The ISO standard 25010 which is also called systems and software quality requirements and evaluation (SQUARE) is based on the earlier form of ISO 9126. According to ISO 9126, quality is defined as a set of features and characteristics of product or service that bears on its ability to satisfy the stated or implied needs [7]. Moreover, ISO/IEC 9126 defines a high-level quality attributes in which quality measurements are based on procedures that are recommended in ISO 15999 [8]. ISO 9126-1 specifies three models of software product related to the three views of quality: an internal quality model, an external quality model, and a quality-in-use model [9].

As for the ISO 25010, SQUARE, it describes the software product quality requirements [10]. ISO 25010 consists of two models which are product quality model and quality-in-use model. ISO 25010 defines product quality model which was used for this study as:

> "*A product quality model composed of eight characteristics (which are further subdivided into sub characteristics) that relate to static properties of software and dynamic properties of the computer system. The model is applicable to both computer systems and software products*" [10].

ISO 25010 quality model presents the software quality attributes in a hierarchical manner [11]. The quality model divides product quality into characteristics, each of which is composed of several sub-characteristics. The product quality model consists of (1) Functional Suitability, (2) Performance Efficiency, (3) Compatibility, (4) Usability, (5) Reliability, (6) Security, (7) Maintainability, and (8) Portability which are broken down into 31 sub characteristics with a set of internal and external measures to quantitatively assess these quality characteristics [10]. Sub factors of quality model are explained in detail in part 3.1 of this study.

According to Behkamal et al., the defined characteristics of ISO model are applicable to every kind of software. Moreover, hierarchical structure, universal expressions and terms, simple and exact definitions, and having criteria for evaluation are the most important characteristics of ISO model [6].

2.3   Mobile Application Quality Practices

As a mobile application quality product, researches have been focused on proposing practices to analyze, to measure and to test mobile applications in order to assess the quality.

Standard-Based Mobile Application Product Assessment: The validity of the ISO software quality model were used and supported by many of the studies that include not only desktop software applications but also for mobile applications. Six major factors of ISO 9126 were used to assess the quality attributes of the HTML5 bases smart phone applications in Hasan, Zaidi, and Haider's study in 2012 [12]. Furthermore, mobile application quality model that includes functionality, usability, efficiency, maintainability, data integrity and portability as major characteristic and suitability, security, adaptability and extensibility as sub characteristic in Zahra, Khalid, and Javed study [13]. Moreover, Franke and Kowalewski stated that developers cannot focus on all qualities which are described in McCall's, Boehm, and ISO 9126 quality models, and proposed a mobile software quality model which includes usability, data persistence, efficiency, flexibility, adaptability, portability, and extensibility quality characteristics and applied on two android mobile applications to evaluate the quality of those applications[14]. As for the users' acceptance perspective, application interface design, performance of application, battery efficiency, features of mobile device, application and connectivity cost, user lifestyle, and quality of service are some of the factors that affect any mobile applications' quality [15]. Kutar & Hussain also studied the quality of mobile applications from the users' perspective by only using usability metric, and proposed effectiveness, efficiency, and satisfaction quality characteristics which are divided into seventeen usability guidelines to evaluate the mobile application quality from the usability perspective [16].

Metric-Oriented Mobile Application Product Assessment: In order to measure the performance efficiency and mobile application quality, a set of metrics were stated to monitor statically source code of mobile applications by Ryan and Rossi in their study [17]. As for the performance efficiency issue, a key performance metrics were proposed by Pandi and Charaf by using resource management as an input to measure the performance of the application [18]. Furthermore, Goal Question Metric was used to evaluate the usability of mobile applications by Hussain and Ferneley [19].

Test-Based Mobile Application Quality Assessment: As testing a mobile application is another type of assessing the quality, Franke & Weise proposed a software quality framework which is based on existing models, metrics, patterns, methods and tools for testing of mobile applications [20]. Moreover, a quality framework to test mobile application was proposed Wang, Jiang, and Wei by mentioning that achieving high level user satisfaction and adapting for variety of mobile device are key success factors of a mobile application [3]. Also, a review of testing requirements which help to test applications in both emulators and mobile devices was proposed by Dantas [21]. Moreover, an adaptive random test case generation technique was proposed to produce black-box test cases for mobile applications [22].

2.4   B2C Mobile Application Quality Practices

Garofalaki et al. evaluated the business-to-customer mobile applications with four quality attributes, which are functionality, usability, reliability and efficiency, with three characteristic dimensions of m-commerce systems which are (1) presentation which describes how a product is shown to the end user, (2) navigation which includes the variety of mechanisms to the user for accessing information and services of the mobile commerce system, and (3) purchasing which refers to commercial transaction facilities [23]. The authors answered the question whether m-commerce system can be both well designed as well as high quality system or not. Gupta and Madan extended Garofalaki study's by adding two more quality characteristics which are maintainability and portability, and also defined the security attributes, which includes confidentiality, security mechanism, replay attack prevention, that affect the quality of business-to-customer mobile application [24].

Andreou et al. are the ones that were looking the both key design and development factors of mobile commerce applications in their study by mentioning dimensions which are technical issues affecting the quality and user requirements from the consumer's satisfaction perspective [25]. The authors stated in their study that interference, low bandwidth, high delays and large delay variation, lower security, frequent disconnections were listed as key technical issues which influence the performance of mobile applications and ubiquity, personalization, flexibility, and localization are the key user requirements to assess the mobile consumer's satisfaction [26].

3   Approach for This Study

In order to analyze the business to customer mobile application quality, this study has five steps as follows:

- Step 1: Choosing ISO 25010 product quality model as a basis after literature review of most well-known quality models.
- Step 2: Identifying quality characteristics of a business to customer mobile applications by using Garofalakis, Stefani, & Stefanis' study.
- Step 3: Choosing a group of experts from mobile application development area.
- Step 4: Assigning importance degree of the characteristics, quality factors and sub-factors of the b2c mobile application.
- Step 5: Developing the quality criteria.

3.1   Choosing ISO 25010 Product Quality Model as a Basis

ISO 25010 quality model, which was defined in the literature session of this study, has eight quality characteristics that includes Functional Suitability, Performance Efficiency, Compatibility, Usability, Maintainability, Portability, Security, and Reliability. An overview of the defined characteristics and sub characteristics of this product model is shown in Figure 1. Definition of the quality factors and sub-factors are given below:

Functional Suitability: Functional suitability is *"degree to which a product or system provides functions that meet the stated and implied needs when used under specified conditions"* [10].This quality factor consists of three sub-factors which are functional completeness, functional correctness, and functional appropriateness. Functional completeness means that whether all the functions cover user needs and objectives or not. Functional correctness means that application's results are correct. Functional appropriateness means that applications' functions facilitate the user objectives and needs.

Performance Efficiency: Performance efficiency is *"relative to the amount of resources used under stated conditions"* [10]. It consists of three quality sub-factors: Time behavior shows the degree of application's response and processing time. Resource utilization describes the amounts and types of resources which are used by application. Capacity means the maximum limits of application in order to achieve requirements.

Compatibility: Compatibility is "the degree to which a product, system or component can exchange information with other products, systems or components, and/or perform its required functions, while sharing the same hardware or software environment" [10]. It includes two sub-factors which are co-existence and interoperability. Co-existence means application can perform its functions effectively while sharing common resources with other applications. Interoperability is degree of application's ability to interact with the specified systems.

Usability: Usability is *"degree to which a product or system can be used by specified users to achieve specified goals with effectiveness, efficiency and satisfaction in a specified context of use"* [10]. It has six sub-factors: Appropriateness recognizability means that users are aware of the application provides their needs. Learnability shows the degree of users' effort in order to use the application effectively. Operability defines the users' effort for operation and control in the application. User error protection provides users with not making errors. User interface aesthetics shows the degree of attractive and interactive user interface for the user. Accessibility shows that application can be used widest range of people even who have disabilities.

Reliability: Reliability is *"the degree to which a system, product or component performs specified functions under specified conditions for a specified period of time"* [10]. Reliability quality factor consists of four sub-factors: Maturity shows that degree of the application provides the needs of reliability. Availability means that application is available and usable when necessary for use. Fault tolerance is the ability of application to cope with any software faults. Recoverability shows the degree of application's recover capability in case of any failure.

Security: Security is *"the degree to which a product or system protects information and data so that persons or other products or systems have the degree of data access appropriate to their types and levels of authorization"* [10]. Security quality factor has five sub-factors: Confidentiality means that application's data is only accessible by users who have access rights. Integrity displays that application prevents unauthorized access. Non-repudiation means actions can be proven in order not to repudiate later. Accountability shows the degree of traceability of any actions that are performed by the user. Authenticity means that any actions that are done by the user in the application could be proven.

Maintainability: It is *"degree of effectiveness and efficiency with which a product or system can be modified by the intended maintainers"* [10]. It consists of two sub-factors: Modularity is the degree of any changes in one component has minimal impact on other components in the application. Reusability shows the any component of the application can be used in any other component.

Portability: It is *"the degree of effectiveness and efficiency with which a system, product or component can be transferred from one hardware, software or other operational or usage environment to another"* [10]. It has six sub-factors: Adaptability means that application can be adapted effectively to different environments without any additional effort. Installability defines the users' effort for the installing the application. Replaceability means that application can be changed by another application. Analyzability is the effort to find out any bugs or failures and to identify any parts of the application that should be modified. Modifiability means application can be effectively modified without any bugs. Testability shows the effort to validate modification of application.

3.2   Characteristics of B2C Mobile Applications

In order to identify quality characteristics of b2c mobile applications, first literature survey was conducted and tried to find out if there is any instrument available to measure the characteristic of b2c mobile application. According to Creswell, reviewing the literature should be conducted whether there is already instrument available or not [26]. From the literature, Garofalakis, Stefani, Stefanis, & Xenos study selected as a baseline. As stated in B2C Quality Practices section, the authors gathered the characteristics of m-commerce system which includes both b2c and b2b applications in three dimensions which are presentation, navigation, and purchasing. Moreover, authors also evaluated those characteristics with four quality characteristics of ISO 9126 which are functionality, usability, efficiency, and reliability.

Presentation: It describes how a product is shown to the end user. It includes seven characteristics of application which are product's description, use of text, use of colors, use of graphics, clarity, text inputting, and appropriateness of presentation.

Navigation: Navigation has variety of mechanisms that provide user with accessing information and services of the application. It consists of six characteristics of application which are navigation mechanism, access keys, use of links, help, undo functions, user oriented hierarchy.

Purchasing: It has ten characteristics of application which are shopping cart as a metaphor, security mechanism, pricing mechanism, alternative payment methods, authentication, personalization, error recovery, error tolerance, operation response time, accuracy of the operations.

Although Garofalakis' et al. study has 25 sub characteristics, some of the sub characteristics are grouped and shortened for this study, and three sub characteristics which are appropriateness, operation response time, and accuracy of the operations characteristics were added to online survey. Moreover, Garofalakis' et al. study discussed correlation of the m-commerce characteristics with only four quality factors. However, this study tries to find out importance degree of m-commerce characteristics, and ISO 25010 quality factors separately which makes this study important and different.

3.3   Group of Software Expert Views

In this study, mobile application developers' who have computer science background viewpoints were considered. In order to achieve that, purposive sampling method which participants are selected on the basis of researcher' prior information about participants, instead of random sampling was used. For this study, 34 mobile application developers were chosen to answer online survey. The questionnaire was sent them by email. They were asked to give importance degree of each characteristic and quality factor between 1 and 5. Moreover, if the participants have no idea about characteristic or factor, s/he could select option 6 which shows s/he has no idea about the criteria (1= Not Important, 2=Low Level Important, 3=Medium Level Important, 4=High Level Important, 5=Critical Level Important, 6= No Idea). It is important to provide "No Idea" option which helps to prevent distribution of participants' responses in medium level importance if they have not any idea about the characteristics or factors.

Demographic information about the participants' department is shown in Table 1 Distribution of Participants' University Departments which displays that all of the participants have computer science background.

Table 1. Distribution of Participants' University Departments

Departments	Frequency	Percent	Valid Percent	Cumulative Percent
Computer Education and Instructional Technology	4	11,8	11,8	88,2
Computer Engineering	19	55,9	55,9	55,9
Computer Programming	5	14,7	14,7	70,6
Computer Technology & Information Systems	1	2,9	2,9	73,5
Elecrtrical and Electronics Engineering	1	2,9	2,9	97,1
Information Systems	1	2,9	2,9	91,2
Information Technology	1	2,9	2,9	94,1
Mathematics	1	2,9	2,9	100
Teacher Training in Computer and Control	1	2,9	2,9	76,5
Total	34	100	100	

Moreover, it is important to note that only 2 (5,9%) mobile application developers have 0-1 experience year, 16 (47,1%) have 1-3 experience years, and 16 (47,1%) have 3+ experience years on mobile application development area.

4   Results

The questionnaire which has both characteristics of mobile commerce applications, quality factors and sub-factors of application based on ISO 25010 quality model was conducted with 34 mobile application developers.

As for the importance degree of characteristics of mobile commerce application, results can be analyzed from the three dimension perspective. The most important characteristic of presentation dimension as shown in Table 2 is use of graphics with 55,9 percent critical importance and it is followed by product's description with 41,2% percent critical importance. As for the least critical importance in the presentation dimension, it can be seen that use of text has least critical importance with 17.6 percent.

Table 2. Participants' Responses to Presentation Dimension in Questionnaire Items

Items *	(1) %	(2) %	(3) %	(4) %	(5) %	(6) %
Product's description	2,9	0,0	14,7	41,2	41,2	0,0
Use of Text	0,0	2,9	38,2	41,2	17,6	0,0
Use of Colors	0,0	0,0	23,5	41,2	35,3	0,0
Use of Graphics	0,0	0,0	8,8	35,3	55,9	0,0
Clarity	0,0	0,0	2,9	55,9	38,2	2,9
Appropriateness of Presentation	0,0	0,0	14,7	55,9	26,5	2,9

As seen from Table 3, the most important characteristic of navigation dimension is navigation mechanism with 52.9 percent critical importance and it is followed by access keys with 41.2 percent critical importance. Also, it can be seen from the results that help is not critically important characteristic with 14,7 percent critical importance, and it has the highest percent for the low importance degree with 14,7 percent.

Table 3. Participants' Responses to Navigation Dimension in Questionnaire Items

Items *	(1) %	(2) %	(3) %	(4) %	(5) %	(6) %
Navigation Mechanism	0,0	2,9	14,7	29,4	52,9	0,0
Access keys	0,0	2,9	20,6	29,4	41,2	5,9
Use of Links	0,0	5,9	41,2	26,5	20,6	5,9
Help	2,9	14,7	50,0	17,6	14,7	0,0
Undo functions	0,0	2,9	38,2	38,2	17,6	2,9
User oriented hierarchy	0,0	0,0	14,7	47,1	38,2	0,0

As for the purchasing dimension, accuracy of the operations (76,5%) and security mechanism (73,5%) are the most critically important characteristics of the application as seen in Table 4. Furthermore, operation response time, authentication and errors tolerance have the same critical importance with 41.2 percent. As for the least importance, it can be seen from the results that personalization has the least critical importance with 20,6 percent, and it has the second highest value which is 14,7 percent about low degree importance after shopping cart-metaphor criteria (17,6%).

Table 4. Participants' Responses to Purchasing Dimension in Questionnaire Items

Items *	(1) %	(2) %	(3) %	(4) %	(5) %	(6) %
Shopping cart –Metaphor	0,0	17,6	23,5	29,4	29,4	0,0
Security mechanism	2,9	0,0	5,9	17,6	73,5	0,0
Pricing Mechanism	0,0	2,9	20,6	44,1	32,4	0,0
Alternative payment methods	2,9	11,8	20,6	38,2	26,5	0,0
Authentication	2,9	8,8	5,9	41,2	41,2	0,0
Personalization	2,9	14,7	38,2	23,5	20,6	0,0
Error recovery	0,0	0,0	17,6	41,2	38,2	2,9
Errors tolerance	0,0	0,0	17,6	25,3	41,2	5,9
Operation Response time	0,0	0,0	17,6	41,2	41,2	0,0
Accuracy of the operations	0,0	0,0	2,9	20,6	76,5	0,0

Table 5. Participants' Responses to M-Commerce Quality Factors in Questionnaire Items

Items *	(1) %	(2) %	(3) %	(4) %	(5) %	(6) %
Functional Suitability	0,0	0,0	2,9	64,7	32,4	0,0
Reliability	0,0	0,0	2,9	29,4	67,6	0,0
Performance efficiency	0,0	0,0	14,7	53,9	32,4	0,0
Usability	0,0	0,0	0,0	50,0	50,0	0,0
Security	0,0	0,0	14,7	23,5	61,8	0,0
Compatibility	0,0	11,8	17,6	47,1	23,5	0,0
Portability	0,0	20,6	26,5	41,2	8,8	2,9
Maintainability	0,0	5,9	8,8	50,0	35,3	0,0

When the importance degree of quality factors were analyzed from the Table 5, it is obvious that reliability is the most important quality factor by critical importance degree with 67,6 percent. Also, it is followed by security factor with 61,8 percent critical importance degree. This result confirms the purchasing dimension result about the security mechanism which has 73,5 percent critical importance degree. Moreover, usability factor has 50 percent for both high degree importance and critical degree importance. Furthermore, it is important note that even though functional suitability has 32,4 percent critical importance degree it has the highest high importance degree with 64,7 percent. On the contrary, portability is the least critical importance degree with 8.8 percent and highest low importance degree with 20.6 percent.

As for the importance degree of quality sub-factors seen from Table 6, recoverability (47,1%), fault tolerance (44,1%) and functional correctness (44,1%) are the important ones that have the highest critical level importance. Considering that recoverability and fault tolerance are sub-factors of reliability factor, it confirms the quality factors result as reliability has the highest critical importance degree. Moreover, functional completeness (55,9%), functional appropriateness (52,9 %) and functional correctness (50,0 %) have high degree importance which might also confirm why functional suitability has high importance degree with 64.7 percent. Furthermore, it can be seen from the results that sub factors of the portability which are adaptability, installability and replaceability are not critically important.

Table 6. Participants' Responses to M-Commerce Quality Sub Factors in Questionnaire Items

Items *	(1) %	(2) %	(3) %	(4) %	(5) %	(6) %
Functional Appropriateness	0,0	0,0	14,7	52,9	29,4	2,9
Functional Correctness	0,0	0,0	2,9	50,0	44,1	2,9
Functional Completeness	0,0	0,0	17,6	55,9	23,5	2,9
Maturity:	0,0	0,0	14,7	50,0	32,4	2,9
Availability:	0,0	0,0	14,7	52,9	26,5	5,9
Fault tolerance:	0,0	0,0	20,6	35,3	44,1	0,0
Recoverability:	0,0	2,9	8,8	38,2	47,1	2,9
Timebehaviour:	0,0	5,9	14,7	38,2	41,2	0,0
Resource Utilization	0,0	8,8	26,5	41,2	20,6	2,9
Capacity	0,0	8,8	20,6	50,0	17,6	2,9
Appropriateness Recognisability	0,0	8,8	23,5	55,9	11,8	0,0
Learnability	0,0	5,9	26,5	32,4	35,3	0,0
Operability	0,0	0,0	35,3	35,3	26,5	2,9
User Error Protection	0,0	2,9	20,6	38,2	38,2	0,0
User Interface Aesthetics	0,0	0,0	5,9	52,9	41,2	0,0
Accessibility	0,0	2,9	38,2	32,4	23,5	2,9
Confidentiality	0,0	2,9	23,5	32,4	41,2	0,0
Integrity	0,0	0,0	23,5	50,0	23,5	2,9

Table 7. (*Continued*)

Accountability	0,0	11,8	17,6	41,2	29,4	0,0
Authenticity	0,0	11,8	8,8	50,0	29,4	0,0
Co-existence	2,9	20,6	23,5	29,4	20,6	2,9
Interoperability	0,0	11,8	23,5	38,2	23,5	2,9
Modularity	2,9	8,8	20,6	41,2	20,6	5,9
Reusability	0,0	5,9	26,5	44,1	23,5	0,0
Analyzability	0,0	2,9	29,4	41,2	26,5	0,0
Modifiability	0,0	5,9	14,7	44,1	32,4	2,9
Testability	0,0	2,9	20,6	52,9	23,5	0,0
Adaptability	5,9	14,7	26,5	38,2	14,7	0,0
Replaceability	2,9	11,8	29,4	35,3	20,6	0,0
Installability	2,9	11,8	32,4	35,3	17,6	0,0

5   Discussions and Conclusion

This research study analyzes both b2c mobile applications' characteristics and ISO 25010 product quality model to help both development of more qualified mobile applications and analyzing the mobile application quality process. At first, literature review was conducted to analyze both software quality models and mobile application quality models. Later as b2c mobile applications are the specific domain of this study, characteristics of mobile commerce applications were discussed with three dimensions which are presentation, navigation, and purchasing. Choosing ISO 25010 quality model and Garofalaki et al. study's as a baseline, the importance degree of both characteristics and quality factors of the product analyzed with the help of expert views. From the results, these characteristics and quality factors can be grouped so that more specific model can be produced. Moreover, characteristics and quality factors which has critical and high degree importance should be considered by developers and quality assurance teams as shown in results part.

As a limitation of this study and to give idea for the future studies, it will be good to consider customer perspective as this study includes only mobile application developer participants. Different views can express the overall quality of the product. To illustrate, from the user's perspective, usability of the system is the most important one whereas from the developer and maintainers view analysis ability and maintainability are the most important ones [6]. Furthermore, it might be a future study to look for the relationship among dimensions. For example, does presentation dimension positively influence on navigation and purchasing?

References

1. Gartner, Inc. Gartner Says Worldwide Mobile Application Store Revenue Forecast to Surpass $15 Billion in (2011),
   `http://www.gartner.com/it/page.jsp?id=1529214` (retrieved)
2. "Mobile Applications - Quality Matters" Dave Donovan. EzineArticles,
   `http://ezinearticles.com/?Mobile-Applications—Quality-Matters&id=6666537`
3. Wang, Y., Jiang, M., Wei, Y.: A Software Quality Framework for Mobile Application Testing. In: The Fourth International Conference on Advances in System Testing and Validation Lifecycle (2012)
4. Conder, S., Darcey, L.: Android Wireless Application Development, 2nd edn. Addison-Wesley (2011)
5. Cavano, J.P., McCall, J.: A framework for the measurement of software quality. SIGMETRICS Perform. (1978)
6. Behkamal, B., Kahani, M., Akbari, M.K.: Customizing ISO 9126 quality model for evaluation of B2B applications. Information and Software Technology (2013)
7. Software engineering —Product Quality - Part1: Quality Model, International Standard Organization Std. 9126 (2001)
8. ISO. Software engineering – Software product Quality Requirements and Evaluation (SQuaRE)– Measurement reference model and guide (ISO/IEC 25020:2007). International Standards Organization (2007)
9. Cheikhi, L., Abran, A.: Investigation of the Relationships Between the Software Quality Models of the ISO 9126 Standard: An Empirical Study Using Taguchi Method. Systems and Software Engineering Process (2012)
10. ISO/IEC 25010:2011: Systems and software engineering - Systems and software Quality Requirements and Evaluation (SQuaRE) - System and software quality models (2011)
11. Stefani, A., Stefanis, V., Garofalaki, M.X.J.: Quality Attributes of Consumer-Based M-Commerce Systems. In: IEEE International Conference (2007)
12. Zaidi, M., Hasan, N.H.Y.: Smart Phones Application development using HTML5 and related technologies: A tradeoff between cost and quality. International Journal of Computer Science Issues (2012)
13. Zahra, S., Khalid, A., Javed, A.: An Efficient and Effective New Generation Objective Quality Model for Mobile Applications. I. J. Modern Education and Computer Science (2013)
14. Franke, D., Kowalewski, S.: A Mobile Software Quality Model. In: 12th International Conference (2010)
15. Wac, K., Fiedler, M., Ickin, S.: Factors Influencing Quality of Experience of Commonly Used Mobile Applications. IEEE Communications Magazine (2012)
16. Hussain, A., Kutar, M.: Usability Metric Framework for Mobile Phone Application. In: The 10th Annual PostGraduate Symposium on The Convergence of Telecommunications, Networking and Broadcasting (2009)
17. Ryan, C., Rossi, P.: Software, performance and resource utilisation metrics for context-aware mobile applications. In: Proceedings of the 11th IEEE International Software Metrics Symposium (2005)
18. Pandi, K., Charaf, H.: Mobile performance metrics for resource management. In: Proceedings of the International Conference on System Science and Engineering. IEEE (2013)

19. Hussain, A., Ferneley, E.: Usability metric for mobile application: a goal question metric (GQM) approach. In: Proceedings of the 10th International Conference on Information Integration and Web-based Applications & Service (2008)
20. Franke, D., Weise, C.: Providing A Software Quality Framework For Testing of Mobile Applications. In: Fourth IEEE International Conference (2011)
21. Dantas, V.L.L., Marinho, F.G., da Costa, A.L., Andrade, R.M.C.: Testing requirements for mobile applications. In: Proceedings of the 24th International Symposium on Computer and Information Sciences (2009)
22. Liu, Z., Gao, X., Long, X.: Adaptive random testing of mobile application. In: Proceedings of the 2010 2nd International Conference on Computer Engineering and Technology (ICCET) (2010)
23. Stefani, A., Stefanis, V., Garofalaki, M.X.J.: Quality Attributes of Consumer-Based M-Commerce Systems. In: IEEE International Conference (2007)
24. Gupta, A., Madan, P.: Impact of Security and Quality Attributes of 3-G Based M-Commerce Systems Based on B2C Operation (2011)
25. Andreou, S.A., Leonidou, C., Chrysostomou, C., Pitsillides, A., Samaras, G., Schizas, C.N.: Key issues for the design and development of mobile commerce services and applications. Int. J. Mobile Communications (2005)
26. Creswell, J.W.: Educational Research: Planning, conducting, and evaluating quantitative and qualitative research, 4th edn. Pearson, Boston (2012)

An Investigation on User Preferences of Mobile Commerce Interface Design in Saudi Arabia

Lulwah AlSuwaidan and Abdulrahman A. Mirza

Collage of Computer and Information Science, Department of Information Systems,
King Saud University, P.O. Box. 51178 Riyadh 11534, K.S.A
llalsuwaidan@gmail.com, amirza@ksu.edu.sa

Abstract. Mobile commerce user interface has different issues affecting overall attitude towards the participation in mobile commerce shopping. There is a lack in the literature that has identified problems, elements, and characteristics of user interface preferences in mobile commerce from the Saudi Arabian customers' point of view. Although some research has proposed user interface frameworks and models, the problem is in the incompatibility of these current models to the new era of mobile technology especially in Saudi Arabia. In addition, the new platforms of smartphones have the ability to adapt with user's needs which add a kind of challenge for mobile commerce developers. In this paper, we will present a framework consisting of basic elements for successful Mobile commerce interface design. Methodology used in collecting users' requirements and preferences was conducted by distributing a questionnaire to a group of people from Saudi Arabia who are active mobile commerce shoppers.

Keywords: Mobile Commerce, m-commerce, user interface, Smartphone, mobile Apps.

1 Introduction

Electronic Commerce or E-commerce has created a new and exciting new format for shopping. It uses new electronic technologies, and is mainly based on the Internet. Many companies created their websites to easily communicate with their customers and provide them with products/services that they have. Accordingly, creating a user-friendly website interface was a challenge for companies to meet customers' satisfaction. Therefore, they tend to apply web usability principles to enable m-commerce[1].

Early generation mobile devices had limited capabilities in accessing the Internet, for instance, resolution, screen size, and other limitations that affect the overall representation of commerce sites. Nowadays, the greater reach and bandwidth in telecommunications services at lower costs is facilitating the growth of m-commerce. Such telecommunications advancements have enabled customers to utilize mobile devices for purchasing purposes very easily and quickly. All these developments have lead commercial companies to think of m-commerce applications to keep connected with customers. According to Saudi Communications and Information Technology Commission (CITC) the total number of mobile subscriptions was around 51 million by

I. Awan et al. (Eds.): MobiWis 2014, LNCS 8640, pp. 275–285, 2014.

the end of 2013, with a penetration rate of around 170% [2]. This means that there is a great potential for the m-commerce market in Saudi Arabia.

There are a lot of interests in developing a well organized, clear, and optimized interfaces for m-commerce. Nowadays, smartphones and their mare advanced capabilities and features make mobile commerce more powerful. As these devices have many features, mainly in the simplicity and anytime/anywhere access, this allows merchants to think seriously about targeting customers through smartphone devices. However, m-commerce in smartphones can be an application or through accessing a mobile version of current websites. Mobile commerce for smartphones has had some major limitations in user interface design. Consequently, this paper aims to collect customers' needs through a questionnaire in order to help user interface designers in determining the key elements that attract customers in m-commerce applications interface. Then, the analysis result will help in determining the best representation of mobile commerce. Also, it will assist in reaching a high level of user satisfaction.

User interface motivations for m-commerce were studies by [3]. They determined these motivations by studying m-commerce customer preferences in the United Kingdom. They found that technologies needed to implement mobile commerce are available, and users' engagement in this new form of commerce was increasing rapidly. Moreover, mobile phones capabilities are increasingly becoming smarter, easier, and more capable of connecting to the Internet. However, a good percentage of mobile users are still unwilling to start utilizing m-commerce services. This might have a negative impact on m-commerce growth.

This paper is organized into four main sections. First, literature review to discover the current state of mobile commerce and issues related to user interface design. Second, methodology used in collecting customers' attitudes towards m-commerce and its user interface. The third section covers the determined results after analyzing the collected data. The following section will present a proposed model for the m-commerce user interface design and its different elements. .

2   Literature Review

Mobile commerce is defined by Chan & Fang [4] as "the use of wireless technology, particularly handheld mobile devices and mobile Internet, to facilitate transaction, information search, and user task performance in business-to-consumer, business-to-business, and intra-enterprise communications". Another definition provided by Laudon & Traver [5] "refers to the use of wireless digital devices to enable transactions on the web". Nowadays, due to the availability of wireless technology, mobile devices especially smartphones have provided a much more attractive medium for those interested in doing online shopping.

The popularity of smartphones has been increased due the improvements in the mobile devices such as larger screen sizes, higher display resolutions, light-weighted devices, and a more user friendly functionalities than before [6]. This emerged technology facilitates e-commerce transactions. In [5] Laudon & Traver it is stated that around 13 Billion Dollars of business revenues are generated from mobile commerce advertisements, location-based services, e-book sales, app sales, and entertainment. This can interpret how mobile commerce becomes an essential part in all kinds of business.

Chan & Fang [7] discussed the issues related to designing mobile commerce interface. Technological issues such as bandwidth and Internet connection was one of these issues since some interface elements require high-speed Internet connections. Input and output format is also another technological trend in smartphones. In addition, they claimed that user goals and tasks effect how the application interface looks like. For example, making a hotel or a flight reservation should be as easy as possible and consume less time. Moreover, Chan & Fang [7] demonstrated the content presented in mobile commerce such as information, navigation, amount of graphics and text, and structure. They also mentioned the poor quality of existing web site commerce and the need to introduce mobile commerce channels. The challenge is always in the unification between e-commerce and m-commerce.

The aforementioned issues have an impact over the customers' attitude towards mobile commerce. The attitude issue has been discussed by Su & Adams [8]. They measured the attitude in terms of cultural and environmental factors in two countries, China and the UK. They concluded with a model of the factors affecting the attitude towards mobile commerce. The factors were political, social, economical, and technological. Therefore, the question is "Are the customers ready for mobile commerce?" This question was asked by Persaud & Azhar [9] to measure how customers are willing to get into mobile commerce. The work resulted in a set of motivations for using mobile commerce: consumers' shopping style, brand trust, and value.

Chang et al. [10] argued that companies/firms should identify the critical success factors of mobile commerce. This will assist in identifying measures and strategies to successfully develop mobile commerce. The critical success factors as stated by [10] consist of services customization and business/services offerings. In addition, Chiang & Liao [6] stated the factors that influence customers to trust mobile transactions. These factors are: credibility, privacy, security, time-criticality, responsiveness, service quality, interactivity, and, reliability. Specifically, privacy and security are two factors that are related to each other. Once the application provides secure services, this is claimed to influence an improved level of privacy [11].

The concerns have not been limited to specifying issues and factors of the interface of mobile commerce, but also directed to measuring and evaluating of existing interfaces. In this matter, Cooharjananone et al. [12] presented a work in Thailand to evaluate interfaces in smartphones by comparing two different methods of interface representation: text-based and graphic-based interfaces. The study was focused on three main aspects; ease of use, intention to use, and risk. They determined that the languages provided within the application and menu icons were more important factors that influenced customer and end user satisfaction. In terms of customer personalization, Georgiadis [13] was focused in his study in personalizing user interface issues. He concentrated on the importance of matching user preferences and device constraints in m-commerce applications. Therefore, customers can add alerts, notifications, push-based mobile messaging, and others. For the issue of navigation, Jones et al. [14] made an experiment to measure the navigation and scrolling in small screens versus large ones. They found that navigation and scrolling are much easier in large screens rather than that in small screens [14].

Mobile commerce needs a certain set of technologies to work well. Since it is mobile, it certainly needs effective and efficient wireless networks. In [15], Lee et al. revealed the need of technologies and disciplines for m-commerce systems. They divided the m-commerce system into six components: mobile commerce applications, mobile station, mobile middleware, wireless network, wired network, and host computers. Mobile commerce applications have two sets of programs: client, and server side programs. Mobile station presents user interfaces to the end users and displays the processing results later using the interfaces. The main role of mobile middleware is to encrypt the communication in order to provide high level of security for transactions. User's transactions are passed through a wireless network either by access point or base station. A wired network component is optional for m-commerce systems because servers mostly reside in wired networks. A host computer processes, produces, and stores all the information for mobile commerce applications. It is similar to that used in e-commerce.

Mobile commerce plays a crucial role in making purchasing decisions. In 2013, Kalnikaite et al. [16] evaluated how shopping apps that overwhelm shoppers with information related to the purchased products affect shoppers' decisions. The study proposed using embedded technologies such as barcode scanner to provide simple information and feedbacks. The study found that when information is presented in an easy and simple manner, this would affect the buying decision. Also, the type of information provided, for example for supermarket shoppers, such as calories, fat, health nutrition, comparisons between products, and customers' reviews and ratings, are very helpful for shoppers to make the right decision. In this regard, Ku et al. [17]have investigated how a recommender system user interface is important in affecting customers' decision making. The chosen approach by [17] was conjoint analysis to differentiate between consumers' preference for the recommender system in an e-commerce interface.

Although, most existing e-commerce concentrated on the functions provides via mobile commerce, Huang et al. [18] focused on designing task-oriented mobile commerce rather than functional-oriented interface. The reason was to guarantee the nonfunctional requirements such as portability, reliability, and maintainability that have an impact on the system overall usability. The scenario-based design framework is composed of five steps: defining problem scenarios, developing activity scenarios, designing information scenarios, designing interaction scenarios, and evaluating prototypes.

3   Research Methodology

This paper is studying the Saudi Arabian customer attitude towards mobile commerce user interfaces. The results collected from the questionnaire will help determine customer preferences of mobile interfaces in commerce applications. Generally, customers are the most important elements in commerce and business sectors. User interface design is considered an important way to give a good impression about m-commerce applications. If customers feel comfortable and can easily reach what they want, they will proceed to make a purchase. Otherwise, there is a high chance that they will leave the site and not return again. To avoid this issue, we distributed a questionnaire to a set of regular m-commerce users to determine their preferences in a mobile commerce interface. The study covered different aspects such as preferences for Mobile commerce interface, customer personalization, navigation, and interface view.

The intended study specifically targeted those who are interested in doing purchases through m-commerce applications. Also, targeted participants were expected to be technology savvy and hence should have some awareness of good interface design principles.. The study participants included both males and females, however, the percentage of targeted female participants was much greater than male participants since females in Saudi Arabia, as a result of the cultural structure of the country, and their inability to drive, are most likely to take advantage of m-commerce applications. Our targeted sample size included members of the Saudi community aged between 18-60 years.

The questionnaire was created and distributed as an electronic version using Google Forms which is a good tool to create, collect responses, and analyze results. This electronic questionnaire was distributed in various ways using social networking, e-mails, and messages to collect reasonable responses. Nowadays, electronic surveys are more popular since it allows researcher to collect more responses than printed copy.

4   Results and Data Analysis

This section covers results and analysis of collected study data.

4.1   Data Collection

The questionnaire was completed by 155 persons, 22 had no previous experience with m-commerce and hence were removed from the study. Hence, the number of responses to be included in this study were from 133 participants who had previous experience with m-commerce applications. Table 1 shows general information of the study sample. As shown in Table 1, the percentage of female participants is almost 87%. Moreover, and as can be seen from the same table, the largest group of participants is that between the ages of 19 and 35, at slightly above 82%. Participants with a Bachelor's degree and those with post-graduate degrees are almost equal with 48.87% and 46.61% respectively.

Table 1. Demographic Analysis of the Sample

General Information	
Category	Percentage (%)
Gender	
Male	13.53%
Female	86.47%
Ages	
Below 19	1.50%
19 – 35	85.71%
36 – 60	12.78%
Education	
Secondary	4.51%
Bachelor	48.87%
Post graduate	46.61%

Table 2 shows list of points covered in the questionnaire. It consists of the most desirable features that customers/users feel should be available in m-commerce application interfaces. This section of the questionnaire is divided into ten categories of measurements.

— First category measures how products lists are presented in home panel or main page. Questionnaire asked customers/users for their preferences in arranging product lists either by list of categories or as a vertical list.
— Second category measures how to present product and its details. This point gave three options of product displays, either product's image, text only, or, other. For the "other" option, participants were allowed to write their option.
— Third, product pricing is considered a critical element in e-commerce and particularly in m-commerce. In this point, we asked the participants about their preferences regarding pricing representation, should it be displayed or not?.
— Fourth, we asked if customers would like to be able to view additional detailed information about each product, or the ability to view a 3D image of the product.
— Fifth, how should the products be sorted and displayed. Should they be sorted based on the best seller, the most recently introduced, the least price, all products with no specific sorting, or, based on user's own defined priority.
— Sixth, usage aimed to measure how frequently the sample tends to use mobile commerce applications.
— Seventh, a measure of the participants' desirability in customizing the application's screen to match their interface preferences.
— Eight, the shopping cart is another issue in e-commerce in general and most customers feel wary about security and how to complete their purchasing operations. The questionnaire asked participants how they prefer to complete their purchasing, once an item is selected, or after all items have been selected and the customer is ready to check-out.

— Ninth, category measures the navigation process in m-commerce. What is the preferred way to navigate from one page to another? Participants were asked if they prefer to have a submenu in each page, return back to main page always, or, backtracking their moves until reaching a specific point from which they can choose a different track of pages.

— Tenth, security and privacy are among the most important issues that customers are concerned about when shopping online. The questionnaire asked participants if they prefer to allow the application to save their personal and payment information for further use, or if they prefer to provide them in each purchasing process.

Table 2. Sample preferences of mobile commerce interface

Mobile commerce Interface Preferences			
Category	Percentage(%)	Category	Percentage (%)
Products List Representation (Menu)		**Usage**	
Categories of products	86.46%	Frequent	20.30%
Vertical lists	12.78%	Sometimes	45.11%
Product View		Rare	34.58%
Image	84.21%		
Text	4.51%	**Screen Customization**	
Other (Both image & text)	9.77%	Yes	77.45%
Other (Video)	1.50%	No	22.55%
Display Product Price		**Purchases and Checkout**	
Yes	99.24%	All products	87.96%
No	0.75%	Each product	12.03%
Additional Product Information		**App Browsing**	
Yes	96.24%	Home Page	9.77%
No	3.75%	Backward	35.33%
Product Display Priority		Dynamic Submenu	54.88%
Best sellers	16.54%	**Security**	
Newest	52.63%	Save Data	65.41%
Least price	3.00%	Do not save	34.58%
No Order	21.05%		
Other (User Priority)	6.76%		

4.2   Data Analysis

In terms of representation and design of Mobile commerce applications, the questionnaire asked some questions about the fundamental elements of m-commerce interfaces that the Saudis prefer when shopping through this media.. As can be seen in Table 2, a great majority of participants at 86.46% have indicated that they prefer to see products listed according to categories such as fashion, electronic, books, movies, music, materials, etc., rather than having them as random vertical lists. 84.21% indicated that they like to view products listed as images, 4.5% prefer to view them as text, while, 9.77% preferred the "Other" option and indicated image and text as how they like to view products. Moreover, 52.63% of the participants like to have the newest products displayed to them, followed by 21% who did not have any specific ordering of products, followed by 16.54% who would like to see products ordered with best sellers first. An "Other" option was given to which 6.76% of the participants indicated that they would like to have the opportunity to select their own ordering scheme. This indicates that this is an important choice, and it should have been provided as one of the main options to choose from. The desire to see products listed based on the least price first was the least popular, with only 3% selecting this option.

When the shoppers choose one of the products, 96.24% of the sample prefer to have more detailed information regarding the chosen product. This information is considered very useful for customers to know about the product that they are willing to buy. For instance, information about materials used, colors, size, or any supported information that helps customers make a buying decision. Pricing is also another very important element that almost all shoppers at 99.24% have indicated as a must have.

Customization is another great feature that can be added to mobile commerce sites. It refers to the ability to add, edit, move, and remove any elements as needed by customer, so, he/she has the full authority to build his/her own m-commerce interface. When the questionnaire asked about the ability to customize mobile commerce application, 77.44% have responded with "yes", while the remaining, 22.55%, said no.

When customers/users finished browsing the app and found what they wanted, they do the next step by finalizing the trading and completing the payment process. Almost 88% of the participants prefer to add selected products into a shopping cart and then checking out once done shopping. Only 12% indicated that they like to make immediate payment, once each single product is selected.

When m-commerce shoppers are browsing the site for products they might need to go back to check another item or another category. The questionnaire asked the sample to what they prefer when need to check another page. Almost 55% of the study sample have indicated that they prefer to have a dynamic submenu on each page from which they can jump to any other page. 35.33% indicated that they prefer to track back their steps going back to the previous pages, and only 9.77% said that they would like to go the Home page and start again from there.

Storing customer's personal and payment information within application or site for further use are typically considered as a major security issues in m-commerce and e-commerce. However, when the questionnaire asked about that matter, 65.41% of the respondents said that they do not mind that the application saves their information for further use, while only 34.58% said they prefer to enter their payment and personal information every single time. This result means that m-commerce merchants need to provide highly secured databases and payment processes for their customers.

5   Proposed Prototype

In previous section a discussion of the main preferable elements of mobile commerce application interface have been presented. The nine elements are the most crucial elements for successful mobile commerce application interface. Figure 1 shows a representation of these elements. Therefore, this paper aimed to investigate the customers' needs for mobile commerce application interface. Also, it aims at proposing an interface prototype that may be considered as a standard for mobile commerce application interfaces. This prototype preserves customer satisfaction since businesses/merchants can examine their mobile commerce application interfaces under consideration of this prototype. Meeting all or part of the prototype elements optimize mobile commerce interfaces.

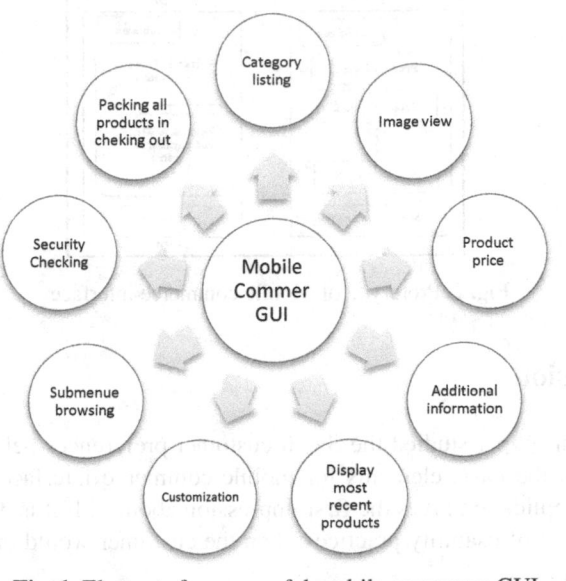

Fig. 1. Elements for successful mobile commerce GUI

The proposed prototype ensures the fundamental elements that should be included in designing mobile commerce interface as illustrated in Figure 2. Part A of this Figure shows the main panel when customers access the application. Category is the arranging method used in the main panel/page within photo illustrates of each category. To simplify accessing the shopping cart, it should be available in all panels to allow customers to check what they selected. The submenu is also available in all panels to easily discover all the parts of the application. Part B represents the page when a customer chooses one of the items. It has a photo of that item, related information, product price, special offers, and a button to add it to the shopping cart. If customer is finished discovering the items and wanted to make payment, part C illustrates this by having information of all selected items within the total pricing. Finally, when everything is settled, customers have to complete their purchasing by filling out personal, addressing, and payment information as shown in part D.

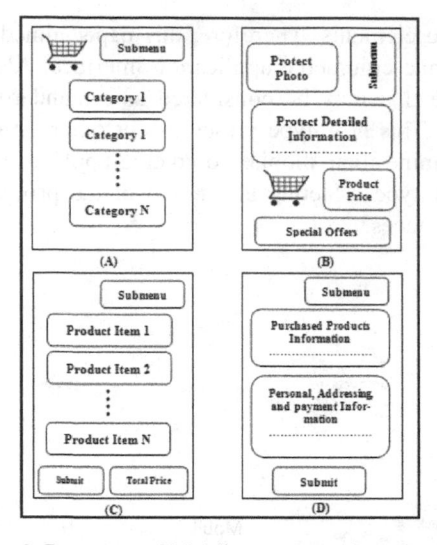

Fig. 2. Prototype of Mobile commerce interface

6   Conclusion

In conclusion, this paper studied the Saudi customer preferences behind mobile commerce and found the basic elements for mobile commerce interfaces. User interface for any mobile application gives the first impression about it. If it is designed well and includes high level of usability practices, then the customer would proceed to continue using this App.

This paper measured shoppers' preferences of interface for mobile commerce. The basic elements that should be taken into consideration when designing the interfaces are: ability to customize the interface, ability to save payment and personal information, user profiling for recommendations, products viewing as images, browsing/navigation ability, and supported information for each product. In addition, at the end of this work, we proposed a prototype that illustrated the main elements of mobile commerce interface. All in all, this paper mainly represents m-commerce interface preferences of Saudi Arabian shoppers.

References

1. Huang, I., Li, M.: Research on C2C e-commerce website usability evaluation system. In: 2010 IEEE 11th International Conference on Computer-Aided Industrial Design & Conceptual Design (CAIDCD), Zhenjiang, China (2010)
2. ICT Indicators Report, Communication and Information Commission, Riyadh (2013)
3. Hunaiti, Z., Tairo, D., Sedoyeka, E., Elgazzar, S.: Factors Facing Mobile Commerce Deployment in United Kingdom. In: Handheld Computing for Mobile Commerce: Applications, Concepts and Technologies, pp. 109–122. Information Science Reference, Hershey (2010)

4. Chan, S.S., Fang, X.: Interface Design Issues for Mobile Commerce. In: Electronic Commerce: Concepts, Methodologies, Tools, and Applications, pp. 250–257. Information Science Reference, Hershey (2008)
5. Laudon, K.C., Traver, C.G.: E-Commerce 2011 Business. Technology. Pearson, Society, Harlow, England (2011)
6. Chiang, I.-P., Liao, Y.-S.: Exploring the Key Success Factors of Mobile Commerce in Taiwan. In: 26th International Conference on Advanced Information Networking and Applications Workshops, Fukuoka (2012)
7. Chan, S.S., Fang, X.: Interface Design Issues for Mobile Commerce. In: Electronic Commerce: Concepts, Methodologies, Tools, and Applications, pp. 250–257. IGI Global, Hershey (2008)
8. Su, Q., Adams, C.: Consumers' attitudes toward Mobile Commerce: a Model to Capture the Cultural and Environment Influences. International Journal of E-Services and Mobile Applications 2(1), 1–25 (2010)
9. Persaud, A., Azhar, I.: Innovative mobile marketing via smartphones: Are consumers ready? Marketing Intelligence & Planning 30(4), 418–443 (2012)
10. Chang, S.I., Peng, T.C., Hung, Y.C., Chang, I.C., Hung, W.H.: Critical Success Factors of Mobile Commerce Adoption: A Study Based on the System Life Cycle and Diamond Model. In: Eighth International Conference on Mobile Business, Dalian, Liaoning, China (2009)
11. Sheng, H., Nah, F.F.-H., Siau, K.: An Experimental Study on Ubiquitous commerce Adoption: Impact of Personalization and Privacy Concerns. Journal of the Association for Information Systems 9(6), 344–376 (2008)
12. Cooharojananone, N., Muadthong, A., Limniramol, R., Tetsuro, K., Hitoshi, O.: The Evaluation of M-Commerce Interface on Smart Phones in Thailand. In: 13th International Conference on Advanced Communication Technology (ICACT), Phoenix Park, Republic of Korea (2011)
13. Georgiadis, C.K.: Adaptation and Personalization of User Interface and Content. In: Human Computer Interaction: Concepts, Methodologies, Tools, and Applications, pp. 393–403. Information Science Reference, Hershey (2009)
14. Jones, M., Marsden, G., Mohd-Nasir, N., Boone, K., Buchanan, G.: Improving Web Interaction on Small Displays, http://www8.org/w8-papers/1b-multimedia/improving/improving.html (accessed 2013)
15. Lee, C.-W., Hu, W.-C., Yeh, J.-H.: Mobile Commerce Technology. In: Encyclopedia of Information Science and Technology, pp. 2584–2589. Information Science Reference, Hershey (2009)
16. Kalnikaite, V., Bird, J., Rogers, Y.: Decision-making in the aisles: informing, overwhelming or nudging supermarket shoppers? Personal and Ubiquitous Computing 17(6), 1247–1259 (2013)
17. Ku, Y.-C., Peng, C.-H., Yang, Y.-C.: Consumer Preferences for the Interface of E-Commerce Product Recommendation System. In: Nah, F.F.-H. (ed.) HCIB 2014. LNCS, vol. 8527, pp. 526–537. Springer, Heidelberg (2014)
18. Huang, E.Y., Lin, Y.-J., Huang, T.K.: Task-Oriented M-Commerce Interface Design. In: Stephanidis, C. (ed.) HCII 2013, Part I. CCIS, vol. 373, pp. 36–40. Springer, Heidelberg (2013)

Exploring Social Influence and Incremental Online Persuasion on Twitter: A Longitudinal Study

Agnis Stibe

Department of Information Processing Science,
Faculty of Information Technology and Electrical Engineering,
P.O. Box 3000, FI-90014 University of Oulu, Finland
agnis.stibe@gmail.com

Abstract. This paper outlines the second phase of an ongoing longitudinal research initiative aimed at exploring and describing why people use Twitter the way they do and what factors change their behaviors and attitudes over time. In a repeated online survey, 501 valid responses were collected from Twitter users. A comparative analysis of findings from both surveys verified persistent online persuasion patterns influencing both user behavior related to content generation and tweeting frequency, as well as user attitudes about Twitter being an influential tool to use in calling for action outside the virtual world. A comprehensive analysis of responses from 49 individuals who had participated in both surveys revealed underlying factors that had prompted changes in what they thought about Twitter, as well as their use behaviors. Further findings emphasized the role of social influence design principles and their capacity to explain changes that Twitter users had experienced over the period of two years.

Keywords. Twitter, online persuasion, social influence, design principles, user behavior, incremental, longitudinal.

1   Introduction

Online social networks increasingly change the ways in which people communicate, collaborate, consume, and create [2]. They transform the ways organizations manage their relationships with markets and societies, creating new possibilities and challenges for various aspects of business operations from traditional marketing and electronic commerce to more sophisticated participatory design and co-creation with customers. Such transformations increase the necessity for organizations to embrace new ways of maintaining customer relationships and monitoring their behaviors.

Research on social networks has been a rapidly growing area for many years. However, recently, it has experienced significant acceleration [2]. Studies have been carried out in various contexts, including business [27], health [29], education [17], disasters [7], and even revolutions [22]. Among other social networks, Twitter has demonstrated its relevance within an organizational context [14] because it enables the development of virtual customer environments, in which online interest groups can form around particular brands [10], thus facilitating the co-design of products.

I. Awan et al. (Eds.): MobiWis 2014, LNCS 8640, pp. 286–300, 2014.

Several studies have addressed the adoption [5] and continued usage [8] of Web 2.0, including Twitter. However a large part of existing research is focused on statistical descriptions of Twitter itself [4]. In addition to Twitter, studies that are simply based on extensive analyses of available log data [1], such as the content of tweets and other parameters, further attempt to explain the behaviors and attitudes of Twitter users are needed. According to Aral et al. [2], further research based on the recurrent metering of the attitudes and behaviors of Twitter users is necessary in order to study their dynamics and design social media strategies, especially those focusing on the individual level [2].

Therefore, this study outlines the second phase of an ongoing longitudinal research initiative aimed at exploring, understanding, and explaining why people use Twitter the way they do and what factors change their behaviors and attitudes over time. The motivation behind this phase was to discover the underlying factors and persuasive design principles that influence what people think about Twitter and their use behaviors. Ultimately, the aim was to uncover how social interactions on Twitter can influence peoples' behaviors and attitudes outside the virtual world. The research questions for this study were posed as follows:

RQ1: What types of persistent online persuasion patterns exist on Twitter that can change the behaviors and attitudes of users over time?

RQ2: What factors affect these changes and how they are interlinked on an individual level?

2   Background

Earlier research highlighted Twitter's ability to disseminate news and other information regarding both online trends and real-world events quickly and broadly [24]. Such online networking capabilities often facilitate the fast circulation of last-minute information, thus attracting considerable commercial and consumer interest. Thus, Twitter can be seen as an interesting channel via which companies can develop brands and improve their customer service [4]. The existing body of knowledge about Twitter contains various types of studies. A large part of it is based on descriptive and statistical research about this social network, such as the identification of different user types [18], social networks on Twitter [16], "retweeting" behaviors as conversational practice [6], and collaboration via Twitter [15]. Recent studies have been based on a partial least squares path modeling approach, which was intended to examine Twitter use [23] and use continuance [4] behaviors.

Social patterns observed on Twitter differ from known behaviors on other social networks [19]. This includes an asynchronous type of relationship between Twitter users, which permits them to select whom to follow without any obligation to be followed in return. This principle has liberated Twitter use behavior, thus making it less predictable than other social networks with synchronous types of relationships at the core of systems design. The major social interaction on Twitter is reading through an instantly updated feed of tweets, a chronologically ordered list of all messages openly posted by the users one is following. On the one hand, this seemingly light functionality may have simplified the user experience on this social network. On the other hand, this may hinder the recognition of the actual behavioral patterns of Twitter users. Thus, studies are required to uncover all potentially hidden consequences of human behavior and social influence, e.g., the interest groups formed.

A myriad of studies related to online social networking have been conducted previously, but only very recently has an organizing framework for social media research been reported [2]. The underlying intention was to help scholars frame their research initiatives in a systematic way. The framework proposed a conceptualization of the social media landscape as an intersection of four types of activities that users or producers can undertake and three levels of analysis at which these activities can be investigated. According to the research questions stated earlier, the most relevant activity from the proposed framework was "design and features," which is aimed at describing how consumers and organizations use or design specific social media features. On the level of "users and society," this activity is focused on studying user interactions with specific features and the user behaviors affected by their design, while on the level of "platforms and intermediaries," it concentrates on how these features can be designed to influence user behavior.

The functionality, design, and dynamic social processes govern how social networks affect the behaviors and attitudes of their users. For instance, organizations can create word-of-moth peer influence and social contagion by designing features around their products [3]. Firms can also manage the strength of network effects by adjusting features embedded in software, together with appropriate network seeding [11]. Finally, users' statuses, similarities, and desire to differentiate affect their content generation behavior [31].

3   Research Methodology

This study has a longitudinal character. The initial online survey of Twitter users was carried out in June of 2010 [26]. Two years later, for the purposes of the second phase of this ongoing longitudinal research initiative, the survey instrument was improved, and another survey was conducted in July of 2012. A link to the online survey was promoted via Twitter. Respondents who had reported their usernames in the first survey were invited to participate in the second with specially designed tweets containing their usernames. In the second round, 501 valid responses were collected. Based on the identical Twitter usernames, 49 respondents were identified to be the same in both surveys. The repeated survey mainly contained the same questions about the habits, thoughts, behaviors, and attitudes of Twitter users, but in the second round, specific questions aimed at measuring users' attitudes toward the presence of social influence factors on Twitter were included. Particular questions were constructed to reveal persuasion patterns on Twitter, e.g., How long have you been using Twitter? How often do you tweet? What do you consider yourself on Twitter: a reader, retweeter, responder, or content generator? Do you think that Twitter is a powerful tool to call for action outside the virtual world? Do some user-created communication and behavioral rules exist on Twitter? What is the level of credibility on Twitter?

The newly incorporated statements were designed to capture users' attitudes about social influence design principles [25] on Twitter. E.g., Twitter allows me to compare my behavior with other users (social comparison). There are norms on Twitter that should be followed by me (normative influence). I can discern other active users while using Twitter (social facilitation). I can cooperate with other users on Twitter (cooperation). I can compete with other users on Twitter (competition). Twitter users receive public recognition for their merits (recognition).

The sample from the second survey was very similar to the sample from the original survey in terms of gender, age, and education. The length of use naturally differed because two more years that has passed between both surveys. More descriptive statistics about the new sample are provided in Table 1, which also contains descriptive statistics for 49 repeated respondents.

Table 1. Descriptive statistics for the new sample of 501 total and 49 repeated respondents

		New sample		Repeated	
		N=501	%	N=49	%
Gender	Male	237	47.3	17	34.7
	Female	264	52.7	32	65.3
Age	Less than 20 years	68	13.6	5	10.2
	20 to 24 years	195	38.9	15	30.6
	25 to 29 years	112	22.4	14	28.6
	30 to 34 years	60	12.0	7	14.3
	35 to 39 years	33	6.6	4	8.2
	40 years or more	33	6.6	4	8.2
Education	Studies in school	49	9.8	4	8.2
	Secondary school	158	31.5	14	28.6
	Bachelor	198	39.5	22	44.9
	Master	95	19.0	9	18.4
	Doctoral	1	0.2	-	-
The length of Twitter use	Less than 6 month	23	4.6	-	-
	6 months to 1 year	50	10.0	-	-
	1 to 2 years	148	29.5	5	10.2
	2 to 3 years	187	37.3	23	46.9
	More than 3 years	93	18.6	21	42.9

4   Incremental Online Persuasion

The findings from the initial survey in 2010 revealed several incremental online persuasion patterns that influenced the behaviors and attitudes of Twitter users over time [26]. Before comparing the results from both surveys, the same analysis methods were applied to the dataset of the 501 newly gathered respondents. As previously, the data analysis was carried out with SPSS software, which is widely used for statistical analysis in the social sciences. Descriptive statistics were used, especially cross-tabulation, which is the process of creating a contingency table from the multivariate frequency distribution of statistical variables. The results of the statistical data analysis provided support for the existence of significant relationships between the duration of Twitter use and behavior or attitude changes in Twitter users for several questions.

4.1   Content Generation on Twitter

The question about content generation behavior remained exactly the same as in the original survey [26], i.e., "As a Twitter user, do you consider yourself a...," and the responses was measured using a four-point ordinal scale with the following response options: "Reader," "Retweeter" (reader who also retweets), "Responder" (retweeter who also replies and comments), and "Generator" (responder who also generates new content). The Pearson chi-square test was used to assess the dependence of the column and row variables (Table 2).

Table 2. The relationship between length of use and content generation on Twitter

How long have you been using Twitter?	As a Twitter user, you consider yourself a:			
	Reader	Retweeter	Responder	Generator
Less than 6 month	17.4% (n=4)	39.1% (n=9)	30.4% (n=7)	13.0% (n=3)
6 months to 1 year	6.0% (n=3)	38.0% (n=19)	42.0% (n=21)	14.0% (n=7)
1 to 2 years	9.5% (n=14)	24.3% (n=36)	44.6% (n=66)	21.6% (n=32)
2 to 3 years	5.9% (n=11)	19.8% (n=37)	44.4% (n=83)	29.9% (n=56)
More than 3 years	3.2% (n=3)	14.0% (n=13)	40.9% (n=38)	41.9% (n 39)

According to the cross-tabulation, followed by a Pearson chi-square test, there was a dependent relationship showing very clearly that experienced users generate more content than new users ($\chi^2(12) = 34.569$, p = .001). Especially remarkable was the growth in the percentage of generators from each category of users according to their length of Twitter use. There were only 13.0% generators among new users (less than 6 months), 14.0% generators among slightly more experienced Twitter users (more than 6 months and less than 1 year), 21.6% generators among even more experienced users (between 1 and 2 years), 29.9% generators among users with Twitter experience between 2 and 3 years, and 41.9% generators among the most experienced group of Twitter users (3 years or more). To conclude, this finding provides additional support for a previously tested assumption that the longer one uses Twitter, the more one's behavior regarding content generation changes. Persuaded incrementally, Twitter users become more responsive and more ready to generate new content.

4.2   Frequency of Tweeting

Also, the question about the frequency of tweeting behavior remained exactly the same as in the original survey [26], i.e., "You tweet:," but the responses were measured using a six-point ordinal scale (instead of the original five-point ordinal scale) with the following response options: "Do not tweet," "Once in several months,"

"Sometimes during a month," "Several times a week," "Every day," and "Several times a day." The first five response options remained exactly the same as in the original survey. Only the sixth response option was added to the measurement scale for this question. Because only 5.2% of the responses were in the first two categories, the first three categories were combined under the name of "Sometimes during the month and less." The Pearson chi-square test was used to assess the dependence between variables (Table 3). According to the cross-tabulation followed by a Pearson chi-square test, there was a dependent relationship emphasizing that the amount of tweeting has increased over time ($\chi^2(12) = 27.177$, p = .007).

Table 3. The relationship between length of use and frequency of tweeting

How long have you been using Twitter?	You tweet:			
	Sometimes a month or less	Several times a week	Every day	Several times a day
Less than 6 month	21.7% (n=5)	52.2% (n=12)	17.4% (n=4)	8.7% (n=2)
6 months to 1 year	34.0% (n=17)	38.0% (n=19)	16.0% (n=8)	12.0% (n=6)
1 to 2 years	20.3% (n=30)	44.6% (n=66)	18.9% (n=28)	16.2% (n=24)
2 to 3 years	16.6% (n=31)	32.1% (n=60)	23.0% (n=43)	28.3% (n=53)
More than 3 years	11.8% (n=11)	36.6% (n=34)	22.6% (n=21)	29.0% (n=27)

This provides support for the presumption that experienced users tweet more than new users and that this behavior develops incrementally. Especially significant growth was seen in the percentage of respondents tweeting several times a day from each category of users according to their length of Twitter use: 8.7% of new users (less than 6 months), 12.0% of users using Twitter for more than 6 months and less than 1 year, 16.2% of users with Twitter experience between 1 and 2 years, 28.3% of users with Twitter experience between 2 and 3 years, and 29.0% of the most experienced users (3 years or more) tweeted several times a day. Similarly to the finding from the initial survey [26], this result obviously contributed to the persistent incremental nature of this behavior.

4.3 Call for Action Outside the Virtual World

The borderlines between the virtual and real worlds are continuously converging. To investigate this interplay, exactly the same question was asked in the second survey as in the first [26]: "Do you think Twitter is a powerful tool to call for action outside the virtual world?" However, in the second survey, a seven-point scale was used for measuring the responses: "Strongly disagree," "Disagree," "Somewhat disagree," "Undecided," "Somewhat agree," "Agree," and "Strongly agree." In order to exclude cells with expected counts less than the required minimum for the Pearson chi-square test, the first three responses were combined under "Disagree," and last two responses were combined under "Agree" (Table 4). The Pearson chi-square test results reveal that Twitter has been perceived by respondents as an influential tool to call for action offline, i.e., outside of the virtual world, and that experienced users were more ready to take action based on their communication via Twitter ($\chi^2(12) = 25.352$, p = .013) than other users. Again, this provides additional support for the previously tested assumption that experienced users are more responsive to taking action in the real world after receiving a call to action on Twitter. The analysis seems to demonstrate that this change in the attitude and behavior of Twitter users happens incrementally over time depending on the length of Twitter use. In addition, Twitter also provides a convenient mechanism for spreading calls to action via retweeting.

Table 4. The relationship between length of use and reported attitude regarding whether Twitter is an influential tool to call for action outside the virtual world

How long have you been using Twitter?	Do you think that Twitter is an influential tool to call for action outside the virtual world?			
	Disagree	Undecided	Somewhat agree	Agree
Less than 6 month	8.7% (n=2)	21.7% (n=5)	39.1% (n=9)	30.4% (n=7)
6 months to 1 year	10.0% (n=5)	4.0% (n=2)	52.0% (n=26)	34.0% (n=17)
1 to 2 years	10.1% (n=15)	8.1% (n=12)	43.9% (n=65)	37.8% (n=56)
2 to 3 years	5.3% (n=10)	3.7% (n=7)	36.4% (n=68)	54.5% (n=102)
More than 3 years	7.5% (n=7)	6.5% (n=6)	43.0% (n=40)	43.0% (n=40)

4.4   Summarized Results from Both Surveys

In Table 5, the key findings from both surveys are summarized. They explicitly emphasize persistent incremental online persuasion patterns on Twitter that can affect user behaviors or attitudes. Thus, these findings provide an answer to research question RQ1.

Table 5. Incremental online persuasion patterns on Twitter [26]

How long have you been using Twitter?	Year 2010 (N=403)	Year 2012 (N=501)
Content generation behavior	$\chi^2(9)=29.789$, p=.000	$\chi^2(12)=34.569$, p=.001
Frequency of tweeting behavior	$\chi^2(6)=18.059$, p=.006	$\chi^2(12)=27.177$, p=.007
Attitude about Twitter being influential	$\chi^2(6)=18.551$, p=.005	$\chi^2(12)=25.352$, p=.013

5   Factors Influencing User Behavior and Attitude on Twitter

In order to find answers to research question RQ2, the sample of 49 repeated respondents was examined. It provided an excellent opportunity for a comprehensive data analysis regarding changes in the behaviors and attitudes of Twitter users on an individual level. Before carrying out the following analysis with repeated respondents, first, it was ensured that the variables and their measurement scales were consistent across both years. Second, for each original variable, two new variables were created, one that implied a general change in an attitude or behavior over time and another that implied a more detailed change in an attitude or behavior over time. For example, when the variable measuring content generation behavior on Twitter is examined, for each respondent, this variable had two measures, one from the year 2010 and another from the year 2012. To record the change in this behavior over time, a new variable (CONT^3) was created. Then, for each of the 49 respondents, their change in terms of this particular behavior was coded into a measurement scale with three categories: behavior decreased (1), remained the same (2), or increased (3) over time. To record more a detailed change in the same behavior over time, an additional variable (CONT^5) was created. Then, again, for each of the 49 respondents, their change in this particular behavior was coded into a five-point measurement scale: behavior decreased more than one step (1), behavior decreased only one step (2), behavior remained the same (3), behavior increased one step (4), or behavior increased more than one step (5) over time. This was done for all repeated variables.

All other variables used in the following analysis were collected only during the second survey, and they were measured on the following seven-point scale: "Strongly disagree," "Disagree," "Somewhat disagree," "Undecided," "Somewhat agree," "Agree," and "Strongly agree."

5.1   Analysis of Variance

The dataset containing the 49 repeated respondents was examined with a one-way analysis of variance (ANOVA), which has typically been used to determine significant differences between the means of three or more independent groups. Also, post-hoc testing was done to compare multiple groups. Both Fisher's LSD (least significant difference) and Tukey's HSD (honestly significant difference) post-hoc tests are commonly accepted among statisticians, and the logic behind them is the same. However, Tukey's HSD post-hoc test can be used only when sample sizes are equal, which is not true in the design of this research. Therefore, Fisher's LSD post-hoc test was selected to determine significant differences between the means of the paired groups.

It was consistently ensured that the data met all six assumptions that should be tested before and while running the one-way ANOVA. It was ensured that all independent variables consisted of three categorical, independent groups; all observations were independent; there were no significant outliers; there was homogeneity of variances; all dependent variables were measured at interval level; and they were approximately normally distributed for each category of the related independent variable. The assumption of homogeneity of variance was tested using Levene's test, which provides an F statistic and a significance value (p value). When the data failed to meet the homogeneity of variances assumption ($p < .05$), a Welch ANOVA was carried out instead of a one-way ANOVA, and a Games-Howell pot-hoc test was carried out instead of a Fisher's LSD post-hoc test.

The following subsections provide the analysis of Twitter users grouped by changes in their behaviors and attitudes that they had reported at both measurement time points, i.e., whether their reported behavior or attitude had decreased, remained the same, or increased over time. The comparisons of these groups were performed based on their scores for various factors measured in this study. The objective was to reveal significant differences between groups and to uncover the percentage of variance explained (R^2) by other factors in a particular behavior or attitude change.

5.2   User Behavior Associated with Content Generation on Twitter

The differences between groups of Twitter users were studied based on changes in their behaviors associated with content generation ($CONT^3$), i.e., whether their specific behaviors had decreased, remained the same, or increased over time (Table 6).

First, the comparison of the aforementioned groups revealed that the frequency of tweeting ($FREQ^5$) was significantly increased for Twitter users who reported an increase in content generation behavior. Second, the comparison of the same groups revealed that the attitude change associated with credibility on Twitter ($CRED^5$) was significantly increased for Twitter users who reported increased, rather than decreased, content generation behavior.

Table 6. Content generation behavior on Twitter ($CONT^3$)

	Levene's	ANOVA	Decreased	Remained	Increased	p	R^2
$FREQ^5$	2.5 (.093)	3.1 (.053)		2.83±0.53	3.44±0.88	.017[*]	12%
$CRED^5$	2.9 (.064)	5.1 (.010)	2.60±0.52		3.89±1.17	.003[**]	18%
$INFL^5$	1.8 (.164)	4.3 (.019)	2.70±0.67	3.27±0.52		.005[**]	16%
SC	4.7 (.014)	5.9 (.009)	5.60±0.70	4.40±1.61		.007[**]	11%
NI	4.5 (.016)	4.9 (.019)		4.70±1.75	5.78±0.83	.042[*]	9%
SF	1.8 (.172)	2.2 (.124)	5.80±0.92		4.56±1.67	.043[*]	9%

Levene's test and ANOVA results are reported as: F statistic (p value)
Post-hoc test results are in columns: Decreased, Remained, Increased
Significance values of post-hoc test results are in columns: $p^{**} < .01$, $p^* < .05$

Third, the comparison of the groups revealed that the attitude change regarding whether Twitter is an influential tool to call for action outside the virtual world ($INFL^5$) was significantly increased for Twitter users who reported the same or decreased content generation behavior. Fourth, the comparison of the groups based on their reported attitude at the second measurement point regarding whether Twitter allows them to compare their behaviors with those of other users (SC) revealed that this attitude was significantly increased for Twitter users who reported decreased, rather than the same, content generation behavior.

Fifth, the comparison of the groups based on their reported attitude in the second measurement point regarding whether there are norms on Twitter that should be followed (NI) revealed that this attitude was significantly increased for Twitter users who reported an increased, rather than the same, content generation behavior. Sixth, the comparison of the groups based on their reported attitudes at the second measurement point regarding whether they can discern other active users on Twitter (SF) revealed that this attitude was significantly increased for Twitter users who reported decreased, rather than increased, content generation behavior.

5.3   User Behavior Associated with Frequency of Tweeting

The differences between groups of Twitter users were studied based on their changes in behavior associated with the frequency of tweeting ($FREQ^3$), i.e., whether their behaviors had decreased, remained the same, or increased over time (Table 7). First, the comparison of the abovementioned groups revealed that the view that followers form interest groups on Twitter ($GROU^3$) was significantly increased for Twitter users who reported an increased, rather than a decreased, frequency of tweeting. Second, the comparison of the same groups based on their reported attitude at the second measurement point regarding whether they can cooperate with other users on Twitter (CR) revealed that this attitude was significantly increased for Twitter users who reported the same, rather than a decreased, frequency of tweeting.

Table 7. Frequency of tweeting ($FREQ^3$)

	Levene's	ANOVA	Decreased	Remained	Increased	p	R^2
$GROU^3$	0.5 (.584)	3.1 (.057)	2.82±0.98		3.88±0.99	.018*	12%
CR	0.2 (.860)	3.8 (.030)	5.09±1.14	6.00±0.91		.010*	14%
RE	6.2 (.004)	8.3 (.002)	2.82±1.25		4.50±0.53	.003**	16%
FUTU	1.8 (.172)	2.2 (.124)	6.27±0.65	6.73±0.45		.014*	13%

Third, the comparison of the groups based on their reported attitude at the second measurement point regarding whether Twitter users receive public recognition for their merits (RE) revealed that this attitude was significantly increased for Twitter users who reported an increased, rather than a decreased, frequency of tweeting. Fourth, the comparison the same groups based on their reported attitude at the second measurement point regarding whether they will use Twitter hereafter (FUTU) revealed that this attitude was significantly increased for Twitter users who reported the same, rather than a decreased, frequency of tweeting behavior.

5.4   User Attitude Associated with Interest Groups on Twitter

The differences between groups of Twitter users were studied based on their attitude changes regarding whether followers form interest groups on Twitter ($GROU^3$), i.e., whether their attitude regarding this being true had decreased, remained the same, or increased over time. First, the comparison of the aforementioned groups revealed that the attitude changes regarding whether there are unwritten behavioral and communication rules on Twitter ($RULE^5$) were significantly increased for Twitter users who reported an increased, rather than the same, attitude regarding whether followers form groups of interests on Twitter (Table 8). Second, the comparison of the same groups based on their reported attitude at the second measurement point regarding whether they can compete with other users on Twitter (CT) revealed that this attitude was significantly increased for Twitter users who reported an increased, rather than the same, attitude regarding whether followers form interest groups on Twitter.

Table 8. Attitude associated with interest groups on Twitter ($GROU^3$)

	Levene's	ANOVA	Decreased	Remained	Increased	p	R^2
$RULE^5$	0.9 (.410)	3.5 (.040)		2.48±0.87	3.21±0.89	.018*	13%
CT	3.2 (.049)	6.1 (.011)		3.26±1.80	5.36±1.39	.004**	20%

5.5   User Attitude Associated with Credibility on Twitter

The differences between groups of Twitter users were studied based on their attitude changes associated with credibility on Twitter (CRED³), i.e., whether their specific attitudes had decreased, remained the same, or increased over time (Table 9).

Table 9. Attitude associated with credibility on Twitter (CRED³)

	Levene's	ANOVA	Decreased	Remained	Increased	p	R^2
RULE⁵	2.1 (.138)	3.5 (.038)	3.23±0.72	2.38±1.02		.012*	13%

The comparison of these groups revealed that the attitude change regarding whether there are unwritten behavioral and communication rules on Twitter (RULE⁵) was significantly increased for Twitter users who reported a decreased, rather than the same, attitude regarding credibility on Twitter.

6   Discussion and Contribution

In the current study, the factors affecting users' behaviors and attitudes on Twitter were explored, focusing on incremental online persuasion patterns, interrelating factors, and social influence design principles [25]. Initially, two behaviors and one attitude of Twitter users were found that changed along with the length of Twitter use. These findings revealed the same online persuasion patterns that were discovered in the initial study two years earlier [26]. Thus, this study provided additional support for the presence of these patterns on Twitter.

Two patterns indicated that both users' content generation and tweeting frequency behaviors were significantly associated with their length of Twitter use. Respondents with longer Twitter experiences reported stronger confidence in being real content generators and more frequent tweeters. Zeng and Wei [31] have described user-generated content as the lifeblood of social networks. Similarly, organizations can benefit from engaging customers in content-generation behaviors [21]. At the same time, they can expect incremental social networking activity from users with longer experiences on Twitter. In particular, users' behaviors associated with tweeting frequency can serve as content relevance indicators for organizations [28]. Finally, organizations can target more experienced Twitter users to facilitate the adoption of a product, service, or opinion [12]. The third pattern indicated that users with more experience on Twitter had stronger attitudes regarding this social network being influential in terms of calls for action outside the virtual world. This finding demonstrated that there is evidence for a significant link between such attitudes among more experienced Twitter users and their potential behaviors in the real world. Marketers can differentiate the way they approach this group to increase the effectiveness of future campaigns. Inside organizations, such people can play key roles in accelerating organizational changes, including the adoption and use of novel information systems and mobile applications.

To reveal the factors behind these patterns and changes in users' behaviors and attitudes, a comprehensive analysis was conducted that produced many interesting and relevant findings. First, it was found that changes in content generation behavior were influenced by six factors: one behavioral factor, changes in tweeting frequency; two attitudinal factors, changes in Twitter credibility and shifts in opinions about Twitter being an influential tool in terms of calls for action outside the virtual world; and three social influence factors, namely social comparison, normative influence, and social facilitation. Second, it was found that changes in tweeting frequency were influenced by four factors: two attitudinal factors, namely intentions to use Twitter in the future and shifts in opinions regarding interest groups on Twitter, and two social influence factors, namely cooperation and recognition. Third, it was found that changes in respondents' attitudes about interest groups on Twitter were influenced by shifts in their opinions about unwritten behavioral and communication rules on Twitter, as well as the social influence factor of competition. Finally, it was found that changes in respondents' attitudes about Twitter's credibility were influenced by shifts in their opinions about unwritten behavioral and communication rules on Twitter.

There were found two types of relationships between factors: those that maintained a change with the same direction for both related factors, e.g. if one factor increased, then the other increased as well, and those that had changes with opposite directions, e.g., if one factor increased, then the other factor decreased. This principle was applied to only those groups in each factor that revealed significant differences between two groups in terms of the dependent variables. Almost all the discovered relationships implied unidirectional changes, with the exception of the following three: (1) the relationship between attitudes about credibility and unwritten behavioral rules on Twitter, and (2) the relationship between content generation behavior and social comparison, and (3) that between content generation and social facilitation.

Especially interesting were the findings that revealed significant differences between neighboring groups, such as decreased-remained and remained-increased, rather than the maximum-distance relationships of the decreased-increased differences. Consequently, the relationship between attitudes about credibility and unwritten behavioral rules has revealed that Twitter users who thought that Twitter was less credible after two years had stronger opinions about the presence of unwritten behavioral and communication rules on Twitter than those that did not change their opinion about credibility over that time period. Similarly, those respondents who decreased their content generation behavior over the two years had stronger opinions about the presence of social comparison on Twitter than those who did not change their content-generation behaviors.

Finally, the same respondents also had stronger opinions about the presence of social facilitation on Twitter than those who increased their content generation behavior. These findings have shown a potential negative effect for social comparison and social facilitation on content generation behaviors. The effect of social comparison can be partially explained by a human tendency to compare themselves with others when social norms are not available [13]. However, social facilitation typically has a negative effect when complicated tasks are performed [30]. Those respondents who increased their content generation behavior over two years also expressed stronger opinions about the presence of normative influence on Twitter than those who did not change their content generation behavior. Humans tend to seek norms and follow them [9].

Twitter users who decreased their tweeting frequency over two the years also scored lower regarding the presence of cooperation on Twitter than those who did not change their tweeting frequency behaviors. Those respondents who increased their tweeting frequency over the two years also scored higher regarding the presence of recognition on Twitter than those who decreased their tweeting frequency. Finally, Twitter users who came to agree with the view that interest groups exist on Twitter over the two years also scored higher regarding the presence of competition on Twitter than those that did not change their attitudes regarding interest groups on Twitter. These aforementioned social influence principles, namely cooperation, competition, and recognition, have been described as interpersonal motivating factors. The first two are driven by the human tendency to cooperate and compete, but the latter reflects people's enjoyment of having their accomplishments recognized and appreciated by others [20].

7   Conclusions

During this second phase of an ongoing longitudinal research initiative, the initial survey [26] instrument was improved, and another online survey was conducted to collect data about the behaviors and attitudes of Twitter users. Altogether, 501 responses were collected, of which 49 were identified as repeated respondents at both measurement times. Within the full sample, significant evidence was found for three incremental online persuasion patterns that persisted on Twitter over a period of two years. Then, within the smaller sample, factors were found that influence these patterns and other opinions about Twitter and were measured.

Although this research has highlighted several notable findings, some limitations should be acknowledged. Both of the surveys were carried out in Latvia, so cultural factors might limit the generalizability of findings. Both samples were similar in terms of their characteristics and sufficient in terms of their size, but larger samples containing more respondents with shorter experiences on Twitter, especially those containing older age groups, would strengthen the results of such a study.

In conclusion, this study has provided valuable and interesting findings that can be used as building blocks for further studies related to online persuasion techniques, incremental behavior change patterns in social networks, interrelated attitudinal changes on Twitter, and the effects of social influence design principles [25] on users of information systems. In particular, some of the preliminary data analysis results indicated a potential interplay between social influence factors on Twitter. This provides relevant insights for the next phase of this longitudinal research initiative. For practitioners, these findings could be instrumental in harnessing social influence through online social networks, outlining social media strategies for online persuasion, and designing socially influencing systems.

Acknowledgements. The author would like to thank Ilze Bērziņa, Jouni Markkula, Gregory Moody, Harri Oinas-Kukkonen, and Seppo Pahnila, who helped with this research, which was partly supported by the Foundation of Nokia Corporation, the Doctoral Program on Software and Systems Engineering, and the Someletti Research Project on Social Media in Public Space (grant 1362/31), provided by Tekes, the Finnish Funding Agency for Technology and Innovation.

References

1. Achananuparp, P., Lim, E.P., Jiang, J., Hoang, T.A.: Who is Retweeting the Tweeters? Modeling, Originating, and Promoting Behaviors in the Twitter Network. ACM Transactions on Management Information Systems (TMIS) 3(3), 13 (2012)
2. Aral, S., Dellarocas, C., Godes, D.: Introduction to the Special Issue—Social Media and Business Transformation: A Framework for Research. Information Systems Research 24(1), 3–13 (2013)
3. Aral, S., Walker, D.: Creating Social Contagion through Viral Product Design: A Randomized Trial of Peer Influence in Networks. Management Science 57(9), 1623–1639 (2011)
4. Barnes, S.J., Böhringer, M.: Modeling Use Continuance Behavior in Microblogging Services: The Case of Twitter. Journal of Computer Information Systems 51(4), 1 (2011)
5. Bjørn-Andersen, N., Hansen, R.: The Adoption of Web 2.0 by Luxury Fashion Brands. In: Proceedings of CONFIRM, Paper 34 (2011)
6. Boyd, D., Golder, S., Lotan, G.: Tweet, Tweet, Retweet: Conversational Aspects of Retweeting on Twitter. In: Proceedings of the 43rd Hawaii International Conference on System Sciences, Koloa, HI, USA (2010)
7. Chatfield, A.T., Brajawidagda, U.: Twitter Tsunami Early Warning Network: A Social Network Analysis of Twitter Information Flows. In: Proceedings of the 23rd Australasian Conference on Information Systems, Geelong, Victoria, Australia, pp. 1–10 (2012)
8. Chen, S.C., Yen, D.C., Hwang, M.I.: Factors Influencing the Continuance Intention to the Usage of Web 2.0: An Empirical Study. Computers in Human Behavior 28(3), 933–941 (2012)
9. Cialdini, R.B., Kallgren, C.A., Reno, R.R.: A Focus Theory of Normative Conduct: A Theoretical Refinement and Reevaluation of the Role of Norms in Human Behavior. In: Zanna, M.P. (ed.) Advances in Experimental Social Psychology (24), pp. 201–234. Academic Press, New York (1991)
10. Culnan, M.J., McHugh, P.J., Zubillaga, J.I.: How Large US Companies Can Use Twitter and Other Social Media to Gain Business Value. MIS Quarterly Executive 9(4), 243–259 (2010)
11. Dou, Y., Niculescu, M., Wu, D.J.: Engineering Optimal Network Effects Via Social Media Features and Seeding in Markets for Digital Goods and Services. Inform. Systems Res. 24(1), 164–185 (2013)
12. Fang, X., Hu, P.J.H., Li, Z.L., Tsai, W.: Predicting Adoption Probabilities in Social Networks. Information Systems Research 24(1), 128–145 (2013)
13. Festinger, L.: A Theory of Social Comparison Processes. Human Relations 7(2), 117–140 (1954)
14. Fosso Wamba, S., Carter, L.: Twitter Adoption and Use by SMEs: An Empirical Study. In: The 46 Hawaii International Conferences on System Sciences (HICSS), Maui, Hawaii, USA (2013)

15. Honeycutt, C., Herring, S.C.: Beyond Microblogging: Conversation and Collaboration Via Twitter. In: Proceedings of the 43rd Hawaii International Conference on System Sciences, Koloa, HI, USA (2010)
16. Huberman, B.A., Romero, D.M., Wu, F.: Social Networks that Matter: Twitter under the Microscope. First Monday 14(1) (2009), http://firstmonday.org/htbin/cgiwrap/bin/ojs/index.php/fm/article/view/2317/2063 (retrieved on April 12, 2013)
17. Junco, R., Elavsky, C.M., Heiberger, G.: Putting Twitter to the Test: Assessing Outcomes for Student Collaboration, Engagement and Success. British Journal of Educational Technology (2012)
18. Krishnamurthy, B., Gill, P., Arlitt, M.: A Few Chirps about Twitter. In: Proceedings of the First Workshop on Online Social Networks, Seattle, WA, USA, pp. 19–24 (2008)
19. Kwak, H., Lee, C., Park, H., Moon, S.: What is Twitter, a Social Network or a News Media? In: Proceedings of the 19th World-Wide Web (WWW) Conference, Raleigh, NC, USA, April 26-30 (2010)
20. Malone, T.W., Lepper, M.: Making Learning Fun: A Taxonomy of Intrinsic Motivations for Learning. In: Snow, R.E., Farr, M.J. (eds.) Aptitude, Learning and Instruction: III. Conative and Affective Process Analyses, pp. 223–253. Erlbaum, Hillsdale (1987)
21. Miller, A.R., Tucker, C.: Active Social Media Management: The Case of Health Care. Information Systems Research 24(1), 52–70 (2013)
22. Oh, O., Tahmasbi, N., Rao, H.R., Vreede, G.D.: A Sociotechnical View of Information Diffusion and Social Changes: From Reprint to Retweet. In: Joey, F.G. (ed.) Proceedings of the 33th International Conference on Information Systems, Orlando, FL, USA (2012)
23. Ou, C.X., Davison, R.M., Cheng, N.C.: Why Are Social Networking Applications Successful: An Empirical Study of Twitter. In: Proceedings of the 15th Pacific Asia Conference on Information Systems (PACIS) (2011)
24. Pervin, N., Fang, F., Datta, A., Dutta, K., Vandermeer, D.: Fast, Scalable, and Context-Sensitive Detection of Trending Topics in Microblog Post Streams. ACM Transactions on Management Information Systems (TMIS) 3(4), 19 (2013)
25. Stibe, A., Oinas-Kukkonen, H.: Using Social Influence for Motivating Customers to Generate and Share Feedback. In: Spagnolli, A., Chittaro, L., Gamberini, L. (eds.) PERSUASIVE 2014. LNCS, vol. 8462, pp. 224–235. Springer, Heidelberg (2014)
26. Stibe, A., Oinas-Kukkonen, H., Bērziņa, I., Pahnila, S.: Incremental Persuasion Through Microblogging: A Survey of Twitter Users in Latvia. In: Proceedings of the 6th International Conference on Persuasive Technology: Persuasive Technology and Design: Enhancing Sustainability and Health, p. 8. ACM (2011)
27. Vatrapu, R.: Understanding Social Business. In: Emerging Dimensions of Technology Management, pp. 147–158. Springer India (2013)
28. Wirtz, B.W., Piehler, R., Ullrich, S.: Determinants of Social Media Website Attractiveness. Journal of Electronic Commerce Research 14(1) (2013)
29. Young, M.M.: Twitter Me: Using Micro-blogging to Motivate Teenagers to Exercise. In: Winter, R., Zhao, J.L., Aier, S. (eds.) DESRIST 2010. LNCS, vol. 6105, pp. 439–448. Springer, Heidelberg (2010)
30. Zajonc, R.B.: Social Facilitation. Science 149, 269–274 (1965)
31. Zeng, X., Wei, L.: Social Ties and User Content Generation: Evidence from Flickr. Inform. Systems Res. 24(1), 71–87 (2013)

A Regional Exploration and Recommendation System Based on Georeferenced Images

Chandan Kumar[1], Sebastian Barton[1], Wilko Heuten[2], and Susanne Boll[1]

[1] University of Oldenburg, Oldenburg, Germany
{chandan.kumar,sebastian.barton,susanne.boll}@uni-oldenburg.de
[2] OFFIS - Institute for Information Technology, Oldenburg, Germany
wilko.heuten@offis.de

Abstract. Socially tagged images contain rich spatial information about the culture and environment that could exemplify the composition of regions and provide a useful geovisual assessment. Flickr is one of such prominent data sources capable of making sense of the geospatial world. In several spatial decision scenarios such as touring a new city, end-users are interested in the characterization and comparison of relevant geographic regions. But the current means of interfaces limit the end users on visual abstraction and comparison of relevant geographic regions. In this work we propose a system that generates the makeup of a region based on geospatial tagged images of the region. We can then use the relevant metadata to identify and compare other suitable regions which exhibit a similar fingerprint of images. The developed interface allows the user to get a good regional overview, and also to drill in and compare selected regions.

1   Introduction

There is a great need of geographic information in several touristic and spatial decision making scenarios. Web services such as TripAdvisor[1], or Expedia[2] can be used by people to inform themselves about popular landmarks or points of interest. However, in some planning and decision making processes, the interest lies not in specific places, but rather in the makeup of regions, e.g., a person might have a very little time to travel across different popular spots in a foreign city, instead would like to find most interesting region to spend some quality time. The choice of region could be influenced by his past experience of being in an interesting region. Exploration of geographic regions and their comparison was found as one of the key desires of current local search users [6]. There have been some recent efforts to recommend interesting regions for end users based on query by example scenarios [5,4]. These approaches provide a facility based overview of geographic regions using georeferenced entities from the OpenStreetMap or spatial Web documents. However, there are several other media

---

[1] http://www.tripadvisor.com
[2] http://www.expedia.com

I. Awan et al. (Eds.): MobiWis 2014, LNCS 8640, pp. 301–308, 2014.
© Springer International Publishing Switzerland 2014

sources which contain relevant geospatial content and could better present the visual characteristics of geographic regions. Specifically in touristic scenarios, users look for more visually appealing features that can attract their attention as well as provide a useful comparison of regions. In this work we propose the use of geospatial images for this purpose. Nowadays huge numbers of photographs on the Web are associated with geocoordinates. Such geo-referenced photos can be categorized geographically or displayed on a map interface to provide a rich spatial context.

Geo-referenced images have been a great source to characterize the spatial appearance of the world [3]. Billions of images shared on websites such as Flickr[3] serve as a growing record of our society and surroundings. Interaction with such collections could provide visual as well as social significance. Effective utilization of such information has been one of the most challenging tasks in the multimedia research community [10]. Following this trend, our work goes in the direction of making use of such visual and spatially significant data for characterization and comparisons of relevant geographic regions.

In this paper we present a map based interface to explore and compare the geographic regions of interest via the collection of georeferenced pictures from Flickr. We go beyond the conventional Flickr interface and propose to access its database with queries by spatial example. In an evaluation study, we compare the proposed interface with other modes of regional characterization such as facility and keyword based visualizations. We conducted the experiment to investigate the overall suitability and user satisfaction of these interfaces. The study results provided us generous indication on the acceptability of image based characterization for regional search and exploration.

2   Related Work

There has been various research efforts which considers geographic location information associated with photographs. Toyama et. al. [11] proposed a map-based system for browsing a global collection of georeferenced photos. Several similar map-based image browsing applications exist[4], which use "geo-tagged" images from Flickr. Most of the theses systems focus on generic browsing of images compared to regional characterizations and comparisons.

Making use of the metadata associated with Georeferenced images have also been a common aspects of various approaches [8,9,2]. Mamei et. al. [7] used the metadata associated with the photos, and the tags that have a high correlation could be displayed according to their spatial occurrence on a map. Nguyen and Schumann [8] proposed 'Taggram' to explore geo-data on maps through a tag cloud-based visualization. They make use of the frequently occurring tags from the large data set of Flickr. Such approaches represent the Flickr data with most interesting tags, however their visualization is only based on tags, and they miss

---

[3] https://www.flickr.com
[4] http://geobloggers.com or http://mappr.com

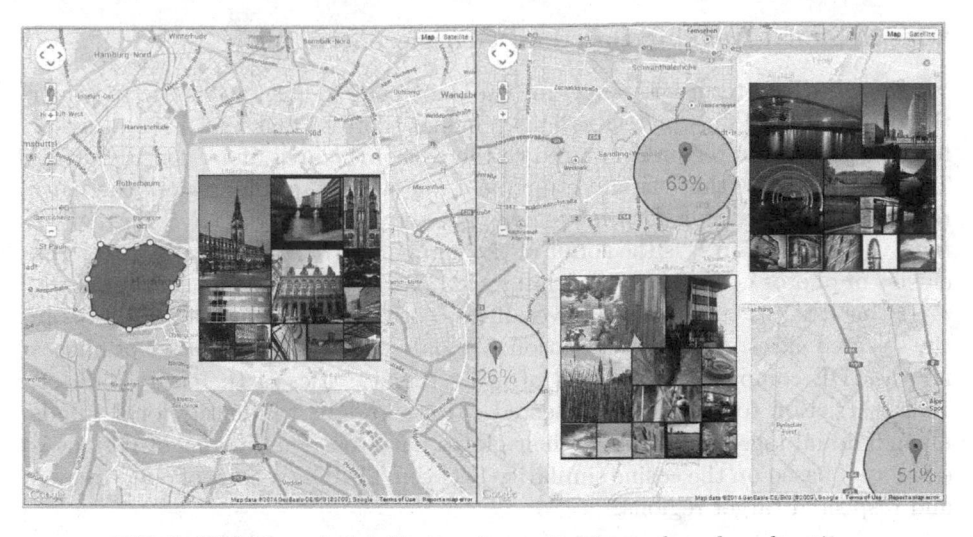

Fig. 1. Flickr based visualization for regional search and exploration

out on effective visual presentation of photos itself. In this work we showcase that an image based representation could be more appealing for end users compared to keyword/tag based visualization of geographic regions.

3   Regional Search and Exploration Based on Georeferenced Flickr Images

In this work our focus is on the representation of geographic regions, and their classification is based upon the availability of geo-located images. The basic design has been adapted from the regional search interfaces [5] where users could select a particular city or multiple cities for the spatial exploration. Figure 1 shows the Web interface of proposed system, where two German cities Hamburg and Munich were selected by the user. In the following subsections we describe the functionality of the system in more detail.

3.1   Selection of Regional Preferences

Figure 1 shows an example of user selected region of interest via a polygon query in the city Hamburg (map in the left). Having specified the query region of interest, users could select several location preferences in a destination city via clicking markers on the map interface. The system defines the target regions by encircling the area around the user selected locations with the same diameter as the query region polygon. In Figure 1 user selected 3 markers on the city map of Munich. The target region in the centre of city is most relevant with the similarity of 63%, and consequently has the dark green tone.

3.2   Regional Ranking Based on Georeferenced Tags

We use TF-IDF (term frequency, inverse document frequency) metric to prefer the popular tags. This metric assigns a higher score to tags that have a higher frequency within a region compared to the rest of the area under consideration. The assumption is that the more unique a tag is for a specific region, the more representative the tag is for that region. The term frequency $tf(R,t)$ for a given tag t within a region R is the count of the number of times t was used within the cluster of photos georeferenced within region R: The inverse document frequency $idf(t)$ for a tag t, computes the overall ratio of the tag t amongst all photos in the selected cities under consideration. We only consider a limited set of photos for the IDF computation, instead of using the statistics of the entire dataset. This restriction to the current selected cities allows us to identify local trends for individual tags, regardless of their global patterns. The ranking of regions is estimated based on the cosine similarity between TF-IDF vectors of query region and respected target regions.

3.3   Image Oriented Visual Analysis and Comparison

Users could view the most interesting photos of a region in a grid window. We provide the collection of images sorted according to their relevance for the selected region. They are sorted in descending order according to their interestingness. Then, the size of the images is adjusted. The image for the tag with the highest TF-IDF is the largest and the images are getting smaller with decreasing relevance. The presented overview was the result of user centre design process where we have experimented with different layouts, numbers and sizes of images.

The image overview could also be a relevant assistance in analyzing the similarity between regions. In the example shown in Figure 1, the query region from Hamburg consists of several pictures of interesting architectures, cathedrals, and touristic areas near the river; similarly the target region in Munich with 63% similarity contains the images of beautiful spots around the lake and architectural buildings. In comparison the other region in Munich which is just 26% similar to query region contains images mostly related to nature, greenery and food. It is evident that different people could be attracted to different regions based on the visual summary of regions.

3.4   Interaction with Image Overview

Users might like to interact with the regional overview of images. There is a possibility of enlarged view of images in an overlay (Figure 2). For automatic recognition of this function the icon of the mouse will change to a magnifying mouse icon when the cursor is on the image of interest. The associated tags are displayed at the bottom of the image since it provides valuable additional information to the image. In the lower left corner there is Flickr icon which navigates to the Flickr page, and is primarily the source of evidence of the image that provides relevant information such as the author and the time, the

Fig. 2. The overlay with mouse above the Flickr-icon

image was taken. Additionally, it is possible to display the next or the previous images from the preview window directly in the overlay. The system attempts to determine the most suitable images for a region, however there could be scenarios when users could find the pictures not attractive or inappropriate. In this case user could click the thumbs down icon on the lower right corner of the image to remove this picture and replace it with another one from the same category of pictures. The navigation elements are arranged intuitively and even for inexperienced internet users self-explanatory. Users could also view exact geocoordinate positions of the picture on map while hovering over the pictures in grid.

3.5   Data Description

We used raw geospatial data from the Flickr API [5], which we collect in a Lucene[6] index database. For the collection of regional images we follow the Yahoo's guidance to divide the world into regions. Each region has a unique identifier, which is known as WOEID (**W**here **o**n **E**arth **Id**entifier)[7]. Using a WOEID Finder we first determined the identifiers for many German cities. With this identification the Flickr database can be searched for images in a particular region. The analysis of the database indicated that some users have uploaded thousands of images on Flickr using the same tags and the same geo-data. Hence we store one photo per user and region into the database.

4   Evaluation

We conducted an experiment to investigate how the geotagged images are able to support regional search and exploration. We intend to find out the general

---

[5] http://www.flickr.com/services/api

[6] https://lucene.apache.org

[7] http://developer.yahoo.com/geo/geoplanet/guide/concepts.html

perspective of end users, however one of the main objectives of our work is to investigate how image based visualization perform against other popular regional visualizations. We had chosen two baselines, first is the criteria based heatmap visualization of OpenStreetMap, since it provides a relevant regional overview with facility distribution [5]. Figure 3a shows its example, where the pie charts is used to visualize the relative ratio of different categories inside a region. The second baseline is from tag based visualization perspective (Figure 3b). This view displays the most popular keywords from websites that are assigned to the specified region [4]. It is interesting to select such visualization since most of the current geovisualization approaches make use of such tag clouds to display the spatial characterization of regions [3,1].

4.1   Method

10 volunteers (8 male, 2 female) participated in our study. They were aged between 24 and 51 years (mean 29.3, SD 10.95). To evaluate the application, we had given two scenario to the participants: The first was to use the interface and compare two regions in different cities that are already well known to the user. In the second scenario the participant had to start a new comparison, i.e., to compare a well-known city with an unknown. The scenarios was as follows: *Due to a business trip you are going to a foreign city. From previous trips to other cities, you already know some regions that have attracted you before. Select a query region on the map that you really liked in a known city. Arbitrarily set three markers on the destination city for comparison. Since your time is limited, you only have time to visit one specific region in the destination city. Based on the recommendations of the application make a decision for a region you would visit.*

The participants were asked about how far the application could assist in their spatial decision making. We intend to evaluate the similarity and visualization capabilities of the proposed visualizations. Hence the users were first asked if they agree with the calculated percentage similarity of regions, secondly if they like the visual presentation of regions. Most of the assessments were made on seven point Likert scales, which should be rated from *strongly disagree* to *strongly agree*.

4.2   Results

Overall 9 of the 10 participants mentioned that the system could help them to find a region that they want to visit. When being asked about which perspective could provide the best impression of a foreign region (multiple answers were allowed), the Criteria-view received 5 votes in comparison to 8 votes for Flickr representation. The similarity assessment was judged by 9 of the participants, since one of the participant was not able to rate the results. The median of the satisfaction for the Criteria-view was 6 (IQR=0), for the Keyword-view it was 5 (IQR=2), and for the Flickr-view it was 5 (IQR=0).

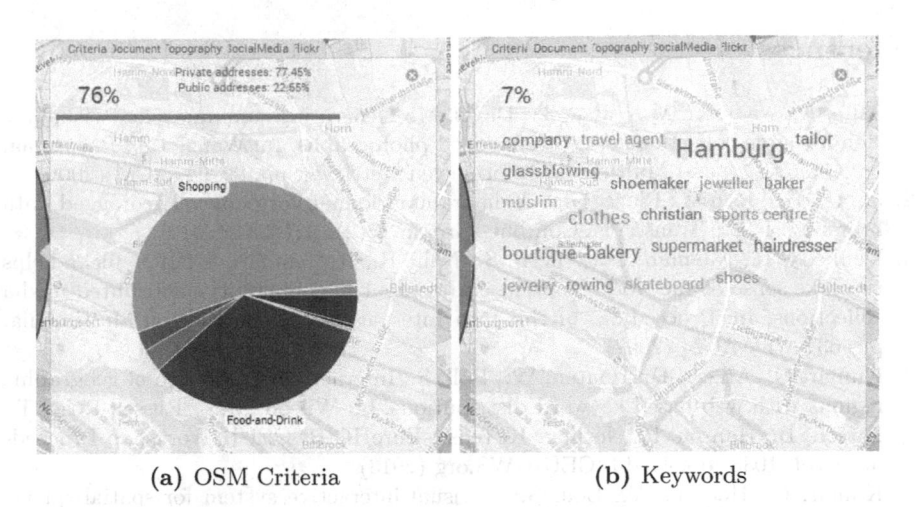

(a) OSM Criteria   (b) Keywords

Fig. 3. The two baseline views at Hamburg harbour

All of the participants were able to judge the visual presentation of regional search. The median satisfaction for the Criteria-view was 5 (IQR=2), the Keyword-view was 5 (IQR=1), and for the Flickr-view it was 6 (IQR=1). The student t-test statistics shows that the Flickr view provides significantly better visual presentation of geographic regions as compared to Criteria-view ($p = .01$) and Keyword-view ($p = .05$). However in the similarity assessment between geographic regions, Criteria-view performed better than Flickr-view($p = .04$). The estimation of similarity was based on the tags associated with images. These tags are assigned by the users who upload the images to Flickr, so the vocabulary of tags differs significantly among the users which could result in non-optimal text similarity metric. However, for Criteria-view the similarity is based on OSM fixed set of categories, and the users could easily access the similarity based on the categorical pie chart overview.

5   Conclusion

In this paper we proposed interactive visual interfaces for end-users to specify, analyze, and compare the geographic regions of interest via the collection of georeferenced pictures from Flickr. The relevance estimation of geographic regions is based on the meta-data associated with the images. The proposed interface provides the easy overview and exploration of spatial characteristics of regions; however, due to the erroneous user supplied tags it is limited on similarity estimation of regions. The integration of all interfaces, i.e. use of different multimedia sources could be a move forward to satisfy the diversity of users.

Acknowledgment. The authors are grateful to the DFG SPP 1335 'Scalable Visual Analytics' priority program, which funds the project UrbanExplorer.

References

1. Jaffe, A., Naaman, M., Tassa, T., Davis, M.: Generating summaries and visualization for large collections of geo-referenced photographs. In: Wang, J.Z., Boujemaa, N., Chen, Y. (eds.) Multimedia Information Retrieval, pp. 89–98. ACM (2006)
2. Jo, H., Hee Ryu, J.: Placegram: A diagrammatic map for personal geotagged data browsing. IEEE Trans. Vis. Comput. Graph. 16(2), 221–234 (2010)
3. Kennedy, L., Naaman, M., Ahern, S., Nair, R., Rattenbury, T.: How flickr helps us make sense of the world: context and content in community-contributed media collections. In: Proceedings of the 15th International Conference on Multimedia, pp. 631–640. ACM (2007)
4. Kumar, C., Ahlers, D., Heuten, W., Boll, S.: Interactive exploration of geographic regions with web-based keyword distributions. In: Wilson, M.L., Russell-Rose, T., Larsen, B., Hansen, P., Norling, K. (eds.) EuroHCIR. CEUR Workshop Proceedings, vol. 1033, pp. 11–14. CEUR-WS.org (2013)
5. Kumar, C., Heuten, W., Boll, S.: A visual interactive system for spatial querying and ranking of geographic regions. In: Lindstaedt, S.N., Granitzer, M. (eds.) I-KNOW, p. 30. ACM (2013)
6. Kumar, C., Poppinga, B., Haeuser, D., Heuten, W., Boll, S.: Geovisual interfaces to find suitable urban regions for citizens: A user-centered requirement study. In: Proceedings of the 2013 ACM Conference on Pervasive and Ubiquitous Computing Adjunct Publication, pp. 741–744. ACM (2013)
7. Mamei, M., Rosi, A., Zambonelli, F.: Automatic analysis of geotagged photos for intelligent tourist services. In: Callaghan, V., Kameas, A., Egerton, S., Satoh, I., Weber, M. (eds.) Intelligent Environments, pp. 146–151. IEEE Computer Society (2010)
8. Nguyen, D.-Q., Schumann, H.: Taggram: Exploring geo-data on maps through a tag cloud-based visualization. In: Banissi, E., Bertschi, S., Burkhard, R.A., Counsell, J., Dastbaz, M., Eppler, M.J., Forsell, C., Grinstein, G.G., Johansson, J., Jern, M., Khosrowshahi, F., Marchese, F.T., Maple, C., Laing, R., Cvek, U., Trutschl, M., Sarfraz, M., Stuart, L.J., Ursyn, A., Wyeld, T.G. (eds.) IV, pp. 322–328. IEEE Computer Society (2010)
9. Nguyen, D.-Q., Tominski, C., Schumann, H., Ta, T.-A.: Visualizing tags with spatiotemporal references. In: Banissi, E., Bertschi, S., Burkhard, R.A., Cvek, U., Eppler, M.J., Forsell, C., Grinstein, G.G., Johansson, J., Kenderdine, S., Marchese, F.T., Maple, C., Trutschl, M., Sarfraz, M., Stuart, L.J., Ursyn, A., Wyeld, T.G. (eds.) IV, pp. 32–39. IEEE Computer Society (2011)
10. Quack, T., Leibe, B., Van Gool, L.: World-scale mining of objects and events from community photo collections. In: Proceedings of the 2008 International Conference on Content-Based Image and Video Retrieval, pp. 47–56. ACM (2008)
11. Toyama, K., Logan, R., Roseway, A.: Geographic location tags on digital images. In: Proceedings of the Eleventh ACM International Conference on Multimedia, pp. 156–166. ACM (2003)

Author Index